VISUAL QUICKSTART GUIDE

DHTML AND CSS

FOR THE WORLD WIDE WEB, 2ND EDITION

Jason Cranford Teague

Peachpit Press

Visual QuickStart Guide
DHTML and CSS for the World Wide Web, 2nd Edition
Jason Cranford Teague

Peachpit Press
1249 Eighth Street
Berkeley, CA 94710
510/524-2178
800/283-9444
510/524-2221 (fax)

Find us on the World Wide Web at: www.peachpit.com

Peachpit Press is a division of Addison Wesley Longman

Copyright © 2001 by Jason Cranford Teague

Editor: Nancy Davis and Rebecca Gulick
Production Coordinator: Connie Jeung-Mills
Copyeditor: Kathy Simpson
Technical Editor: Ben Fisher
Compositor: Owen Wolfson
Indexer: Karin Arrigoni
Cover and interior design: The Visual Group

ISBN 0-201-73084-7
9 8 7 6 5 4 3 2 1

Printed and bound in the United States of America

 Printed on recycled paper

*For Jocelyn and Dashiel, who are making
my life more dynamic every day.*

Special thanks to:

Tara, my soulmate and best critic.

Rebecca, who dotted my i's and made sure everything made sense.

Nancy, who got this project started.

Kathy, for catching all of my mistakes.

Connie, for making it look right.

Simon, who edited the first edition.

Ben, whose attention to technical details is unsurpassed.

Mom, Dad, and Nancy, for making me who I am.

Pat and Red, my biggest fans.

Johnny, whose ongoing support is always appreciated.

Charles Dodgson (Lewis Carroll) for writing *Alice in Wonderland*.

John Tenniel, for his inspiring illustrations of *Alice in Wonderland*.

Judy, Boyd, Dr. G and The Teachers of America. Keep up the good work.

Nabih at Nabih's Computer Systems who rescued my hard drive not once but twice during the writing of this book.

Douglas Adams, so long and thanks for all the books.

The The, The Cure, Siouxsie and the Banshees, The Beatles, Blur, Cracker, Danielle Dax, Nine Inch Nails, KMFDM, The Pogues, The Ramones, New Model Army, The Cocteau Twins, The Cranes, The Sisters of Mercy, The Smiths, Bauhaus, Bad Religion, This Mortal Coil, and Dead Can Dance, whose noise helped keep me from going insane while writing this book.

TABLE OF CONTENTS

Introduction   **xiii**

PART 1:   **CASCADING STYLE SHEETS**   **1**

Chapter 1:   **Understanding CSS**   **3**
What Is a Style? 5
What Are Cascading Style Sheets? 6
Versions of CSS 9
Types of CSS Rules 11
The Parts of a CSS Rule 12
Kinds of HTML Tags 14

Chapter 2:   **CSS Basics**   **17**
Adding CSS to an HTML Tag 18
Adding CSS to a Web Page 20
Adding CSS to a Web Site 23
(re)Defining an HTML Tag 29
Defining Classes to Create Your Own Tags 31
Defining IDs to Identify an Object 33
Creating Your Own Inline HTML Tags 35
Creating Your Own Block-Level HTML Tags 37
Defining Tags with the Same Rules 39
Defining Tags in Context 41
Making a Definition !important 43
Inheriting Properties from a Parent 45
Managing Existing or Inherited Property Values . 47
Determining the Cascade Order 49
Setting the CSS for Printing 51
Adding Comments to CSS 54
Style-Sheet Strategies 55

Chapter 3:   **Font Controls**   **57**
Understanding Typography on the Web 58
Using Type on the Web 59
Setting the Font 61
Downloading Fonts 63
Using Browser-Safe Fonts 65
Setting the Font Size 67
Making Text Italic 69

Setting Bold, Bolder, Boldest 71
Creating Minicaps 73
Setting Multiple Font Values 74

Chapter 4:   **Text Controls**   **77**
Adjusting Kerning 78
Adjusting Word Spacing 79
Adjusting Leading 80
Setting Text Case 82
Aligning Text Left, Right, and Center 83
Aligning Text Vertically 85
Indenting Paragraphs 87
Decorating Text 89
Controlling White Space 91
Setting Page Breaks for Printing 93

Chapter 5:   **List and Mouse Controls**   **95**
Setting up a List 96
Setting the Bullet Style 98
Creating a Hanging Indent 99
Creating Your Own Bullets 100
Changing the Mouse Pointer's Appearance 102

Chapter 6:   **Color and Background Controls**   **105**
Setting the Background 106
Setting Individual Background Properties 109
Setting a Foreground Color 114

Chapter 7:   **Border and Margin Controls**   **115**
Understanding the Element's Box 116
Setting the Width and Height of an Element . . . 118
Setting an Element's Margins 121
Setting an Element's Border 124
Decorating an Element's Border 126
Setting an Element's Padding 129
Setting a Table's Borders and Margins 131
Wrapping Text Around an Element 133
Preventing Text from Wrapping 135
Telling an Element How to Display (or Not) 137

Chapter 8:   **Positioning Controls**   **139**
Understanding the Window 140
Setting the Positioning Type 142
Setting the Position from the Top and Left 146
Setting the Position from the Bottom
    and Right 149
Stacking Objects (3-D Positioning) 151

Nesting an Absolute Element in a
Relative Element 153
Nesting a Relative Element in an
Absolute Element 155

Chapter 9: Visibility Controls   157
Setting the Visibility of an Element 158
Setting the Visible Area of an
Element (Clipping) 160
Setting Where the Overflow Goes 162

PART 2: DYNAMIC HTML   165

Chapter 10: Understanding DHTML   167
What Is Dynamic HTML? 168
The Flavors of DHTML 169
Why Should I Use DHTML? 171
Flash vs. DHTML 173

Chapter 11: The Document Object Model   177
Understanding the DOM: Road Map to
Your Web Page 178
Creating an Object 180
Understanding Event Handlers 181
Detecting an Event 183
How the DOM Works 185
Using Feature Sensing 191
Detecting the DOM Type 192
Building a Cross-Browser DOM 194
Using the Cross-Browser DOM 197
Netscape 4 and Nested Layers 199

Chapter 12: Learning About Your Environment   203
Detecting the Browser's Name and Version 204
Detecting the Operating System 206
Finding the Screen Dimensions 208
Finding the Number of Colors 210
Finding the Browser Window's Dimensions 212
Finding the Visible Page Dimensions 213
Finding the Page's Location and Title 215
Finding the Page's Scroll Position 216
Finding an Object's Dimensions 218
Finding an Object's Top and Left Positions 220
Finding an Object's Bottom and Right Positions 222
Finding an Object's 3-D Position 224
Finding an Object's Visibility State 226
Finding an Object's Visible Area 228

Chapter 13: Dynamic Techniques: The Basics **233**

Making Objects Appear and Disappear 234
Moving Objects from Point to Point 236
Moving Objects By a Certain Amount 238
Moving Objects in 3-D 240
Scrolling a Web Page 243
Changing an Object's Visible Area 245

Chapter 14: Dynamic Techniques: Advanced **247**

Making a Function Run Again 248
Passing an Event to a Function 251
Creating a Global Event Handler 252
Animating an Object 254
Finding Your Location on the Screen 257
Identifying an Object on the Screen 259
Dynamic Content Between Frames 261
Moving the Browser Window 264
Opening a New Browser Window 266
Changing a Window's Size 270

Chapter 15: Dynamic Techniques: CSS **273**

Changing a Definition 274
Changing an Object's Class 276
Adding a New Rule 278
Disabling a Style Sheet 280

Chapter 16: Netscape Layers **283**

What Is a Netscape Layer? 284
Creating a Layer 285
Importing External Content with
    Netscape Layers 288
Accessing Layers with JavaScript 290
Modifying Layers with JavaScript 294
Providing Content for Nonlayer Browsers 296

Chapter 17: Internet Explorer for Windows **297**

Fading Between Objects 298
Transitions Between Pages 299
Making an Element Blur 301
Making an Object Wave 302

PART 3: USING DHTML AND CSS TOOLS   **303**

Chapter 18: GoLive Primer   **305**
The GoLive Interface 306
Adding CSS 310
Adding a Layer (Floating Box) 314
Adding DHTML Animation 316

Chapter 19: Dreamweaver Primer   **319**
The Dreamweaver Interface 320
Adding CSS 324
Adding a Layer 328
Adding Animation 330

PART 4: DYNAMIC WEB SITES   **333**

Chapter 20: Understanding the Dynamic Web   **335**
What Makes a Web Site Dynamic? 336
What Is Hypertext? 338
Dynamic by Design 339
Understanding Layout on the Web 340
Navigation Do's and Don'ts 343

Chapter 21: Creating a Dynamic Web Site   **347**
Step 1: Define 348
Step 2: Design 351
Step 3: Build 356

Chapter 22: Web Page Layout   **359**
Netscape CSS Bug Fix 360
Setting the CSS for the OS 362
Creating Headlines 364
Creating a Fixed Header 366
Creating a Sidebar 368
Setting a Dynamic Header and Footer 370
Making Your Own Frame Borders 372
Opening and Closing Frames 374
Keeping Pages Framed 380
Looking Good in Print (on the Web) 383

Chapter 23: Importing External Content   **385**
Combining ilayers and iframes 386
Using Server-Side Includes 388
Using an External JavaScript File 389
Viewing Someone Else's External Content 390

Chapter 24: Web Site Navigation   393

Setting Link Styles 394
Setting Multiple Link Styles 397
Creating Drop-Down Menus 399
Creating a Sliding Menu 404
Creating a Remote Control 407
Creating a Clamshell Menu 411
Creating a Breadcrumb Menu 415
Navigation for Nondynamic Browsers 421
Educating the Browser 422

Chapter 25: Controls   425

Creating Your Own Scroll Bars 426
Creating Your Own Back Button 433
Creating a Slide Show 434
Creating Pop-Up Hypertext 438
Using Form Input for Dynamic Actions 441
Creating Contextual Forms 443
Drag-and-Drop Objects 446
Swapping Images 449
Creating a Smart Menu 454

Chapter 26: Special Effects   459

Creating Drop Caps 460
Creating a Simple Drop Shadow 462
Creating an Advanced Drop Shadow 464
Fading HTML Text 467
Follow the Mouse Pointer 471
Floating Objects 475
Creating Transparent Graphics in PNG Format . . 478
Creating a Clock 483

Chapter 27: Multimedia   485

Adding Sound 486
Adding a GIF Animation 488
Adding a Flash Animation. 495
Adding Video 501
Adding a Java Applet 504

Chapter 28: Debugging Your Code   507

Troubleshooting CSS 508
Validating Your CSS 511
Troubleshooting JavaScript 513
Cross-Browser Conundrums 517

Chapter 29: The Future of the Dynamic Web   **519**
Why Standards Matter 520
Extensible Markup Language (XML) 522
Extensible Hypertext Markup
      Language (XHTML) 525
Synchronized Multimedia Integration
      Language (SMIL) 529
Scalable Vector Graphics (SVG) 531
What's Next: CSS Level 3 532

Appendix A: The DHTML and CSS Browsers   **533**
Internet Explorer 534
Netscape Navigator 535
Other Browsers 536

Appendix B: CSS Quick Reference   **537**

Appendix C: DHTML Quick Reference   **547**
Reserved Words 550

Appendix D: Browser-Safe Fonts   **553**

Appendix E: Tools of the Trade   **559**
Software 560
Online 563

Appendix F: Further Resources   **565**
Web Sites: Technology and Standards 566
Web Sites: Design and Theory 570
Web Sites: Examples 572
Books, Magazines, and Other Publications 574

Index   **577**

INTRODUCTION

Creating Web pages used to be simple. You learned a few tags, created a few graphics, and presto: Web page. Now, with streaming video, JavaScript, CGI, Shockwave, Flash, and Java, the design of Web pages may seem overwhelming to anyone who doesn't want to become a computer programmer.

Enter dynamic HTML (DHTML) and cascading style sheets (CSS), technologies that give you—the Web designer—the ability to add pizzazz to your Web pages as quickly and easily as HTML does. With DHTML, you don't have to rely on plug-ins that the visitor might not have—or rely on complicated programming languages (except maybe a little JavaScript). For the most part, DHTML is created the same way as HTML and requires no special software.

What Is This Book About?

In the years since Netscape Navigator and Internet Explorer began supporting DHTML and CSS capabilities, the Web itself has changed significantly. The browser wars, the dot-com explosion (and subsequent crash), and the Web's enormous growth in popularity have led to a shakedown of the technologies that are regularly used to create Web sites. Both DHTML and CSS, however, remain two standards being used to create some of the best Web sites around.

In this book, I will show you the best ways to implement DHTML and CSS so that the broadest spectrum of the Web-surfing population can view your Web sites. To help organize the information, I have split this book into four parts:

- **Part 1** details how to use CSS to control the appearance of the content on Web pages. I will show you accurate ways to control the various aspects of how your Web page displays.

- **Part 2** deals with how to use the Document Object Model (DOM) with CSS and JavaScript to create basic dynamic functions. I will show you how to create a DOM that will allow you to run dynamic functions in most browsers with as little redundant code as possible.

- **Part 3** concentrates on how to create DHTML and CSS with two of the most popular Web-page-editing programs on the market: Adobe GoLive and Macromedia Dreamweaver. Although you do not have to use these programs to create Web sites with CSS and DHTML, they can make your life easier.

- **Part 4** will show you how to design a site with DHTML and CSS, and describes some of uses for these technologies. In addition, I will show you ways to debug your code and introduce you to some emerging dynamic technologies.

Who Is This Book For?

If the title of this book caught your eye, you're probably already well acquainted with the ins and outs of the Internet's most popular offshoot, the World Wide Web (or perhaps you're just a severely confused arachnophile). To understand this book, you need to be familiar with HTML (Hypertext Markup Language). You don't have to be an expert, but you should know the difference between a `<p>` tag and a `<br>` tag. In addition, several chapters call for more than a passing knowledge of JavaScript.

That said, the more knowledge about HTML and JavaScript you can bring to this book, the more you will get out of it.

WHO IS THIS BOOK FOR?

Everyone Is a Web Designer

Forget about 15 minutes of fame: In the future, everyone will be a Web designer. As the Web continues to expand, a growing number of people are choosing this medium to get their message—whatever it may be—out to the rest of the world. Whether they are movie buffs extolling the virtues of *The Third Man* or multinational corporations extolling the virtues of their companies, individuals and companies see the Web as the way to get the message out.

The fact is, just as everyone who uses a word processor is at some level a typographer, as the Web grows in popularity, everyone who uses it to do more than passively view pages will need to know how to design for the Web.

Learning DHTML and CSS is your next step into the larger world of Web design.

Values and Units

Throughout this book, you will need to enter different values to define different properties. These values come in various forms, depending on the need of the property. Some values are straightforward—a number is a number—but others have special units associated with them.

Values in chevrons (<>) represent a type of value (**Table i.1**). Words that appear in the code font are literal values and should be typed exactly as shown.

Length values

Length values come in two varieties:

◆ **Relative lengths,** which vary depending on the computer being used (**Table i.2**).

◆ **Absolute values,** which remain constant regardless of the hardware and software being used (**Table i.3**).

I generally recommend using pixel sizes to describe font sizes for the greatest stability between operating systems and browsers.

Color values

You can describe color on the screen in a variety of ways (**Table i.4**), but most of these descriptions are just different ways of telling the computer how much red, green, and blue is in a particular color.

Table i.1

Value Types		
VALUE TYPE	WHAT IT IS	EXAMPLE
<number>	A whole	1, 2, 3
<length>	A measurement of distance or size	1in
<color>	A chromatic expression	red
<percentage>	A proportion	35%
<URL>	The absolute or relative path to a file on the Web: http://www.mySite.net/ bob/graphics/image1.gif	

Table i.2

Relative Length Values			
NAME	TYPE OF UNIT	WHAT IT IS	EXAMPLE
em	Em dash	Width of the letter M for that font	3em
ex	x-height	Height of the lowercase x of that font	5ex
px	Pixel	Based on the monitor's resolution	125px

Table i.3

Absolute Length Values			
NAME	TYPE OF UNIT	WHAT IT IS	EXAMPLE
pt	Point	Generally used to describe font size. 1pt = 1/72 of an inch.	12pt
pc	Picas	Generally used to describe font size. 1pc ~ 12pt.	3pc
mm	Millimeters		25mm
cm	Centimeters		5.1cm
in	Inches	1 inch = 2.54cm	2.25in

Table i.4

Color Values		
NAME	WHAT IT IS	EXAMPLE
#RRGGBB	Red, green, and blue Hex-code value of a color (00-99,AA-FF)	#CC33FF or #C3F
rgb	Red, green, and blue (#R,#G,#B) numeric values of a color (0–255)	rgb(204,51,255)
rgb(R%,G%,B%)	Red, green, and blue percentage values of a color (0%-100%)	rgb(81%,18%,100%)
name	The name of the color	Purple

VALUES AND UNITS

Percentages

Many of the properties in this book can have a percentage as their value. The behavior of this percentage value depends on the property being used.

URLs

A Uniform Resource Locator (URL) is the unique address of something on the Web. This resource could be an HTML document, a graphic, a CSS file, a JavaScript file, a sound or video file, a CGI script, or a variety of other file types. URLs can be *local*, which simply describes the location of the resource relative to the current document; or *global*, which describes the absolute location of the resource on the Web and begins with http://.

In addition, throughout the book, I use links in the code examples. I used the number sign (#) as a placeholder in links that can be directed to any URL you want:

```
<a href="#">Link</a>
```

The number sign is shorthand that links to the top of the current page. Replace these with your own URLs as desired.

However, in some links, placing any URL in the href will interfere with the DHTML functions in the example. For those, I used the built-in JavaScript function void():

```
<a href="javascript:void('')">Link</a>
```

This function simply tells the link to do absolutely nothing.

✔ Tip

■ Certain colors always display properly on any monitor. These colors are called the browser-safe colors. You'll find them fairly easy to remember because their values stay consistent. For hex, you can use any combination of 00, 33, 66, 99, CC, or FF. For numeric values, use 0, 51, 102, 153, 204, or 255. For percentages, use 0, 20, 40, 60, 80, or 100.

VALUES AND UNITS

Reading This Book

For the most part, text, tables, figures, code, and examples should be self-explanatory. But you need to know a few things to understand this book.

CSS value tables

In Part 1, each section that explains a CSS property includes a table to give you a quick reference to the different values the property can use, as well as the browsers and CSS levels with which those values are compatible (**Figure i.1**). The compatibility column displays the first browser version of Netscape and Internet Explorer that supported the value. **Table i.5** lists the browser abbreviations I used.

Table i.5

Browser Abbreviations	
ABBREVIATION	BROWSER
IE3	Internet Explorer 3
IE4	Internet Explorer 4
IE5	Internet Explorer 5
N4	Netscape 4
N6	Netscape 6

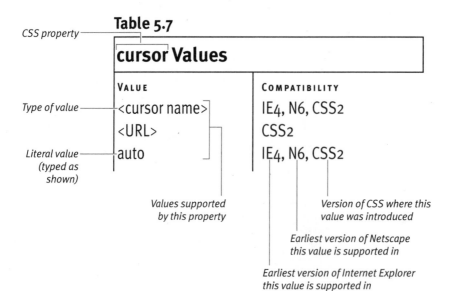

Figure i.1 The property tables in Part 1 of this book show you the values available with a property, the earliest browser version the value is available in, and which version of CSS the value was introduced in. Keep in mind, though, that even if the value is available in a particular version of the browser, it may not be available in all operating systems. Appendix B shows which operating systems a particular value works in and if there are any problems.

The code

For clarity and precision, I have used several layout techniques to help you see the difference between the text of the book and the code.

Code looks like this:

```
<style>
    p { font-size: 12pt; }
</style>
```

All code in this book is presented in lowercase (see the sidebar "Uppercase or Lowercase Code"). In addition, quotes in the code always appear as straight quotes (" or '), not curly quotes (" " or '). There is a good reason for this distinction: Curly quotes (also called smart quotes) will cause the code to fail.

Important lines of code that I discuss on a certain page are emphasized by appearing in red in the code sample.

When you type a line of code, the computer can run the line as long as needed, but in this book, lines of code have to be broken to make them fit on the page. When that happens, I use this gray arrow (→) to indicate that the line of code is continued from above, like this:

```
.title { font: bold 28pt/26pt times,
→ serif;'color: #FFF; background-color:
→ #000;'background-image: url(bg_
→ title.gif); }
```

I often begin a numbered step with a line of code. This is intended as a reference to help you pinpoint where that step applies in the larger code block that accompanies the task.

Uppercase or Lowercase Code?

All the HTML code, properties, and values in this book are lowercase. Although HTML code can be uppercase or lowercase, an up-and-coming standard called XHTML requires all code to be lowercase (see "XHTML" in Chapter 29). XHTML is likely to be the future markup language for the Web, and to begin the transition now, I have started placing all my code in lowercase.

READING THIS BOOK

What Tools Do You Need for This Book?

The great thing about DHTML is that, like HTML, it doesn't require any special or expensive software. DHTML code is just text, and you can edit it with a program such as SimpleText (Mac OS) or NotePad (Windows). You do need to have one of the Version 4.0 browsers, however, to run most DHTML code.

Appendix E includes a list of extremely helpful (and mostly free) utilities and tools that I recommend to anyone who creates Web sites.

In addition, a couple of programs make life with DHTML and CSS much easier by automating many of the tedious and repetitive tasks associated with Web design. I recommend using Adobe GoLive or Macromedia Dreamweaver. Part 3 of this book can help you decide which program is better for you.

Web Sites for This Book

I hope you'll be using a lot of the code from this book in your Web pages, but watch out—retyping information can lead to errors. Some books include a fancy-shmancy CD-ROM containing all the code from the book, and you can pull it off that disk. But guess who pays for that CD? You do. And CDs aren't cheap.

But if you bought this book, you already have access to the largest resource of knowledge that ever existed: the Web. And that's exactly where you can find the code from this book.

This is my support site for this *Visual QuickStart Guide* (**Figure i.2**):

www.webbedenvironments.com/dhtml/

continues on next page

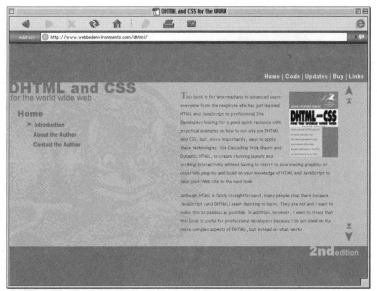

Figure i.2 The *DHTML and CSS for the World Wide Web: Visual QuickStart Guide* support Web site, open 24 hours a day.

You can download the code and any important updates and corrections from here. The site also includes other articles I have written about the Web.

If you do type the examples from the book, you might find that some do not work without the support files I used to create them. No worries—at the support site, you will find the various examples, which you can view live to compare results.

You have DHTML questions? I have DHTML answers. You can contact me at `vqs-dhtml@webbedenvironments.com`.

Also, be sure to visit Peachpit Press' own support site for the book:

`www.peachpit.com/vqs/DHTML`

Built with DHTML

In addition to the support site, I have set up a list of the most current DHTML-capable browsers at:

`www.webbedenvironments.com/dhtml/builtwith/`

You can use the "Built with DHTML" logo (**Figure i.3**) to link to this Web page from your own DHTML Web site to help visitors find the right browser.

Figure i.3 Built with DHTML. Use this logo on your Web site to link to the list of DHTML-capable browsers I have set up.

PART 1

CASCADING
STYLE SHEETS

Chapter 1:   Understanding CSS   3

Chapter 2:   CSS Basics   17

Chapter 3:   Font Controls   57

Chapter 4:   Text Controls   77

Chapter 5:   List and Mouse Controls   95

Chapter 6:   Color and Background Controls 105

Chapter 7:   Border and Margin Controls   115

Chapter 8:   Positioning Controls   139

Chapter 9:   Visibility Controls   157

UNDERSTANDING CSS

Figure 1.1 The CSS logo.

Let's face it: HTML is not exactly a designer's dream come true. It is imprecise, unpredictable, and not terribly versatile when it comes to presenting the diverse kinds of content that Web designers demand of it.

Then again, HTML was never intended to deliver high-concept graphic content and multimedia. In fact, it was never really intended to be anything more than a glorified universal word processing language delivered over the Internet—and a pretty limited one at that.

HTML is a markup language that was created to allow authors to define the structure of a document for distribution on the Web. That is, rather than being designed to show the style of what is being displayed, it is intended only to show how the page should be organized.

Over time, new tags and technologies have been added to HTML that allow greater control of the structure and appearance of documents—things such as tables, frames, justification controls, and JavaScript—but what Web designers can't do with fast-loading HTML, they have had to hack together using slow-loading graphics.

It's not a very elegant system.

So when Web developers started clamoring for the World Wide Web Consortium to add greater control of Web page design, the W3C introduced cascading style sheets (CSS) to fill the void in straight HTML (**Figure 1.1**).

Now, you are probably thinking, "Oh, great—just when I learn HTML, they go and change everything." But never fear: CSS is as easy to use as HTML. In fact, in many ways it's easier, because rather than introducing more HTML tags to learn, it works directly with existing HTML tags to tell them how to behave.

Take the humble <bold> tag, for example. In HTML, it does one thing and one thing only: it makes text darker. But using CSS, you can "redefine" the bold tag so that it not only makes text darker, but also displays text in all caps and in a particular font to really add emphasis. You could even make the <bold> tag *not* make text bold.

In this chapter, you'll learn how CSS works and the principles involved in creating them. In subsequent chapters, you'll learn how to apply all the individual properties.

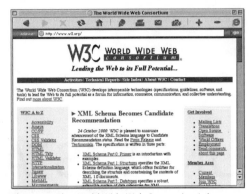

Figure 1.2 The World Wide Web Consortium's home page: www.w3.org.

What Is the World Wide Web Consortium?

The World Wide Web Consortium (W3C) is an organization that sets many of the standards that browser manufacturers eventually use to create their products (**Figure 1.2**).

Created in 1994, the W3C has a mission to "to lead the World Wide Web to its full potential by developing common protocols that promote its evolution and ensure its interoperability."

The W3C is made up of more than 400 member organizations around the world. These organizations include vendors of technology products and services, content providers, corporate users, research laboratories, standards bodies, and governments.

According to the W3C's Web site, the consortium has three goals:

1. *Universal Access*: "To make the Web accessible to all by promoting technologies that take into account the vast differences in culture, education, ability, material resources, and physical limitations of users on all continents."

2. *Semantic Web*: "To develop a software environment that permits each user to make the best use of the resources available on the Web."

3. *Web of Trust*: "To guide the Web's development with careful consideration for the novel legal, commercial, and social issues raised by this technology."

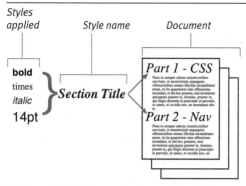

Styles applied

bold
times
italic
14pt

Style name

} *Section Title*

Document

Part 1 - CSS

Nam tu semper aderas misericorditer saeviens, et amarissimis aspargens offensionibus omnes illicitas iucunditates meas, ut ita quaererem sine offensione iucundari, et ubi hoc possem, non invenirem quicquam praeter te, domine, praeter te, qui fingis dolorem in praecepto et percutis, ut sanes, et occidis nos, ne moriamur abs te.

Part 2 - Nav

Nam tu semper aderas misericorditer saeviens, et amarissimis aspargens offensionibus omnes illicitas iucunditates meas, ut ita quaererem sine offensione iucundari, et ubi hoc possem, non invenirem quicquam praeter te, domine, praeter te, qui fingis dolorem in praecepto et percutis, ut sanes, et occidis nos, ne

Figure 1.3 Styles being applied to a section title in a word processing program tag.

What Is a Style?

Most word processors today include a way to make changes to text not just on a word-by-word basis, but also throughout an entire document by means of styles.

Styles collect all the different attributes, such as format and size, that you want to apply to similar types of text—titles, headers, captions, and so on—and give these groups of attributes a common name. Suppose that you want all the section titles in your document to be bold, Times font, italic, and 14-point. You could assign all those attributes to a style called Section Title (**Figure 1.3**).

Whenever you type a section title, all you have to do is use the Section Title style, and all those attributes are applied to the text in one fell swoop—no fuss, no mess. Even better, if you decide later that you really want all those titles to be 18-point instead of 14-point, you just change the definition of Section Title. The word processor then changes the appearance of all the text marked with that style throughout the document.

What Are Cascading Style Sheets?

CSS brings to the Web the same "one-stop shopping" convenience for setting styles that is available in most word processors. You can set a CSS in one central location to affect the appearance of HTML tags on a single Web page or across an entire Web site.

Although the CSS methodology works with HTML, it is not HTML. Rather, CSS is a separate code that enhances the abilities of HTML by allowing you to redefine the way that existing HTML tags work (**Figures 1.4** and **1.5**).

For example, the paragraph tag container, <p>...</p>, basically does one thing: It puts a space between two paragraphs. Using CSS, however, you can change the nature of the paragraph tag so that it also makes all the text within the paragraph bold, Times font, italic, and 14-point (**Figure 1.6**). As you can with word processor styles, you can also choose to change the definition of the <p> tag and all paragraphs on a Web page.

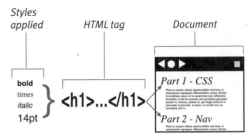

Figure 1.4 Styles being applied to an HTML tag.

Figure 1.5 An HTML page using CSS to add an image in the background, position the content down and to the right, and format the text.

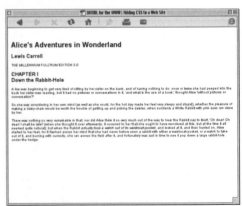

Figure 1.6 The same code displayed without the benefit of CSS. The page still displays, but without the formatting of Figure 1.5.

Table 1.1

CSS Properties		
PROPERTY	WHAT YOU CONTROL	FOR MORE INFO
Font	Letter form, size, boldface, italic	Chapter 3
Text	Kerning, leading, alignment, case	Chapter 4
List & Mouse	Bullets, indentation	Chapter 5
Color	Borders, text, bullets, rules, backgrounds	Chapter 6
Background	Behind the page or behind a single element on the page	Chapter 6
Border & Margin	Margins, padding, borders, width, height	Chapter 7
Positioning	Exact placement on the screen	Chapter 8
Visibility	Whether one element appears and how much of it is showing	Chapter 9

Figure 1.7 The W3C's logo.

Table 1.1 shows some of the things you can do with CSS and where to find more information.

✔ Tip

■ The power of CSS comes from its capability to mix and match different rules from different sources to tailor your Web pages' layout to your exact needs. In some ways, it resembles computer programming—which is not too surprising, because a lot of this stuff was created by programmers instead of designers. But when you get the hang of it, CSS will become as natural as putting together a sentence.

Who Owns CSS?

On January 12, 1999, Microsoft Corp. (www.microsoft.com) was granted U.S. Patent #5,860,073. This particular patent, titled *Style sheets for publishing system(s)*, covers "the use of style sheets in an electronic publishing system." Sound familiar?

The inventors listed in this patent claim to have developed a system whereby "text, or other media such as graphics, is poured into the display region," at which time style sheets—defined as "a collection of formatting information, such as fonts and tabs"—are applied. This patent seems to overlap concepts laid out in the W3C's specifications for CSS (**Figure 1.7**) and the Extensible Stylesheet Language (XSL), which have been in development at least since 1994.

sidebar continues on next page

Who Owns CSS? *continued*

What does this mean? It means that Microsoft can now claim as its intellectual property several of the key concepts that make Web-browser technology possible. Theoretically, if you want to use these technologies—or any technology based on them—you now need to sign a licensing agreement with Microsoft. Imagine a world in which every Web site using CSS, dynamic HTML (DHTML), and XSL has to be Microsoft-certified.

The situation may never get that bad, however. Microsoft has reported that it will offer "free and reciprocal" licensing agreements to anyone who wants to use "its" technology, adding that it is not even clear whether a license will be necessary.

A brief analysis of the patent shows that it has two major flaws, which the W3C and the Web Standards Project (www.webstandards.org) have already been quick to point out:

1. "The existence of prior art," referring to the fact that style sheets were proposed with the first Web browsers coming out of CERN laboratories in 1994. In fact, style sheets have been around since the 1960s, when they were used for print publications. At best, Microsoft is a Johnny-come-lately to the concept.

2. The W3C's own licensing ensures that the standards developed under its banner are universally available and royalty-free. Because the W3C first developed the concept of style sheets, its license should hold precedence.

Microsoft had representatives on the committees that created these standards, and its own patent refers to documents produced by the W3C regarding CSS, so it seems highly improbable that this patent would stand up to much scrutiny.

George Olsen of the Web Standards Project questions whether the patent should have been granted in the first place, "because [there] are a number of prior examples of similar technology, including the original proposal for CSS," he says. Also, it is assumed that any organization—Microsoft included—with representatives in the W3C will detail any current or pending patents that might affect the W3C standards under consideration, which this patent certainly did. Yet the W3C first heard of the patent on February 4, 1999, when information about the patent was made publicly available.

So what does this mean *to you*? Probably, not much. The W3C has published CSS as an open standard, and the genie is already out of the bottle.

So far, I haven't heard of Microsoft serving anyone a cease-and-desist order for using CSS on a Web site. Still, the point of having an open standard is to allow interested parties to contribute without one entity taking all the credit. Let's hope that this patent won't put a chill on future CSS development.

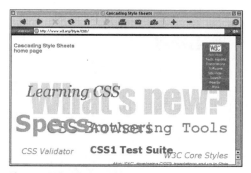

Figure 1.8 The W3C's CSS home page
(www.w3.org/Style/CSS/).

Versions of CSS

CSS has evolved over the past several years under the guidance of the W3C (**Figure 1.8**) into its current version, referred to as Level 2. Although most modern browsers support the most recent version, older browsers support combinations of older versions of CSS. Appendix B details which browsers support which CSS properties:

♦ **CSS Level 1 (CSS1).** The W3C Consortium released the first official version of CSS in 1996. This early version included the core capabilities associated with CSS, such as the capability to format text, to set fonts, and to set margins. Netscape 4 and Internet Explorer 3 and 4 support Level 1—almost.

♦ **CSS-Positioning (CSS-P).** Web designers needed a way to position elements on the screen precisely. CSS1 had already been released, and CSS Level 2 was still off in the distance, so the W3C released a stop-gap solution: CSS-Positioning. This standard was intended to be a proposal that the various parties concerned could debate for a while before it became official. Netscape and Microsoft jumped on these proposals, however, and included the preliminary ideas in their version 4 browsers. Do both Netscape and Internet Explorer support CSS-P? Sort of. Although most of the basic features are supported in both of the "name-brand" browsers, several features were left out.

♦ **CSS Level 2 (CSS2).** The most recent version of CSS came out in 1998. Level 2 includes all the attributes of the previous two versions, plus an increased emphasis on international accessibility and the capability to specify media-specific CSS. Internet Explorer 5 and Netscape 6 support Level 2.

continues on next page

◆ **CSS Level 3 (CSS3).** This standard is still under development, and even after it's released, it usually takes a few years for browsers to support a standard. The most exciting new addition to CSS3 undoubtedly will be Scalable Vector Graphics (SVG). This is a format that allows you to include shapes (lines, circles, splines, and so on) as vectors rather than bitmaps, bringing the power of vector-based graphics and typography to the Web. See "Understanding Typography on the Web" in Chapter 3 for more details on vector versus bitmap text and "What's Next: CSS Level 3" in Chapter 29 for more details on CSS3.

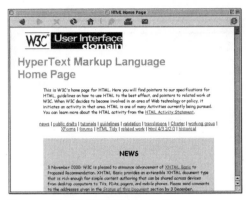

Figure 1.9 The W3C's HTML home page.

✔ Tip

■ CSS is not the only type of style sheet available for the Web. Netscape 4, for example, also supports JavaScript style sheets. CSS, however, is the most commonly used style sheet, and it has been endorsed by the W3C.

CSS and HTML 4.01

The latest version of the Hypertext Markup Language, HTML 4.01, was released in December 1999 by the W3C. HTML 4.01 includes the style-sheet methodology (previously maintained as a separate standard) as part of the HTML specification (**Figure 1.9**).

This does not mean that CSS is HTML; it simply means that HTML now relies on the capabilities of CSS.

Many of the design-related HTML tags, if not abandoned by the new HTML standard, are slated to be made obsolete in favor of CSS. The W3C calls this situation "deprecation." Although the tags still work, they are on the way out.

The W3C's thinking is this: Style sheets should be used to "relieve HTML of the responsibilities of presentation."

Translation: Don't bug us with requests for more HTML tags to do layout. Use style sheets instead.

That's probably a good idea. It means that anybody can use HTML tags, whether she is Jo Web Designer or not. But ol' Jo can reassign standard HTML tags to do whatever she wants them to do.

You can find further information about HTML at **www.w3.org/MarkUp/**.

Types of CSS Rules

The best thing about cascading style sheets is that they are amazingly simple to set up. They don't require plug-ins or fancy software—just rules. A CSS rule defines what the HTML should look like and how it should behave in the browser window.

You can set up rules to tell a specific HTML tag how to display its content, or you can create generic rules and then apply them to tags at your discretion.

There are three types of CSS rules:

1. **HTML selector.** The text portion of an HTML tag is called the *selector*. h3, for example, is the selector for the <h3> tag. The HTML selector is used in a CSS rule to redefine how the tag displays (see "(Re)Defining an HTML Tag" in Chapter 2). Example:

   `p { font: bold 12pt times; }`

2. **Class.** A *class* is a "free agent" rule that can be applied to any HTML tag at your discretion. You can name the class anything you want (see Appendix C). Because it can be applied to multiple HTML tags, a class is the most versatile type of selector (see "Defining Classes to Create Your Own Tags" in Chapter 2). Example:

   `.myClass { font: bold 12pt times; }`

3. **ID.** ID rules work much like class selectors, in that they can be applied to any HTML tag. ID selectors, however, are usually applied only once on the page to a particular HTML tag to create an object for use with a JavaScript function (see "Defining IDs to Identify an Object" in Chapter 2). Example:

   `#object1 { position: absolute; top:`
   `→ 10px; }`

✔ Tips

- Don't confuse the selector of an HTML tag with its attributes. In the following tag, for example, img is the selector, and src is an attribute.

  `<img src="picture.gif">`

- Although the paragraph tag (<p>) is often used without its closing </p> tag, the closing tag *must* be included if you want to define something using CSS. CSS rules will generally be applied only to HTML tags that have open and close tags, but there are a few exceptions, such as the image tag.

The Parts of a CSS Rule

All rules, regardless of where they are located or what type they are, have the following three parts:

- **Selectors** are the alpha/numeric characters that identify a rule. The selector can be an HTML tag selector, a class, or an ID.

- **Properties** identify what is being defined. There are several dozen properties, each one responsible for an aspect of the page content's behavior and appearance.

- **Values** are assigned to a property to define its nature. A value can be a keyword such as "yes" or "no," a number, or a percentage. The type of value used depends solely on the property to which it is assigned.

After the selector, the rest of a CSS rule consists of the properties and their values, which together I will refer to as a *definition*. **Figure 1.10** illustrates the general syntax of a rule.

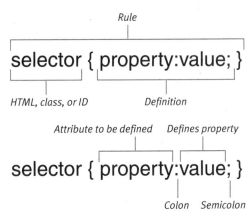

Figure 1.10 The basic syntax of a CSS rule.

Tags or Selectors: What's the Big Difference?

An HTML selector is the text part of an HTML tag—the part that tells the browser what type of tag it is. So when you define an HTML selector using CSS, you are, in fact, redefining the HTML tag. Although the two elements, tag and selector, seem to be identical, they aren't: If you used the full HTML tag—brackets and all—in a CSS rule, the tag would not work. So it's important to keep these two ideas separate.

✔ Tips

■ Although you do not have to include a semicolon with the last definition in a list, experience shows that adding this semicolon can prevent headaches later. If you decide to add something to the definition and forget to put in the required semicolon before the addition, you may cause the rule to fail completely. Not just that one definition, but all the definitions in the rule will fail to be used (see "Troubleshooting CSS" in Chapter 28).

■ Although Netscape 4 and above and Internet Explorer 3 and above support CSS, none of these browsers supports all the CSS capabilities, and the support varies depending on the browser version. When you use CSS, check Appendix B to see whether a particular property is supported by a browser.

Where to Put CSS Rules

You can set up rules in three places:

◆ **In an HTML tag** within the body of your document, to affect a single tag in the document. This type of rule is often referred to as an *inline* rule (see "Adding CSS to an HTML Tag" in Chapter 2).

◆ **In the head of a document,** to affect an entire Web page. This type of rule is called an *embedded* rule (see "Adding CSS to a Web Page" in Chapter 2).

◆ **In an external document** that is then linked or imported into your HTML document(s), to affect an entire Web site. This type of rule is called an *external* rule (see "Adding CSS to a Web Site" in Chapter 2).

The position of a rule in relationship to the document and other CSS rules determines the scope of the rule's effect on the document (see "Determining the Cascade Order" in Chapter 2).

THE PARTS OF A CSS RULE

Kinds of HTML Tags

Not all CSS definitions can be applied to all HTML tags. Whether a particular CSS property can apply depends on the nature of the tag. For the most part, whether a property can be applied to a particular tag (or not) is fairly obvious.

You wouldn't expect the text-indent property, which indents the first line of a paragraph, to apply to an inline tag such as bold, for example. When you do need some help in this area, Appendix B tells you which properties can be used with a particular kind of HTML tag.

Table 1.2

Selectors for Block-Level Tags	
SELECTOR	**HTML USE**
blockquote	Quote style
center	Center text
dd	Definition description
dfn	Defined term
dir	Directory list
div	Logical division
dl	Definition list
dt	Definition term
h1-7	Header levels 1-7
li	List item
ol	Ordered list
p	Paragraph
table	Table
td	Table data
th	Table head
tr	Table row
ul	Unordered list

Uppercase or Lowercase Tags?

HTML tags are not case-sensitive. That is, the browser does not care whether the selectors (the text) in the tags are uppercase or lowercase. Most people prefer to use uppercase for tags, because this makes them stand out from the surrounding content.

I counted myself in that camp until the release of the XHTML standard (see "XHTML" in Chapter 29). One important characteristic of XHTML is that it *is* case-sensitive, and all selectors *must* be in lowercase. Therefore, to prepare for what is likely to be the next evolutionary step of HTML, I have started using lowercase selectors in all my HTML tags.

Table 1.3

Selectors for Inline Tags

SELECTOR	HTML USE
a	Anchored link
b	Boldface
big	Bigger text
cite	Short citation
code	Code font
em	Emphasis
font	Font appearance
i	Italic
pre	Preformatted text
span	Localized style formatting
strike	Strikethrough
strong	Strong emphasis
sub	Subscript
sup	Superscript
tt	Typewriter font
u	Underlined text

Table 1.4

Selectors for Replaced Tags

SELECTOR	HTML USE
img	Image embed
input	Input object
object	Object embedding
select	Select input area
textarea	Text input area

Note: Netscape 4 does not recognize CSS applied directly to these tags.

Besides the <body> tag, there are three basic types of HTML tags:

◆ **Block-level** tags place a line break before and after the element. **Table 1.2** lists the block-level tag selectors that CSS can use.

◆ **Inline** tags have no line breaks associated with the element. **Table 1.3** lists the inline-tag selectors that CSS can use.

◆ **Replaced** tags have set or calculated dimensions. **Table 1.4** lists the replaced-tag selectors that CSS can use.

CSS Basics

Figure 2.1 An HTML page using CSS to add an image in the background, position the content down and to the right, and format the text.

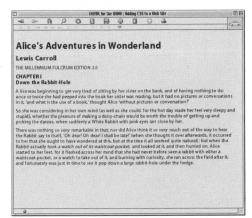

Figure 2.2 The same code displayed without the benefit of CSS. The page still displays, but without the formatting of Figure 2.1.

CSS lets you control your documents' appearance, but the big advantage of using CSS instead of just creating new HTML tags to do the same job is that by changing a definition in a single, centrally located CSS rule, you change the appearance of all the tags controlled by that rule (**Figures 2.1** and **2.2**).

If the rule is in the head of a particular document, the change affects that page. If the rule is in an external file, the change affects every page to which that file is linked—potentially, an entire Web site. On the downside, some browsers don't understand CSS, but they are becoming increasingly rare. Fortunately, they just ignore the CSS code and display the HTML as if it didn't exist. The page may not look as good without CSS, but at least it won't look any worse.

In this chapter, you'll learn how to set up CSS in a variety of places and methods for different effects.

Adding CSS to an HTML Tag

Although CSS means never having to set the appearance of each tag individually, you still have the freedom to set styles within individual tags. This is especially useful for overriding other styles set for the page, if you need to, on a case-by-case basis.

Figure 2.3 shows the general syntax for adding a style directly to an HTML tag, while **Figure 2.4** shows the code's results.

To set the style properties of individual HTML tags:

1. `<h1 style=`

   Type `style=` in the HTML tag you want to define (**Code 2.1**).

2. `"font: small-caps bold italic 2.5em`
   → `'minion web' Georgia, 'Times New`
   → `Roman', Times, serif; color: red;"`

   In quotes, type your style-definition(s) `property : value`, with a semicolon (;) separating individual definitions. Make sure to close the definition list with quotation marks.

3. `> Alice's Adventures in Wonderland`
   → `</h1>`

   After closing the tag, add the content to be styled. Then, if necessary, close the tag pair with the corresponding end tag.

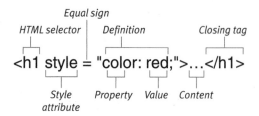

Figure 2.3 The general syntax for defining styles directly in an HTML tag.

Figure 2.4 The styles have been placed directly into the tags.

Code 2.1 Each tag receives instructions on how the content within it should behave, by means of the style attribute.

```
                    code
<html>

<body style ="background:white
→ url(alice23.gif) no-repeat; font-family:
→ arial,helvetica,geneva,sans-serif;
→ word-spacing: 1px;position: relative;
→ top:185px; left:165px; width:480px;">

<br>

<h1 style="font:small-caps bold  italic
→ 2.5em 'minion web' Georgia, 'Times New
→ Roman', Times, serif">Alice's Adventures
→ in Wonderland</h1>

<h2 style="font: bold  1.5em 'minion web'
→ Georgia, 'Times New Roman', Times, serif">
→ Lewis Carroll</h2>

<p style="style: italic; font-family:
→ monospace;">THE MILLENNIUM FULCRUM EDITION
→ 3.0</p>

<h3>CHAPTER I

<br>Down the Rabbit-Hole</h3>

<p><span style="font: 300%/100% serif;
→ color: #999999; margin-right: -3px;
→ ">A</span> lice was beginning to get very
→ tired of sitting by her sister on the
→ bank...</p>

<p>So she was considering in her own
→ mind...</p>

<p>There was nothing so <i>very</i>
→ remarkable in that...</p>

</body>

</html>
```

✔ Tips

■ Beware: Although Netscape supports styles in a tag, a bug in Netscape 4 may cause it to ignore any styles applied to tags after one that contains a directly applied style.

■ Although you do not gain the benefit of the universal style changes, using CSS in individual HTML tags is nevertheless very useful when you want to override universally defined styles. (See "Determining the Cascade Order" at the end of this chapter.).

■ I've also shown how you can define the **<body>** tag in this example, but be careful— this can lead to more problems than it's worth (see "Managing Existing or Inherited Property Values" later in this chapter). In addition, both Netscape and Internet Explorer balk at many properties in the body tag, especially positioning properties.

■ So as not to confuse the browser, it is best to use double quotes (") around the definition list, and single quotes (') for any values in the definition list, such as font names with spaces.

■ One common mistake I make is to confuse the equal sign (=) with the colon (:). Remember that although the style attribute in the tag uses an equal sign, CSS definition lists *always* use a colon.

■ You can also apply common styles to an entire Web page (see the following section, "Adding CSS to a Web Page") or to multiple Web pages (see "Adding CSS to a Web Site" later in this chapter).

ADDING CSS TO AN HTML TAG

Adding CSS to a Web Page

The main use for CSS is to define style rules for an entire document. To do this, you include your style rules in the head of the document nested within a style container (**Figure 2.5**).

While the results of adding style in this manner can look identical to adding the styles directly to an HTML tag (**Figure 2.6**), placing styles in a common location allows you to change the styles in a document from one place.

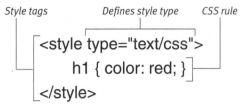

Style tags   *Defines style type*   *CSS rule*

```
<style type="text/css">
       h1 { color: red; }
</style>
```

Figure 2.5 The general syntax of a CSS style placed in the <head> of an HTML document.

Figure 2.6 Although this figure is a doppelganger for Figure 2.4, the CSS used to create it is located in the <head> of the document rather than in each individual tag.

Code 2.2 Although the result of this code (Figure 2.6) may look identical to the preceding example (Figure 2.4), the style rules are collected in the <head> of the document, where they affect all tags within the HTML document.

```
                    code
<html>
<head>
    <style type="text/css">
        body  {
                background:  white
                → url(alice23.gif) no-repeat;
                word-spacing: 1px; }

        #content {
                position: relative;
                top: 190px;
                left: 165px;
                width: 480px;
                font-family: arial,helvetica,
                → geneva,sans-serif; }

        h1 {
                font:small-caps bold  italic 2.5em
                → 'minion web' Georgia, 'Times
                → New Roman', Times, serif;
                color: red; }

        h2  {
                font: bold 1.5em 'minion web'
                → Georgia, 'Times New Roman',
                → Times, serif;
                font-size: 1.5em }

        .dropcap {
                font: 300%/100% serif;
                color: #999999;
                margin-right: -3px; }
    </style>
</head>
<body>
    <div id="content">
<br>
    <h1>Alice's Adventures in Wonderland</h1>
    <h2>Lewis Carroll</h2>
                    (code continues on next page)
```

To set the style for tags in an HTML document:

1. **<style type="text/css">**

   Type the opening <style> tag in the <head> of your document, defining the **type** as **"text/css"**. This defines the following styles as being not just any style, but CSS (**Code 2.2**).

2. **h1 {**

   Open your rule by typing the selector for the tag to be defined, followed by a curly bracket ({). The selector can be any of the following:

   ▲ An HTML tag selector (such as h1; see "(re)Defining an HTML Tag")

   ▲ A class selector (such as myClass; see "Defining Classes to Create Your Own Tags")

   ▲ An ID selector (such as #object1; see "Defining IDs to Identify an Object")

   ▲ A group of selectors separated by commas (such as h1,h2,myclass; see "Defining Tags with the Same Rules") to receive a common definition list

   ▲ A group of selectors separated by spaces (such as h1 myclass object1; see "Defining Tags in Context") to receive contextual definitions

3. **font: small-caps bold italic 2.5em → 'minion web' Georgia, 'Times New → Roman', Times, serif; color: red;**

   Type the definition(s) to be assigned to this rule **property: value**, with a semicolon (;) separating individual definitions in the list.

4. Close the rule with a curly bracket (}).

5. Repeat steps 2-4 for all the selectors you want to define.

6. **</style>**

   Close the style definition by typing the </style> end tag.

   continues on next page

✔ Tips

- You don't have to include `type="text/css"`, because the browser should be able to determine the type of style being used. I always put it there, however, to allow browsers that do not support a particular type of style sheet to avoid the code. It also clarifies to other humans the type being used.

- I recommend using the HTML comment tags `<!--...-->` to hide your CSS from non-CSS-capable browsers. Otherwise, these browsers may display the style sheet in the window as text, which is not very attractive.

- You can also apply styles directly to an individual HTML tag (see "Adding CSS to an HTML Tag") or to multiple Web pages (see "Adding CSS to a Web Site").

Code 2.2 *continued*

```
                     code
    <p style="style: italic; font-family:
    → monospace;">THE MILLENNIUM FULCRUM
    → EDITION 3.0</p>

    <h3>CHAPTER I

    <br>Down the Rabbit-Hole</h3>

    <p><span class="dropcap">A</span> lice
    → was beginning to get very tired of
    → sitting by her sister on the bank...'</p>
<p>So she was considering in her own
→ mind...</p>
<p>There was nothing so <i>very</i>
→ remarkable in tha...</p>
</div>
</body>
</html>
```

Formatting CSS

You will notice throughout this book that I format CSS definitions in a variety of ways. Sometimes, all the definitions are on a single line; other times, there is a line break after the semicolon. Line breaks do not affect the CSS as long as they follow this general syntax:

`selector {property1:value; property2:` `→ value; property3:vaule;}`

The difference in format comes down mostly to preference. I usually like to space my CSS definitions out a bit, to make them easier to scan. Also, spacing things out helps when you are trying to spot mistakes.

Most HTML editing programs, such as Adobe GoLive, allow you to set how the CSS should be formatted, so you can keep your code consistent.

Adding CSS to a Web Site

A major benefit of CSS is that you can create a style sheet for use not just with a single HTML document, but throughout an entire Web site. You can apply this external style sheet to a hundred HTML documents— without having to retype the information.

Establishing an external CSS file is a two-step process. First, set up the rules in a text file; then link or import this file into an HTML document, using either the <link> tag or @import (**Figure 2.7**).

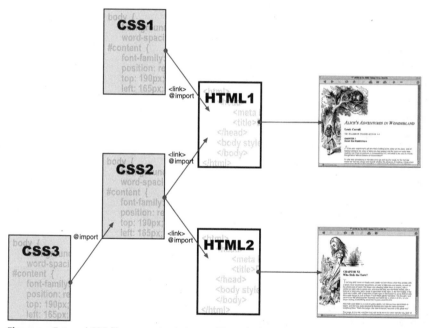

Figure 2.7 External CSS files can not only be used in multiple HTML files, as shown with CSS2, but an external CSS file can be imported (but not linked) into another external CSS file, as shown with CSS3. Linked or imported CSS files, however, act exactly as if you had typed the code into the file they are linked or imported into.

To set up an external CSS file:

1. Create a new file, using word processing or other software that allows you to save as a text file; Notepad or SimpleText will do (**Code 2.3**).

Do *not* use <style> tags in an external CSS file. This will prevent it from working on most browsers.

2. h1 {

Add CSS rules to the page by typing the selector for the tag to be defined, followed by a curly bracket ({). The selector can be any of the following:

▲ An HTML tag selector (such as h1; see "(re)Defining an HTML Tag")

▲ A class selector (such as .myClass; see "Defining Classes to Create Your Own Tags")

▲ An ID selector (such as #object1; see "Defining IDs to Identify an Object")

▲ A group of selectors separated by commas (such as h1,h2,myclass; see "Defining Tags with the Same Rules") to receive a common definition list

▲ A group of selectors separated by spaces (such as h1 myclass object1; see "Defining Tags in Context") to receive contextual definitions

Notice that you do *not* use the <style> tag here. Using that tag in this document will keep it from working in an HTML document.

3. font: small-caps bold italic 2.5em
→ 'minion web' Georgia, 'Times New
→ Roman', Times, serif;
   color: red;

Type the definition(s) to be assigned to this rule property: value, with a semi-colon (;) separating individual definitions in the list.

Code 2.3 filename.css: The external CSS "filename.css" contains definitions that will be used to create the layout in Code 2.4 and Code 2.5.

```
                        code
h1  {
    font: italic small-caps bold 2.5em
    → "minion web Georgia", "Times New Roman",
    → Times, serif;
color: red; }
h2  {
font: bold 1.5em "minion web Georgia",
→ "Times New Roman", Times, serif;  }
```

Code 2.4 The external CSS "filename2.css" contains additional definitions that will be used to create the layout in Code 2.4 and Code 2.5. Remember, you can call these files anything you want. I used "filename" as an example.

```
code
body  {
     background:  white url(alice23.gif)
     → no-repeat;
     word-spacing: 1px; }
#content  {
     font-family: arial, helvetica, geneva,
     → sans-serif;
     position: relative;
     top: 190px;
     left: 165px;
     width: 480px; }
.dropCap {
font: 300%/100% serif;
color: #999999;
margin-right: -3px; }
```

*Defines the link
to a stylesheet*   *URL for external file*

`<link rel="stylesheet" href="filename.css">`

Figure 2.8 The general syntax for linking to an external style sheet.

Figure 2.9 While this page may look exactly the same as Figures 2.6 and 2.4, the CSS used to create is now mostly located in external files that have been linked to.

4. Close the rule with a curly bracket (**}**).

5. Repeat steps 2–4 for all the selectors you want to define.

6. Save this document as `filename.css`, where *filename* is whatever you want to call this file, and *.css* is an extension to identify the file type. You can create and link to as many external CSS files as you want (**Code 2.4**).

7. Attach this file to an HTML file, using `<link>`, or to an HTML file or another CSS file using `@import`.

External style-sheet files can be used with any HTML file through the `<link>` tag. Linking a CSS file affects the document just as though the styles had been typed directly in the head of the document. **Figure 2.8** shows the general syntax for linking style sheets, while **Figure 2.9** shows the results of linking to a style sheet.

To link to an external CSS file:

1. `<link>`

Within the `<head>`...`</head>` of your HTML document, open your `<link>` tag and then type a space (**Code 2.5**).

2. `rel="stylesheet"`

Tell the browser that this will be a link to a style sheet.

3. `href="filename.css"`

Specify the location, either global or local, of the CSS file to be used, where *filename* is the full path and name (including extension) of your CSS document.

Code 2.5 The majority of the styles applied to this HTML document are being linked to from the external CSS files called filename.css and filename2.css, shown in Code 2.3 and Code2.4. The one exception is the <body> tag. It is being defined locally to tailor the background image for this page (Figure 2.9).

```
code
<html>
<head>
   <link rel="stylesheet" href="filename.css">
   <link rel="stylesheet" href="filename2.css">
   <style media="screen" type="text/css">
        body   { background: white url(alice23.gif) no-repeat;  }
   </style>
</head>
<body>
   <div id="content">
   <br>
   <h1>Alice's Adventures in Wonderland</h1>
   <h2>Lewis Carroll</h2>
   <p style="style: italic; font-family: monospace;">THE MILLENNIUM FULCRUM EDITION 3.0</p>
   <h3>CHAPTER I
   <br>Down the Rabbit-Hole</h3>
   <p><span class="dropCap">A</span> lice was beginning to get very tired of sitting by her
   → sister on the bank...</p>
   <p>So she was considering in her own mind...</p>
   <p>There was nothing so <i>very</i> remarkable in that...</p>
   </div>
</body>
</html>
```

URL for external file

@ import url(filename.css);

Figure 2.10 The general syntax for importing an external style sheet.

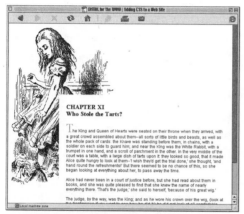

Figure 2.11 The same CSS files have been used to create this page as were used for Figure 2.9. This time, however, the files have been imported rather than linked to. In addition, a different background image has been defined for the <body> than the one used in the Figure 2.10.

4. `>`

Close the `<link>` tag with a chevron (`>`).

5. `<link rel="stylesheet type"`
`→ href="filename2.css">`

Repeat steps 1–5 to add as many style sheets as you want to link to.

6. `<style type="text/css">...</style>`

Add any additional styles in the head, using the `<style>` tag. You can place a `<style>` tag *before* the `<link>` tags, if you desire.

Another way to bring external style sheets into a document is to use the `@import` statement. Although this method is not supported in Netscape 4, it can be used to put external CSS files in an HTML document file, as well as in other external CSS files for Internet Explorer and Netscape 6. **Figure 2.10** shows the general syntax for the `@import` statement while **Figure 2.11** shows the results of importing the style sheet.

To import an external CSS file:

1. `<styletype="text/css">`

Within the head of your HTML document, open a style container (**Code 2.6**).

2. `import url(filename.css);`

Import the CSS file. The filename is the URL of the CSS document to be used. The URL can be global, in which case it would start with http://; or it could be local, pointing to a file on the same computer.

3. `@import url(filename2.css);`

Repeat step 3 for as many external CSS documents as you want to link.

4. `body {background: white url`
`→ (alice40.gif) no-repeat;`
`}`

You can include additional CSS rules here, if needed (see the previous section, "Adding CSS to a Web Page").

5. `</style>`

Close the style definition with a style end tag.

✔ Tips

■ Alternatively, you can place the `<link>` tag directly in an external style sheet. The imported file will be included as part of that external CSS file.

■ Because Netscape 4 does not support the `@import` statement, it generally is preferable to use the `<link>` method. You can use @import with Netscape 6.

■ Although the external CSS filename can be anything you want it to be, it's a good idea to use a name that will remind you of what these styles are for. The name navigation.css, for example, probably is a more helpful name than ss1.css.

Code 2.6 This example uses @import instead of `<link>` to add CSS files to this HTML document. The overall effect is identical, except that @import does not work in Netscape 4.

```
code
<html>
<head>
<style media="screen" type="text/css">
@import url(filename.css);
        @import url(filename2.css);
        body  {
            background: white
            → url(alice40.gif) no-repeat;
        }
</style>
</head>
<body>
<div  id="content">
        <br>
        <h2>CHAPTER XI<br>
        Who Stole the Tarts?</h2>
        <p><span class="dropCap">T</span>he
        → King and Queen of Hearts were
        → seated on their throne...</p>
</div>
</body>
</html>
```

■ A CSS file should not contain any HTML tags (even the `<style>` tag) or other content, with the exception of comments and imported styles.

■ You do not have to use the .css extension with CSS files. You could have just called this file *filename*, and it would have worked just as well. Adding the extension, however, can prevent confusion.

■ Linked style sheets in Netscape 4 often disappear if the document has to be reloaded from the computer's cache. To fix this problem, see "Netscape CSS Bug Fix" in Chapter 22.

Figure 2.12 The general syntax used to define the styles for an HTML tag.

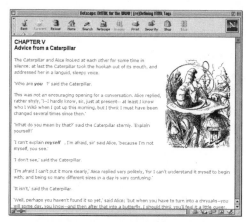

Figure 2.13 Several HTML tags have been redefined. Paragraphs <p> now display their text as gray, 12px size with 1.5 spaces between each line, and using the Verdana font. In addition, images <img> will justify to the right, and italic <i> text will appear bold.

(re)Defining an HTML Tag

Most HTML tags already have built-in definitions. Take the bold tag, for example; its built-in property is the equivalent of `font-weight: bold`.

Figure 2.12 shows the general syntax for a complete CSS rule using an HTML selector.

By adding new definitions to the bold tag's selector, b, you can change the ... tag pair to have just about any effect you want on the content between them (**Figure 2.13**).

HTML selectors can be defined within the <style>...</style> tags in the head of your document (see "Adding CSS to a Web Page" earlier in this chapter) or in an external CSS file that is then imported or linked to the HTML document (see the previous section, "Adding CSS to a Web Site").

To define an HTML selector:

1. `p {`

Start with the HTML selector whose properties you want to define, and add a curly bracket ({) to open your rule (**Code 2.7**).

2. `color: #666666;`
    `font-size: 12px;`
    `line-height: 18px;`
    `font-family: Verdana, Arial,`
    `→ Helvetica, Geneva, sans-serif;`

Type your property definition(s). You can add as many definitions as you want, but the properties have to work with the HTML tag in question. You cannot use text indent, for example, to define the bold tag. Check out Appendix B to see which properties can be used to redefine which tags.

3. `}`

Close your definition list with a curly bracket (}). Forget this, and it will ruin your day!

✔ Tips

■ After you redefine an HTML tag, all instances of the tag throughout the entire document are affected automatically.

■ The syntax is slightly different for redefining an individual HTML tag within a document (see "Adding CSS to an HTML Tag" earlier in this chapter).

■ Redefining a tag does not override that tag's preexisting properties. Thus, `<b>` still makes text bold no matter what other styles are added to it (see "Managing Existing or Inherited Property Values").

Code 2.7 Normally, the `<p>` tag simply puts a space between paragraphs. Add a few styles, however, and the `<p>` tag changes the color of the text, the font family, the font size, and the line spacing—not bad for one little tag (Figure 2.13).

```
                        code
<html>
<head>
<style type="text/css">
p {
color: #666666;
    font-size: 12px;
    line-height: 18px;
    font-family: Verdana, Arial, Helvetica,
    → Geneva, sans-serif; }
img { float: right;}
i { font-weight: bold; }
</style>
</head>
<body>
<div align="left">
<h3>CHAPTER V<br>
Advice from a Caterpillar</h3>
</div>
<p><img src="alice15.gif" width="200"
→ height="264" border="0">The Caterpillar
→ and Alice looked at each other for some
→ time in silence: at last the Caterpillar
→ took the hookah out of its mouth, and
→ addressed her in a languid, sleepy
→ voice.</p>
<p>'Who are <i>you</i>?' said the
→ Caterpillar.</p>
</body>
</html>
```

■ The `<body>` tag can also be redefined in this manner. Although theoretically, it acts likes a block-level tag (see "Kinds of HTML Tags" in Chapter 1), Internet Explorer for Windows does not accept any positioning controls in the `<body>` tag.

If you want to position your entire page, you need to place the whole thing in a CSS layer and position it that way (see "Creating Your Own Block-Level HTML Tags" later in this chapter).

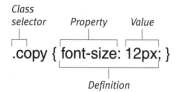

Figure 2.14 The general syntax of a CSS class.

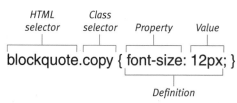

Figure 2.15 The general syntax of a dependent class. The definitions for this version of copy will only work if applied to a <blockquote> tag.

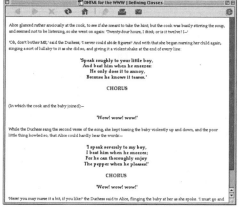

Figure 2.16 The class "copy" has been applied to all of the <p> tags, making the font 12px size, 1.5 spaces between lines, and Trebuchet MS font. The <blackquote> has its own version of "copy" as a dependent class to make the text bold, 14px size, a tighter line height, Book Antiqua font, and centered.

Defining Classes to Create Your Own Tags

Using a class selector gives you the ability to set up an independent style that you can then apply to any HTML tag.

Figures 2.14 and **2.15** show the general syntax of a CSS class rule.

Unlike an HTML selector, which automatically defines a particular type of tag, a class is given a unique name that is then specified in the HTML tag or tags you want to use it in with the style attribute (**Figure 2.16**).

Class rules can be defined within the <style>...</style> tags in the head of your document (see "Adding CSS to a Web Page" earlier in this chapter) or in an external CSS file that is then imported or linked to the HTML document (see "Adding CSS to a Web Site" earlier in this chapter).

Dependent Classes

A class can be directly associated with an HTML selector, in which case it is a dependent class. That means the class selector can be used only with that particular HTML tag. **Figure 2.15** shows the basic syntax of a dependent class.

Why would you want to tie a class to only one tag? A dependent class allows you to add to an existing class specific styles that are enacted only if the class is in a particular tag. You might want the class **copy** to generally be a certain font and size, but if **copy** is inside of a **blockquote** tag you can set it to be larger and bold.

To define a class selector:

1. `.copy {`

Type a dot (`.`) and a class name; then open your definition with a curly bracket (`{`).

The class name can be anything you choose, as long as you use letters and numbers.

`copy` is an independent class, so you can use it with any HTML tag you want, with one stipulation: The properties set for the class must work with the type of tag you use it with (**Code 2.8**).

2. `font-size: 12px;`
`line-height: 150%;`
`font-family: "Trebuchet MS",`
`→ Arial, Helvetica, Geneva,`
`→ sans-serif`

Type your definition(s) for this class, making sure to separate definitions with a semicolon (`;`).

3. `}`

Type a curly bracket (`}`) to close your rule.

A class will not work until it is specified inside an HTML tag within a document, as in the following exercise.

To apply your class to an HTML tag:

◆ `<p class="copy">...</p>`

Add `class="className"` to the tag to which you want to apply the class. Notice that although when you defined the class in the `<style>...</style>` tags, it started with a dot (`.`), you do *not* use the dot when referencing the class name in a tag.

✔ Tips

■ You can mix a class with ID and/or inline rules (see "Adding CSS to an HTML Tag" and the following section "Defining IDs to Identify an Object") within an HTML tag.

Code 2.8 A class style can be set up to be applied to any HTML tag, as with copy, or only to specific HTML tags, as with `blockquote.copy`.

```
<html>
<head>
    <style type="text/css">
.copy {
    font-size: 12px;
    line-height: 150%;
    font-family: "Trebuchet MS", Arial,
    → Helvetica, Geneva, sans-serif; }
blockquote.copy {
    font-weight: bold;
    font-size: 14px;
    line-height: 16px;
    font-family: "Book Antiqua", "Times New
    → Roman", Georgia, Times, serif;
    text-align: center; }
</style>
</head>
<body>
    <p class="copy">Alice glanced rather
    → anxiously at the cook...</p>
    <p class="copy">'Oh, don't bother ME,'
    → ...</p>
    <blockquote class="copy">
    <p>
    'Speak roughly to your little boy, <br>
    And beat him when he sneezes:<br>
    He only does it to annoy,<br>
    Because he knows it teases.'<br><br>
    CHORUS</p>
    </blockquote>
</body>
</html>
```

■ A class name can not be a JavaScript reserved word. See Appendix C for the list.

■ You can use classes with `<div>` and `<span>` tags to create your own HTML tags (see "Creating Your Own Inline HTML Tags" and "Creating Your Own Block-Level HTML Tags" later in this chapter).

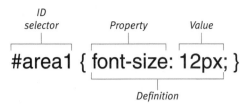

Figure 2.17 The general syntax for an ID.

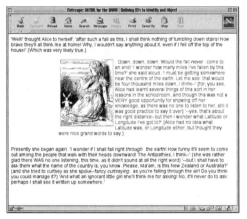

Figure 2.18 By setting the left margin, "area1" has been shifted over to the right, while "image1" has been set to float to the left.

Defining IDs to Identify an Object

Like the class selector, the ID selector can be used to create unique styles that are independent of any particular HTML tag. Thus, they can be assigned to any applicable HTML tag. **Figure 2.17** shows the general syntax of IDs.

IDs are the cornerstone of dynamic HTML (DHTML), in that they allow JavaScript functions to identify a unique object on the screen. This means that unlike a class, an ID should normally be used only once on a page to define a single element as an object. This object then can be manipulated with JavaScript (**Figure 2.18**).

An ID can be defined within the `<style>...</style>` tags in the head of your document (see "Adding CSS to a Web Page" earlier in this chapter) or in an external CSS file that is then imported or linked to the HTML document (see "Adding CSS to a Web Site" earlier in this chapter).

To define an ID:

1. #area1 {

ID rules always start with a number sign (#) and then the name of the ID. The name can be a word or any set of letters or numbers you choose (**Code 2.9**).

2. color: red; margin-left: 9em;
→ position: relative;

Type your definition(s) for this class, making sure to separate definitions with a semicolon (;).

You can use an ID with any type of property, but ID selectors are best used to define unique objects on the screen.

3. }

Type a curly bracket (}) to close your rule.

An ID will not work until it is specified with an individual HTML tag within a document, as in the following exercise.

To apply an ID to an HTML tag:

◆ <p id="area1">...</p>

Add id="idName" to your HTML tag of choice, as shown in Code 2.9. The value of the ID attribute will be the name of the ID selector you created, as explained earlier in this chapter. Notice, though, that although the number sign (#) is used to define an ID, it is not included for referencing the ID in the HTML tag.

✔ Tips

■ You can mix an ID with a class and/or inline rules (see "Adding CSS to an HTML Tag" and "Defining Classes to Create Your Own Tags" earlier in this chapter) within an HTML tag.

■ An ID name cannot be a JavaScript reserved word. See Appendix C for the list.

Code 2.9 The ID area1 is used to define an area of the document to be manipulated (Figure 2.18).

```
code
<html>
<head>
    <style type="text/css">
#area1 {
                color: red;
                margin-left: 9em;
                position: relative; }
#image1 { float :left; }
</style>
</head>
<body>
    <p>'Well!' thought Alice to herself,
    → 'after such a fall as this, I shall
    → think nothing of tumbling down stairs!
    → ...</p>
    <p id="area1"><img id="image1"
    → src="alice06.gif" width="163"
    → height="200" border="0">Down, down,
    → down. Would the fall <i>never</i> come
    → to an end!...</p>
<p>Presently she began again. 'I wonder if I
→ shall fall right <i>through</i> the
→ earth!...</p>
</body>
</html>
```

■ The difference between IDs and classes will become apparent after you've learned more about using CSS positioning and after you've used IDs to create CSS layers. IDs are used to give each element on the screen a unique name and identity. This is why an ID is typically used only once, for one element in a document, to make it an object that can be manipulated with JavaScript.

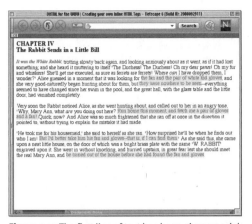

Figure 2.19 The first line of text has been given special treatment and important passages in the text have been highlighted.

Code 2.10 To set up your own inline tags, you must set up a class or ID that can then be applied to a <span> tag. In this example, I've set up an ID to define what the first line of a paragraph should look like and a class that can be used to highlight sections of the text (Figure 2.19).

```
<html>
<head>
<style type="text/css">
#firstline {
color: red;
font: italic bold 14px/100%  "Book Antiqua",
→ "Times New Roman", Georgia, Times,
→ serif; }
span.highlight   { background-color:
→ #ffcccc; }
</style>
</head>
<body>
<h3>CHAPTER IV<br>
The Rabbit Sends in a Little Bill</h3>
<p><span id="firstline">It was the White
→ Rabbit</span>, trotting slowly back
→ again, and looking anxiously about as it
→ went, as if it had lost something; and
→ she heard it muttering to itself 'The
→ Duchess! The Duchess! Oh my dear paws!
→ Oh my fur and whiskers! She'll get me
```

(code continues on next page)

Creating Your Own Inline HTML Tags

You have already seen how you can change the way that HTML tags work using CSS. Yet almost all HTML tags contain some existing properties that you either have to accept or redefine (see "Managing Existing or Inherited Property Values" later in this chapter). For example, the <b> tag automatically behaves as if "font-weight: bold" has been set.

What do you do if you want to start from scratch? Although you can't create your own HTML tags per se, you can use either the <span> or <div> tag, along with classes and IDs, to get close.

The <span> tag has no inherited properties; it serves as a blank slate for the purposes of creating your own inline tag (**Figure 2.19**).

In this example (**Code 2.10**), I've set up two styles. The first style is a class that you can use to give the first line of a paragraph extra emphasis. The second style turns the background behind the element pink to highlight it on the page.

CSS rules can be defined within the <style>...</style> tags in the head of your document (see "Adding CSS to a Web Page" earlier in this chapter) or in an external CSS file that is then imported or linked to the HTML document (see "Adding CSS to a Web Site" earlier in this chapter).

35

To create an inline tag:

1. #firstline {...}

span.highlight {...}

Create either an ID or class style rule (see "Defining Classes to Create Your Own Tags" or "Defining IDs to Identify an Object" earlier in this chapter).

2. <span id="firstline">...</span>

<span class="highlight">...</span>

In the HTML, add the **ID** and/or **Class** attribute to a **<span>** tag (see "(re)Defining an HTML Tag" earlier in this chapter).

✔ Tips

■ Remember that the CSS rules can be placed either in the head of your document or in an external file that is then linked or imported into the document.

■ Notice that the class selector in the example has the HTML selector **span** before it. This limits the **<span>** tags use, so that these definitions apply only if the class is used in a **<span>** tag. CSS2 also allows you to define an ID as being relevant only for a specific tag type. Unfortunately, Netscape 4 does not support this capability and ignores the ID if you try it.

Code 2.10 *continued*

```
   executed, as sure as ferrets are ferrets!
   Where <i>can</i> I have dropped them, I
   wonder?' Alice guessed in a moment that it
   was looking for <span class="highlight">
   the fan and the pair of white kid
   gloves</span>, and she very good-naturedly
   began hunting about for them, but<span
   class="highlight"> they were nowhere to
   be seen</span>--everything seemed to have
   changed since her swim in the pool, and
   the great hall, with the glass table and
   the little door, had vanished completely.
   </p>
</body>
</html>
```

Figure 2.20 The title for the page has been placed in red letters in a block with a black background, while the content for the page is in the block with a gray background.

Code 2.11 To set up your own block-level tags, you first have to set up a class or ID tag, which you can use to apply to a <div> tag. In this example, I've set up an ID for the title of the page and a class for the content of the page. Figure 2.20 shows the result.

```
<html>
<head>
<style type="text/css">
#title9   {
color: red;
background-color: black;
layer-background-color: #000000;
padding: 5px;
font: 1.45em Arial, Helvetica, Geneva,
→ sans-serif;
position: absolute;
top: 10px;
left: 10px;
width: 200px; }

div.content   {
color: black;
background-color: #cccccc;
layer-background-color: #cccccc;
padding: 10px;
```

(code continues on next page)

Creating Your Own Block-Level HTML Tags

In the preceding section, you saw how you could create your own tag from scratch that could be nested within other tags: an inline tag. But you often need to be able to set up a "block" that separates itself from other content in the document (**Figure 2.20**).

Because the <div> tag's only inherent property is that it has a break above it and below it, it's useful for creating a paragraph-style tag without having to upset the <p> tag.

In this example (**Code 2.11**), I have set up two styles. The first one is an ID used to define the appearance and position of the title block on the page, and the second one is used to define the appearance and position of the content block on the page.

CSS rules can be defined within the <style>...</style> tags in the head of your document (see "Adding CSS to a Web Page" earlier in this chapter) or in an external CSS file that is then imported or linked to the HTML document (see "Adding CSS to a Web Site" earlier in this chapter).

To create a block-level tag:

1. `#title9 {...}`

`div.content {...}`

Create either an ID or class style rule (see "Defining Classes to Create Your Own Tags" or "Defining IDs to Identify an Object" earlier in this chapter).

2. `<div id="title9">...</div>`

`<div class="content">...</div>`

In the HTML, add the ID and/or class attribute to a `<div>` tag (see "(re)Defining an HTML Tag" earlier in this chapter).

✔ Tips

■ Remember that the CSS rules can be placed either in the head of your document or in an external file that is then either linked or imported into the document.

■ Theoretically, you could use the paragraph tag `<p>` instead of the `<div>` tag. Paragraphs are regularly used throughout a document, however, and many browsers have difficulty applying positioning styles to the `<p>` tag.

■ When you start using CSS with JavaScript to create dynamic documents, you should become very familiar with this technique. DHTML relies on *layers* created by using the `id` attribute within a `<div>` tag to create objects that can be manipulated with JavaScript.

Code 2.11 *continued*

```
                    code
font: 12px/14px "Book Antiqua", "Times New
→ Roman", Georgia, Times, serif;
position: absolute;
top: 10px;
left: 220px;
width: 350px; }
</style>
</head>

<body>
<div id="title9">
<h3>CHAPTER IX<br>
The Mock Turtle's Story</h3>
</div>

<div class="content">
<p>'You can't think how glad I am to see
→ you again, you dear old thing!' said
→ the Duchess, as she tucked her arm
→ affectionately into Alice's, and they
→ walked off together.</p>
</div>
</body>
</html>
```

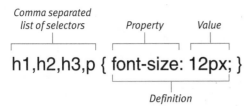

Comma separated list of selectors — Property — Value

h1,h2,h3,p { font-size: 12px; }

Definition

Figure 2.21 The general syntax for a list of selectors all receiving the same definition list.

Figure 2.22 The headers and paragraph are all the same font and margins.

Defining Tags with the Same Rules

If you want two or more selectors to have the same definitions, just put the selectors in a list separated by commas. The general syntax for a definition grouping is shown in **Figure 2.21**.

You can define qualities in the list and then add rules for each HTML selector individually, if you like (**Figure 2.22**).

CSS rules can be defined within the `<style>...</style>` tags in the head of your document (see "Adding CSS to a Web Page" earlier in this chapter) or in an external CSS file that is then imported or linked to the HTML document (see "Adding CSS to a Web Site" earlier in this chapter).

To group definitions:

1. h1,h2,h3,p {...}

Type the list of HTML selectors, separated by commas (**Code 2.12**). These selectors all receive the same definitions.

2. h3 {...}

You can then add or change definitions for each selector individually to tailor it to your needs. If you are overriding a definition set in the group rule, make sure these rules come after the group rules in your CSS (see "Determining the Cascade Order").

✔ Tips

■ IDs and/or classes can also be defined in the list:

h1,h2,.dropcap {...}

■ Grouping selectors like this can save a lot of time and repetition. But be careful—by changing the value of any of the properties in the definition, you change that value for every tag in the list.

Code 2.12 Save time by combining selectors in a list separated by commas to be given a common set of definitions (Figure 2.22).

```
                      code
<html>
<head>
<style type="text/css">
h1,h2,h3,p {
        font-family: "Book Antiqua", "Times
        → New Roman", Georgia, Times, serif;
            margin-left: 10px;
            font-variant: small-caps; }
h1,h2,.dropcap {
            font-size: 1.5em;
            line-height: 100%;
            color: red; }
h3  {
            margin-top: 25px;
            border-top: 2px solid black; }
p { font-variant: normal; }
</style>
</head>
<body>
   <h1>Alice's Adventures in Wonderland</h1>
      <h2>Lewis Carroll</h2>
<h3>CHAPTER I<br>
Down the Rabbit-Hole</h3>
<p><span class="dropCap">A</span> lice was
→ beginning to get very tired of sitting by
→ her sister on the bank...</p>
</body>
</html>
```

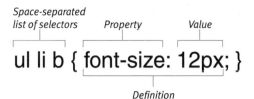

Figure 2.23 General syntax for a contextual rule.

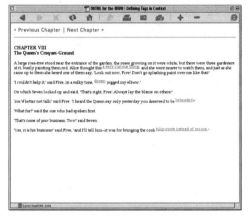

Figure 2.24 Although all these links use the *<a>* tag, there are two distinct link styles on the page depending on where the links appear.

Defining Tags in Context

When a tag is surrounded by another tag, one inside another, we call the tags *nested*. In a nested set, the outer tag is called the *parent*, and the inner tag is the *child*. You can use CSS to create a rule for a tag if it is the child of another particular tag or tags.

Figure 2.23 shows the general syntax of contextual selectors.

In this example (**Code 2.13**), I've set up the link tags so that they will have a completely different appearance depending on whether the link is in a *<p>* tag or in a *<div>* tag with the menu class (**Figure 2.24**).

Code 2.13 Context-sensitive CSS allows you to set the styles of HTML tags depending on their parents' characteristics. In this example, I've set up two versions of the link style: one to be used if the link is within a paragraph; the other to be used if a link is within a *<div>* tag with the menu class (Figure 2.24).

```
<html>
<head>
<style type="text/css">
p a:link {
          color: red;
          text-decoration: underline; }
div.menu a:link {
color: #900;
font-weight: bold;
text-decoration: none; }
div.menu { font: bold 16px  "Trebuchet MS", Arial, Helvetica, Geneva, sans-serif; }
p { font: 12px "Book Antiqua", "Times New Roman", Georgia, Times, serif; }
</style>
```

(code continues on next page)

To set up a contextual selector:

1. `p a:link {...}`

   `div.menu a:link {...}`

   Type the HTML selector of the parent tag, followed by a space. You can type as many HTML selectors as you want for as many different parents as the nested tag will have, but the last selector in the list is the one that receives all the styles in the rule.

2. `<div class="menu"><a href="#">...`
   `→ </a></div>`

   `<p><a href="#">...</a></p>`

   If, and only if, the `<link>` tag occurs within a paragraph, it appears bright red. And if, and only if, the link is in a `<div>` tag with the menu class, it appears darker crimson with no underlining.

✔ Tip

- Like grouped selectors, contextual selectors can include class selectors (dependent or independent) and/or ID selectors in the list, as well as HTML selectors.

Code 2.13 *continued*

```
</head>
<body>
<div class="menu">
<a href="#">&lt; Previous Chapter</a> |
→ <a href="#">Next Chapter &gt;</a>
</div>
<hr>
<h3>CHAPTER VIII<br>
The Queen's Croquet-Ground</h3>
<p>A large rose-tree stood near the entrance
→ of the garden: the roses growing on it
→ were white, but there were three gardeners
→ at it, busily painting them red. Alice
→ thought this <a href="#">a very curious
→ thing</a>, and she went nearer to watch
→ them, and just as she came up to them she
→ heard one of them say, 'Look out now,
→ Five! Don't go splashing paint over me
→ like that!'</p>
</body>
</html>
```

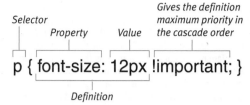

Figure 2.25 The general syntax for making a definition important.

Figure 2.26 Because the <p> tag defines its font size as important, it overrides the later font size set for the "copy" class, making the text 16px instead of 10px. Because both the <p> tag and copy have !important set for the font family, however, copy takes precedence (see "Determining the Cascade Order" later in this chapter) and the font is Times instead of Arial.

Making a Definition !important

The !important value can be added to a definition to give it the maximum weight in determining the cascade order (see "Determining the Cascade Order" later in this chapter). **Figure 2.25** shows the basic syntax for using !important.

In this example (**Code 2.14**), I have redefined the <p> tag and made the font-size and font-family definitions !important. I have also defined a class called **copy** that is applied to the paragraph tags with the font family in it defined as !important. As a result (**Figure 2.26**), the paragraph text uses the font-size definition from the paragraph-tag rule, but uses the font family and color definition from the **copy** rule.

CSS rules cab be defined within the <style>...</style> tags in the head of your document (see "Adding CSS to a Web Page" earlier in this chapter) or in an external CSS file that is then imported or linked to the HTML document (see "Adding CSS to a Web Site" earlier in this chapter).

To force a definition to always be used:

1. `p {`

Open a CSS rule with a selector and a curly bracket (`{`). You can use an HTML selector class or ID.

2. `font-size: 16px !important;`

Type a style definition, a space, `!important`, and a semicolon (`;`) to close the definition.

3. `font-family: arial, helvetica,`
`→ geneva, sans-serif !important;`
`→ color: black; }`

Add any other definitions you desire for this rule, making them `!important` or not as you desire, and then close the rule with a curly bracket (`}`).

4. `p.copy{...}`

Add any other rules you desire, making their definitions `!important` as needed.

✔ Tips

- Netscape 4 does not support `!important`.

- One common mistake is to place the `!important` *after* the semicolon in the definition. This causes the browser to ignore the definition and, possibly, the whole rule.

- Many browsers allow users to define their own style sheets for use by the browser. Although making a definition `!important` should override any user-defined styles— even a user's `!important` definitions—I have not found this to be the case in any browser I have tested. In fact, a user-defined style sheet *always* overrides an author-defined style sheet.

Code 2.14 A definition set as `!important` gets top priority when it comes time to determine which definitions are applied to the HTML. In this example, I've set up two rules. The first defines the font size, font family, and color of the <p> tag; the second defines a class called copy for use with the <p> tag, which sets the font size, font family, and text color. Although the copy class should override the font size set in the <p> tag, using `!important` changes this so that the <p> tags definition takes precedence (Figure 2.26).

```
code
<html>
<head>
<style type="text/css">
p    {
font-size: 16px  !important;
font-family: arial, helvetica, geneva,
→ sans-serif  !important;
color: black; }
p.copy {
font-size: 10px;
font-family: "Times New Roman", Georgia,
→ Times, serif !important;
color: red; }
</style>
</head>
<body>
    <h3>CHAPTER X<br>
The Lobster Quadrille</h3>
<p class="copy">The Mock Turtle sighed
→ deeply, and drew the back of one flapper
→ across his eyes...</p>
</body>
</html>
```

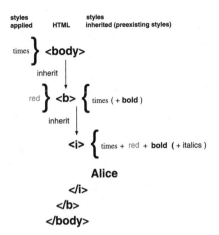

styles applied   HTML   styles inherited (preexisting styles)

times } **<body>**

inherit ↓

red } **<b>** { times (+ **bold**)

inherit ↓

<i> { times + red + **bold** (+ italics)

Alice

</i>

</b>

</body>

Result

Alice

Figure 2.27 The <body> tag is set to the Times font style. This is inherited by the <b> tag, which also has a color style set to red and a pre-existing font weight style of bold. The <i> tag inherits all of these styles and adds its own pre-existing italic style.

Inheriting Properties from a Parent

No, this is not the *Visual QuickStart Guide to Real Estate*. All HTML tags that can be controlled with CSS, except the <body> tag, have a parent—a container tag that surrounds it.

HTML tags generally assume the styles of any tags that are nested within their parent. This is called inheritance of styles. A color set for the <body> tag, for example, will be used as the color for all tags in the body (**Code 2.15** and **Figures 2.27** and **2.28**).

continues on next page

Code 2.15 The <body> tag sets the font style and background color. The font style is inherited by the <p> tag—because the <body> is its parent—but it changes the background color. The <i> tag inherits the <body> styles but also defines its own background color (Figure 2.28).

```
code

<html>
<head>
<style type="text/css">
        body {font: 16pt/20pt times,serif; color: red; background-color: → #999999;}
        p {background-color: #cccccc;}
        i {background-color: #ffffff;}
</style>
</head>
<body>
<p>She waited for some time without hearing anything more: at last came a rumbling of little
→ cartwheels, and the sound of a good many voices all talking together: she made out the words:
→ <i> 'Where's the other ladder?--Why, I hadn't to bring but one; Bill's got the other--Bill!
→ fetch it here, lad!--Here, put 'em up at this corner--No, tie 'em together first--they don't
→ reach half high enough yet--Oh! they'll do well enough; don't be particular-- Here, Bill! catch
→ hold of this rope--Will the roof bear?--Mind that loose slate--Oh, it's coming down! Heads
→ below!'</i> (a loud crash)--'Now, who did that?--It was Bill, I fancy--Who's to go down the
→ chimney?--Nay, I shan't! you do it!--That I won't, then!--Bill's to go down--Here, Bill! the
→ master says you're to go down the chimney!'</p>
</body>
</html>
```

In some cases, a property is not inherited by its nested tags—for example, obvious properties such as margins, width, and borders. You will probably have no trouble figuring out which properties are inherited and which are not. You wouldn't expect every nested element to have the same amount of padding as its parent, for example.

If you have any doubts, though, check out Appendix B, which lists all the properties, as well as whether or not they are inherited.

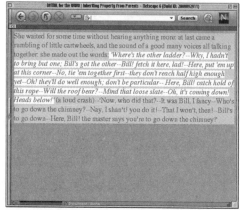

Figure 2.28 Both the <p> and <i> tags inherit the red and Times styles from the <body> tag. The <p> tag overrides the <body> tag's background color with a lighter gray, however, and the <i> tag overrides the <p> tag's background color with white.

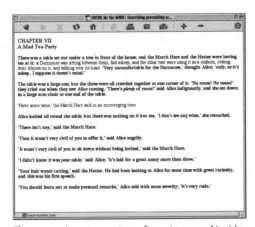

Figure 2.29 In a strange turn of events, normal text is bold and bold text is normal.

Managing Existing or Inherited Property Values

By redefining a selector, you do not cause it to lose any of its inherent attributes. A tag redefined with CSS keeps its specified properties. All those properties display, unless the specific existing properties that make up its appearance are changed (**Figure 2.29**).

With CSS, you could make the <b> tag a larger font size and italic, as follows:

```
b {font-size: larger; font-style: italic;}
```

Even though it is not specified in the CSS definition, this text would still be bold. You could, however, set the <b> tag not to be bold by changing the font-weight property, as follows:

```
p b {font-weight: normal;}
```

This overrides the <b> tag's natural state (see **Code 2.16**) whenever bold text is being set within a paragraph.

continues on next page

Code 2.16 In this example, the <p> tag will make text bold unless the text is actually within a <b> tag. In that case, the inherited bold from the <p> tag is overridden, as well as the <b> tag's own inherent boldness (Figure 2.29).

```
<html>.
<head>
    <style type="text/css">
        p { font-weight: bold; }
        p b { font-weight: normal; }
        .nobold { font-weight: normal; }
    </style>
</head>
<body>
<h3>CHAPTER VII<br>
A Mad Tea-Party</h3>
<p>There was a table set out under a tree in front of the house, and the March Hare and the
→ Hatter were having tea at it: a<b>Dormouse was sitting between them, fast asleep, and the other
→ two were using it as a cushion, resting their elbows on it, and talking over its head.</b> 'Very
→ uncomfortable for the Dormouse,' thought Alice; 'only, as it's asleep, I suppose it doesn't
→ mind.'</p>
```

(code continues on next page)

Properties that are inherited from a parent tag (see the previous section, "Inheriting Properties from a Parent") can likewise be overturned: Simply reset the property in the nested tag's definition list, either in the head style list or directly in a particular tag.

The class `.noBold` in Code 2.16, for example, can be applied to a `<p>` tag to override its font-weight definition, which, in this example, has been set to bold.

✔ Tip

■ Netscape is a bit uncooperative when it comes to getting rid of existing values. You can adjust them, but you can't override them. Even if you set the bold tag's font weight to normal, it still appears bold in Netscape.

Code 2.16 *continued*

```
                        code
<p>The table was a large one, but the three
→ were all crowded together at one corner of
→ it: 'No room! No room!' they cried out
→ when they saw Alice coming. 'There's
→ <i>plenty</i> of room!' said Alice
→ indignantly, and she sat down in a large
→ arm-chair at one end of the table.</p>

<p class="noBold">'Have some wine,' the March
→ Hare said in an encouraging tone.</p>
</body>
</html>
```

Determining the Cascade Order

Within a single Web page, style sheets may be linked, imported, embedded, or even inlined.

But many browsers allow visitors to have their own style sheets, which they can use to override yours. It's guaranteed, of course, that style sheets from two or more sources being used simultaneously will have conflicting definitions. Who comes out on top? Why do you think they call them cascading style sheets?

The following rules determine the cascade order when style sheets conflict.

1. The existence of the !important attribute

   Including !important with a definition gives it top billing when being displayed (see "Making a Definition !important" earlier in this chapter).

   Many browsers allow the user to define their own style sheets for use by the browser. In theory, if both the page author and the visitor have included !important in their definitions, the author's definition wins. All the browsers I have tested, however, give preferential treatment to styles defined by the user.

2. The source of the rules

   Again, in theory, an author's style sheets override a visitor's style sheets unless the visitor uses the !important value. In practice, however, most browsers favor a user's style sheet when determining which definitions are used for a tag.

   continues on next page

3. Specificity

The more specific a rule is, the higher its cascade priority. So the more HTML, class, and ID selectors a particular rule has, the more important it is. In determining this priority, ID selectors count as 100, classes count as 10, and HTML selectors are worth only 1. With this formula, the selectors OL OL OL.cool would be weighted at 13 (1+1+1+10=13), whereas P would be 1. This priority setting may seem a bit silly, but it allows context-sensitive and ID rules to carry more weight, keep ensuring that they will be used.

4. Last one in the pool wins

CSS gives priority to the last rule listed, in order. This is especially useful if you include a definition in line to override style settings listed in the head.

5. Existing or inherited properties

Any styles that are inherent to the tag or inherited from parent tags are applied (see "Managing Existing or Inherited Properties" earlier in this chapter).

Following these rules with **Code 2.17** and **2.18**, we get the results shown in **Figure 2.30**.

Code 2.17 global.css: This version provides the default CSS to be used in the Web site, and defines a rule for the <h3> tag.

```
h3 { color: blue; }
```

Code 2.18 index.html: The external file global.css is linked to this HTML file. It's defining the color for <h3> tags, but it is overridden in the <style> tag. The color set in the <h3> tag itself overrides all other color definitions (Figure 2.30).

```
<html>
<head>
<link rel="stylesheet" href="global.css">
    <style type="text/css">
h3 { color: lime; }
</style>
</head>
<body>
<h3 style="color: red">CHAPTER X<br>
    The Lobster Quadrille</h3>
        <p>The Mock Turtle sighed deeply...</p>
</body>
</html>
```

Figure 2.30 The <h3> tag is set to have its text appear in blue, and then lime. But the text displays in red, since it is the last color to be defined.

Figure 2.31 What the screen displays is completely different than...

Setting the CSS for Printing

When most people think of Web pages, they think of them displayed on a screen (**Figure 2.31**). But sooner or later, most people want to print at least some Web pages (**Figure 2.32**). What looks good on the screen, however, does not always look good when printed.

CSS lets us tell the browser to use different style sheets depending on whether the Web page is headed to the computer monitor or to the printer.

Figure 2.32 ...what the printer prints.

To specify a style sheet for a particular medium:

1. Create two external style sheets: one optimized for use on a computer screen and the other tailored for the printed page (see "Adding CSS to a Web Site" earlier in this chapter).

In this example, the screen version (**Code 2.19**) has white text on a black background—which, although it looks cool on the screen, would not only look messy if printed, but also eat through the toner cartridge. The print version (**Code 2.20**) reverses this with black text on a white (paper) background.

Code 2.19 screen.css: This defines how the HTML page in Code 2.21 should be displayed on the screen.

```
body    {
    color: white;
    font-family: arial, helvetica, geneva,
    → sans-serif;
    background: black url(alice23.gif)
    → no-repeat;
    word-spacing: 1px;
    position: relative;
    top: 200px;
    left: 165px;
    width: 480px; }
h1,h2 {
    font:small-caps bold  italic 2.5em
    → 'minion web' Georgia, 'Times New
    → Roman', Times, serif; }
h2  {
    font-style: normal;
    font-variant: normal;
    font-size: 1.5em; }
.dropCap {
font: 300%/100% serif;
color: #999999; }
```

Code 2.20 print.css: This defines how the HTML page in Code 2.21 should display when printed.

```
body      {
    color: black;
    font-size: 10pt;
    line-height: 12pt;
    font-family: "Book Antiqua", "Times New
    → Roman", Georgia, Times, serif;
    background: white no-repeat;
    text-align: justify;
    position: relative;
    top: 10px;
    left: 40px;
    width: 575px; }
h1,h2  {
    color: black;
    font: italic small-caps bold 2.5em
    → "minion web Georgia", "Times New
    → Roman", Times, serif; }
```

(code continues on next page)

Code 2.20 *continued*

```
                      code
h2   {
    color: black;
    font-style: normal;
    font-variant: normal;
    font-size: 1.5em; }
.dropCap {
color: #999999;
    font: 300%/100% serif; }
```

Code 2.21 index.html: The HTML code links to two different CSS files: One is to be used if the file is output to the screen; the other is to be used if the file is output to a printer. Figure 2.31 shows the result for the screen; Figure 2.32 shows the printed result.

```
                      code
<html>
<head>
<link rel="stylesheet" href="print.css"
→ media="print">
<link rel="stylesheet" href="screen.css"
→ media="screen">
</head>
<body>
<br>
<h1>Alice's Adventures in Wonderland</h1>
<h2>Lewis Carroll</h2>
<p style="font-family: monospace;">
→ THE MILLENNIUM FULCRUM EDITION 3.0</p>
<h3>CHAPTER I
<br>Down the Rabbit-Hole</h3>
<p><span class="dropCap">A</span>lice was
→ beginning to get very tired of sitting by
→ her sister on the bank...</p>
<p>So she was considering in her own
→ mind...</p>
<p>There was nothing so <i>very</i> remarkable
→ in that...</p>
</body>
</html>
```

2. `<link rel="stylesheet" href=`
`→ "print.css" media="print">`

In the head of your HTML document, type a `<link>` tag that references the print version of the CSS and define `media` as `print` (**Code 2.21**).

3. `<link rel="stylesheet" href=`
`→ "screen.css" media="screen">`

Immediately after the `<link>` tag to the printer version of the CSS, add another `<link>` tag that references the screen version of the CSS, and define `media` as `print`.

✔ Tips

■ Unfortunately, Netscape 4 does not support media-based CSS. You can link to a printer-friendly version of the Web page, however, and use a different external CSS file that looks better when printed (see "Looking Good in Print (On the Web)" in Chapter 22).

■ The order in which the different CSS files are added to the document is critical, due to the cascade order of styles. If the browser does not understand the `media` reference, it uses both style sheets.

■ Although several media types including aural (speech), Braille, projection, and handheld are available, none is supported by currently available browsers.

SETTING THE CSS FOR PRINTING

Adding Comments to CSS

Like any other part of an HTML document, style sheets can have comments. A comment does not effect code; comments only add notes or give guidance to anyone viewing your code. You can include comments in the head of an HTML document or in an external CSS file, as shown in **Code 2.22**.

If your comment is only one line, you can use a slightly different format, as shown in the following exercise.

To include single-line comments in a style sheet:

1. `//`

Start a comment line by typing two slashes (/).

2. Sets the general apperance of code tags

Type your comments. In this format, you can use any letters or numbers and symbols, but you cannot include line breaks.

To include multiple-line comments in a style sheet:

1. `/*`

To open a comment area in a style sheet, type a slash (/) and an asterisk (*).

2. tag= HTML tags

Type your comments. You can use any letters or numbers, symbols, and even line breaks (Return or Enter key presses).

3. `*/`

Close your comment by typing an asterisk (*) and a slash (/).

Code 2.22 You can use comments to add useful notes to a page without interfering with the code.

```
// Sets the general apperance of code tags
code
{
font-family: monaco,courier,monospace;
font-size: 10pt;
line-height: 12pt;
margin-left: 2em;
}


/* While this sets the apperance of special
→ cases for code
              selector= HTML tags
              rule= the CSS Rule that
              → defines the apperance
              comment= Comments in the
              → CSS */
code.selector { color: #009900;}
code.rule { color: #990099;}
code.comment { color: #cc0000;}
```

✔ Tips

- You cannot nest comments.

- The double slashes of a single-line comment often stand out better when you're skimming a document, making them easier to find. You can add as many additional slashes as you like, but the minimum is two:

  `////// Your Note Here!`

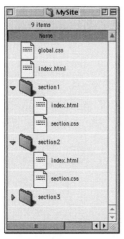

Figure 2.33 A typical tiered file structure that allows different HTML pages to use a global CSS file and then tailor the styles for the particular section with a sectional CSS file. Notice that both sections use a file called "section.css" and not ones called "section1.css" or "section2.css." This allows us to move HTML files between sections without needing to change the URLs used to link or import the documents.

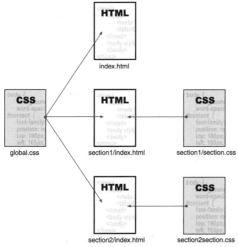

Figure 2.34 This diagram shows how the different HTML files will be linked to the associated CSS files. "global.css" is linked to all three files, while each section's individual "section.css" is linked to refine the page's layout.

Style-Sheet Strategies

Here are some useful tips for constructing a site with CSS:

◆ Wherever possible, place your styles in external style sheets (see "Adding CSS to a Web Site" earlier in this chapter).

◆ The power of CSS is that you can place your styles in one common location and change an entire Web site from one place (**Figure 2.33**).

◆ At the top level of your Web site, define a default global.css style sheet that can be applied to your entire Web site.

Generally speaking, you will want certain characteristics to be ubiquitous throughout your Web site. You may want all your level-1 headers to be a certain size and font, for example (**Figure 2.34**).

◆ Refine styles at sublevels with a section.css style sheet.

By doing this, each section can change or add to the global style sheet. For example, you have already set the size and font for your <h1> tags in the global style sheet, but each section's headers are color-coded. This is your chance to set the color for each section individually.

◆ Use different .css files for distinctive uses.

Placing all your CSS in one file can lead to larger files and longer download times if you use a lot of CSS. Instead, consider splitting your CSS into several files and importing them on an as-needed basis for each page.

continues on next page

◆ Place styles in the <head> after the JavaScript.

Although you can place the <style>...</style> pair anywhere in the head of your document, it's best to place it in one consistent location to make it easier to find. I usually place mine at the bottom, because—well, that's where I put it. Wherever you put your code, be consistent.

◆ Avoid using styles in tags unless you have a compelling reason.

Again, the great thing about CSS is that you can apply styles to multiple tags and change those styles throughout a Web site on a whim. If you define the style directly in the tag, you lose this ability.

FONT CONTROLS

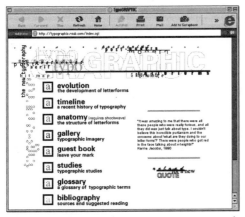

Figure 3.1 typoGRAPHIC (www.typographic.rsub.com) is a great source for learning about the power of typography both on and off the Web.

Figure 3.2 counterSPACE (www.studiomotiv.com/counterspace) also provides insight into typography, all in a beautiful Flash interface.

Typography is one of your most powerful tools for presenting organized, clean-looking documents. For that matter, type is your best tool for presenting chaotic, grungy-looking documents.

The fonts you use go a long way toward getting your message across in just the way you want—whether that message is classical, grunge, or anything in between. Boldface, italic, and other typographic effects help designers guide a visitor's eye around the page (**Figures 3.1** and **3.2**).

CSS gives you the ability to control the appearance of fonts, also known as the *letterforms*, in your Web pages. But with CSS, you can set more than just the font family, boldface and italic attributes, and the limited font sizes available with HTML tags. CSS allows you to go a step further and set generic font families, various levels of boldness, different types of italic, and any font size, using the standard point notation used in the print world.

Understanding Typography on the Web

A *type style* (commonly referred to as a *font family* on the Web) is a category of typefaces (*fonts*) that have similar characteristics. For the Web, there are five basic font families (**Figure 3.3**).

Font Family	Example
serif	Times New Roman
sans-serif	Helvetica and Arial
monospace	Courier New
cursive	*Apple Chancery*
fantasy	Webdings (⌐ 🏠 ⚙ ♥ ① ●◼ ?)

Figure 3.3 The generic font families and some common examples of each.

◆ **Serif** A *serif* is the small ornamentation at the end of a letter that gives it a distinguishing quality. Serifs are holdovers from the days of stonecutting and pen strokes. They often improve legibility by making individual letters stand out from their neighbors. Serif fonts generally are best suited for the display of larger text or for smaller printed text. They are not so good for smaller text on a screen, because the serifs often obscure the letter.

◆ **Sans serif** As you might guess, *sans-serif* fonts are those fonts without serifs. Although the characters are less distinctive, sans-serif fonts work better for smaller text on a screen.

◆ **Monospace** Although *monospace* fonts can have serifs or not, they are distinguished by the fact that each letter occupies the same amount of space. The lowercase letter *l*, for example, is much thinner than the uppercase letter *M*. In nonmonospace fonts, the letter *l* occupies less space than the *M*, but a monospace font adds extra space around the *l* so that it occupies the same space as the *M*. Monospace fonts work best for text that has to be exactly (but not necessarily quickly) read, such as programming code, in which typos can spell disaster.

◆ **Cursive** *Cursive* fonts attempt to mimic cursive handwriting, usually in a highly stylized manner. Cursive fonts are best reserved for decoration; they are not very good for reading large chunks of text.

◆ **Fantasy** Decorative fonts that don't fit into any of the preceding categories are referred to as *fantasy* fonts. These fonts usually are extremely ornamental or, in the case of Dingbats, are illustrations or icons. Like cursive fonts, fantasy fonts are best reserved for decoration. You should choose fantasy fonts carefully to reinforce the look and feel of your Web site.

Using Type on the Web

Theoretically, you can use any font you want on the Web, but there are three distinctive ways to present text, each with its own strengths and weaknesses:

◆ **HTML text** The text that you type in your HTML document acts, for the most part, like the text in a word processor. The advantages of HTML text are that it is easy to edit if changes are required, and it can adjust to the width of the screen on which it is being viewed. But HTML text has some severe limitations for design purposes.

By and large, most of the textual control is left up to the visitor's browser, and you can't do things like run text vertically rather than horizontally. Even more stifling is the fact that you are limited to the fonts that are available on the visitor's machine (see "Using Browser-Safe Fonts" later in this chapter). Thus, if you have a specific font on your machine that you want to use, but the person viewing your site doesn't have that font on her machine, you are out of luck.

CSS gives designers greater control of many common typographic features (such as line and word spacing), but even with CSS, HTML text is severely limited, particularly in the special-effects department. This is why many designers turn to text in graphics to get the look they want.

◆ **Graphic text** Unlike HTML text, graphic text is a graphic (GIF or JPEG) that just happens to have text in it. This means that you can do anything you want in terms of how the text looks and can use any font you want, whether the site visitor has it on his machine or not.

continues on next page

You also have all the limitations that go along with using graphics, such as larger file sizes (larger graphics mean slower download times) and the difficulty of editing graphic text. Graphics also take up a set amount of screen space and may be cut off if the visitor's screen is not large enough.

◆ **Vector text** Vector text combines the best of both worlds. Like HTML text, it is easy to change and can position itself dynamically, depending on the screen size. But like graphic text, vector text allows you to apply special effects easily (on a slightly more limited scale), and you can use any font that you want.

Currently, the only universal way to get vector text into a Web site is to use Macromedia's Flash plug-in. The World Wide Web Consortium (W3C) is working on standards that will allow browsers to display vector text (and graphics) just as they would HTML text.

On the horizon is the Scalable Vector Graphics (SVG) format, which is now a standard from the W3C and is being pushed by its chief developer, Adobe Systems Inc. Although SVG allows the use of vector graphics integrated into HTML documents, like Flash, it relies on a browser plug-in to be displayed. But the Flash plug-in has been out for more than three years, so you can guess which format your users are most likely to be able to use.

Code 3.1 You can specify as many fonts in your definition as you want. Separate names with a comma, and place quotes around font names that contain more than one word.

```
                        code
<html>
<head>
        <style type="text/css">
            h1 {font-family: times,"Times
            → New Roman", palatino, serif;}
            h3 { font-family: "Courier New",
            → Courier, Monaco, monospace; }
            .copy {font-family: Arial,
            → Helvetica, Geneva, sans-serif; }
</style>
</head>
<body>
        <hr>
        <h1>ALICE'S ADVENTURES IN WONDERLAND
        → </h1>
        <h3>Lewis Carroll</h3>
    <hr>
        <h3>CHAPTER I<br>
        Down the Rabbit-Hole</h3>
        <p class="copy">Alice was beginning...
        → </p>
        <p class="copy">So she was
        → considering...</p>
        <p class="copy">There was nothing...
        ...</p>
</body>
</html>
```

Setting the Font

The font you use to display your text can make a powerful difference in how readers perceive your message. Some fonts are easier to read on the screen; others look better when printed. The font property allows you to determine the visual effect of your message by choosing the font for displaying your text.

In this example (**Code 3.1** and **Figure 3.4**), the level-1 header has been assigned to the Times font.

To define the font in a rule:

1. `font-family:`

   Type the property name, followed by a colon (:).

2. `times`

   Type the name of the font you want to use.

3. `,"Times New Roman", palatino`

   If you want, you can type a list of fonts separated by commas.

continues on next page

Figure 3.4 The font for the title, subtitle, and text of the page have all been set, thus overriding the default font set in the browser.

4. , serif;

After the last comma, type the name of the generic font family for the particular style of font you are using. **Table 3.1** lists generic values for font families. Although including this value is optional, doing so is a good idea.

✔ Tips

■ When you provide a list of fonts, the browser tries to use the first font listed. If that one isn't available to the browser, it works through the list until it encounters a font that is installed on the visitor's computer. If there are no matches, the browser displays the text in the user's default font. The advantage of specifying a generic font is that the browser tries to display the text in the same style of font, even if the specific ones you list are not available.

■ Fonts that contain a space in their names must be enclosed in quotation marks (example: "New York").

■ Check out "Using Browser-Safe Fonts" later in this chapter for a list of the fonts that generally are available to browsers.

■ Theoretically, Internet Explorer and Netscape allow you to download a particular font to the visitor's computer and then specify the font by using the family-name property. See the next section, "Downloading Fonts," for details.

Table 3.1

font-family Values	
VALUE	**COMPATIBILITY**
\<family-name\>	IE3, N4,CSS1
\<generic-family\>	IE3, N4,CSS1
serif	IE3, N4,CSS1
sans-serif	IE3*, N4,CSS1
cursive	IE4, N4,CSS1
fantasy	IE4, N4,CSS1
monospace	IE4, N4,CSS1

* IE4 for the Mac

Using CSS vs. the Font Tag

The most common way to set a font face is by using the font tag, as follows:

```
<font face="arial,helvetica">Blah,
→ blah, blah</font>
```

But the font tag is on the way out. The most recent version of the HTML specification from the W3C does not include this tag, noting that fonts should be handled by CSS.

There are two basic problems with the font tag:

◆ You have to add this tag every time you set a font, which can significantly increase file size.

◆ If you need to change the font attributes, you have to change the attributes in every tag.

CSS solves both of these problems by allowing you to redefine how existing tags treat the text they contain, rather than adding more tags, and by allowing you to control these behaviors from a single line in the document.

Code 3.2 @fontface is used to define the name and location of a font to be downloaded to the user's computer.

```
                        code
 <html>

 <head>

    <style type="text/css">

        @font-face { font-family: Garamond;
        ⇢ src: url(Garamond.eot); }

        h2 {font-family: Garamond, "Times New
        ⇢ Roman", Georgia, Times, serif ;}

    </style>

 </head>

 <body>

    <h2>Chapter VIII<br>The Queen's
    ⇢ Croquet-Ground</h2>

 <p class="copy">A large rose-tree...</p>

 </body>

 </html>
```

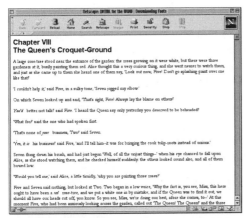

Figure 3.5 The text is displayed in Garamond, which has been downloaded like a graphic rather than residing on the user's computer.

Downloading Fonts

The Holy Grail of Web-based typography is downloadable fonts. Imagine if, rather than having to rely on the limited list of browser-safe fonts or having to create graphics just to get the typeface you want to use, you could send the font to the visitor's computer automatically.

Actually, the CSS Level 2 standard allows for downloadable fonts. In this example (**Code 3.2** and **Figure 3.5**), I've set up the font Garamond to be downloaded and then used in the level-2 header tag.

To download a font:

1. @font-face {

    Type @font-face.

2. font-family: Garamond;

    Type the font-family property and the name of the font.

3. src: url(Garamond.eot);}

    Type the location of the font file.

4. h2 {font-family: Garamond, "Times New
    ⇢ Roman", Georgia, Times, serif ; }

    Reference the font that you named in step 2. I also recommend including a list of alternative fonts, just in case the specified font does not download.

continues on next page

DOWNLOADING FONTS

✔ Tips

- The bad news is, of course, that you can't download any old font file. Fonts have to be specially processed, and the processing is different in Internet Explorer and Netscape (see the sidebar below, "Where Are All the Fonts?").

- To make matters even worse, when testing this technique in Netscape 4, I found that if the font file did not download, the browser ignored other fonts in the list and used the browser's default font.

Where Are All the Fonts?

Why don't we see downloaded fonts all over the Web? There are several impediments to simple font delivery:

- Many fonts are not free. There is some concern among font creators that if their fonts are distributed via the Web, they will not be compensated. This assumes that users can download and reuse fonts without having to pay for them.

- Windows and Mac fonts are incompatible. You would have to include versions for both platforms.

- Font files can be quite large and, thus, take a while to download.

Netscape and Internet Explorer have introduced schemes to overcome these problems and allow font downloading for Web pages. The problem is that you can't simply queue a font like a graphic and have it download. Instead, you have to process the font for the Web. Unfortunately, Netscape and Microsoft came up with incompatible—not to mention difficult—systems for creating downloadable fonts.

For Internet Explorer, you have to convert your fonts to .eot format, using a program called WEFT (`www.microsoft.com/typography/web/embedding/weft2/`). This program, however, is Windows-only software.

For Netscape, you have to purchase software from Bitstream Inc. to convert your fonts to TrueDoc format (`www.truedoc.com`). According to Bitstream, this format works in both Netscape and Internet Explorer but is extremely buggy.

So until we see easy-to-create downloadable fonts that work for both browsers and platforms, we are stuck using browser-safe fonts.

Using Browser-Safe Fonts

Look around the Web, and what do you see? Two fonts: Helvetica and Times. Virtually every site whose designers made an effort to control the display of text uses either Helvetica (or its Windows equivalent, Arial) or Times. This situation came about for one simple reason: Virtually every computer has these two fonts or some variant of them.

I am sick of them.

Don't get me wrong—these are great fonts, easy to read at many sizes. But as I said earlier, typography adds a language to text that goes far beyond the written word.

Right now, Web-based typography seems to be mired in using Times for serif fonts and Helvetica/Arial for sans-serif fonts. This arrangement mutes the power of typography, and all Web pages begin to look the same.

What are the alternatives to the "terrible two"? That depends on the computer the person visiting your site is using. Mac and Windows computers have certain standard fonts that should always be installed. In addition, Internet Explorer (which comes installed on most computers these days) includes several common fonts.

continues on next page

I have compiled a list of browser-safe fonts that should be available on the different platforms. These fonts are the ones supplied by Apple for the Mac (**Table 3.2**), by Microsoft for Windows (**Table 3.3**), and by Microsoft for Internet Explorer (Windows and Mac) (**Table 3.4**).

As you can see, there are certainly more than two choices. Appendix D also lists these fonts with examples of what they should look like, and lists fonts that are similar looking.

Table 3.2

Mac System Fonts

FONT NAME	STYLES
Apple Chancery*	
Capitals*	
Charcoal	
Chicago	
Courier	bold, bold italic, italic
Gadget*	
Geneva	
Helvetica	bold, bold italic, italic
Hoefler Text*	bold, bold italic, italic
Monaco	
New York	
Palatino	bold, bold italic, italic
Sand*	
Skia*	
Symbol	
Techno*	
Textile*	
Times	bold, bold italic, italic

*= as of System 8.5

Table 3.3

Windows System Fonts

FONT NAME	STYLES
Abadi MT Condensed Light*	
Arial Black*	bold, bold italic, italic
Book Antiqua*	bold, bold italic, italic
Calisto MT*	bold, italic
Century Gothic*	bold, bold italic, italic
Comic Sans MS*	bold
Copperplate Gothic Bold	
Copperplate Gothic Light	
Courier New	bold, bold italic, italic
Lucid Console*	
Lucida Handwriting Italic*	
Lucida Sans Unicode*	italic
News Gothic MT*	bold, italic
OCR A Extended*	
Symbol	
Tahoma*	bold
Times New Roman	bold, bold italic, italic
Verdana*	bold, bold italic, italic
Webdings*	
Wingdings	

*= as of Windows 98

Table 3.4

Internet Explorer Fonts (Windows/Mac)

FONT NAME	STYLES
Andale Mono	
Arial Black	
Comic Sans MS	bold
Georgia*	bold, bold italic, italic
Impact	
Minion Web*	bold, italic
Trebuchet MS*	bold, bold italic, italic
Verdana	bold, bold italic, italic
Webdings*	

*= as of IE 5

NOTE: Internet Explorer installs these fonts, so they may not be available to Netscape users. Still, because many computers come with IE installed, it's a safe bet that these fonts will be on your visitor's machine.

8pt 12pt 24pt 48pt

Figure 3.6 A few font sizes.

Code 3.3 The font size for the class copy has been set to 12 pixels, blockquotes will appear with a 2-em indent, and level-3 header tags will appear large(er) than the parent's text—which, in this case, is the default size set for the browser.

```
                        code
<html>
<head>
    <style type="text/css">
        .copy { font-size: 12px; }
        blockquote { font-size: 2em; }
        h3 { font-size: large; }
    </style>
</head>
<body>
<h3>CHAPTER II<br>
The Pool of Tears</h3>
<p class="copy">'Curiouser and curiouser!'
→ ...</p>
    <blockquote>
        ALICE'S RIGHT FOOT, ESQ.<br>
        HEARTHRUG,<br>
        NEAR THE FENDER,<br>
          (WITH ALICE'S LOVE).
    </blockquote>
</body>
</html>
```

Setting the Font Size

HTML gives you seven font sizes, but these are all relative to a default size set by the visitor. With CSS, you can specify the size of the text on the screen by using several notations or methods, including the traditional point-size notation, percentage, absolute size, and even a size relative to the surrounding text. **Figure 3.6** shows text in different sizes.

In this example (**Code 3.3** and **Figure 3.7**), I define the class copy to use a font size of 12 pixels and then apply it to paragraphs of text.

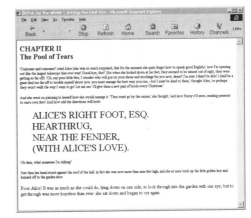

Figure 3.7 The size of the font helps determine its legibility and the emphasis it receives on the page. Titles usually are larger than copy, but some text needs a little more attention.

To define the font size in a rule:

1. `font-size:`

   Type the `font-size` property, followed by a colon (:).

2. `12px;`

   Type a value for the font size, which could be any of these options:

   ▲ A **length unit** (usually, the font size in points).

   ▲ An **absolute expression** that describes the font size. The expressions are `xx-small`, `x-small`, `small`, `medium`, `large`, `x-large`, and `xx-large`.

   ▲ `smaller` or `larger`, to describe the font size in relation to its parent element (see "Inheriting Properties from a Parent" in Chapter 2).

   ▲ A **percentage**, representing how much larger the text is in proportion to the size of its parent element (75%, for example).

See **Table 3.5** for a list of font-size values and their browser compatibility.

✔ Tips

■ Although the maximum-size font you can use depends on the visitor's computer, try to stay below 50-point fonts, to be safe.

■ Don't limit yourself to the small letters available with HTML. CSS allows you to create dramatic effects for titles by using large letters that download as quickly as any other text.

Table 3.5

font-size Values	
VALUE	COMPATIBILITY
<length>	IE4, N4, CSS1
<percentage>	IE4, N4, CSS1
smaller	IE4, N4, CSS1
larger	IE4, N4, CSS1
xx-small	IE4, N4, CSS1
x-small	IE4, N4, CSS1
small	IE4, N4, CSS1
medium	IE4, N4, CSS1
large	IE4, N4, CSS1
x-large	IE4, N4, CSS1
xx-large	IE4, N4, CSS1

Pixels and Points

`pt` is the abbreviation for *point*, which is one way of referring to a font's relative size. A 12-point font is a fairly average size and is comfortable for most readers.

Point sizes are a common way to denote a font's size. The size of a point, however, varies slightly between operating systems, so a font set to 12 point in Windows appears larger than the same font set to 12 point on a Mac.

I occasionally set fonts by using the point size (especially if the page is being printed), but I usually prefer to specify font sizes by using `px`, which defines the size in pixels. Pixels are still a little unreliable, but they usually are more accurate than point size.

Although there is not a one-to-one correlation between pixels and points, `12px` is roughly the same size as `12pt`.

normal *italic oblique*

Figure 3.8 Italic or oblique?

Code 3.4 Although the book's title and paragraphs within a blockquote are italicized, the italics tag is set so that it will *not* make text italicized.

```
<html>
<head>
<style type="text/css">
.booktitle, blockquote p { font-style: italic; }

i { font-style: normal; }
</style>
</head>
<body>
<h1>An excerpt from <span class="booktitle">
→ Alice in Wonderland</span></h1>
<p><i>How doth the little--</i>&quot;' and
→ she crossed her hands on her lap...</p>
<blockquote>
<p>'How doth the little crocodile</p>
<p>Improve his shining tail,</p>
</blockquote>
</body>
</html>
```

Making Text Italic

The two kinds of styled text —*italic* and *oblique*—are often confused. An italic font refers to a special version of a particular font, redesigned with more pronounced serifs and usually a slight slant to the right. An oblique font is simply a font that is slanted to the right by the computer (**Figure 3.8**).

With the font-style element, you can define a font as italic, oblique, or normal. When a font is set to italic but does not have an explicit italic version, the font defaults to oblique.

In this example (**Code 3.4** and **Figure 3.9**), the class booktitle and any paragraphs within a blockquote are italicized. The italic tag, however, has been overridden to normal.

Figure 3.9 Book titles and quotes are generally italicized to set them off.

To set font-style in an HTML tag:

1. `font-style:`

   Type `font-style` property name, followed by a colon (:).

2. `italic;`

   Type a value for the `font-style`. Your options are (**Table 3.6**):

   ▲ `italic,` which displays the type in an italic version of the font

   ▲ `oblique,` which slants the text to the right

   ▲ `normal,` which overrides any other styles set

✔ Tips

■ Many Web designers underline words to draw visual attention to them. I recommend using italic or oblique text instead. Underlining often causes the page to look cluttered. More important, underlined text might be confused with hypertext links.

■ Italicized text generally fits into a more compact space than does nonitalic text (called *roman* in traditional typesetting terms) and could be used to save screen space. But be careful—at small point sizes, italic can be difficult to read on the screen.

Table 3.6

font-style Values	
VALUE	COMPATIBILITY
normal	IE4, N4, CSS1
italic	IE4, N4, CSS1
oblique	IE4, N6, CSS1

MAKING TEXT ITALIC

normal **bold**

Figure 3.10 The difference between normal and bold text is evident here.

Figure 3.11 All the text has been set to bold except italicized words, which are a normal weight.

Setting Bold, Bolder, Boldest

In straight HTML, text is either bold or not. CSS provides several more options that allow you to set different levels of boldness for text. Many fonts have various weights associated with them; these weights have the effect of making the text look more or less bold. CSS can take advantage of this feature (**Figure 3.10**).

In this example (**Code 3.5** and **Figure 3.11**), I've created a class called bolder to make text bolder than the surrounding text.

Code 3.5 The bolder class is used to boldface text. Italics within a paragraph have been set to nonbold.

```
<html>
<head>
<style type="text/css">
.bolder { font-weight: bolder; }
p i { font-weight: normal; }
</style>
</head>
<body>
<b>More from <i>Alice in Wonderland</i></b>
<p><span class="bolder">'I wish I hadn't cried so much!'...</span></p>
<p><span class="bolder">Just then she heard <i>something</i> splashing about in the pool a little
→ way off...</span></p>
<p><span class="bolder">'Would it be of any use, now,'</p>
<p><span class="bolder">'Perhaps it doesn't understand English,'</span></p>
<p><span class="bolder">'Not like cats!'
→ </span></p>
</body>
</html>
```

To define bold text in a CSS rule:

1. `font-weight:`

   Type the `font-weight` property name, followed by a colon (:).

2. `bolder;`

   Type the value for the `font-weight` property, using one of these options (**Table 3.7**):

   ▲ `bold`, which sets the font to boldface.

   ▲ `bolder` or `lighter`, which set the font's weight to be bolder or lighter relative to its parent element's weight.

   ▲ A value from `100` to `900`, in increments of 100. This value increases the weight, based on alternative versions of the font that are available.

   ▲ `normal`, which overrides other weight specifications.

✔ Tip

■ Use `font-weight` to add emphasis to text, but use it sparingly. If everything is bold, nothing stands out.

Table 3.7

font-weight Values	
VALUE	COMPATIBILITY
normal	IE4, N4, CSS1
bold	IE3, N4, CSS1
lighter	IE3, N6, CSS1
bolder	IE3, N6, CSS1
100-900	IE4*, N4*, CSS1

Depending on available font weights

Font-Weight Numbers

Most fonts do not have nine weights, so if you specify a `font-weight` value that is not available, another weight is used, based on the following system:

◆ `100` to `300` use the next-lighter weight, if available, or the next-darker

◆ `400` and `500` may be used interchangeably

◆ `600` to `900` use the next-darker weight, if available, or the next-lighter

Normal MINICAPS

Figure 3.12 All the letters are capitals, but the first letter is larger than the rest.

Code 3.6 The level-2 header tag is set to display in small caps.

```
                    code
<html>
<head>
<style type="text/css">
h2 { font-variant: small-caps; }
</style>
</head>
<body>
<h2>Chapter III<br>
A Caucus-Race and a Long Tale</h2>
<p>They were indeed a queer-looking
→ party...</p>
        <p>The first question of course was,
        → how to get dry again...</p>
        <p>At last the Mouse...</p>
        <p>'Ahem!' said the Mouse...</p>
        <p>'Ugh!' said the Lory, with a
        → shiver.</p>
        <p>'I beg your pardon!'...</p>
<p>'Not I!' said the Lory hastily.</p>
</body>
</html>
```

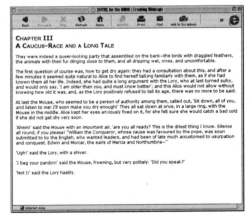

Figure 3.13 Using minicaps for the title is an elegant way to set it off from the rest of the text.

Creating Minicaps

Minicaps are useful for emphasizing titles. With minicaps, lowercase letters are converted to uppercase, but in a slightly smaller size than regular uppercase letters (**Figure 3.12**).

In this example (**Code 3.6** and **Figure 3.13**), the <h2> tag is used to create a distinctive book title in minicaps.

To make a rule for minicaps:

1. `font-variant:`

   Type the `font-variant` property name, followed by a colon (:).

2. `small-caps;`

   Type the value of the `font-variant` property, using one of these options (**Table 3.8**):

   ▲ `small-caps`, which sets lowercase letters as smaller versions of true uppercase letters

   ▲ `normal`, which overrides other `font-variant` values that might be inherited

✔ Tip

■ Minicaps are best reserved for titles or other special text; they are hard to read at smaller sizes.

Table 3.8

font-style Values	
VALUE	COMPATIBILITY
normal	IE4, N6, CSS1
small-caps	IE4, N6, CSS1

Setting Multiple Font Values

Although you can set font properties independently, it is often useful, not to mention more concise, to put all font elements in a single definition. To do this, you use the font property.

This example (**Code 3.7** and **Figure 3.14**) shows a level-1 header tag being defined, along with a class called copy that will be applied to paragraphs of text. In addition, the level-3 header tag is defined with the shorthand font style (see the sidebar "Using the Visitor's Styles" on the next page).

To define several font attributes simultaneously in a rule:

1. font:

   Type the font property name, followed by a colon (:). Then type the values in the following steps (**Table 3.9**):

2. italic

   Type a font-style value, followed by a space (see "Making Text Italic" earlier in this chapter).

3. small-caps

   Type a font-variant value, followed by a space (see the previous section, "Creating Minicaps").

4. bold

   Type a font-weight value, followed by a space (see "Setting Bold, Bolder, Boldest" earlier in this chapter).

5. 26px

   Type a font-size value (see "Setting the Font Size" earlier in this chapter).

Code 3.7 The h1 tag and copy class have had the various font styles set at the same time, while the h3 tag uses a shorthand value to mimic the caption style.

```
code
<html>
<head>
<style type="text/css">
h1 { font: italic small-caps bold 26px/32px
→ "minion web", "Times New Roman", Times,
→ serif; }
h3 { font: caption; }
.copy { font: 10px/20px Arial, Helvetica,
→ Geneva, sans-serif; }
</style>
</head>
<body>
<hr>
<h1>Alice's Adventures In<br>
Wonderland</h1>
<h3>Lewis Carroll</h3>
<hr>
<h3>CHAPTER I<br>
Down the Rabbit-Hole</h3>
<p class="copy">Alice was beginning...</p>
<p class="copy">So she was considering...</p>
<p class="copy">There was nothing so
→ <i>very</i>...</p>
</body>
</html>
```

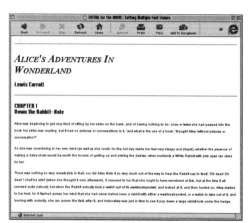

Figure 3.14 You can set all the font properties (and the line height) in a single definition and even instruct the page to use styles defined by the visitor's computer.

Table 3.9

font Values	
VALUE	COMPATIBILITY
<font-family>	IE4, N4, CSS1
<font-style>	IE4, N4, CSS1
<font-variant>	IE4, N4, CSS1
<font-weight>	IE4, N4, CSS1
<font-size>	IE4, N4, CSS1
<font-height>	IE4, N4, CSS1
<visitor-style>	IE5, N6, CSS2

6. /32px

Type a forward slash (/), a line-height value, and a space (see "Adjusting Leading" in Chapter 4).

7. "minion web", "Times New Roman", → Times, serif

Type a font-family value (refer to "Setting the Font" earlier in this chapter).

✔ Tips

- If you don't want to set a particular value in the list, don't include it. The browser will use its default value instead.

- The font attribute is a real time-saver, and I try to use it as often as possible. WYSIWYG programs such as GoLive and Dreamweaver, however, tend to default to using the individual attributes.

Using the Visitor's Styles

Wouldn't be nice if you could match the font styles that the user visiting your page is already using in his browser? Internet Explorer 5 and Netscape 6 allow you to do this by simply declaring the font style to be one of the following keywords (such as font: icon;):

- ◆ Caption: the font style being used by buttons
- ◆ Icon: the font style being used to label icons
- ◆ Menu: the font style being used in drop-down menus and menu lists
- ◆ Message-box: the font style being used in dialog boxes
- ◆ Small-Caption: the font style being used for labeling small controls
- ◆ Status-bar: the font style being used in the window's status bar

TEXT CONTROLS

Text is everywhere around us. Text can be used for everything from listing the ingredients in breakfast cereal to writing an ode to a Grecian urn. It is the best system that humans have yet devised for relating complex thoughts.

Many people think of text as being simply a way of recording spoken words, but typography adds a language to text that goes far beyond the written word.

Typography affects how text appears by controlling not only the shapes and sizes of the letters being used (the font), but also the spaces between letters, words lines, and paragraphs. On the Web, typography has taken on the challenges of displaying text on a computer screen to wide audiences.

Unfortunately, many of the challenges of typography on the Web have come about as a result of a need to circumvent the limitations of the medium.

In this chapter, I'll show you ways to present text using CSS to open up the screen and improve legibility, as well as draw interest.

Adjusting Kerning

Kerning refers to the amount of space between letters in a word. More space between letters often improves the readability of the text. On the other hand, too much space can hamper reading by making individual words appear less distinct on the page.

In this example (**Code 4.1** and **Figure 4.1**), extra space is being added between the letters of the word *stretching*.

To define kerning:

1. letter-spacing:

Type the letter-spacing property, followed by a colon (:) in the CSS definition list.

2. 2em;

Type a value for the letter-spacing property (**Table 4.1**), using either:

▲ A **length value,** such as 2em, which sets the absolute space between letters

▲ normal, which overrides inherited spacing attributes

✔ Tip

■ A positive value for letter-spacing adds more space to the default amount; a negative value closes the space. A value of 0 does not add or subtract space but prevents justification of the text (see "Aligning Text Left, Right, and Center" later in this chapter).

Code 4.1 Here, I've used letter spacing for a dramatic effect to stretch the word *stretching*.

```
                         code
<html>

<head>

<style type="text/css">

.stretch { letter-spacing: 2em; }

    </style>

</head>

<body>

An enormous puppy was looking down at her with
→ large round eyes, and feebly <span class=
→ "stretch">stretching</span> out one paw,
→ trying to touch her. 'Poor little thing!'
→ said Alice, in a coaxing tone, and she
→ tried hard to whistle to it; but she was
→ terribly frightened all the time at the
→ thought that it might be hungry, in which
→ case it would be very likely to eat her up
→ in spite of all her coaxing.

</body>

</html>
```

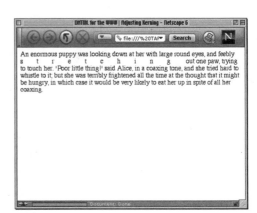

Figure 4.1 This text does what it says.

Table 4.1

letter-spacing Values	
VALUE	**COMPATIBILITY**
normal	IE4*, N6, CSS1
\<length\>	IE4*, N6, CSS1

* Mac version only; not available in Windows

Code 4.2 I've set up a class for the title to space out the words (and the letters). In addition, this code uses a negative value in <p> tags to press the text together, and overrides that setting with a positive tag in <p> tags with the copy class.

```
code

<html>
<head>
<style type="text/css">
.title {
word-spacing: 8px;
letter-spacing: 4px; }
p { word-spacing: -8px; }
p.copy {
          word-spacing: 4px;
          letter-spacing: 1px; }
</style>
</head>
<body>
       Yet more<span class="title"> Alice in
→ Wonderland</span>
       <p>'We indeed!' cried the Mouse, who
→ was trembling down to the end of
→ his tail. 'As if I would talk on
→ such a subject! Our family always
→ <i>hated</i> cats: nasty, low,
→ vulgar things! Don't let me hear
→ the name again!'</p>
       <p class="copy">'I won't indeed!'
→ said Alice...</p>
       <p>So she called softly after it...</p>
       <p>It was high time to go...</p>
</body>
</html>
```

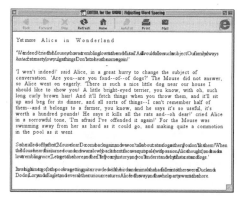

Figure 4.2 The space between letters is stretched slightly for a more relaxed appearance and, further down, compressed to be made illegible.

Adjusting Word Spacing

Just like adjusting kerning, adjusting word spacing can both help and hinder legibility. Adding a little space between words on the screen can help make your text easier to read, but too much space interrupts the path of the reader's eye across the screen and, therefore, interferes with reading.

In this example (**Code 4.2** and **Figure 4.2**), some of the words are being pressed illegibly close together, and others are separated to give the text a looser appearance.

To define word spacing:

1. `word-spacing`:

   Type the property name, followed by a colon (`:`) in the CSS definition list.

2. `8px`;

   Set the value for word spacing (**Table 4.2**), using either:

   ▲ A **length value** representing the amount of space between words (`8px`, for example)

   ▲ `normal`, which overrides inherited values

✔ Tip

■ A positive value for word spacing adds more space to the default, and a negative value closes the space. A value of 0 neither adds nor subtracts space but prevents justification (see "Aligning Text Left, Right, and Center" later in this chapter).

Table 4.2

word-spacing Values	
VALUE	COMPATIBILITY
normal	IE4*, N6, CSS1
<length>	IE4*, N6, CSS1

* Mac version only; not available in Windows

Adjusting Leading

Anybody who has ever typed a term paper knows that these papers usually have to be double-spaced, to make reading easier and to allow space for comments to be written on the page. Space between lines (*leading*) also can be increased for a dramatic effect by creating areas of negative space between the text. The line-height property adds space between the baselines (the bottoms of most letters) of lines of text.

In this example (**Code 4.3** and **Figure 4.3**), the copy has been double-spaced, and the citation text has its line height set slightly above the font size.

To define leading in a rule:

1. line-height:

Type the property name, followed by a colon (:), in the CSS definition list.

2. Type the value for the line height (**Table 4.3**), using one of these options:

▲ A **number** to be multiplied by the font size to get the spacing value (2 for double spacing, for example).

▲ A **length value**, such as 24px. The space for each line of text is set to this size regardless of the designated font size. So if the font size is set to 12px and the line height is set to 24px, the text will be double-spaced.

▲ A **percentage**, which sets the line height proportionate to the font size being used for the text.

▲ normal, which overrides inherited spacing values.

Code 4.3 Text with the class copy will be double-spaced while the <cite> tag will have less than a single space between each line.

```
<html>
<head>

<style type="text/css">
        .copy {
        line-height: 2;
            font-size: 12px; }
p cite {
            line-height: 14px;
        font-size: 12px; }
    </style>
</head>
<body>
    <p class="copy">After a time she heard a
    → little pattering of...</p>
            <p><cite>Alice took up the fan and
            → gloves</cite>
            <p class="copy">'I'm sure I'm not
            → Ada...</p>
</body>
</html>
```

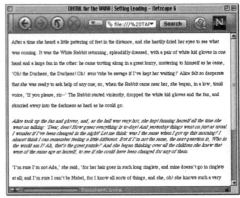

Figure 4.3 The text is double-spaced for regular text. The leading is closer for quotes.

Table 4.3

line-height Values	
VALUE	COMPATIBILITY
normal	IE3, N4, CSS1
<number>	IE4, N4, CSS1
<length>	IE3, N4, CSS1
<percentage>	IE3, N4, CSS1

✔ Tips

- Adding space between lines of text enhances legibility—especially in large amounts of text. Generally, a line height of 1.5 to 2 times the font size is appropriate for most text.

- To double-space text, set the line-height value as either 2 or 200%. Likewise, 3 or 300% results in triple-spaced text.

- You can use a negative value to smash text lines together. Although this effect may look neat, it probably won't ingratiate you with your readers.

- Line height can also be defined in the font property (see "Setting Multiple Font Values" in Chapter 3).

Setting Text Case

When you're dealing with dynamically generated output, you can never be sure whether the text will appear in uppercase, lowercase, or a mixture. With the `text-transform` property, you can control the ultimate case of the text no matter what it is to begin with.

In this example, the names of the characters have been typed in the HTML (**Code 4.4**) in lowercase characters. When displayed in the browser (**Figure 4.4**), however, the text is transformed into its correct format.

To define the text case:

1. `text-transform:`

    Type the `text-transform` property name, followed by a colon (:), in the CSS definition list.

2. `capitalize`

    Type one of the following values (**Table 4.4**) to specify how you want the text to be treated:

    ▲ `capitalize` sets the first letter of each word in uppercase

    ▲ `uppercase` forces all letters to be uppercase

    ▲ `lowercase` forces all letters to be lowercase

    ▲ `none` overrides inherited text-case values and leaves the text as is

✔ Tips

■ If you want specific text to be uppercase, you should type it as uppercase, so that older browsers won't be left out.

■ The `text-transform` property probably is best reserved for formatting text that is being created dynamically. If the names in a database are all uppercase, for example, you can use `text-transform` to make them more legible when displayed.

Code 4.4 The class name, if invoked, will force words to be displayed in initial caps.

```
<html>
<head>
    <style type="text/css">
        .name { text-transform: capitalize; }

        h2  { text-transform: uppercase; }
</style>
</head>
<body>
    <h2>Dramatis Personae</h2>
    <p class="name">alice</p>
    <p class="name">the rabbit</p>
    <p class="name">the queen of hearts</p>
    <p class="name">cheshire cat</p>
    <p class="name">the mad hatter</p>
    <p class="name">the march hare</p>
    <p class="name">the dormouse</p>
</body>
</html>
```

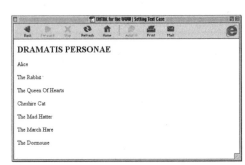

Figure 4.4 Even though the text is lowercase in the HTML, it's displayed in uppercase in the browser.

Table 4.4

text-transform Values	
VALUE	COMPATIBILITY
capitalize	IE4, N4, CSS1
uppercase	IE4, N4, CSS1
lowercase	IE4, N4, CSS1
none	IE4, N4, CSS1

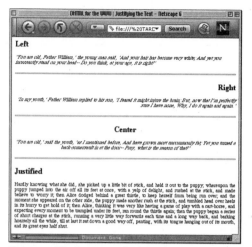

Figure 4.5 Aligning text to the left side, the right side, in the center, or equally on both sides.

Aligning Text Left, Right, and Center

Traditionally, text is either aligned at its left margin or fully justified (often called *newspaper style*, in which text is aligned at both left and right margins). In addition, for emphasis or special effect, text can be centered on the screen or even right-justified. The text-align property gives you control of the text's alignment and justification (**Figure 4.5**).

To define text alignment:

1. text-align:

   Type the property name, followed by a colon (:), in the CSS definition list (**Code 4.5**).

continues on next page

Code 4.5 I'm setting up classes for all the various justifications.

```
<html>
<head>
<style type="text/css">
.left { text-align: left; }

.justify { text-align: justify; }

.center { text-align: center; }

.right { text-align: right; }
</style>
</head>
<body>
        <h2 class="left">Left</h2>
        <p class="left"><i>'You are old, Father William...</i></p>
        <hr>
        <h2 class="right">Right</h2>
        <p class="right"><i>'In my youth...</i></p>
        <hr>
        <h2 class="center">Center</h2>
        <p class="center"><i>'You are old,' said the youth...</i></p>
        <hr>
        <h2 class="justify">Justified</h2>
        <p class="justify">Hardly knowing what she did...</p>
</body>
</html>
```

2. `left;`

Set one of the following alignment styles (**Table 4.5**):

- ▲ `left` to align the text on the left margin
- ▲ `right` to align the text on the right margin
- ▲ `center` to center the text within its area
- ▲ `justify` to align the text on both the left and right sides

✔ Tip

- ■ Fully justifying text may produce some strange results on the screen, because spaces between words must be added to make each line the same length. In addition, there is considerable debate about whether full justification helps or hinders readability.

Table 4.5

text-align Values	
VALUE	COMPATIBILITY
left	IE3, N4, CSS1
right	IE3, N4, CSS1
center	IE3, N4, CSS1
justify	IE3, N4, CSS1

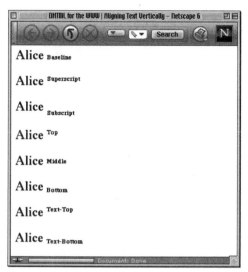

Figure 4.6 There are a variety of ways to align text relative to other text on the screen.

Code 4.6 Here I'm setting up a class for each of the vertical alignments.

```
<html>
<head>
    <style type="text/css">
.superscript {
vertical-align: super;
font-size: 12px;}
.baseline {
vertical-align: baseline;
font-size: 12px;}
.subscript {
vertical-align: sub;
font-size: 12px;}
.top {
vertical-align: top;
font-size: 12px;}
.middle{
font-size: 12px;
vertical-align: middle }
.bottom {
vertical-align: bottom;
font-size: 12px;}
```
(code continues on next page)

Aligning Text Vertically

With the `vertical-align` property, you can specify the position of inline elements relative to the text around it, either above or below. This means that `vertical-align` can be used only with inline element selectors—tags without a break before or after them, such as the anchor (`<a>`), image (`<img>`), bold (`<b>`), and italic (`<i>`) tags.

Figure 4.6 shows how the different vertical-alignment types should look.

To define vertical alignment:

1. `vertical-align:`

   Type the property name, followed by a colon (`:`), in the definition list (**Code 4.6**).

2. `super;`

   Type a value for the vertical alignment of the text (**Table 4.6**). Choose one of these options:

   ▲ `super`, which superscripts the text above the baseline.

   ▲ `sub`, which subscripts the text below the baseline.

   ▲ `baseline`, which places the text on the baseline (its natural state).

   ▲ A **relative value** from **Table 4.7** that sets the element's alignment relative to its parent's alignment. To align the top of your text with the top of the parent element's text, for example, type `text-top`.

   ▲ A **percentage** value, which raises or lowers the element's baseline proportionate to the parent element's font size (**25%**, for example).

continues on next page

✔ Tips

- Superscript and subscript are used for scientific notation. To express the Pythagorean theorem, for example, you would use superscripts:

  $a^2 + b^2 = c^2$

  A water molecule might be expressed with subscripts as follows:

  H_2O

- Superscript is also great for footnotes in the text, which can then be anchor-linked to notes at the bottom of the current page or to another Web page.

Table 4.6

vertical-align Values	
VALUE	COMPATIBILITY
super	IE4, N6, CSS1
sub	IE4, N6, CSS1
baseline	IE4, N6, CSS1
<relative>	IE5*, N6, CSS1
<percentage>	IE5**, N6, CSS1

*IE5.5 in Windows
** Mac version only; not available in Windows

Table 4.7

Setting an Element's Position Relative to the Parent Element	
TYPE THIS	TO GET THE ELEMENT TO ALIGN LIKE THIS
top	Top to highest element in line
middle	Middle to middle of parent
bottom	Bottom to lowest element in line
text-top	Top to top of parent element's text
text-bottom	Bottom to bottom of parent element's text

Code 4.6 *continued*

```
.texttop {
vertical-align: text-top;
font-size: 12px;}
.textbottom {
vertical-align: text-bottom;
font-size: 12px; }
.normal {
font-weight: bold;
font-size: 24px; }
</style>
</head>
<body>
    <p class="normal">Alice <span class="baseline">Basline</span></p>
    <p class="normal">Alice <span class="superscript">Superscript</span></p>
    <p class="normal">Alice <span class="subscript">Subscript</span></p>
    <p class="normal">Alice <span class="top">Top</span></p>
    <p class="normal">Alice <span class="middle">Middle</span></p>
    <p class="normal">Alice <span class="bottom">Bottom</span></p>
    <p class="normal">Alice <span class="texttop">Text-Top</span></p>
<p class="normal">Alice <span class="textbottom">Text-Bottom</span></p>
</body>
</html>
```

Figure 4.7 Paragraphs stand out better when they are indented.

Indenting Paragraphs

At last, the Web can indent paragraphs! Indenting the first word of a paragraph several spaces (traditionally, five) is the time-honored method of introducing a new paragraph.

On the Web, however, indented paragraphs haven't worked because most browsers compress multiple spaces into a single space. Instead, paragraphs have been separated by an extra line break.

Now, with the `text-indent` property, you can specify extra spaces at the beginning of the first line of text in a paragraph (**Figure 4.7**).

To define text indentation in a rule:

1. `text-indent:`

   Type the property name, followed by a colon (`:`), in the CSS definition list (**Code 4.7**).

continues on next page

Code 4.7 The class copy is set up to indent paragraphs of text 10% of the total screen width. So the wider the screen, the wider the indent.

```
code
<html>
<head>
<style type="text/css">
p.copy  {
text-indent: 10%; }
</style>
</head>
<body>
    <h3>CHAPTER IV<br>
        The Rabbit Sends in a Little Bill</h3>
<br>
    <p class="copy">'But then,' thought Alice...</p>
    <p class="copy">'Oh, you foolish Alice!'...</p>
    <p class="copy">And so she went on...</p>
    <p class="copy">'Mary Ann! Mary Ann!'...</p>
    <p class="copy">Presently the Rabbit came up to the door...</p>
    <p class="copy">'<i>That</i> you won't' thought Alice...</p>
    <p class="copy">Next came an angry voice...</p>
</body>
</html>
```

2. 10%;

Type a value for the indent, using either of these options (**Table 4.8**):

▲ A **length value**, such as 2em. This amount will create a nice, clear indent.

▲ A **percentage** value, which indents the text proportionate to the paragraph's width (10%, for example).

✔ Tips

■ You can set the margin of a paragraph to 0 to override the <p> tag's natural tendency to add space between paragraphs.

■ Because indenting is more common in the print world than online, you may want to consider using indents only for the printer-friendly versions of your page (see "Looking Good in Print [On the Web]" in Chapter 22).

Table 4.8

text-indent Values	
VALUE	COMPATIBILITY
<length>	IE3, N4, CSS1
<percentage>	IE3, N4, CSS1

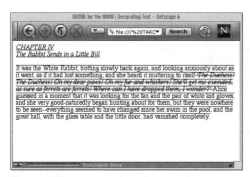

Figure 4.8 There are a variety of ways to decorate your text, but the most useful is underlining. Striking through text is also useful for text that you want to show as being deleted.

Decorating Text

Text decoration allows you to adorn the text in one of four ways. Used to add emphasis, these decorations attract the reader's eye to important areas or passages in your Web page (**Figure 4.8**).

To decorate a selector's text:

1. `text-decoration:`

   Type the property name, followed by a colon (:), in the CSS definition list (**Code 4.8**).

   continues on next page

Code 4.8 Emphasized text will be underlined unless it is in a paragraph, in which case it will have a line through it and a line over it, which it inherits from the <p> tag.

```
<html>
<head>
<style type="text/css">
em { text-decoration: underline; }
p em  { text-decoration: line-through; }
p { text-decoration: overline; }
</style>
</head>
<body>
                <em>CHAPTER IV<br>
      The Rabbit Sends in a Little Bill</em>
   <p>It was the White Rabbit, trotting slowly back again, and looking anxiously about as it went,
 → as if it had lost something; and she heard it muttering to itself<em> 'The Duchess! The
 → Duchess! Oh my dear paws! Oh my fur and whiskers! She'll get me executed, as sure as ferrets
 → are ferrets! Where <i>can</i> I have dropped them, I wonder?' </em>Alice guessed in a
 → moment...</p>
</body>
</html>
```

DECORATING TEXT

2. `Underline;`

Type a value for the decoration style (**Table 4.9**). Choose one of the following:

▲ `underline`, which places a line below the text

▲ `overline`, which places a line above the text

▲ `line-through`, which places a line through the middle of the text

▲ `blink`, which causes the text to blink on and off

▲ `none`, which overrides decorations set elsewhere

Table 4.9

text-decoration Values	
VALUE	COMPATIBILITY
none	IE4, N4, CSS1
underline	IE3, N4, CSS1
overline	IE4, N6, CSS1
line-through	IE3, N4, CSS1
blink	IE4, N4, CSS1

✔ Tips

■ If you want to, and as long as the first value is not none, you can have multiple text decorations by adding more values in a list separated by spaces, as follows:

`underline overline underline blink`

■ Many visitors don't like blinking text, especially on Web pages where they spend a lot of time. Use this decoration sparingly.

■ I've used strikethrough in online catalogs that include sale prices. I show the original price in strikethrough, with the sale price next to it.

■ Setting `text-decoration: none;` overrides link underlines in many browsers, even if the visitor has set her browser to underline links. In my experience, many visitors look for underlining to identify links. Although I don't like underlining for links—it clutters the page, and CSS offers many alternatives to identify links—I receive angry e-mails from visitors when I turn underlining off.

Code 4.9 Adding "white-space: pre" to the paragraph tag means that all of the spaces will be displayed unless the class `.collapse` is used, which then allows only one space between characters.

```
                         code
<html>
<head>


<style type="text/css">
p { white-space: pre; }
.collapse {white-space: normal;}
</style>
</head>
<body>
<p>A        L    I    C    E 'S    RIGH
         T F OO T, E S        Q . </P>
<p CLASS="collapse">H       E      A      R
→ T    H    R U G          ,</p>
<p>(W    I    T    H    A    L    I    C    E    '
→ S    L    O    V    E ).
<img src="alice08.gif" width="200"
→ height="131">
</p>
</body>
</html>
```

Controlling White Space

As mentioned in "Indenting Paragraphs" earlier in this chapter, browsers in the past have collapsed multiple spaces into a single space unless the <pre> tag was used. CSS lets you allow or disallow the collapsing of spaces, as well as designate whether text can break at a space (similar to the <nobr> HTML tag).

In this example (**Code 4.9** and **Figure 4.9**), the text has been spaced in odd configurations. If the white-space attribute were not defined for the style, all those spaces would collapse (**Figure 4.10**).

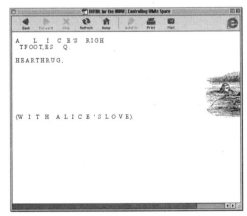

Figure 4.9 White space allows you to space text and graphics exactly the way you want them. Notice that the picture of Alice has been pushed over with spaces.

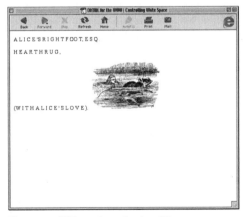

Figure 4.10 Without the style, the white spaces collapse.

To define white space for a selector:

1. `white-space:`

Type the property name, followed by a colon (:), in the CSS definition list.

2. `pre`

Type one of the following values (**Table 4.10**) to designate how you want spaces in text to be handled:

▲ `pre`, which preserves multiple spaces.

▲ `nowrap`, which prevents line wrapping without a break tag.

▲ `normal`, which allows the browser to determine how spaces are treated. This settings usually forces multiple spaces to collapse into a single space.

✔ Tips

■ The text content of any tag that receives the `nowrap` value runs horizontally as far as it needs, regardless of the window's width. The user may be forced to scroll horizontally to read all the text, so this setting is usually frowned upon.

■ `nowrap` is great for keeping lines of text in tables together regardless of the width of the table data cell.

Table 4.10

white-space Values	
VALUE	COMPATIBILITY
normal	IE5*, N4, CSS1
pre	IE5*, N4, CSS1
nowrap	IE5*, N6, CSS1
*IE5.5 for Windows	

Code 4.10 The level-3 header tag <h3> has been set up so that whenever the page is printed, a page break is forced above it.

```
                         code
<html>

<body>

<p>Once more she found herself in the
→ long hall...</p>

<hr>

<h3 style=" page-break-before: always;"
→ >CHAPTER VIII<br>

The Queen's Croquet-Ground</h3>

<p>A large rose-tree stood near...</p>

</body>

</html>
```

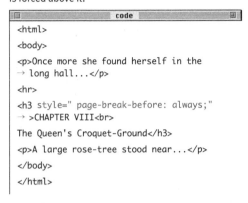

Figure 4.11 On the screen, each section immediately follows the preceding one.

Figure 4.12 When the page is printed, the beginning of the new section forces a page break.

Setting Page Breaks for Printing

One problem you'll encounter when trying to print a Web site is that pages break wherever they happen to break. A Web page may actually contain several printed pages. So the header for a section might appear at the bottom of a page and its text at the top of the next page.

If you want to force a page break when printing a Web page, use the following code to define an HTML tag (see "Adding CSS to an HTML Tag" in Chapter 2).

In this example, the Web page has a new chapter starting (**Figure 4.11**). Normally, when this page is printed, this header might appear anywhere on the page. By adding a page break in the <h3> tag (**Code 4.10**), however, you can force the chapter title to appear at the top of a new page when printed (**Figure 4.12**).

To define a page break for printing:

1. `style type="`

This CSS property works only if it is included in the `style` attribute of an HTML tag.

2. `page-break-before:`

Type the property name, followed by a colon (`:`), in the CSS definition list.

3. `always;`

Type one of the following values (**Table 4.11**) to designate how you want page breaks to be handled:

▲ `always`, which forces a page break before the element

▲ `auto`, which allows the browser to place the page breaks

4. `"`

Add other styles and then close the `style` attribute with quotation marks (`"`).

✔ Tips

■ Remember that this attribute will not work if it is included as part of a CSS rule—only if it is used directly in a tag with the `style` attribute.

■ `page-break-after` works pretty much the same way, but it puts the page break immediately after the tag.

■ Setting page breaks is a key ingredient in "Looking Good In Print (on the Web)" in Chapter 22.

Table 4.11

page-break-before Values	
VALUE	COMPATIBILITY
always	IE4, N6, CSS2
auto	IE4, N6, CSS2

LIST AND MOUSE CONTROLS

One useful feature of HTML is its capability to set up lists that automatically number or bullet themselves. You set up the list, and the browser takes care of the rest. When you add items to the list, the layout adjusts automatically when it's rendered in the window. The available choices, however, are fairly limited with HTML.

CSS gives you many more choices, providing control of the type of marker used to denote the list items, which can be a bullet or an alphanumeric character. You can also create your own bullets and make lists with hanging indents.

The bad news is that Netscape 4 and Internet Explorer 4 do not support many of these features. In addition, for the features that it does support, Netscape 4 does not allow you to use just any HTML tag; it only allows you only to redefine the `<li>` tag.

In this chapter, I'll show you not only how to whip your lists into shape by using CSS, but also how to change the mouse pointer into a variety of shapes.

Setting up a List

You can set all the attributes for a list in one line of code by using the `list-style` property. This gives you access to the `list-style-type`, `list-style-position`, and `line-style-image` properties.

In this example (**Code 5.1**), I've set up a list of cities to which I would like to travel one day and have given them an exciting bullet to add emphasis (**Figure 5.1**).

To define multiple list-style attributes for a selector:

1. `li {`

Set up the list item selector to be redefined. Because of the limitation in Netscape 4, it is best to stick with the `<li>` tag.

2. `list-style:`

Type the `list-style` property, followed by a colon (`:`), and then the list-style values as listed below and in **Table 5.1**.

3. `circle`

Type a `list-style-type` value listed in **Table 5.2**, followed by a space, or type `none` if you want no marker to appear (see the next section, "Setting the Bullet Style," for more information.

4. `inside`

Type a `list-style-position` value, followed by a space. Use either of the following:

▲ `inside`, which aligns subsequent lines of wrapped text with the bullet

▲ `outside`, which aligns subsequent lines of wrapped text with the first letter in the first line of the text

See "Creating a Hanging Indent" later in this chapter for more information.

Code 5.1 All the list-style properties are set at the same time.

```
<html>
<head>
    <style type="text/css">
        li {list-style: url(bullet1.gif)
        ⇢ circle inside ; }
</style>
</head>
<body>
    <h3>places to go</h3>
<ul>
        <li>london
        <li>paris
        <li>tokyo
        <li>new york
        <li>slippery creek
</ul>
</body>
</html>
```

Figure 5.1 Keep your lists in line by using CSS.

Table 5.1

list-style Values	
VALUE	COMPATIBILITY
<list-style-type>	IE4, N4, CSS1
<list-style-position>	IE4, N6, CSS1
<list-style-image>	IE4, N6, CSS1

Table 5.2

list-style bullets	
NAME	APPEARANCE (VARIES DEPENDING ON SYSTEM)
disc	●
circle	○
square	■
decimal	.
upper-roman	I
lower-roman	i
upper-alpha	A
lower-alpha	a

Figure 5.2 An arrow bullet.

5. `url(bullet1.gif)`

Next, type a `list-style-image` value. To include your own bullet, you first have to create the bullet graphic (**Figure 5.2**) and then tell the browser where the graphic is located. This location is either the complete Web address or the local file name of the image. (See "Creating Your Own Bullets" later in this chapter for more information.)

6. `;}`

Close the definition with a semicolon (`;`). Then, type in any other definitions for this rule and close it with a curly bracket (`}`).

✔ Tips

■ Because each of the multiple values in the preceding exercise is a different type, not all values must be present for this definition to work. Values omitted are set to the default. The following example works just fine:

`list-style: inside;`

■ If the visitor has turned off graphics in the browser, or if a graphical bullet does not load for some reason, the browser uses the `list-style-type` instead.

SETTING UP A LIST

Setting the Bullet Style

The list-style property gives you control of the type of bullet to be used for list items—not just circles, discs, and squares, but also letters and numerals and dots. Oh, my!

In this example (**Code 5.2**), I have set up my shopping list, using different bullet styles for different types of items (**Figure 5.3**).

To define the bullet style:

1. li.grocery {

    Type the selector you are defining. For this example, I've set up a dependent class called **grocery** that is associated with the list <li> tag. It's important to remember that in Netscape, you can change only the list tag with these properties.

2. list-style-type:

    Type the list-style-type property, followed by a colon (:) and one of the values below and in **Table 5.3**.

3. disc

    Type one of the bullet names listed in Table 5.2, or type **none** if you want no marker to appear.

4. ;}

    Close the definition with a curly bracket (}).

✔ Tip

- You can use list-style-type only with list tags (<li>) in Netscape 4. This arrangement is at odds with the official CSS specs, which state that any HTML tag can be used to make a list as long as it includes the definition display.

Code 5.2 Two classes are created to help with the shopping list. The grocery class uses a disc as its bullet, and computer uses a square.

```
<html>
<head>
    <style type="text/css">
        li.grocery {list-style-type: disc;}
        li.computer {list-style-type: square;}
    </style>
</head>
<body>
    <h3>Shopping list</h3>
    <ul>
        <li class="grocery">Butter
        <li class="grocery">Milk
        <li class="grocery">Cereal
        <li class="computer">5GB Hard drive
        <li class="grocery">Orange juice
        <li class="grocery">Cat Food
        <li class="computer">40MB RAM
        <li class="grocery">Soup
    </ul>
</body>
</html>
```

Figure 5.3 The computer items stand out in the shopping list, because they use a unique bullet.

Table 5.3

list-style-type Values	
VALUE	COMPATIBILITY
<bullet name>	IE4, N4, CSS1
none	IE4, N4, CSS1

Code 5.3 Lists are set to display with a hanging indent unless given the class `inside`, which causes the text to run flush with the bullet.

```
                        code
<html>
<head>
    <style type="text/css">
            li {list-style-position:
            → outside; width="200px";}

            li.inside {list-style-position:
            → inside;}
</style>
        </head>
    <body>
            <ul>
            <li>'A knot!' said Alice, always
            → ready to make herself useful, and
            → looking anxiously about her.
            → 'Oh, do let me help to undo it!'
            <li class="inside">'I shall do
            → nothing of the sort,' said the
            → Mouse, getting up and walking
            → away. 'You insult me by
            → talking such nonsense!'
            <li>'I didn't mean it!' pleaded
            → poor Alice. 'But you're so
            → easily
            offended, you know!'
        <li>The Mouse only growled in reply.
</UL>
</body>
</html>
```

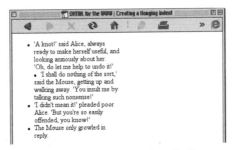

Figure 5.4 The bullet stands out from the list text.

Table 5.4

list-style-position Values	
VALUE	COMPATIBILITY
inside	IE4, N6, CSS1
outside	IE4, N6, CSS1

Creating a Hanging Indent

Often, the text of an item in a bulleted list is longer than one line. By using the `list-style-position` property, you can specify the position of wrapping text in relation to the bullet. Wrapped text that is indented to start below the first letter of the first line of text is called a *hanging indent*.

In this example (**Code 5.3**), I have set up the bullets with two position styles: one to create a hanging indent and the other to align the text with the bullet (**Figure 5.4**).

To define the line position for wrapped text in a list item:

1. `li.inside {`

    Set up your selector. For this example, you'll create an independent class called `inside`, which, when used with a list tag, will make the listed text fall flush with the bullet.

2. `list-style-position:`

    Type the `list-style-position` property, followed by a colon (:).

3. `inside`

    Type one of the following keywords to determine how you want the text to be indented (**Table 5.4**):

    ▲ `inside`, which aligns subsequent lines of wrapped text with the bullet

    ▲ `outside`, which aligns subsequent lines of wrapped text with the first letter in the first line of the text

4. `;}`

    Close the definition with a semicolon (;) and a curly bracket (}).

✔ Tip

■ Generally, bulleted lists that have a hanging indent (outside position) stand out much better than those without a hanging indent (inside position).

Creating Your Own Bullets

You're not limited to the preset bullet styles built into the browser (see "Setting the Bullet Style" earlier in this chapter). You can also use your own graphics as bullets, in GIF, JPEG, and PNG (for supporting browsers only) formats.

In this example (**Code 5.4**), I've set up a list of things to do (**Figure 5.5**) and added emphasis with the arrow bullet created earlier in the chapter (Figure 5.2).

To define your own graphic bullet:

1. li{

Start your definition with a list selector.

2. list-style-image:

Type in the list-style-image property name, followed by a colon (:).

3. url(bullet1.gif);

To include your own bullet, you have to tell the browser where your bullet graphic is located. This location is either the complete Web address or the local file name of the image. In this example, bullet1.gif is a local file.

Alternatively, type none, which instructs the browser to override any inherited bullet images (**Table 5.5**).

Code 5.4 These list items will have an image in front of them rather than a standard bullet.

```
<html>
<head>
    <style type="text/css">
        li {list-style-image: url(bullet1.gif);
        → margin-left: 20px;}
    </style>
</head>
<body>
        <h2>Things to do</h2>
    <ul>
        <li>write book
        <li>make examples
        <li>edit book
        <li>take holiday in bahammas
        <li>drink pina colladas
    </ul>
</body>
</html>
```

Figure 5.5 Why settle for the same old bullets? Create your own with CSS.

Table 5.5

list-style-image Values	
VALUE	COMPATIBILITY
<url>	IE4, N6, CSS1
none	IE4, N6, CSS1

4. ;}

Close the definition with a semicolon (;). Then type any other definitions for this rule and close it with a curly bracket (}).

✔ Tips

- Netscape 4 does not support the list-style-image property. Therefore, I recommend always including a backup list-style-type in case the image cannot be used.

- Graphic bullets are a great way to enhance the appearance of your page while minimizing download time.

- Keep in mind that the text being bulleted has to make space for the graphic you use. A taller graphic will force more space between individual bulleted items, and a wider graphic will force bulleted items farther to the right.

CREATING YOUR OWN BULLETS

Changing the Mouse Pointer's Appearance

Normally, the mouse pointer's appearance is determined by the browser. The browser changes the mouse pointer depending on the current content over which the mouse pointer happens to be resting.

If the pointer is over text, for example, the pointer becomes a text selector. Or if the browser is working and the visitor can't do anything, the pointer becomes a timer, letting the visitor know she needs to wait.

Sometimes, it's useful to override the browser's wishes and set the appearance of the pointer yourself.

In this example (**Code 5.5**), I have set up different pointer types that depend on the type of object or link over which the pointer is hovering (**Figures 5.6, 5.7,** and **5.8**).

Code 5.5 Because the link leads to a help screen, I've set the appearance to use the help class. In addition, images will have a move pointer, and the entire page will use a pointer that is generally used when resizing the window from the top-left corner.

```
<html>
<head>
    <style type="text/css">
        .help {cursor: help;}
        body {cursor: nw-resize;}
        img {cursor: move;}
    </style>
</head>
<body>
    <h3>CHAPTER VIII<br>
    The Queen's Croquet-Ground</h3>
    <p><img src="alice30.gif" width="200"
 → height="272" border="0" align="left">A
 → large rose-tree stood near the entrance
 → of the garden...</p>
    <p>'I couldn't <a class="help" href="#">
 → help</a> it,' said Five, in a sulky tone;
 → 'Seven jogged my elbow.'</p>
</body>
</html>
```

Figure 5.6 The mouse pointer is still an arrow in most places in the window, but it looks different from the standard arrow.

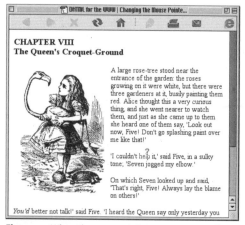

Figure 5.7 When the mouse pointer passes over the help link, it becomes a question mark.

Figure 5.8 When the mouse pointer is over an image, it changes to the resize pointer. This feature will come in handy when you make your magnetic-poetry kit (see "Drag-and-Drop Objects" in Chapter 25).

Table 5.6

Pointer Names	
NAME	**APPEARANCE** (VARIES DEPENDING ON OS)
crosshair	+
hand*	🖑
pointer	🖑
move	✛
n-resize	▲
ne-resize	◥
e-resize	▶
se-resize	◢
s-resize	▼
sw-resize	◣
w-resize	◀
nw-resize	◤
text	I
wait	⌚
help	?

* IE only; same as pointer

To set the mouse pointer's appearance:

1. `cursor:`

   Type the `cursor` attribute, followed by a colon (`:`), in the CSS definition list.

2. `help`

   Type one of the mouse-pointer names listed in **Table 5.6**, or type `auto` if you want the browser to decide which mouse pointer to use (**Table 5.7**).

✔ Tips

■ According to the CSS standards, you should also be able to create your own mouse pointer by using any normal Web graphic, as follows:

   `cursor: url(myPointer.gif);`

   Unfortunately, none of the browsers currently supports this feature. Sorry.

■ Although it's fun to play around with switching the mouse pointers, I've tested this feature on my own Web site and have gotten several e-mails asking me to cut it out. Most Web users have learned to recognize what particular pointers are for and when they should appear. Breaking these conventions tends to confuse people.

Table 5.7

cursor Values	
VALUE	**COMPATIBILITY**
<cursor name>	IE4, N6, CSS2
<URL>	CSS2
auto	IE4, N6, CSS2
none	IE4, N6, CSS2

COLOR AND BACKGROUND CONTROLS

HTML has allowed us to set background colors and graphics almost since its beginnings. This capability, however, was limited to the background of the entire Web page. You could play around with the background colors of table cells, but that was still very confining.

CSS lets you define the background color and graphic for any individual element on the page, giving you much greater versatility when it comes to designing your Web pages. In fact, this may be the most significant advancement that CSS offers.

Setting the Background

You can use the background property to define the background image and color for the entire page or the background image and color immediately behind any individual element on the page (**Code 6.1** and **Figure 6.1**).

To define the background:

1. background:

Start your definition by typing the background property, followed by a colon (:), and then the following background values (**Table 6.1**).

Figure 6.1 The background for the page (the telescoping Alice) appears to the extreme right of the page, and the header has its own distinctive background: a rough texture that repeats only on the left side and is flat gray in the rest.

Code 6.1 This code sets up a background image for the entire page through the <body> tag. The image will be fixed on the right side and not repeat. In addition, the <h3> tag will have its own background image, which repeats only down from the top on the left side of the element.

```
<html>
<head>
    <style media="screen" type="text/css">
        body  { background: white url(alice05.gif) no-repeat fixed right top; }
        h3  {
            background: #999999 url(background_rough.gif) repeat-y left top;
            color: white;
            width: 60%;
            padding: 20px }
        p { width: 60%; }
</style>
</head>
<body>
    <h3>CHAPTER II<br>
The Pool of Tears</h3>
    <p>'Curiouser and curiouser!' cried Alice...</p>
    <p>And she went on planning...</p>
    <p>Oh dear, what nonsense I'm talking!'</p>
    <p>Just then her head struck...</p>
    <p>Poor Alice!...</p>
    <p>'You ought to be ashamed of yourself...</p>
    <p>After a time she heard a little pattering...</p>
</body>
</html>
```

Table 6.1

background Values	
VALUE	COMPATIBILITY
<background-color>	IE4, N4, CSS1
<background-image>	IE4, N4, CSS1
<background-repeat>	IE4, N4, CSS1
<background-attachment>	IE4, N6, CSS1
<background-position>	IE4, N6, CSS1

More Background on Backgrounds

Netscape and Internet Explorer disagree on how far the background extends in an element. Internet Explorer extends the element's background all the way across the screen; Netscape extends the background only as far as the end of the element's content. To overcome this problem, set the width of the element either in pixels or as a percentage so that both browsers have a consistent width for the element (see "Setting the Width and Height of an Element" in Chapter 7).

2. `white`

Type a value for the color you want the background to be, followed by a space. This value can be the name of the color, a hex color value, or an RGB value.

Alternatively, you could type `transparent`, which tells the browser to use the default color set by the browser.

3. `url(alice05.gif)`

Type a URL for the location of the background image, followed by a space. This location is the image file (GIF, JPEG, or PNG) that you want to use as the background and is either a complete Web address or a local filename.

Alternatively, you can type `none` instead of a URL. `none` instructs the browser not to use a background image.

4. `repeat-y`

Type a keyword defining how you want your background to repeat, followed by a space. You can use one of these options:

▲ `repeat` instructs the browser to repeat the graphic throughout the background of the element.

▲ `repeat-x` instructs the browser to repeat the background graphic only horizontally. In other words, the graphic repeats in one straight horizontal line along the top of the element.

▲ `repeat-y` instructs the browser to repeat the background graphic only vertically. In other words, the graphic repeats in one straight vertical line along the left side of the element.

▲ `no-repeat` causes the background graphic to appear only once and not tile.

continues on next page

5. fixed

Type a keyword to specify how you want the background to be treated when the page scrolls, followed by a space. You can use these options:

▲ fixed instructs the browser not to scroll the background content with the rest of the elements (**Figure 6.2**)

▲ scroll instructs the background graphic to scroll with the element

6. right top;

Type two values, separated by a space, to specify where you want the background to appear in relation to the top-left corner of the element. You can use one of these values:

▲ A **length value,** such as –10px. The values can be positive or negative. The first number tells the browser the distance the element should appear from the left edge of its parent; the second value specifies the position from the top edge of the parent.

▲ A **percentage value,** such as 25%. The first percentage indicates the horizontal position proportional to the parent element's size; the second value indicates the vertical position proportional to the parent element's size.

Figure 6.2 Although the text has scrolled, the background image for the page (the telescoping Alice) stays in the same place.

✔ Tips

■ The ability to place graphics behind any element on the screen is a very powerful tool for designing Web pages; it frees you from the constraints of having to create new graphics whenever text changes. You can combine the versatility of HTML text with graphics to create stunning effects (see "Creating Headlines" in Chapter 22).

■ The default state for an element's background is **none**, so the parent element's background image and/or color will show through unless the background color or background image for that particular element is set.

■ The background attribute allows you to set all of the background properties at once. The following sections will show you how to set each attribute individually.

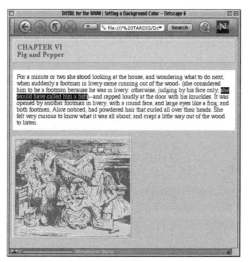

Figure 6.3 Background colors have been applied to various elements on the screen. Notice that a pink color has been set for the image. This color shows through where the image has been made transparent.

Setting Individual Background Properties

Although you can set all the background properties with the background property (see the previous section, "Setting the Background"), you can also set each of the background properties individually.

Setting a background color

The ability to set the background color for an HTML page has been around almost since the first Web browsers. With CSS, however, you can define the background color for not only the entire page, but behind individual elements as well (**Code 6.2** and **Figure 6.3**).

Code 6.2 The background color for the page has been set to gray. Other CSS definitions (<img>, <h3>, <p> with the copy class, and the highlight class) override this background color.

```
<html>
<head>
    <style type="text/css">
        body { background-color: #cccccc;}
        img  {background-color: #ff9999;}
        h3 {position:relative; background-color: #ff9999; layer-background-color: #ff9999;
        → padding: 10px;}
        p.copy {position:relative; background-color: rgb(100%, 100%, 100%); layer-background-color:
        → rgb(100%, 100%, 100%);  padding: 10px;}
        .highlight {background-color: black; color: white;}
    </style>
</head>
<body>
<h3>CHAPTER VI<BR>
    Pig and Pepper</h3>
    <p class="copy">For a minute or two she stood looking at the house, and wondering...</p>
    <img src="alice21.gif" width="300" height="248" border="0">
</body>
</html>
```

To define the background color of an element:

1. `background-color:`

Start your definition by typing the property, followed by a colon (:).

2. `#cccccc`

Type a value for the color you want the background to be (**Table 6.2**). This value can be the name of the color, a hex color value, or an RGB value.

Alternatively, you could type `transparent`, which tells the browser to use the default color set by the browser.

✔ Tip

■ The default state for an element's background color is **none**, so the parent element's background will show through unless the background color or image for that particular element is set.

Table 6.2

background-color Values	
VALUE	COMPATIBILITY
<color>	IE4, N4, CSS1
transparent	IE4, N4, CSS1

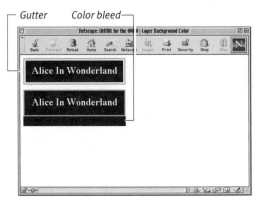

Figure 6.4 In the first title, although the background color has been set, a clear gutter appears between the element and the element's border. In the second title, the `layer-background` property has been set to fill the gutter, but now the color sticks out on the bottom. Infuriating, isn't it?

Background Color in Netscape

Netscape 4 has a bug when it comes to background colors. Although the color will appear behind the element, a clear gutter appears between an element and any border you set for that element (**Figure 6.4**).

The good news is that you can add the Netscape-specific attribute `layer-background-color` to overcome this problem:

`layer-background-color: black;`

This code adds color to the gutter area as long as the element has its position attribute set (see "Setting the Positioning Type" in Chapter 8).

The bad news is that even this solution is buggy. The color tends to stick out on the top and/or bottom of the element and can look odd in some designs, especially if you include a border (Figure 6.4). My advice is to live with the gutter.

Figure 6.5 The background image (Alice) appears on the left side of the screen, and the text has been pushed over to the right.

Setting a background image

CSS offers you the flexibility to not only set the background graphic for a page or element on the page, but also dictate how that background graphic should be repeated and positioned. (**Code 6.3** and **Figure 6.5**).

Code 6.3 In this code, a background image is defined for the <body> of the page. In turn, this image is instructed not to repeat, fixed, and moved up and to the left by using negative values with the position. Additionally, the <h3> tag has been defined with a rough background graphic that is repeated just across the top of the element. Finally, so that the text does not overlap the background image, all text has been offset 200 pixels.

```
<html>
<head>
    <style type="text/css">
        body    {
            background-image: url(alice05.gif);
            background-repeat: no-repeat;
            background-attachment: fixed;
            background-position: -10px -5px;
        }
        h3  {
            background-image: url(background_rough.gif);
            background-repeat: repeat-x;
            background-position: -20px -2px;
            margin-left: 200px;
        padding: 10px; }
        .copy { margin-left: 200px; }
</style>
</head>
<body>
    <h3>CHAPTER II<br>
The Pool of Tears</h3>
    <p>'Curiouser and curiouser!' cried Alice...</p>
</body>
</html>
```

SETTING INDIVIDUAL BACKGROUND PROPERTIES

To define the position of a background image:

1. `background-image: url(alice05.gif);`

   Type the `background-image` property, and define an URL for the location of the image. This location is the image file (GIF, JPEG, or PNG) that you want to use as the background and is either a complete Web address or a local filename.

   Alternatively, you can type none instead of an URL to instruct the browser not to use a background image (**Table 6.3**).

2. `background-repeat: no-repeat;`

   Type the `background-repeat` property, followed by a colon (:); then define how you want your background to repeat by typing one of the following options (**Table 6.4**):

   ▲ repeat instructs the browser to repeat the graphic throughout the background of the element.

   ▲ repeat-x instructs the browser to repeat the background graphic only horizontally. In other words, the graphic repeats in one straight horizontal line along the top of the element.

   ▲ repeat-y instructs the browser to repeat the background graphic only vertically. In other words, the graphic repeats in one straight vertical line along the left side of the element.

   ▲ no-repeat causes the background graphic to appear only once and not tile.

3. `background-attachment: fixed;`

   Type the `background-attachment` attribute, followed by a colon (:); then define how you want the background to be treated when the page scrolls by typing one of the following options (**Table 6.5**):

   ▲ fixed instructs the browser not to scroll the background content with the rest of the elements (**Figure 6.6**).

Table 6.3

background-image Values	
VALUE	COMPATIBILITY
<url>	IE4, N4, CSS1
none	IE4, N4, CSS1

Table 6.4

background-repeat Values	
VALUE	COMPATIBILITY
repeat	IE4, N4, CSS1
repeat-x	IE4, N4, CSS1
repeat-y	IE4, N4, CSS1
no-repeat	IE4, N4, CSS1

Table 6.5

background-attachment Values	
VALUE	COMPATIBILITY
scroll	IE4, N6, CSS1
fixed	IE4, N6, CSS1

Figure 6.6 Although the text has scrolled down, the background image stays in place.

Table 6.6

background-position Values	
VALUE	COMPATIBILITY
<percentage>	IE4, N6, CSS2
<length>	IE4, N6, CSS2
top	IE4, N6, CSS2
center	IE4, N6, CSS2
bottom	IE4, N6, CSS2
left	IE4, N6, CSS2
right	IE4, N6, CSS2

▲ `scroll` instructs the background graphic to scroll with the element.

4. `background-position: -10px -5px;`

Type the background-position property, followed by a colon (`:`). Then type two values—separated by a space—to indicate where you want the background to appear in relation to the top-left corner of the element (usually, the screen). These values can be (**Table 6.6**):

▲ **Length values,** such as `-10px`. The values can be positive or negative. The first number tells the browser the distance the element should appear from the left edge of its parent; the second value specifies the position from the top edge of the parent.

▲ **Percentage values,** such as 25%. The first percentage indicates the horizontal position proportional to the parent element's size; the second value indicates the vertical position proportional to the parent element's size.

▲ **Keywords** (see the sidebar "Positioning in Plain English" in this section).

✔ Tips

■ Sometimes, a repeating background can be really annoying. It may repeat where it's not wanted, or you may want it to tile in only one direction. CSS gives you supreme control of how background graphics appear through the `background-repeat` property.

■ You can mix percentage and length values in the same `background-position` definition, but you cannot mix length or percentages with plain-English keywords.

■ Any background space that does not have a background graphic will be filled with the background color (see "Setting Individual Background Properties" earlier in this chapter).

Positioning in Plain English

Another way to define the position of a background image is by using keywords.

`background-position: center top;`

To position the graphic relative to the size of the window use the following:

1. Type a horizontal-position keyword: `left, center, right`.

2. Type a space, followed by a vertical-position keyword: `top, center, bottom`.

Setting a Foreground Color

By using the color property, you can set the color appearance for an element (**Code 6.4**). Although this property is primarily used to color text, Internet Explorer and Netscape 6 allow you to use color for horizontal rules and form elements as well (**Figure 6.7**).

To define the foreground color:

1. color:

    Type the name of the color property, followed by a colon (:), in the CSS definition list.

2. Red;

    Now type a value for the color you want this element to be (**Table 6.7**). This value can be the name of a color, a hex color value, or an RGB value (see "Values and Units Used in this Book" in the introduction).

✔ Tips

■ Assigning a color to several nested elements can lead to unwanted color changes. The most obvious example is if you set the color in the <body> tag. Internet Explorer 4/5 and Netscape 6 will change the color of *all* elements in the body. Always consider which tags you redefine and how they might affect other tags on your Web page (see "Inheriting Properties from Parents" in Chapter 2).

■ A tag's border color can be set by the color property but can be overwritten by the border-color property (see "Setting an Element's Border" in Chapter 7).

Table 6.7

color Value	
VALUE	COMPATIBILITY
<color>	IE3, N4, CSS1

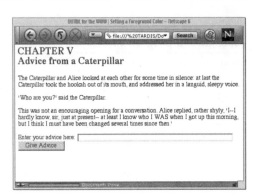

Figure 6.7 The text in the header for this page is red, as is the text in the form elements.

Code 6.4 The <h2> tag is defined to display its text in red.

```
<html>
<head>
<style type="text/css">
        h2 { color: red; }
        form {color: #990000;}
        input {color: rgb(100%, 0%, 0%); }
        .copy{ color: rgb(102,102,102`}
</style>
</head>
<body>
    <h2>CHAPTER V<br>
    Advice from a Caterpillar</h2>
    <p class="copy">The Caterpillar and Alice
    → looked at each other...</p>
    <p class="copy">'Who are you?' said the
    → Caterpillar.</p>
    <p class="copy">This was not an encouraging
    → opening for a conversation...</p>
    <form name="FormName" action="#"
    → method="get">Enter your advice here:
        <input type="text" name="textfieldName"
        → size="48"><br>
        <input type="submit" name="advice"
        → value="Give Advice">
    </form>
</body>
</html>
```

BORDER AND MARGIN CONTROLS

7

In the physical world, atoms are the building blocks for all larger objects. Every type of atom has its own unique properties, but when bonded with other atoms, they create larger structures with properties different from the parts—molecules.

Likewise, HTML tags are the building blocks of your Web page. Each tag has its own unique capabilities, and tags can be combined to create a Web page that is greater than the parts.

Whether a tag is by itself or nested deep within other tags, each tag can be treated as a discrete element on the screen and controlled by CSS.

I use the concept of the box as a metaphor to describe the various things that you can do to an HTML element in a window, whether it is a single tag or several nested tags. This box has several properties—including margins, borders, padding, width, and height—that can be influenced by CSS.

In this chapter, I'll show you how to control the box and its properties.

Understanding the Element's Box

The term *element* refers to the various parts of an HTML document that are set off by HTML container tags. The following is an HTML element:

```
<p>Alice</p>
```

This is another HTML element:

```
<div><p><b>Alice<img src="alice11.gif">
→ </b></p></div>
```

The first example is an element made of a single tag. The second example is a collection of nested tags, and each of those nested tags is in turn an individual element. Remember that nested tags are referred to as the children of the tags within which they are nested; those tags in turn are referred to as the parents (see "Inheriting Properties from Parents" in Chapter 2).

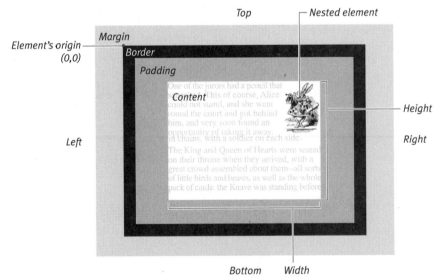

Figure 7.1 An element's box has a margin, a border, and padding on four sides around its central content. The element's width and height can be defined by the author or can be left to the browser's discretion. The origin of an element's box is always its top-left corner.

The following sections give you a closer look at what makes up an element's box.

Parts of the box

All HTML elements have four sides: top, bottom, left, and right (**Figure 7.1**). These four sides make up the element's box, to which CSS properties can be applied. Each side of the box has the following properties:

◆ **Width** and **height,** which are the lengths on a side of the element. Top and bottom are the width; left and right are the height. Parallel sides (left/right and top/bottom) have the same length. If you leave width and height undefined, these distances are determined by the browser (see the next section, "Setting the Width and Height of an Element").

◆ **Margin,** which is the space between the border of the element and other elements in the window (see "Setting an Element's Margins" later in this chapter).

◆ **Border,** which is a rule (line) that surrounds the element. The border is invisible unless its color, width, and style—solid, dotted, dashed, and so on—are set (see "Setting an Element's Border" later in this chapter).

◆ **Padding,** which is the space between the border and the content of the element (see "Setting an Element's Padding" later in this chapter).

Element boxes can also wrap around other elements, embedding an element within another (see "Wrapping Text Around an Element" later in this chapter).

The content

At the center of the box is the content. All other CSS properties (font, text, color, background, and lists) apply to this area. (Note: Background properties also apply to the padded area of an element's box.) The content includes all text, lists, forms, and images you care to use.

Tags or Containers?

You'll see the term *HTML tag* used often, not only in this book, but also all over the Web. A tag is a marker used by HTML (the `<blockquote>` tag, for example) that tells the browser to do something. Very often, a tag also has an associated closing tag that is designated with a slash (/) character (`</blockquote>`, for example, is the closing `<blockquote>` tag). The closing tag shows the browser when to stop doing something. These two tags collectively are known as a *container*. But more often than not, the entire container is referred to as a tag.

Setting the Width and Height of an Element

The width and height of block-level and replaced elements can be specified with the width and height properties (see "Kinds of HTML Tags" in Chapter 1). Usually, the width and height are determined automatically by the browser and default to being 100% of the available width and whatever height is needed to display all the content. You can use CSS, however, to override both the width and height properties (**Code 7.1** and **Figure 7.2**).

Figure 7.2 The width and height for the form box, the image (which looks uncomfortably scrunched), and the text block have all been set. Notice that although the form box conforms to both width and height, the text block seems to have only the width set. Height is ignored unless you define the overflow property (see "Setting Where the Overflow Goes" in Chapter 9).

Code 7.1 You can set the width and/or height of an element by using a variety of different units. The most common method is to use pixels. But you can also use centimeters, millimeters, inches, and points, among other options.

```
<html>
<head>
    <style type="text/css">
        textarea { width: 225px; height: 100px; }
        .copy{ width: 225px;height: 100px;}
        img {width: 5cm;height: 12cm; }
    </style>
</head>
<body>
    <form action="#" method="get">
        <textarea align="left" name="content" cols="40" rows="4">Alice remained looking
        thought→ fully at the mushroom...</textarea>
    </form>
    <img src="alice11.gif"  border="0" align="left">
    <p class="copy">Alice remained looking thoughtfully at the mushroom...</p>
</body>
</html>
```

Table 7.1

width Values	
VALUE	COMPATIBILITY
<length>	IE4, N4, CSS1
<percentage>	IE4, N4, CSS1
auto	IE4, N4, CSS1

Table 7.2

height Values	
VALUE	COMPATIBILITY
<length>	IE4, N6, CSS1
<percentage>	IE4, N6, CSS1
auto	IE4, N6, CSS1

To define the width of an element:

1. `width:`

   Type the `width` property, followed by a colon (`:`), in the CSS definition list.

2. `225px;`

   Type a value for the element's width, which can be any of the following (**Table 7.1**):

   ▲ A **length value**.

   ▲ A **percentage**, which sets the width proportional to the parent element's width.

   ▲ `auto`, which uses the width calculated by the browser for the element. The width usually will be the maximum distance that the element can stretch to the right before hitting the edge of the window or the edge of a parent element.

To define the height of an element:

1. `height:`

   Type the `height` property, followed by a colon (`:`).

2. `100px;`

   Type a value for the element's height, which can be any of the following (**Table 7.2**):

   ▲ A **length value**.

   ▲ A **percentage**, which sets the height proportional to the parent element's height.

   ▲ `auto`, which uses a calculated height determined by the browser. The height will be however much space the element needs to display all the content.

continues on next page

SETTING THE WIDTH AND HEIGHT OF AN ELEMENT

✔ Tips

- You can resize an image (GIF or JPEG) by using the width and height properties, thus overriding the width and height set in the image tag. Doing this will more than likely create a severely distorted image, but that can sometimes be a pretty neat effect.

- Use width and height to keep form fields and buttons a consistent size.

- Although you can set the height of any element, only elements with replaced tags (see "Kinds of HTML Tags" in Chapter 1) will use it. Other tags ignore a height value *unless* you define what should happen to the overflowing content of the element (see "Setting Where the Overflow Goes" in Chapter 9).

- Internet Explorer and Netscape disagree on what the auto width is. Internet Explorer stretches an element's width to the edge of its parent, whereas Netscape extends the width only as far as the content will fill.

- Netscape 4 is buggy when it comes to setting the width of an element. Regardless of what width is set for the element, unless there is enough content to fill the space, Netscape defaults to auto.

Code 7.2 You can set the margins in one definition or on a side-by side basis, either by defining each side individually, as shown in this code, or by listing each side.

```
<html>
<head>
<style type="text/css">
p.paragraphtwo { margin: 5em; }
h2 { margin: 1em }
p.copy {
margin-top:  5em;
            margin-bottom: 10%;
            margin-left:  8em;
            margin-right: 200px; }
</style>
</head>
<body>
    <h2>CHAPTER VII<br>
    A Mad Tea-Party</h2>
    <p class="copy">There was a table set out
    → under a tree in front of the house...</p>
<p class="paragraphtwo">The table was a
large one...</p>
</body>
</html>
```

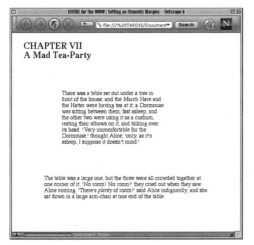

Figure 7.3 The margins around the first block of text have been set relative to the live area of the screen.

Setting an Element's Margins

The margin property allows you to set the space between that element and other elements in the window by specifying one to four values (**Code 7.2**) that correspond to all four sides together, the top/bottom and left/right sides as pairs, or all four sides independently (**Figure 7.3**).

To define the margins of an element:

1. margin:

   Start your definition by typing the margin property, followed by a colon (:), in the definition list.

2. 5em;

   Now type a value for the margin, which can be any of the following (**Table 7.3**):

   ▲ A **length value**.

   ▲ A **percentage**, which creates a margin proportional to the parent element's width.

   ▲ auto, which returns control of the margins to the browser's discretion.

   continues on next page

Table 7.3

margin Values	
VALUE	**COMPATIBILITY**
<length>	IE3, N4, CSS1
<percentage>	IE3, N4, CSS1
auto	IE3, N4, CSS1

✔ Tips

- You can also set each side's margin independently (see "Setting Margins on a Side" on the next page).

- Be careful in setting negative margins around a hypertext link. If one element has margins that cause it to cover the link, the link will not work as expected.

- You can also set margins for the <body> tag, in which case they define the distance at which elements nested in the body should appear from the top and left sides of the browser window.

- Netscape 4 permits only negative values for the top and bottom margins.

- When setting proportional margins, be aware that you might get very different results depending on the size of the user's window. What looks good at a resolution of 640x480 might be a mess at larger screen sizes.

- Netscape 4 has a bug that forces any element with the margins being set to act as a block-level tag (see "Kinds of HTML Tags" in Chapter 1).

Setting negative margins

Although you can use negative margins to create interesting effects for overlapping pieces of text, this method is frowned upon, because the various browsers present different results.

```
margin: -5em;
```

Overlapping text is better achieved with CSS positioning (see Chapter 8, "Positioning Controls").

Setting margins on a side

If you want to set several margins, you can enter up to four values, separated by spaces, as follows:

`margin: 5em auto 5em 25%;`

- One value sets the margin for all four sides.

- Two values set the top/bottom margins and left/right margins.

- Three values set the top margin, the left and right margins (the same), and the bottom margin.

- Four values set each individual margin: top, right, bottom, and left.

You can also set just one side of the box's margin without having to worry about the other three margins. This is especially useful when used with an inline style to override margins set elsewhere. To do this, just specify the margin side you want to define and a legitimate margin value:

```
margin-top: 5em;
margin-bottom: 10%;
margin-left: 8em;
margin-right: 200px;
```

The `auto value` doesn't work for `margin-right` and `margin-left` in Internet Explorer 4 or Netscape 4.

Setting an Element's Border

To set any of the border attributes for all four sides of the box simultaneously, CSS provides the **border** property (**Code 7.3**). You can use **border** to set width, style, and/or color (**Figure 7.4**). You can also set the element's border on each side of the box individually (see the sidebar "Setting Borders on a Side" in this section).

To set the border:

1. border:

Type the **border** property, followed by a colon (:), in the CSS definition list.

2. 20px

Type a **border-width** value, followed by a space. This value can be one of the following (**Table 7.4**):

▲ A **length value**. A value of 0 prevents the border from appearing.

▲ A **relative-size keyword**. Use thin, medium, or thick.

3. double

Type the name of the style you want to assign to your border. (See **Table 7.4** for a complete list of available border styles.)

Alternatively, you can type **none**, which prevents the border from appearing.

4. #990000;

Type a color value, which is the color you want the border to be. This value can be the name of the color, a hex color value, or an RGB value.

Code 7.3 You can set all the border's attributes in one definition for all four sides, or you can set them individually for each side (see the sidebar "Setting Borders on a Side").

```
                         code

<html>
<head>
    <style type="text/css">
p {
        width: 230px;
        border: 20px double #990000;
padding:5px; }
.frame {
        width: 230px;
        border-top: 1mm dotted #990000;
        border-bottom: 3px dashed #990000;
        border-left: 3pt solid #990000;
        border-right: 2pc inset #990000; }
</style>
</head>
<body>
    <div class="frame"><img width="200"
    → height="264" src="alice15.gif"></div>
    <p>This time Alice waited patiently until
    → it chose to speak again...</p>
</body>
</html>
```

Table 7.4

border Values

VALUE	COMPATIBILITY
<border-width>	IE4, N4, CSS1
<border-style>	IE4, N4, CSS1
<border-color>	IE4, N4, CSS1

Figure 7.4 The border around the image has been set to have a different decoration on each side, while the text below it always has a double rule.

✔ Tips

- Most browsers that do not support other border properties usually support this one.

- Netscape 4 has a bug that forces any element with the border being set to act as a block-level tag (see "Kinds of HTML Tags" in Chapter 1).

Setting Borders on a Side

Each border side can also have all its values set independently, as follows:

```
border-top: 1mm dotted #990000;
border-bottom: 3px dashed #990000;
border-left: 3pt solid #990000;
border-right: 2pc inset #990000;
```

This method is especially useful for overriding the border values set by the single `border` property.

Unfortunately, Netscape 4 does not support these properties. Instead, you need to set the properties for each decorative property separately (see the next section, "Decorating an Element's Border").

Decorating an Element's Border

Although you can use the border attribute to set all the border attributes (style, color, and width) at the same time (see the previous section, "Setting an Element's Border"), you can also set each border attribute individually for the box (**Code 7.4** and **Figure 7.5**), and even on each side (**Figure 7.6**).

Code 7.4 You can set the border-decoration attributes (style, color, and width) for all four sides at the same time, or you can define each side independently (see the sidebar "Setting Borders on a Side" on the previous page).

```
code
<html>
<head>
   <style type="text/css">
   .frame {
       border-style: inset;
       border-color:  #ff0000;
       border-width:10px; }
       p.frame {
       border-style: inset;
       border-color:  red;
       border-top-width: 1px;
       border-bottom-width: 2px;
       border-left-width: 4px;
       border-right-width: 8px;
       padding: 5px; }
</style>
</head>
<body>
   <div class="frame">
       <img src="alice06.gif" width="200" height="245">
   </div>
       <p class="frame">Alice was not a bit hurt, and she jumped up on to her feet in a moment...</p>
</body>
</html>
```

Figure 7.5 The attributes for the borders have been mixed and matched.

Figure 7.6 It's hard to see in a two-color book, but trust me—this border is a beautiful, vibrant multicolored extravaganza.

To decorate a border:

1. `border-style: inset;`

   Add a border style with a value from **Table 7.5**. Or type none; which prevents the border from appearing.

2. `border-color: #ff0000;`

   Add a border color with a color value, which is the color you want the border to be (**Table 7.6**). This value can be the name of the color, a hex color value, or an RGB value (see "Values and Units Used in This Book" in the introduction).

continues on next page

Table 7.5

border-style values

VALUE	APPEARANCE	COMPATIBILITY
none		IE4, N4, CSS1
dotted	··················	IE4*, N6, CSS1
dashed	– – – – – – –	IE4*, N6, CSS1
solid	———	IE4, N4, CSS1
double	═══	IE4, N4, CSS1
groove	━━━	IE4, N4, CSS1
ridge	━━━	IE4, N4, CSS1
inset	━━━	IE4, N4, CSS1
outset	▄▄▄	IE4, N4, CSS1

IE 5.5 for Windows

Table 7.6

border-color Values

VALUE	COMPATIBILITY
<color>	IE4, N4, CSS1

DECORATING AN ELEMENT'S BORDER

3. `border-width:10px;`

Add a border width and one the following values (**Table 7.7**):

▲ A **length value**. A length of `0` prevents the border from appearing.

▲ A **keyword**. Use `thin`, `medium`, or `thick`.

✔ Tips

■ You do not have to include all the individual border attributes, but if you don't, their defaults will be used (see Appendix B).

■ Netscape 4 has a bug that forces any element with the border being set to act as a block-level tag (see "Kinds of HTML Tags" in Chapter 1).

Table 7.7

border-width Values	
VALUE	**COMPATIBILITY**
thin	IE4, N4, CSS1
medium	IE4, N4, CSS1
thick	IE4, N4, CSS1
<length>	IE4, N4, CSS1

Decorating Borders on a Side

You do not have to settle for the same border on all four sides. CSS gives you the freedom to define the border's appearance on a side-by-side basis, as follows:

```
border-style: ridge double dotted dashed;
border-width: 20px 15px 10px 5px;
border-color: red green blue purple;
```

To set each side's border properties separately, you can type from one to four values (refer to Figure 7.6).

◆ One value sets the border width for all four sides.

◆ Two values set the border width for the top/bottom and left/right sides.

◆ Three values set the top border width, the border width for the left and right sides (the same), and the bottom border width.

◆ Four values set the border width for each side individually: top, right, bottom, and left.

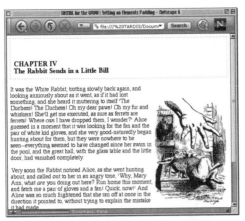

Figure 7.7 The padding moves the element to the bottom-left corner of the box. Note: The element's borders have been turned on so that you can better see the effects of padding.

Setting an Element's Padding

At first glance, padding seems to have an effect identical to margins: It adds space around the element's content. The difference is that padding sets the space between the border of the element and its content, rather than between the element and the other elements in the window (**Code 7.5** and **Figure 7.7**).

Code 7.5 You can use one, two, three, or four values with the padding attribute, depending on which sides you want to set.

```
<html>
<head>
<style type="text/css">
.chpttitle {
padding: 10% 1cm 10px .5em;
border: dashed silver 1px; }
img { padding-top: 25px }

</style>
</head>
<body>
<h3  class="chpttitle">CHAPTER IV<br>
    The Rabbit Sends in a Little Bill</h3>
<p>
<img src="alice12.gif" width="200" height="287" border="0" align="right">It was the White
→ Rabbit...</p>
        <p>Very soon the Rabbit noticed Alice...</p>
        <p>'He took me for his housemaid,'...</p>
</body>
</html>
```

To define padding:

1. `padding:`

Start your definition by typing the `padding` property, followed by a colon (:).

2. `10% 1cm 10px .5em;`

Next, type a value for the element's padding, which can be either of the following (**Table 7.8**):

▲ A **length value**

▲ A **percentage**, which creates padding proportional to the parent element's width

You can type a single value to be set on all sides, type two values for the top/bottom and left/right padding, or type four values to set the top, right, bottom, and left sides.

✔ Tips

■ Padding and margins are easily confused, often because their results look the same if the border is not visible. Remember: Margins separate one element from other elements, but padding is the space between the border and the content of the element.

■ Just as you can set an element's margins on a side (see "Setting Margins on a Side" earlier in this chapter), you can set the padding on a side.

Table 7.8

padding Values	
VALUE	COMPATIBILITY
<length>	IE4, N4, CSS1
<percentage>	IE4, N4, CSS1

Code 7.6 You can use CSS to set table tags, which gives you greater flexibility in table layout.

```
code
<html>
<head>
    <style type="text/css">
    table {
    border: 2px solid red;
    font: 75px  "arial black";
    }
td {
    width: 150px;
    border: 8px inset red;
    align: center;
    text-align: center;
    }
td.lightBG {
    background-color: #cccccc;
    }
td.darkBG {
    background-color: #666666;
    }
</style>
</head>
<body>
<table>
<tr>
<td  class="darkBG">X</td>
<td  class="lightBG">0</td>
    <td class="darkBG">X</td>
</tr>
<tr>
<td  class="lightBG">X</td>
    <td class="darkBG">X</td>
    <td class="lightBG">0</td>
    </tr>
    <tr>
    <td class="darkBG">0</td>
    <td class="lightBG">0</td>
    <td class="darkBG"><br></td>
    </tr>
    </table>
</body>
</html>
```

Setting a Table's Borders and Margins

Tables have become a staple of Web design. They are used to control the layout of almost every Web site you will see, despite the fact that they were never intended to do anything more than display tabular data.

But without tables, the Web might never have taken off as the multimedia medium of choice for millions of users around the world. So it might be surprising to hear that there was a lot of grumbling when Netscape introduced tables with Navigator 1, because they were not part of the World Wide Web Consortium's HTML standards.

Since that time, tables have become the standard for anyone who wants more than a lump of text and graphics on a Web page.

Tables can benefit from CSS; you can set common attributes and change them in one common place without having to go to every <table>, <tr>, or <td> tag and change them individually.

CSS can do many things to make a table layout easier. **Code 7.6** shows how CSS border attributes can be applied to a table (**Figure 7.8**). Although you can use CSS to define tables, all the browser-specific limitations of tables still apply.

continues on next page

✔ Tip

- Netscape 4 does not allow you to use CSS to set the width, height, or border attributes of a table. You can apply backgrounds and other CSS attributes to the content within, however, by defining the `<table>`, `<tr>`, or `<td>` tags.

Figure 7.8 Tic-tac-toe, anyone? The table's appearance is being controlled with easy-to change CSS rather than cumbersome tag attributes.

Wrapping Text Around an Element

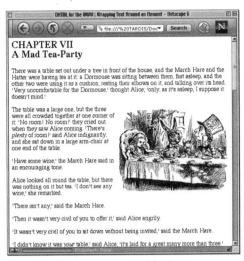

Figure 7.9 The text wraps around the image.

Early in the development of HTML, when the capability to have text flow around a graphic was added, designers everywhere were delighted. Finally, text could wrap around images. CSS takes this technique one step forward by letting you not only flow text around graphics, but also flow text around other blocks of text and text around tables (**Figure 7.9**). You accomplish this feat by using the float property (**Code 7.7**).

Code 7.7 The float property allows you to have either a block of text or a graphic float inside of another block of text. In this example, all images on the page are being defined as floating to the right in the window.

```
<html>
<head>
    <style type="text/css">
img { float: right; }
</style>
</head>
<body>
    <h2>CHAPTER VII<br>
    A Mad Tea-Party</h2>
    <p class="copy">There was a table set out...</p>
<img src="alice25.gif" width="288" height="219" border="0">
        <p>The table was a large one...</p>
        <p>'Have some wine,' the March Hare said in an encouraging tone.</p>
        <p>Alice looked all round the table...</p>
        <p>'There isn't any,' said the March Hare.</p>
        <p>'Then it wasn't very civil of you to offer it,' said Alice angrily.</p>
        <p>'It wasn't very civil of you to sit down without being invited,' said the March
        Hare.</p>
</body>
</html>
```

To define the floating position of a selector:

1. float:

   Start your definition by typing the float property, followed by a colon (:) (**Table 7.9**).

2. right

   Next, type a keyword to tell the browser the side of the screen to which the element should float. Choose one of the following:

   ▲ right aligns this element to the right, causing other elements to wrap on the left.

   ▲ left aligns this element to the left, causing other elements to wrap on the right.

   ▲ none defaults to the parent element's alignment.

✔ Tips

■ In this example, I applied float to an image, which has the same effect as setting the align property in the <img> tag.

■ You can use float with any tag, not just images, to cause text to float around it, so you can have text floating inside other text.

Table 7.9

float Values	
VALUE	COMPATIBILITY
left	IE4, N4, CSS1
right	IE4, N4, CSS1
none	IE4, N4, CSS1

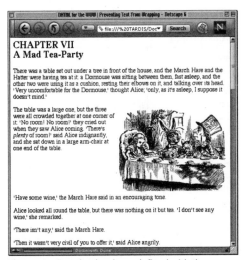

Figure 7.10 Text that has been defined with the nowrap class starts below the image rather than wrapping around it.

Preventing Text from Wrapping

Sometimes, you may find it necessary to override the float property (**Figure 7.10**). Similar to the clear attribute of the HTML break tag, the CSS clear property allows you to specify whether you want to deny floating text to the left, right, or both sides of the element.

To stop text from floating:

1. clear:

Type the clear property, followed by a colon (:), in the CSS rule to start your definition (**Code 7.8**).

continues on next page

Code 7.8 Text given the nowrap class will start after any images.

```
<html>
<head>
    <style type="text/css">
img { float: right; }
.nowrap { clear: right; }
</style>
</head>
<body>
    <h2>CHAPTER VII<br>
    A Mad Tea-Party</h2>
    <p>There was a table set out...</p>
<img src="alice25.gif" width="288" height="219" border="0">
        <p>The table was a large one...</p>
        <p class="nowrap">'Have some wine,' the March Hare said in an encouraging tone.</p>
        <p class="nowrap">Alice looked all round the table...</p>
        <p class="nowrap">'There isn't any,' said the March Hare.</p>
        <p class="nowrap">'Then it wasn't very civil of you to offer it,' said Alice angrily.</p>
        <p>'It wasn't very civil of you to sit down without being invited,' said the March
        → Hare.</p>
</body>
</html>
```

2. left

Choose the side or sides where you want to prevent floating. Type left, right, or both (**Table 7.10**).

Alternatively, you can type none, which overrides other clear properties.

3. <p class="nowrap">...</p>

Now whenever you use this class with an HTML tag, the text will not wrap around other tags, regardless of how their float property is set.

✔ Tip

- It's usually a good idea to set headers and titles so that they don't wrap around other objects.

Table 7.10

clear Values	
VALUE	COMPATIBILITY
left	IE4, N4, CSS1
right	IE4, N4, CSS1
both	IE4, N4, CSS1
none	IE4, N4, CSS1

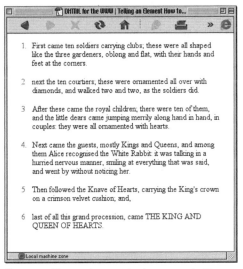

Figure 7.11 The royal procession is enumerated to make it easier to follow.

Telling an Element How to Display (or Not)

You can use the `display` property to define whether an element includes line breaks above and below, is included inline with other elements, is treated as part of a list (**Code 7.9** and **Figure 7.11**), or is displayed at all.

To set the display mode for a selector:

1. `display:`

Start your definition by typing the `display` property, followed by a colon (`:`), in the CSS definition list.

continues on next page

Code 7.9 You can use the `display` property for a variety of purposes. Here, it is used to turn paragraphs into a numbered list of members of the courtly procession.

```
<html>
<head>
    <style type="text/css">
    .list { display: list-item; }
    img {display: none ; }
</style>
        </head>
    <body>
    <img src="alice29.gif" width="200" height="236" border="0" align="right">
    <ol>
        <p class="list">First came ten soldiers carrying clubs...</p>
        <p class="list">next the ten courtiers...</p>
        <p class="list">After these came the royal children...</p>
        <p class="list">Next came the guests...</p>
        <p class="list">Then followed the Knave of Hearts...</p>
        <p class="list">last of all this grand procession, came THE KING AND QUEEN OF HEARTS.</p>
    </ol>
</body>
</html>
```

TELLING AN ELEMENT HOW TO DISPLAY (OR NOT)

2. `list-item`

Type a keyword that defines how this element will display. Choose one of the following options (**Table 7.11**):

▲ `list-item` places a list-item marker on the first line of text, as well as a break above and below. This code allows the item to be used as part of a list.

▲ `block` defines this tag as being a block-level tag and places a line break above and below the element.

▲ `inline` defines this tag as being an inline tag and suppresses line breaks.

▲ `none` causes this element not to display in CSS browsers. It will be as though the content did not exist on the page.

3. `<ol><p class="list">...</p>`

Add the class to a tag. In this example, the `list` class has been added to a `<p>` tag nested in an ordered-list (`<ol>`) tag, turning each paragraph into a line in a numbered list.

✔ Tips

■ Any elements given the value `none` will simply be ignored by a CSS browser. Be careful in using `none`, however. Although it is not an inherited attribute, `none` turns off display of the element as well as any children elements within it.

■ The `display` property should not be confused with `visibility` (see "Setting the Visibility of an Element" in Chapter 9). Unlike the `visibility` property, which leaves a space for the element, `display: none;` completely removes the element from the page although it still loads.

■ Using JavaScript, you can create a simple collapsible menu by changing `display` between `"inline"` to make menu options appear, and `display` `"none"` to make menu options disappear (see "Creating a Clamshell Menu" in Chapter 24).

Table 7.11

display Values	
VALUE	**COMPATIBILITY**
list-item	IE5*, N4, CSS1
block	IE4, N4, CSS1
inline	IE5, N4, CSS1
none	IE4, N4, CSS1
*Mac only	

Pre-loading Images

If you are loading many large graphics in your Web site, you can use the `display` property to preload images on one page for use in another.

For example, if the first page in your site has only a few graphics, but the next page has many, include the `<img>` tags for the graphics on the second page on page 1 but set their `display` to `none`. The graphics will load in the first page but not show up. When the second page loads, the graphics will load from the visitor's cache, which is much faster.

I recommend loading only a few extra graphics on the first page; otherwise, the second page will end up displaying partially loaded images. Use the graphics that will be seen on the page first, and it will look as if your site is loading really fast even with a lot of graphic content.

POSITIONING CONTROLS

A lot of people complain that the Web is too slow; the joke is that *WWW* stands for *World Wide Wait*. Part of the problem is that to construct an attractive Web page, designers often use graphics simply to create text that shows up where the designer wants it.

Another design issue that affects the efficiency of page display is the use of tables to position elements in the browser window or to assemble graphics in jigsaw fashion. Tables take more time to render than content that does not use tables for formatting. The more tables you use, the slower your page displays.

Positioning elements with CSS is more accurate than either graphics or tables, and the results are displayed much faster.

You have already learned how CSS gives you control of composition in terms of creating margins and borders (Chapter 7). Beyond that, CSS allows you to position elements in the window either exactly where you want them (*absolutely*) or in relation to other elements in the window (*relatively*).

This chapter introduces you to the methods of positioning HTML elements by using CSS. In addition, you'll learn how to stack elements on top of one another in 3-D.

Understanding the Window

The browser window is where all the action takes place for Web pages. Within its rectangular confines, everything that you can present to the viewer on the other end is displayed. You can open multiple windows, resize and position windows on the screen, and even break the window into smaller windows called *frames*. Everything that you present, however, is displayed within a browser window (**Figure 8.1**).

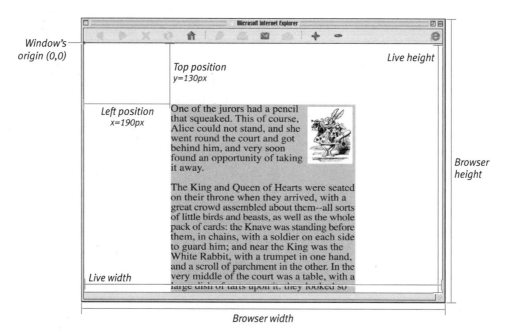

Figure 8.1 The browser window. The element on the gray background has been moved from its normal position to 130 pixels from the top and 190 pixels from the left.

In "Learning About Your Environment" in Chapter 12, I will go into greater detail about the components that make up a window and the screen surrounding it, as well as how to find those values. To understand positioning, however, you need to remember a few important things about the browser window:

- ◆ Like the elements contained within it (see "Understanding the Element's Box" in Chapter 7), the window has a width and height, as well as a top, bottom, left, and right. In fact, you can think of the browser window as being the ultimate element in your Web design—the parent of all other elements. You can define the window with CSS through the <body> tag.

- ◆ Browser windows have two distinct widths and heights. The first is the *browser window* width and height, which is the entire window including any browser controls. The second is the *live browser window* width and height, which includes only the display area of the browser. The live dimensions, obviously, are always less than the full window dimensions. Generally, when I refer to "the window," I'm referring to the live window area.

- ◆ All absolutely positioned elements in the window are positioned either directly (if not nested in another element) or indirectly (if nested in another element) relative to the *origin* of the live window area, which is the top-left corner of the display area in browser windows.

- ◆ The origin of an individual frame in a window is the top-left corner of that particular frame.

- ◆ All relatively positioned elements in the window are positioned relative to the top-left corner of the area where they would have appeared if they had been left alone (also referred to as their normal place in the flow).

Setting the Positioning Type

When you set the attributes of an HTML tag through a selector in a CSS, you, in effect, single out any content within that tag's container as being a unique element in the window (see "Understanding the Element's Box" in Chapter 7). You can then manipulate this unique element through CSS positioning.

An element can have one of four position values—static, relative, absolute, or fixed—although only the first three are commonly available on most browsers (**Code 8.1**). The position type tells the browser how to treat the element when placing it in the window (**Figure 8.2**).

Code 8.1 Currently, there are three cross-browser methods for positioning an element in the window: static, relative, and absolute. In addition, some browsers allow you to set a fixed position.

```
<html>
<head>
    <style type="text/css">
.stat {position: static; font: bold 28pt
→ courier; color: #cccccc;}
.abs {position: absolute; top: 25px;
→ left: 375px; width: 100px; font: bold 35pt
→ helvetica; color: #666666;}
.rel {position: relative; top: 70px;
→ left: 25px; font: bold 12pt times;
→ color: #000000;}
    </style>
</head>
<body>
    <div class="stat">'Oh my ears and
    → whiskers, how late it's getting!'</div>
    <div class="abs">'Oh my ears and
    → whiskers, how late it's getting!'</div>
    <div class="rel"> 'Oh my ears and
    → <span class="rel">whis<span class=
    → "rel">kers</span></span>, how late it's
    → getting!'</div>
</body>
</html>
```

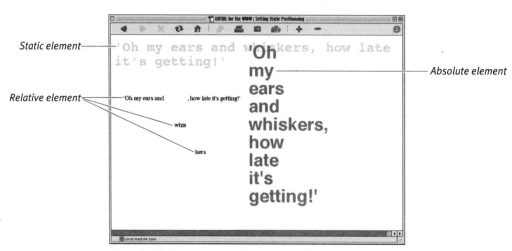

Figure 8.2 Elements being positioned in the window. Notice that the relatively positioned element has relatively positioned elements nested within it, causing the stair-step effect in the text.

Using static positioning

By default, elements are positioned as static in the window unless you define them as being positioned absolutely, relatively, or fixed. Static elements, like the relatively positioned elements explained in the following section, flow into a document one after the next. Static positioning differs, however, in that a static element cannot be explicitly positioned or repositioned.

Using relative positioning

An element that is defined as being relatively positioned will flow into place within the window or within its parent element, just like the default behavior of any other HTML element—that is, it appears after everything that's before it in the HTML and before everything that's after it in the HTML.

You can move a relatively positioned element from its natural position in the window by using the top and left properties. This technique is useful for controlling the way elements appear in relation to other elements in the window.

Using absolute positioning

Absolute positioning creates an independent element—a free agent—separate from the rest of the document, into which you can put any type of HTML content you want. Elements that are defined in this way are placed at an exact point in the window by means of x and y coordinates. The top-left corner of the window or its enclosing element is the origin (that is, coordinates 0,0). Moving an element to a position farther to the right creates a positive x value; moving it farther down creates a positive y value.

SETTING THE POSITIONING TYPE

Using fixed positioning

Before you get too excited, you should know that fixed positioning currently does not work in most browsers. It does not work in Netscape 4 or 6; it does not work in Internet Explorer 4 or 5 for Windows. It does work in Internet Explorer 5 for the Mac, but it's buggy.

Fixing an element's position in the window works almost exactly like absolute positioning: The element is set independently of all other content on the page in a specific position. The big difference is that when the page scrolls in the window, fixed elements stay in their initial positions and do not scroll.

To set an element's position type:

1. `position:`

   Type the `position` attribute in a rule's definition list or in the `style` attribute of an HTML tag.

2. `relative;`

   Type the position-type value, which can be one of the following (**Table 8.1**):

   ▲ `static` flows the content inline, but the position cannot be changed by the `top` and `left` attributes or JavaScript.

   ▲ `relative` places the element inline and allows the position relative to its normal position to be set through the `top` and `left` attributes of JavaScript.

   ▲ `absolute` places the element independently of any other content in its parent. If the element is not nested inside another element, its position will be relative to the body of the document.

   ▲ `fixed` places the element independently of any other content in its parent, the same as an absolutely positioned element. Unlike an absolutely positioned element, when the window is scrolled, the element stays where it is as the rest of the content scrolls. (Remember that `fixed` does not currently work in most browsers.)

Table 8.1

position Values

VALUE	COMPATIBILITY
static	IE4, N4, CSS2
relative	IE4, N4, CSS2
absolute	IE4, N4, CSS2
fixed	IE5*, CSS2

* Not available in Windows

3. `top: 70px;`

Now that the position type has been set, you can set the actual position of the element (see "Setting the Position From the Top and Left" and "Setting the Position from the Bottom and Right" later in this chapter).

In addition, setting the position allows you to set the element's *stacking order* (see "Stacking Objects" later in this chapter), *visibility* (see "Setting the Visibility of an Element" in Chapter 9), and *clipping* (see "Setting the Visible Area of an Element" in Chapter 9).

✔ Tips

- Internet Explorer does not accept position controls in the `<body>` tag. If you need to position the entire body of a Web page, surround all the content with a `<div>` tag and apply positioning to that (see "Nesting a Relative Element in an Absolute Element" later in this chapter).

- After elements have been positioned in the window, you can use JavaScript or other scripting languages to move, hide, or display them (see Part 2 of this book, which discusses DHTML).

- The **fixed** position does not work in Netscape Mac/Windows or in Internet Explorer for Windows. To make matters worse, Internet Explorer 5 for the Mac has a severe bug that makes it useless for creating fixed menus in the window (see the sidebar "Is It Fixed?" at left).

- Browsers that do not understand the **fixed** position type default to `static` for the position type.

- If you are familiar with Netscape's layers (see Chapter 16, "Netscape Layers"), positioning should be familiar. For cross-browser DHTML, however, CSS is used to create layers rather than the `<layer>` tag (see "Creating an Object" in Chapter 11).

Is It Fixed?

The fixed position was introduced with CSS Level 2. It shows a lot of promise for user-interface design, especially in allowing for a fixed menu in the window that's always available to the visitor. Right now, however, it suffers from several problems:

- ◆ fixed is not supported by Netscape and Internet Explorer for Windows. Although you cannot set two different position types for the same element, you can create two different style sheets for each browser (see "Setting the CSS for the OS" in Chapter 22).

- ◆ Although Internet Explorer 5 for the Mac supports fixed, a strange bug causes the link areas of a fixed element to scroll with the rest of the page. So while the graphic or text for a link stays in a fixed position, the invisible area that gets clicked moves.

Setting the Position from the Top and Left

In addition to the margins, which can be specified as part of the box properties (see "Setting an Element's Margins" in Chapter 7), a positioned element can have a **top** value and a **left** value (**Code 8.2**). These values are used to set the element's position from the top and left edges of its parent element or relative to its natural position (**Figures 8.3**, **8.4** and **8.5**).

To define the left and top margins:

1. position: absolute;

To position an element by using the **left** and/or **top** properties, you have to include the **position** property in the same rule.

2. left:

Type the **left** property, followed by a colon (:), in the CSS definition list or in the **style** attribute of an HTML tag.

3. 9em;

Now type a value for how far to the left the element should appear. You can enter any of the following (**Table 8.2**):

▲ A **length value** to define the distance of the element's left edge from the left edge of the window or its parent.

▲ A **percentage value,** such as 55%. The left displacement is relative to the parent element's width.

▲ auto, which allows the browser to calculate the value if the position is set to absolute; otherwise, **left** will be 0.

4. top:

Type the **top** property in the CSS definition list or in the **style** attribute of a tag.

Code 8.2 After you set the position type, you can set the element's top and left distance from its origin. The origin for the element is the window's top-left corner, its parent's top-left corner, or relative to its own top-left corner.

```
<html>
<head>
    <style type="text/css">
#object1 {
        position: absolute;
        top: 125px;
        left: 12em;
        border: silver solid 2px; }
.changeplace {
        position: relative;
        top: 1cm;
        left: 1cm;
        background-color: #ffcccc;}
    </style>
</head>
<body>
    <div id="object1">
        <img src="alice27.gif" width="250"
→ height="225" border="0"
→ align="left">
        <p>'I want a<span class="changeplace">
→ clean cup</span>,' interrupted the
→ Hatter: 'let's all move one place
→ on.'</p>
        <p>He moved on as he spoke, and the
→ Dormouse followed him...</p>
        <p>Alice did not wish to offend the
→ Dormouse again...</p>
        <p>'You can draw water out of a
→ water-well...</p>
    </div>
</body>
</html>
```

Table 8.2

top and left Values	
VALUE	COMPATIBILITY
<length>	IE4, N4, CSS2
<percentage>	IE4, N4, CSS2
auto	IE4, N4, CSS2

Figure 8.3 The element has been absolutely positioned from the top-left corner of the window and the words *clean cup* have been offset from the top and left of their normal positions.

5. 75px;

Type a value for how far from the top the element should appear. You can enter any of the following (**Table 8.2**):

▲ A **length value** to define the distance of the element's top edge from the top edge of the window or its parent.

▲ A **percentage value,** such as 55%. The top displacement will be relative to the window or parent element's width.

▲ auto, which allows the browser to calculate the value if the position is set to absolute; otherwise, top will be 0.

continues on next page

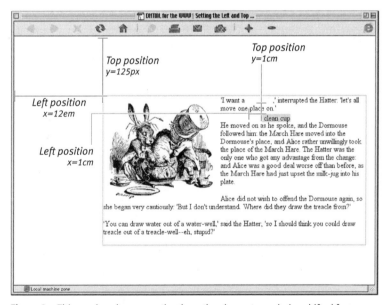

Figure 8.4 This version shows exactly where the elements are being shifted from.

✔ Tips

- You do not have to include both the **top** and **left** definitions.

- You can use negative values to move the content up and to the right instead of down and to the left.

- If an element's position is defined as relative, its margins remain unaffected by the **top** and **left** properties. This means that setting the top and left margins may cause the content to move outside its naturally defined box and overlap other content.

- Although **top** and **left** are not inherited by an element's children, nested elements will be offset along with their parent.

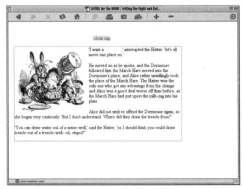

Figure 8.5 The element has been absolutely positioned from the bottom-right corner of the window, and the words *clean cup* have been offset from the bottom and right of their normal positions.

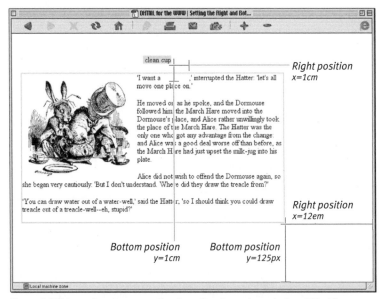

Figure 8.6 This version shows exactly where the elements are being shifted from.

Code 8.3 After you set the position type, you can set the element's right and bottom distance. The positions shift to the right and bottom edges of the element, however, so the origin will be the bottom-right corner instead of the top-left corner. This origin will be the window's bottom-right corner, its parent's bottom-right corner, or the element's own bottom-right corner.

```
code
<html>
<head>
    <style type="text/css">
#object1 {
        position: absolute;
        bottom: 125px;
        right: 12em;
        border: silver solid 2px; }
.changeplace {
        position: relative;
        bottom: 1cm;
        right: 1cm;
        background-color: #ffcccc;}
    </style>
</head>
<body>
    <div id="object1">
        <img src="alice27.gif" width="250"
        → height="225" border="0"
        → align="left">
        <p>'I want a<span class="changeplace">
        → clean cup</span>,' interrupted the
        → Hatter: 'let's all move one place
        → on.'</p>
        <p>He moved on as he spoke...</p>
        <p>Alice did not wish to offend the
        → Dormouse again...</p>
        <p>'You can draw water out of a
        → water-well...</p>
    </div>
</body>
</html>
```

Setting the Position from the Bottom and Right

Although you can accomplish a lot by positioning an element's top and left sides, it can be useful to position the bottom and right sides as well (**Code 8.3**).

CSS Level 2 introduced the capability to set an element's position relative to the right and bottom edges of the element or its surrounding parent (Figure 8.5 and **Figure 8.6**). Currently, these two attributes work only in Netscape 6 and Internet Explorer 5.

To define the right and bottom margins:

1. position: absolute;

   To position an element by using the left and/or top properties, you have to include the position property in the same rule.

2. right:

   Type the right property name, followed by a colon (:).

3. 12em;

   Type a value to indicate how far to the right the right edge of the element should appear. You can enter any of the following (**Table 8.3**):

   ▲ A **length value**, to define the distance of the element's right edge to the right edge of the window or its parent.

   ▲ A **percentage value,** such as 55%. The right displacement will be relative to the parent element's width.

   ▲ auto, which allows the browser to calculate the value if the position is set to absolute; otherwise, right will be 0.

4. bottom:

   Type the bottom property name, followed by a colon (:).

continues on next page

SETTING THE POSITION FROM THE BOTTOM AND RIGHT

149

5. 125px;

Type in a value to specify how far from the bottom the bottom edge of the element should appear. You can enter any of the following (**Table 8.3**):

▲ A **length value** to define the distance of the element's bottom edge from the bottom edge of the window or its parent.

▲ A **percentage value,** such as 55%. The bottom displacement will be relative to the window or parent element's width.

▲ auto, which allows the browser to calculate the value if the position is set to absolute; otherwise, bottom will be 0.

✔ Tips

■ bottom and right do not work in Internet Explorer and Netscape 4.

■ You can combine left or right positioning with top or bottom.

■ What happens if you set the top/left *and* bottom/right positions for the same element? The answer depends on the browser, but Internet Explorer always defaults to the top and left positions.

■ What happens if the bottom position has been set, and the element is longer than the height of the page? Normally, the element would go off the bottom of the window, and you could access the rest of the content by using the scroll bar. If the bottom position of the element has been set, though, the element will be pushed up off the top of the window, and you cannot use the scroll bars to access it. So be careful when setting a bottom position for an element.

Table 8.3

bottom and right Values	
VALUE	COMPATIBILITY
<length>	IE5, N6, CSS2
<percentage>	IE5, N6, CSS2
auto	IE5, N6, CSS2

Code 8.4 Each element is positioned to be offset slightly from the preceding one. The z-index is also set to force element 1 to be on top and then to place elements 2, 3, and 4 underneath.

```
code
<html>
<head>
    <style type="text/css">
        #element1 {
            position: absolute;
            z-index: 3;
            top: 175px;
            left: 255px; }
        #element2 {
            position: absolute;
            z-index: 2;
            top: 100px;
            left: 170px; }
        #element3 {
            position: absolute;
            z-index: 1;
            top: 65px;
            left: 85px; }
        #element4 {
            position: absolute;
            z-index: 0;
            top: 5px;
            left: 5px; }
    </style>
</head>
<body>
    <span id="element1">
        <img src="alice22.gif" width="100"
        → height="147"><br clear="all">
        Element 1
    </span>
    <span id="element2">
        <img src="alice32.gif" width="140"
        → height="201"><br clear="all">
        Element 2
    </span>
    <span id="element3">
        <img src="alice15.gif" width="150"
        → height="198"><br clear="all">
        Element 3
    </span>
    <span id="element4">
        <img src="alice29.gif" width="200"
        → height="236"><br clear="all">
        Element 4
    </span>
</body>
</html>
```

Stacking Objects (3-D Positioning)

Despite the fact that the screen is a two-dimensional area, elements that are positioned can be given a third dimension: a stacking order in relationship to one another.

Positioned elements are assigned stacking numbers automatically, starting with 0 and continuing incrementally with 1, 2, 3, and so on in the order in which the elements appear in the HTML and relative to their parents and siblings. This system is called the *z-index*. An element's z-index number is a value that shows its 3-D relation to other elements in the window.

If the content of elements overlap each other, the element with a higher number in the stacking order appears over the element that has a lower number.

You can override the natural order of the elements (**Code 8.4**) on the page by setting the z-index property directly (**Figures 8.7** and **8.8**).

To define an element's z-index:

1. position: absolute;

   To layer an element in the window, you have to define the position property (see "Setting the Positioning Type" earlier in this chapter).

2. z-index:

   Type the z-index property name, followed by a colon (:), in the same definition list.

   continues on next page

3. 3;

Now type a positive or negative number (no decimals allowed), or 0. This step sets the element's z-index in relation to its siblings where 0 is on the same level (**Table 8.4**).

Alternatively, type auto to allow the browser to determine the element's z-index order.

4. top: 5px; left: 5px; 0;

Type the element's position.

✔ Tips

■ Using a negative number for the z-index causes an element to be stacked that many levels below its parent instead of above.

■ You can change the stacking order of elements by using JavaScript (see "Moving Objects in 3-D" in Chapter 13).

Figure 8.7 This version uses the z-indexes set in the code. Notice that despite the fact that element 1 should be on the bottom of the stack, its z-index has been set to 3, so it appears on top.

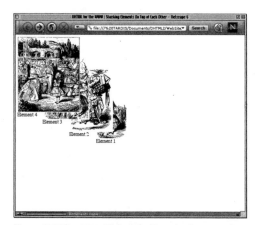

Figure 8.8 The same Web page if you had *not* set the z-index but kept the natural stacking order. Notice that element 1 is now underneath everything else, because its natural z-index is 0.

Table 8.4

z-index Values	
VALUE	COMPATIBILITY
<number>	IE4, N4, CSS2
auto	IE4, N4, CSS2

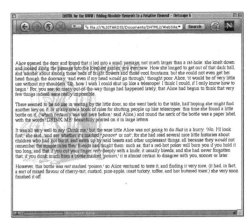

Figure 8.9 The background has been absolutely positioned but is nested in a relatively positioned element. So rather than appearing at the very top of the page, it gets pushed down 75 pixels, along with its parent (the relative element).

Nesting an Absolute Element in a Relative Element

You have seen how an element can be positioned in the window in an exact (absolute) spot. An absolutely positioned element can also be nested within another element that has relative positioning (**Code 8.5**). When you do this, the absolute element flows from an origin at the top-left corner of the relative element rather than the window (**Figure 8.9**).

Code 8.5 Two classes are created, one to be positioned relatively and the other absolutely. Then the absolute class is used in a <div> tag that is nested within a <div> tag that uses the relative class. This sets the absolute element to appear in the background of the relative element, and it will move around as the relative element's position is set. The z-index of the <p> tag is also being set to force text to appear above the absolutely positioned element.

```
                               code
<html>
<head>
    <style type="text/css">
        .relElement {
        position:relative;
            top: 75px;}
        .absElement {
            position: absolute;
            z-index: 0;
            top: 0px;
            left: 0px;
            font-size: 36pt;
            color:  #cccccc; }
        p {
            position: relative;
            z-index: 100}
    </style>
</head>
<body>
```

(code continues on next page)

To set up an absolutely positioned element within a relatively positioned element:

1. `.relElement{...}`

   Create a relatively positioned class.
   I've set up this one to be positioned **75px** from the top of the window.

2. `.absElement {...}`

   Next, create an absolutely positioned class. This one will let the element appear in the top-left corner of its parent and make its text large and gray.

3. `p {...}`

   In this example, content will float above the absolutely placed content, and it has to be relatively positioned with a high-enough z-index to appear above all other content.

4. `<div class="relElement">`
   → `<div class="absElement">...</div>`
   `</div>`

   Now, in the body of the document, surround the absolute elements with a tag by using the `relElement` class. The title is absolutely positioned, but in relation to its parent element and not the window.

✔ Tip

- The preceding technique for combining relatively and absolutely positioned elements can be especially useful if you need to position one or more elements absolutely in relation to one another but not in relation to the window or other elements in the window—for a drop shadow, for example (see "Creating a Simple Drop Shadow" in Chapter 26).

Code 8.5 *continued*

```
      <div class="relElement">
            <div class="absElement">
   Alice In Wonderland
   <br><img src="alice03.gif" width="300"
   → height="284" border="0">
            </div>
            <p>Alice opened the door and found that
            → it led into a small passage...</p>
            <p>There seemed to be no use in
            → waiting by the little door...</p>
            <p>It was all very well to say 'Drink
            → me,'...</p>
            <p>However, this bottle was <i>not</i>
            → marked 'poison,'...</p>
      </div>
   </body>
   </html>
```

Figure 8.10 The relative element is positioned absolutely in the window. This is a great way of creating complex layouts in which you need exact positioning.

Nesting a Relative Element in an Absolute Element

The power of CSS layout comes from its capability to position content precisely in the window. When an absolutely positioned element is nested in a relatively positioned element, the former uses its parent's top-left corner as its origin. Similarly, when a relatively placed element is placed inside an absolutely placed element (**Code 8.6**), it moves with the absolute element (**Figure 8.10**).

Code 8.6 Two classes are created, one defined as being absolutely positioned and the other defined as relatively positioned. The relative class is then used with a `<p>` tag and is nested within a `<div>` tag defined with the absolute class. This allows all the content for this page to be moved over to the right. Notice the string of `<br>` tags at the end of the code outside the absolute element. This string is used to overcome a bug in Internet Explorer that would prevent the scroll bars from appearing.

```
code
<html>
<head>
    <style type="text/css">
.absElement{
    position: absolute;
    left: 100px;
    border-style: none none none solid;
    border-width: 0px 0px 0px 1px;
    border-color: #000000;
    padding: 10px;}
.relElement {
    position: relative;
    float: right;
    font-weight: bold;
    padding: 1em;
    width: 275px; }
    </style>
        </head>
<body>
```

(code continues on next page)

To nest a relative element within an absolute element:

1. `.absElement{...}`

   Create an absolutely positioned class. In this example, I've set up a class that offsets itself 100 pixels to the left and places a thin solid border down the left side of the element.

2. `.relElement {...}`

   Create a relatively positioned class. In this example, the class will float to the right, text will be bold, padding is set to 1 em space, and the element will be 215 pixels wide.

3. `<div class="absElement">`

      `<p class="relElement">...</p>`

   `</div>`

   In the `<body>` of your document, set up a `<div>` tag defined with the absolute class; then place a tag with the relatively positioned class inside that.

✔ Tip

- One problem with having the majority of your content placed in an absolute element is that Internet Explorer will not register the height of the element when the page first loads. The result is that even if the content goes off the bottom of the page, no scroll bar appears. The user can still use the arrow keys to move the page up or down. Alternatively, if the user resizes the page, the scroll bar will appear. The only way to ensure that the scroll bar appears, however, is to place a series of `<br>` tags to force the page down below the fold.

Code 8.6 *continued*

```
<div class="absElement">

    <p class="relElement">
  → <img src="alice37.gif" width="100"
  → height="136" align="right">One of
  → the jurors had a pencil that
  → squeaked...</p>

    <p>The King and Queen of Hearts were
  → seated on their throne when they
  → arrived...</p>

</div>

<br><br><br><br><br><br><br><br><br><br><br>
→ <br><br><br><br><br><br><br><br><br><br>
→ <br><br><br><br><br><br><br><br><br><br>
→ <br><br><br><br><br><br><br><br><br><br>
→ <br><br><br><br><br><br><br>

</body>

</html>
```

VISIBILITY CONTROLS

Although the capability to show and hide elements or parts of elements is one of the cornerstones of dynamic HTML (DHTML), the capability to set the visibility of these elements is a feature of CSS.

Keep in mind, however, that until you learn to change the visibility of an element by using JavaScript (see Chapter 13), the visibility controls will not be of much use.

Setting the Visibility of an Element

The visibility property designates whether an element is visible when it is initially viewed in the window. If visibility is set to hidden, the element is invisible but still takes up space in the document, and a big empty rectangle appears where the element should be (**Figures 9.1** and **9.2**).

To set an element's visibility:

1. position: relative;

   Set the position property to relative or absolute (**Code 9.1**).

2. visibility:

   Type the visibility property name, followed by a colon (:), in the element's CSS definition (**Table 9.1**).

3. hidden

   Now type one of the following keywords to specify how you want this element's visibility to be treated:

   ▲ hidden, which causes the element to be invisible when initially rendered on the screen

   ▲ visible, which causes the element to be visible

   ▲ inherit, which causes the element to inherit the visibility of its parent element

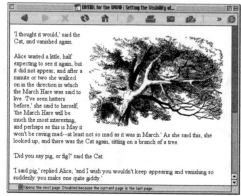

Figure 9.1 In this version, the image's visibility has been left alone, which means that it defaults to visible.

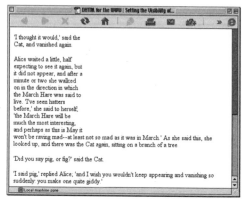

Figure 9.2 This version shows the result of the code. The visibility property has been set to hidden, so there is a blank space where the image should appear.

Code 9.1 The `visibility` property is defined for a class called `hide`, which hides an element in the HTML code.

```
code
<html>
<head>
    <style type="text/css">
        .hide {
            position: relative;
            visibility: hidden;}
    </style>
</head>
<body>
    <span class="hide">
        <img SRC="alice24.gif" WIDTH="350"
        → HEIGHT="238" ALIGN="right">
    </span>
<p>'I thought it would,' said the Cat, and
→ vanished again.</p>
    <p>Alice waited a little, half expecting
    → to see it again...</p>
</body>
</html>
```

Table 9.1

visibility Values

VALUE	COMPATIBILITY
hide	N4*
hidden	IE4, N4, CSS2
show	N4*
visible	IE4, N4, CSS2
inherit	IE4, N4, CSS2

Netscape 4 only; not available in Netscape 6

✔ Tips

■ Though the properties seemingly are similar, `visibility` differs radically from `display`. When `display` is set to `none`, the element is wiped out of the document, and no space is reserved for it.

■ Although CSS2 defines only three values for visibility, Netscape 4 adds two (redundant) values: `show` and `hide`. Netscape 4 can understand the CSS2 values; however, it translates those values into its own lingo, which can cause problems when you are trying to find the visibility state of an object with JavaScript (see "Finding an Object's Visibility State" in Chapter 12). To make matters worse, these values are not available in Netscape 6.

■ I recommend using an ID if you want to define the visibility of a single element on the screen that you might later want to use JavaScript to set to `visible`.

Setting the Visible Area of an Element (Clipping)

Unlike setting the width and the height of an element, which controls its dimensions (see Chapter 7), clipping an element designates how much of that element is visible in the window. The rest of the element's content will still be there, but it will be invisible to the viewer and treated as empty space by the browser (**Figure 9.3**).

To define the clip area of an element:

1. `position: absolute;`

Set the `position` property to relative or absolute (**Code 9.2**).

2. `clip:`

Type the `clip` property name, followed by a colon (`:`).

3. `rect(15 350 195 50)`

Type `rect` to define the shape of the clip as a rectangle, an opening parenthesis (`(`) and four values separated by spaces, and then a closing parenthesis (`)`). The numbers define the top, right, bottom, and left lengths of the clip area, respectively. All these values are distances from the element's origin (top-left corner), not necessarily from the indicated side (**Figure 9.4**).

Each value can be either a number, which is translated into a pixel value, or `auto`, which allows the browser to determine the clip size (usually, 100%).

See **Table 9.2** for the browser compatibility of the values.

Figure 9.3 The Cheshire Cat's face is all that appears from this image. The King, Queen, and Jack have all been clipped away.

Code 9.2 The clip region is defined in the `clipInHalf` class, which is then applied to an element in the HTML code.

```
<html>
<head>
    <style type="text/css">
.clipInHalf    {
        position: absolute;
        clip: rect(15 350 195 50);
        top: 0px;
        left: 0px; }
</style>
</head>
<body>
    <div class="clipInHalf">
        <img  SRC="alice31.gif" WIDTH="379"
        → HEIGHT="480" ALIGN="left">
    </div>
</body>
</html>
```

Table 9.2

clip Values	
VALUE	**COMPATIBILITY**
rect (<topLength>,<rightLength>, <bottomLength>,<leftLength>)	IE4, N4, CSS2
auto	IE4, N4, CSS2

✔ Tips

■ The element's borders and padding will be clipped along with the content of the element.

■ Netscape has difficulty trying to apply clipping directly to many tags, including the image tag. Therefore, it is best to use a <div> or <span> tag when you apply clipping.

■ Currently, clips can be only rectangular, but future versions of CSS promise to support other shapes.

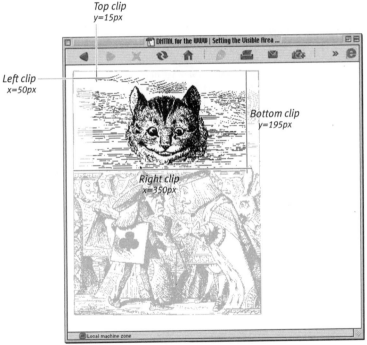

Figure 9.4 The clipping region is defined by four values that detail how far from the origin the top, right, bottom, and left edges of the element's visible area should appear.

SETTING THE VISIBLE AREA OF AN ELEMENT

Setting Where the Overflow Goes

When an element is clipped, or when the width and height are less than the area needed to display everything, some content is not displayed. The overflow property allows you to specify how this extra content is treated (**Figure 9.5**).

To define the overflow control:

1. width: 200px; height: 200px;

   Type a width and/or height to which the element should be restricted (**Code 9.3**). You could also clip the element (see "Setting the Visibility of an Element" earlier in this chapter) (**Table 9.3**).

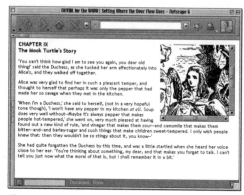

Figure 9.5 Viewers can use the scroll bars to access the overflowing content of the element.

Code 9.3 The class called illustration is set to a height and width of 200 pixels, the overflow (the content that will not fit in this area) is set to auto, and scroll bars will be placed around the element as needed to see the rest of its content. This class is then applied to an element in the HTML code.

```
code
<html>
<head>
    <style type="text/css">
        .illustration{
            width: 200px;
            height: 200px;
            overflow: auto;
            float: right;
            margin: 5px;}
</style>
    </head>
<body>
    <div class="illustration">
        <img  src="alice35.gif" width="401" height="480">
    </div>
        <h3>CHAPTER IX<br>The Mock Turtle's Story</h3>
    <p>'You can't think how glad...</p>
    <p>Alice was very glad to find her...</p>
    <p>'When <i>I'm</i> a Duchess,' she said to herself...</p>
    <p>She had quite forgotten the Duchess by this time...</p>
</body>
</html>
```

Table 9.3

overflow Values	
VALUE	COMPATIBILITY
scroll	IE4, N6, CSS2
hidden	IE4, N6, CSS2
visible	IE4, N6, CSS2
inherit	IE4, N6, CSS2

2. overflow:

Type the overflow property, followed by a colon (:).

3. auto;

Type in one of the following keywords (**Table 9.3**) to tell the browser how to treat overflow from the clip:

▲ scroll, which sets scroll bars around the visible area to allow the visitor to scroll through the element's content.

▲ hidden, which hides the overflow and prevents the scroll bar from appearing.

▲ visible, to cause even the clipped part of the element to show up. This keyword essentially tells the browser to ignore the clipping.

▲ auto, which allows the browser to decide how to treat extra material after clipping.

✔ Tips

■ If the overflow property is not set, most browsers will ignore the height property set for an element.

■ The overflow property is also used to define how clipping overflow is treated.

SETTING WHERE THE OVERFLOW GOES

PART 2

DYNAMIC HTML

Chapter 10:   Understanding DHTML   167

Chapter 11:   The Document Object Model   177

Chapter 12:   Learning About
              Your Environment   203

Chapter 13:   Dynamic Techniques: The Basics   233

Chapter 14:   Dynamic Techniques: Advanced   247

Chapter 15:   Dynamic Techniques: CSS   273

Chapter 16:   Netscape Layers   283

Chapter 17:   Internet Explorer for Windows   297

10

UNDERSTANDING DHTML

As powerful as cascading style sheets are, they aren't really dynamic per se. They give you control of how a document looks when it is first put on the screen, but what about after that?

Web pages created with CSS can have their properties changed on the fly (that is, dynamically) through a scripting language such JavaScript.

The bad news (you knew it couldn't be that easy!) is that Netscape and Internet Explorer have implemented their own dynamic capabilities, which result in cross-browser incompatibilities. The good news is that there is still a lot of overlap between the two, and this is where dynamic HTML, or DHTML, offers advantages.

In this chapter, I'll introduce what makes DHTML dynamic.

What Is Dynamic HTML?

I'll let you in on a little secret: There really isn't a DHTML. At least, not in the way that there is an HTML or a JavaScript. HTML and JavaScript are specific, easily identified technologies for the Web. *Dynamic HTML*, on the other hand, is a marketing term coined by both Netscape and Microsoft to describe a series of technologies introduced in their Version 4.0 Web browsers to enhance the dynamic capabilities of those browsers.

These technologies were created or added in an attempt to overcome what were considered to be the chief limitations of Web pages designed with common HTML. Although the Web was great for delivering pages of text and graphics, those who were used to multimedia were left wanting more.

Adding DHTML to your Web site means that your pages can act and react to the user without continually returning to the server for more data. In programming terms, placing all of the code in the Web page is called *client-side code*. For you, it means not having to learn to program to create interactive Web sites.

What DHTML *Should* Be

Although there is no official or even standard definition of dynamic HTML, a few things are undeniably part of the DHTML mission:

♦ DHTML should use HTML tags and scripting languages without requiring the use of plug-ins or any software other than the browser.

♦ Like HTML, DHTML should work (or at least have the potential to work) with all browsers and on all platforms.

♦ DHTML should enhance the interactivity and visual appeal of Web pages.

Figure 10.1 Netscape's take on DHTML.

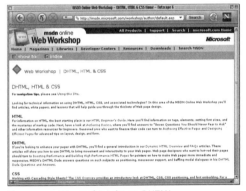

Figure 10.2 Microsoft's take on DHTML.

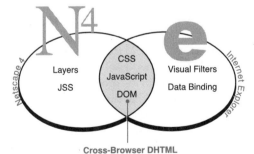

Figure 10.3 Where the two versions of dynamic HTML overlap is where you find cross-browser DHTML, including CSS, JavaScript, and the Document Object Model (DOM).

The Flavors of DHTML

Unfortunately, Microsoft (**Figure 10.1**) and Netscape (**Figure 10.2**) have differing ideas about what technologies should be used to make HTML more dynamic. Fortunately for us, the specifications of these two companies overlap (**Figure 10.3**), and this area of overlap is the primary topic of this book. Why? Because the Web was founded on a very simple premise: The display of Web documents should be indifferent to the software being used.

Evolution and progress mean that newer browsers have had to add technologies not supported by legacy (older) browsers. Still, there is an important tenet to be supported: All users should be able to access the Web, regardless of whose binary code they happen to be running.

Netscape-specific DHTML

Netscape brought several new technologies to the table, hoping to create more dynamic Web pages. Unfortunately, these technologies will never become standards, because CSS does most of the same things and is endorsed by the World Wide Web Consortium (W3C).

JavaScript style sheets (JSS) was introduced in Netscape 4 to offer an alternative to CSS. Like CSS, JSS allows you to define how HTML tags display their content, but JSS uses JavaScript syntax. The only browser that supports JSS, however, is Netscape 4. Not even the latest version of Netscape (version 6) supports this out-of-date technology. As a result, I do not recommend using JSS.

In addition, Netscape offered layers, which were a prototype for CSS positioning controls. Like CSS positioning controls, layers allow you to control the position and visibility of elements on the screen. Again, however, only Netscape 4 supports layers, and Netscape 6 abandoned this technology in favor of CSS positioning. I do not recommend using Netscape layers.

Microsoft-specific DHTML

Much of the Microsoft-specific DHTML is based on proprietary Microsoft software, such as ActiveX technology. Because ActiveX is owned by Microsoft, it is unlikely that it will ever be a cross-browser technology. I do not recommend using ActiveX technologies.

Visual filters let you perform visual effects on graphics and text in your document. If you have ever worked with Photoshop filters, you'll understand the similar ways of visual filters. The problem with these filters is that they are not standard on all browsers, and they are not even supported in all version of Internet Explorer. I do not recommend using visual filters.

Cross-browser DHTML

Where does this leave you? Fortunately, there is a lot more to DHTML than the technologies described in the preceding sections. The most popular browsers today include a slate of technologies that, for the most part, work the same way:

- ◆ **Cascading style sheets (CSS).** CSS allows you to define the properties of any element on the page. Older browsers (such as Netscape 4 and Internet Explorer 4) support CSS Level 1 and CSS-P; the current generation of browsers (such as Internet Explorer 5 and Netscape 6) support CSS Level 2.

- ◆ **JavaScript.** JavaScript allows you to create simple code to control the behavior of Web-page objects. Although Internet Explorer and Netscape do not always agree on the exact implementation of JavaScript, they are close enough that you can work around the inconsistencies.

- ◆ **Document Object Model (DOM).** All DHTML-capable browsers have some version of the DOM that you can use to access the properties of any element-turned-object in the browser window. The problem is that the W3C did not standardize DOM until recently. To be compatible across browsers, your DHTML has to be versatile enough to cope with the legacy DOMs of Netscape 4 and Internet Explorer 4.

Why Should I Use DHTML?

Because you purchased this book, you have already made some commitment to using DHTML. But in case you haven't bought the book and are just flipping through, looking at the cool examples, let me try to make a balanced case for why you should use DHTML in your Web designs—and warn you about some of the troubles you may face.

DHTML advantages

Obviously, DHTML is not without its advantages or no one would use it. It has taken a few years, however, for the power of DHTML to be realized. Here are some advantages to using DHTML:

- **Supported by most browsers.** DHTML is completely or partially supported in Netscape 4/6 and Internet Explorer 4/5, which are used by most of the Web-browsing public. In addition, browsers such as Opera and iCab support or plan to support DHTML.

- **Small file sizes.** Like HTML, DHTML is created with text files, which are smaller than graphic files and generally render faster than alternatives such as Flash and Java.

- **No plug-ins required.** If a browser supports HTML, CSS, JavaScript, and the DOM, it supports DHTML.

- **Easy to learn.** If you are already a Web designer, and you know HTML and JavaScript, you are halfway to knowing DHTML.

- **Fast development.** Many of the tricks that Web designers produced with graphics and JavaScript can be developed faster with DHTML.

continues on next page

◆ **Faster Web experience.** You can use DHTML to hide, show, and change content without having to load new pages. This capability speeds the performance of your site by requiring fewer calls to the server.

◆ **No Java programming required.** Although DHTML can do many of the same things as Java, you do not have to learn a programming language to use it.

DHTML disadvantages

It's not all smooth sailing with DHTML. To use DHTML, you need to understand its weaknesses as well as its strengths.

◆ **Browser and operating-system incompatibilities.** The implementation of CSS, JavaScript, and the DOM varies from browser to browser, and sometimes even between the same browsers on different operating systems. Although I've gone to great pains to present workaround solutions in this book, some browsers can do certain things that others simply cannot do (see "Cross-Browser Conundrums" in Chapter 28).

◆ **Picky, picky, picky.** JavaScript and CSS are notoriously finicky when it comes to syntax. Although HTML is very forgiving if you forget a close tag or nest tags that should not be nested, your entire page may go awry if you have one too many brackets in a JavaScript function or forget a semicolon in a CSS definition list.

◆ **Buggy browsers.** Many browsers have bugs that inexplicably prevent DHTML from working and then suddenly allow it to work. A prime example is Netscape's resize bug. If you resize a Netscape window while it is displaying a page that uses external CSS (see "Adding CSS to a Web Site" in Chapter 2), CSS will not be used when the page is redrawn *until* the page is reloaded (see "Netscape CSS Bug Fix" in Chapter 22). Some bugs have fixes or at least workarounds; others do not.

Flash vs. DHTML

Since their almost simultaneous release about four years ago, both Macromedia Flash and DHTML have seemed to be at odds, vying for Web designers' attention as a way to add interactivity to Web sites.

Although DHTML adds interactivity to Web pages by using HTML, CSS, and JavaScript, Flash is a file format that can be integrated into HTML pages but is a separate technology that is also delivered through Web browsers (see the sidebar "What Is Flash?").

The rest of this book deals with how, where, and why you should use DHTML, but it is also important to understand the strengths and weaknesses of DHTML's chief dynamic competition so that you can better decide which technology to use.

Flash advantages

Flash has scored points with developers for several reasons, not the least of which is its consistency.

◆ **Consistent.** A Flash file will run more or less the same on a Mac using Internet Explorer 5 as it does on a Windows machine running Netscape 4. Unlike HTML, JavaScript, and CSS, which are interpreted by the various companies that make Web browsers, a single company (Macromedia) develops Flash. Thus, there are no cross-browser or operating-system incompatibilities.

◆ **Ubiquitous.** According to Macromedia, 95% of the Web-browsing public has some version of the Flash plug-in installed. Although this figure may be a tad optimistic, there is a good chance that the audience for your Web site will be able to view Flash content that you include in your Web site.

continues on next page

What Is Flash?

Macromedia acquired the vector animation program FutureSplash Animator in 1997, added interactive and scripting capabilities, renamed the program Flash, and positioned it as a way to create dynamic graphic content for the Web. Up until then, graphics on the Web had been fairly lifeless; animated GIFs were the only substantial way to add motion to the browser window.

Flash changed all that by letting Web designers control the appearance and behavior of Web content.

It's important to remember that Flash is both a program (Flash, from Macromedia Inc.) and a file format (which has the extension .swf, pronounced *swif*). The file format is now an open standard. Adobe Systems Inc. has created its own program for creating Flash movies called LiveMotion.

FLASH VS. DHTML

◆ **Attractive.** Flash gives designers a wide range of creative tools to choose among. Also, Flash Web sites win most of the design awards these days.

◆ **Small.** If they are created right, Flash files deliver a lot of dynamic bang for the buck.

Flash disadvantages

Things look good for Flash, but there is another side to the story:

◆ **Difficult to learn and create.** HTML, CSS, and JavaScript can be created with a basic text editor. But to create Flash files, you must purchase and learn to use either Macromedia Flash or Adobe LiveMotion. Both of these programs have a steep learning curve.

◆ **Plug-in phobia.** Although the vast majority of users may have the Flash plug-in, they may not have the most current version; thus, they may not be able to run your cutting-edge Flash movie. To view your site, users have to download the latest version. You could make a similar argument about browsers, but Web surfers traditionally resist downloading plug-ins.

◆ **Usability abuses.** Flash allows greater versatility with the interface design than straight HTML. But with great power comes great responsibility. Designers are more likely to flaunt standard Web interface conventions in Flash designs and this can lead to confusion for the user.

◆ **Bloated downloads.** Although Flash movies can be very small, making them small takes skill and practice. Many enthusiastic designers forget that the people viewing their sites may have slow Internet connections, so downloading these large files can take a long time.

FLASH VS. DHTML

Which Should I Use?

I'm biased on this topic, but I appreciate the simplicity that DHTML offers Web designers. Which technology you select, however, depends on a variety of factors (**Figure 10.4**). Ask yourself the following questions when determining which technology better satisfies your user-interface needs:

◆ **What technology will your audience have?** Will they have DHTML-capable browsers? Will they have the current Flash plug-in installed? Do they have plug-in phobia? The first rule of design is "Know your audience."

continues on next page

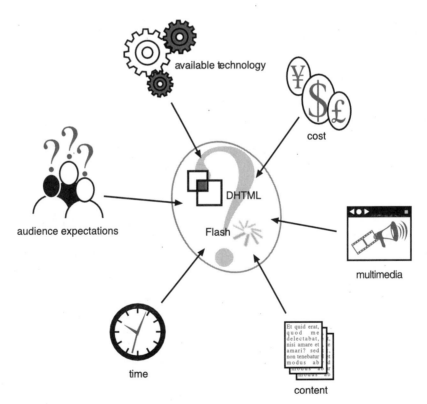

Figure 10.4 In deciding whether to use Flash or DHTML, consider these factors: available technology, cost, multimedia level, content, production and maintenance time, and audience expectations.

FLASH VS. DHTML

- **How much money do you have budgeted?** Unlike DHTML, which has no added costs over HTML, Flash requires that you purchase Flash-creation software (either Flash or LiveMotion). These programs can cost several hundred dollars, not to mention the cost of training.

- **Do you need to use sound, animation, or other media on your site?** Flash is much better than DHTML for creating and presenting multimedia content.

- **Are you presenting a lot of text?** HTML and DHTML are more versatile for presenting large amounts of text. Although Flash has made great strides in its print capability, it still can't hold a candle to HTML.

- **How much development and maintenance time do you have?** Generally, DHTML is faster to create, but this depends on which technology you know better.

- **What are your audience's expectations?** If they want fireworks, Flash is the way to go. If they expect a straightforward site or do not like plug-ins, DHTML is the better option.

The Usability Debate

Noted Web usability guru Jakob Nielsen takes a strong position against Flash. In his essay "Flash: 99% Bad" (`www.useit.com/alertbox/20001029.html`), Nielsen comments that Flash designs have a tendency to break with established Web design conventions, which can lead to confusion for the user.

In response to these allegations, Macromedia set up a Web site (`www.macromedia.com/go/usability`) to address the issues of usability and Flash.

THE
DOCUMENT
OBJECT MODEL

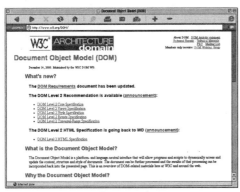

Figure 11.1 The W3C's Document Object Model Web site (www.w3.org/DOM), keeping the Web safe for your DOM.

The capability to change a Web page dynamically with a scripting language is made possible by the Document Object Model (DOM), which can connect any element defined with an ID—an object—to a JavaScript function. This powerful capability allows you to change virtually any property that can be controlled with CSS.

The bad news is that Netscape 4 and Internet Explorer 4 implemented different DOM techniques in their browsers.

The good news is that the most recent versions of both Netscape and Internet Explorer use the DOM standardized by the World Wide Web Consortium (W3C) (**Figure 11.1**).

In this chapter, you'll learn how the legacy DOMs and the W3C's standardized DOM work, and how to create a generic DOM that will work in any DHTML-capable browser. In addition, this chapter introduces you to event handlers that you can use to trigger actions with the DOM.

Understanding the DOM: Road Map to Your Web Page

When you write a letter to someone, you address the envelope, naming the country, the city, the street, the number, and the person for whom the letter is intended. If you put this process in JavaScript, it would look something like this:

```
usa.newyork.sesameST.123.ernie
```

Using this address, you can send a message to the intended recipient. The postal carrier simply uses the address you list and a road map to find the correct location. As long as there are no other Ernies at 123 Sesame Street in New York, you can feel safe that the addressee will receive your message.

If you need to send a message to someone at the same address as Ernie, however, all you have to do is change the name:

```
usa.newyork.sesameST.123.bert
```

Although the addresses are very similar, they are still unique.

The DOM is the "address" through which you can locate any object in your HTML page and then send it a message, using JavaScript. Any element in the window—at least, any element enclosed within HTML tags—can be identified with a `name` or an `id` attribute to give it its own unique address and make it an *object*, rather than simply an *element*.

The DOM describes a path starting with the window itself down through the various objects on the Web page. The following example is the DOM for an image called `button1`:

```
window.document.images.button1
```

This DOM addresses an image in the document in the current window called button1.

If you needed to access an image called button2, you would use this DOM:

```
window.document.images.button2
```

Should I Use a Name or ID?

You can use a name to identify an image in the browser for use with the DOM, as in this example:

```
<img name="button1"
 → src="button_off.png">
```

All other elements have to be identified with an ID, as follows:

```
<div id="layer1"></div>
```

Theoretically, you could also use an ID to identify an image. That technique works in Netscape, but Internet Explorer recognizes only images that have names. So sometimes, you need to include both the ID and the name.

Table 11.1

What the DOM Allows	
CAPABILITY	COMPATIBILITY
Change the CSS properties of an element while it is on the screen	IE4, N6
Change the z-index of elements	IE4, N4
Hide or show elements on the screen	IE4, N4
Control the position of elements relative to the visitor's setup	IE4, N4
Move elements on the screen	IE4, N4
Allow visitors to move objects on the screen	IE4, N4
Reclip the visible area of an element	IE5, N4

CSS Layers?

Often, objects using an ID are referred to as *layers*. These terms can lead to some confusion, however, because the term *layers* was actually coined to describe a similar technology in Netscape (see Chapter 16). Although any HTML tag can be turned into a CSS layer with the addition of the ID attribute, Netscape 4 introduced a `<layer>` tag to achieve a similar result.

The term *layers* seems to be sticking to CSS objects, however, and Netscape layers will soon be a distant memory since the most recent version of Netscape (6) does not support them.

To prevent confusion in this book, I will refer specifically to *Netscape layers* and call CSS layers simply *layers*.

You can use this path to allow a JavaScript function to send that object a message, such as what image it should be displaying (`src`) or what CSS styles it should use (`style`):

```
window.document.images.button1.src=
→ "button_on.gif"
```

At least, that's the grand idea, and it works fine for accessing an image.

Unfortunately, Netscape 4 and Internet Explorer 4 don't agree on the same map to objects defined with CSS; they have different formats for creating addresses to elements on a Web page. It's as though these browsers have two different street systems for reaching the same address when it comes to CSS.

But the W3C recently published a standardized DOM, to which both Netscape 6 and Internet Explorer 5 adhere. Score one for standards!

✔ Tips

- Web pages created with CSS can have their properties changed while they are on the screen (that is, dynamically) through a scripting language and the DOM (**Table 11.1**). Because it is available almost universally, most people use JavaScript as their scripting language. CSS, however, can be affected by any scripting language that your browser can handle—VBScript in Internet Explorer, for example.

- When you send a letter within the same country, you do not need to indicate the country in the address. The post office assumes it's going to some place in the same country. The same is true of indicating which window you are referencing with the DOM. It's simply assumed to be the window the code is in. Instead, you begin the DOM with `document`.

UNDERSTANDING THE DOM

Creating an Object

Simply stated, an *object* is an HTML element (see "Understanding the Element's Box" in Chapter 7) that has been defined with an ID (or, in the case of an image, that has a name). The HTML element has a unique address in the browser window that allows it to be accessed by the DOM.

Identifying an HTML element as an object (**Figure 11.2**) allows you to change any of that element's attributes—at least, to the extent that the browser allows.

To set up an object:

1. `#object1 { position: absolute; }`

   Add an ID rule to your CSS, and define the position as either absolute or relative (see "Defining IDs to Identify an Object" in Chapter 2). You can also add any other definitions you desire, but you must include the position for this layer to be a CSS layer (**Code 11.1**).

2. `<div id="object1">...</div>`

   Apply the ID to an HTML tag—preferably, a `<div>` tag for absolutely positioned layers or a `<span>` tag for relatively positioned layers (see "Creating Your Own Inline HTML Tags" and "Creating Your Own Block-Level HTML Tags" in Chapter 2).

This is Object 1

Figure 11.2 You can act upon the layer dynamically by using JavaScript and the DOM.

Code 11.1 The code sets up a CSS layer by defining a tag with an ID that has had its position type set as either relative or absolute. That's all it takes.

```
<html>
<head>
    <style type="text/css">
    #object1 {
position: absolute;
        top: 100px;
        left: 150px;
        visibility: visible;
        width:210px; }
    </style>
</head>
<body>
    <div id="object1">
        <h3>This is Object 1</h3>
        <img src="alice04.gif" width="200"
        → height="298" border="0">
    </div>
</body>
</html>
```

When this action takes place... *...do this.*

`onmouseover = "toggle(); if (a==b) {x=y; alert('don\'t tread on me!')};"`

Figure 11.3 An event handler.

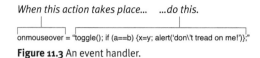

Figure 11.4 This Web page (www.webbedenvironments.com/dhtml/eventhandlers/) contains examples of all the events discussed in this chapter so you can see them in action.

Understanding Event Handlers

In the world of JavaScript, events occur when something happens in the browser window, usually initiated by the visitor. One example is when the visitor moves the mouse pointer over a link; this action generates a `mouseover` event.

Events can also occur when the browser does something, such as loading a new document (`load`) or leaving a Web page (`unload`).

An event handler—which is the event name with the word *on* at the beginning (`onload`)—allows you to define what should happen when a particular event is detected (**Figure 11.3**).

Table 11.2 lists some of the more common event handlers that you will be using. To see these all these events on a single page, visit www.webbedenvironments.com/dhtml/eventhandlers/. I set up this page to demonstrate how the event handlers work (**Figure 11.4**).

Table 11.2

Event Handlers

EVENT HANDLER	WHEN IT HAPPENS	ELEMENTS AFFECTED
onLoad	After an object is loaded	Documents and images
onUnload	After the object is no longer loaded	Documents and images
onFocus	When an element is selected	Documents and forms
onBlur	When an element is deselected	Documents and forms
onMouseOver	When the mouse pointer passes over an area	Links and image map areas
onMouseOut	When the mouse pointer passes out of an area	All*
onClick	When an area is clicked in	All*
onMouseDown	While the mouse button is depressed	All*
onMouseUp	When the mouse button is released	All*
onMouseMove	As the mouse is moved	Document
onKeyDown	While a keyboard key is down	Forms
onKeyUp	When a keyboard key is released	Forms
onKeyPress	When a keyboard key is down and immediately released	Forms
onResize**	When the browser window or a frame is resized	Document
onMove***	When the browser window is moved	Document

* Images and image maps only in Netscape 4   **Not supported by IE4   ***Not supported by IE4/5 or Netscape 6

Event handlers and the DOM

Most changes made in an object's styles with the DOM should be triggered by an event handler. At times, in fact, the JavaScript has to be triggered by an event to work. I have wasted many, many hours trying to figure out what was wrong with my JavaScript, only to find that I had simply forgotten to trigger the script from an event.

This is not to say that you can't run JavaScript outside an event taking place. Many JavaScript functions do dynamic things to the page or window that do not require an event.

✔ Tips

■ Although the `href` *acts* like an `onclick` event handler, it is not, and DHTML code may not run if it is activated from there.

■ If you want a single event to perform multiple tasks, you can add additional JavaScript actions in the quotes separated by a semicolon (;):

`onClick="action1;action2;action3"`

■ The event handler can run JavaScript functions, and you can include JavaScript directly in the quotes as well.

■ At first glance, `onClick` and `onMouseUp` may seem to do the same thing. The `click` event, however, occurs only after the mouse button has been pressed and released. `mouseDown` and `mouseUp` break this action into two separate events, each of which can have a different action associated with it.

Where Does the Event Handler Go?

For the sake of cross-browser compatibility, most of the DHTML examples in this book use event handlers either in a **<body>** tag, **<form>** tag, or link **<a>** tag, because these are the only places where Netscape 4 will generate an event.

Internet Explorer 4/5 and Netscape 6, however, can generate events from any element in the browser window. Thus, any event handler can be placed with a relevant tag. A **<p>** tag, for example, could support the `onmouseover` event.

This Netscape 4-specific limitation puts a huge limitation on cross-browser DHTML. When Netscape 4 is phased out, you should see an explosion of DHTML on the Web.

Figure 11.5 Before the image is rolled over.

Figure 11.6 After the image is rolled over.

Code 11.2 When the visitor moves the mouse over the area of the link with the image (b_off.gif) in it, that image changes its source to a different graphic (b_on.gif).

```
code
<html>
<body>
    <a href="#" onmouseover="document.
    → images.button1.src='b_on.gif'">
        <img src="b_off.gif" name="button1"
        → border="0">
    </a>
</body>
</html>
```

Detecting an Event

An event handler connects an *action* in the browser window to a JavaScript function, which in turn causes some *reaction* in the browser window.

In this example, when the visitor rolls the mouse over (onmouseover) the diamond graphic (**Figure 11.5**), the original graphic is replaced by a triangle graphic (**Figure 11.6**).

To use an event handler:

1. <a href="#"

Start the tag to which you want to add an event handler. This typically will either be a link tag (<a>) or one of the form tags (**Code 11.2**).

2. onmouseover=

In the tag you started in step 1, type a relevant event handler from Table 11.2, followed by an equal sign (=).

3. "document.images.button1.src=
→ 'b_on.gif';"

Type an opening quote ("), the JavaScript you want to be executed when the event occurs, and a close quote ("). The JavaScript can be anything you want it to be, including function calls. If you want to run multiple lines of JavaScript off a single event handler, separate the lines with a semicolon (;), but do *not* use a hard return.

continues on next page

DETECTING AN EVENT

4. Add as many event handlers as you want to the HTML tag by repeating steps 2 and 3.

5. >

Type a closing chevron (>) to close the tag you started in step 1.

6. `<img src="button_off.gif"`
`→ name="button1">`

Add an image, text, or other HTML content that you want to have trigger the event.

7. `</a>`

Type the closing tag for the link or form tag you started in step 1.

✔ Tips

■ If you want an event to perform multiple tasks, add each action inside the quotes, separating actions with a semicolon (;).

■ You can not only use event handlers to run JavaScript functions, but also include JavaScript directly inside the quotes.

How the DOM Works

If you have used any type of scripting language in an HTML page, you have more than likely seen a DOM in action. The DOM works by describing the path from a JavaScript function to an element on the screen, in response to an action in the browser window—an event (**Figure 11.7**).

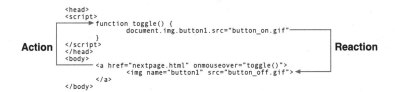

Figure 11.7 This process starts with the visitor's action (the mouseover) and ends with the browser's reaction (changing the graphic). In between, the browser senses the action (event), triggers a function, and uses the DOM to change the image's source to a different graphic file.

Setting up a DOM

The following DOM describes the path, starting with the current document (the window is assumed) and going down to its images and the source location of an image called `button1`: `document.images.button1.src`. You can use this DOM with an event handler such as `onmouseover` (see "Understanding Event Handlers" earlier in this chapter) to change the source of the image being used in the location defined as button1. The upshot is that when the visitor places the mouse pointer over the image, a new image takes its place. This is a common trick on the Web, often referred to as *image swapping* or a *rollover*.

Changing the CSS properties of an object, however, is slightly different from changing an image's source. Although both techniques use a Document Object Model, the DOM for styles is a bit different and varies from browser to browser.

The next few sections describe the three DOMs used to change CSS styles (**Table 11.3**):

◆ **Netscape's Layer DOM**, used only in Netscape 4

◆ **Internet Explorer's All DOM**, used in Internet Explorer 4 and available in Internet Explorer 5

◆ **The W3C's ID DOM**, used in Netscape 6 and Internet Explorer 5

Table 11.3

DHTML-Capable Browsers		
BROWSER	**VERSION**	**DOM**
Netscape	4	Layer
	6	ID
Internet Explorer	4	All
	5	All, ID
Opera	4	ID
	5	ID

Understanding the Object Flow

JavaScript objects are connected in a hierarchical order, with the window at the top and the property being accessed at the bottom. This hierarchy will help you determine the order in which you need to list objects in the DOM. Appendix C has a full object-flow list to help you.

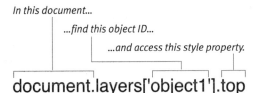

In this document...

...find this object ID...

...and access this style property.

document.layers['object1'].top

Figure 11.8 The Netscape Layer DOM for accessing CSS.

Code 11.3 A JavaScript function using the Netscape Layer DOM. The DOM describes a path to a particular element's position and then reassigns that position.

```
code
<html>
<head>
    <script>
function NAVmoveElement (objectID) {
    document.layers[objectID].left = 120;
    document.layers[objectID].top = 200;
}
    </script>
    <style type="text/css">
    #object1  {
        position: absolute;
        top: 10px;
        left: 10px;
        visibility: visible;
    }
    </style>
</head>
<body>
    <div id="object1">
        <a href="#" onmouseOver=
        → "NAVmoveElement('object1')">
        This script will run in Netscape 4
        → and compatible browsers only.<br>
        <img src="alice04.gif" width="200"
        → height="298" border="0">
        </a>
    </div>
</body>
</html>
```

The Netscape Layer DOM

The Netscape Layer DOM (**Figure 11.8**) allows you to write scripts to control elements created with the <layer> tag (see Chapter 16) and elements created with CSS positioning. This DOM lets you control the position, visibility, and clipping of the element. Changes made in these properties with either layers or CSS positioning occur on the page immediately.

Code 11.3 and **Figure 11.9** show the Layer DOM in action.

Unlike Internet Explorer, Netscape does not provide access to CSS properties other than the positioning controls. Thus, you cannot change the font, text, list, mouse, color, background, border, or margin of an object in Netscape 4 after the page has loaded unless you reload the page.

continues on next page

✔ Tips

- The Layer DOM does not work in Netscape 6. When Netscape started planning its next-generation browser (code-named Mozilla), it decided to start from scratch and attempt to make the browser as standards-compliant as possible. Unfortunately, and to the confusion of many Web designers, this meant abandoning any technologies that were never going to be standards, including the `<layer>` tag and the Layer DOM.

- Although you can get around using the `<layer>` tag in most circumstances, you are stuck with using the Layer DOM in your code and putting up with its many limitations if you want your code to run in Netscape 4.

- Netscape 4 has difficulties directly addressing objects that are nested within other objects (see "Netscape 4 and Nested Layers" later in this chapter).

Figure 11.9 The element is moving from its original position across the screen in response to the function. Keep in mind, however, that this function works only in Netscape 4.

In this document...

...find this object ID...

...and access this style property

document.all['object1'].style.top

Figure 11.10 Internet Explorer's All DOM for accessing CSS.

Code 11.4 A JavaScript function using the Internet Explorer All DOM. The DOM describes a path to a particular element's position and then reassigns that position.

```
<html>
<head>
    <script>
function IEmoveElement () {
    document.all['object1'].style.left = 120;
    document.all['object1'].style.top = 200;
    }
    </script>
    <style type="text/css">
#object1 {
        position: absolute;
        top: 50px;
        left: 10px;
        visibility: visible;
    }
    </style>
</head>
<body>
    <div id="object1">
        <a href="#" onmouseOver=
        → "IEmoveElement()">
        This script will run in Internet
        → Explorer 4, 5 and compatible
        → browsers only.<br>
        <img src="alice04.gif" width="200"
        → height="298" border="0">
        </a>
    </div>
</body>
</html>
```

The Internet Explorer All DOM

The Internet Explorer All DOM (**Figure 11.10**) allows you to write scripts that can access any element on the screen—at least, any element that Internet Explorer understands. These elements includes CSS properties, which let you control the position and visibility of elements on the screen, as well as their appearance. Any changes made in these properties occur on the page immediately, and Internet Explorer re-renders the page to comply.

Thus, any changes made in the font, text, list, mouse, color, background, border, margin, position, or visibility of an object are discernible immediately.

Code 11.4 and **Figure 11.11** show an example of the Internet Explorer DOM in action.

Figure 11.11 The element is moving from its original position across the screen in response to the function. This function works only in Internet Explorer 4 or later.

The W3C ID DOM

The W3C realized that there would be a need to link scripting languages to objects on a Web page, and it diligently began to work out the best method. Unfortunately, the browser manufacturers could not wait, and they introduced their own DOMs before the W3C could set the standard. Better late than never, the W3C released its standardized DOM (**Figure 11.12**), which has been embraced by the browser-building community.

The W3C's ID DOM, or standard DOM, allows you to write scripts that can access any element on the screen. These properties include all CSS properties, which let you control the position and visibility of objects on the screen, as well as their appearance. Any changes made in these properties occur on the page immediately.

Thus, any changes made in the font, text, list, mouse, color, background, border, margin, position, or visibility of an object are discernible immediately.

Code 11.5 and **Figure 11.13** show the standard DOM in action.

Figure 11.13 The element is moving from its original position across the screen in response to the function. This function works only in Internet Explorer 5 and Netscape 6 or later.

In this document...

...find this object ID...

...and access this style property

`document.getElementById('object1').style.top`

Figure 11.12 The W3C's ID DOM for accessing CSS.

Code 11.5 A JavaScript function using the W3C's ID DOM. The DOM describes a path to a particular element's position and then reassigns that position.

```
<html>
<head>
   <script>
function W3CmoveElement () {
   document.getElementById('object1').style.
   → left = 120;
   document.getElementById('object1').style.
   → top = 60;
}
   </script>
   <style type="text/css">
#object1  {
   position: absolute;
   top: 10px;
   left: 10px;
   visibility: visible;
}
</style>
</head>
<body>
   <div id="object1">
      <a href="#" onmouseOver=
      → "W3CmoveElement()">
      This script will run in any browser
      → that uses the W3C's standard<br>
      → for DOM, including → Internet
      → Explorer 5 and Netscape.<br>
      <img src="alice04.gif" width="200"
      → height="298" border="0">
      </a>
   </div>
</body>
</html>
```

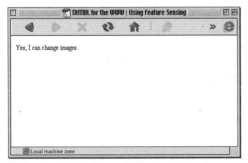

Figure 11.14 This browser can change images.

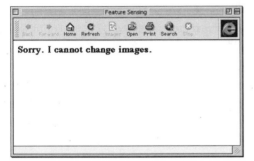

Figure 11.15 Many older browsers, such as Internet Explorer 3, cannot change images. The results now show a different message.

Code 11.6 The code checks to see whether the document.images object is available in the browser.

```
<html>
<body>
    <script language="JavaScript">
if (document.images) {
    document.writeln('Yes, I can change
    → images.');
}
else {
    document.writeln('Sorry. I cannot change
    → images.');
}
    </script>
</body>
</html>
```

Using Feature Sensing

The best way to determine whether the browser that is running your script has what it takes to do the job is to ask it. Finding out whether the browser has the feature(s) you need to use is a lot simpler than it sounds and requires only one added line per function.

In most cases, feature sensing is a better alternative than the more common browser sensing (see "Detecting the Browser's Name and Version" in Chapter 12). If the current version of a browser cannot run your script, who is to say that another, more powerful version of the browser won't be released that can run it? Feature sensing will let any able browser that can run the code run it (**Figures 11.14** and **11.15**).

To sense whether a JavaScript feature is available:

1. if (document.images)

   Within a JavaScript container, set up a conditional statement as shown in **Code 11.6**. Within the parentheses of the if statement, place the DOM for the JavaScript feature you need to use. In this example, you are checking to see whether the browser can handle the image object.

2. { document.writeln('Yes, I can change → 'images.')}

   Within {} brackets, type the JavaScript code you want to be executed if this feature is available on this browser.

3. else { document.writeln → (' Sorry. I can't 'change images.')}

   You can include an else statement specifying the code to be run in the event that the JavaScript feature for which you are testing is not available.

Detecting the DOM Type

Using feature sensing, you can determine the DOM type that your browser is using (**Figures 11.16**, **11.17**, and **11.18**).

To find the DOM type:

1. `var isID=0;`

   Initialize four variables (`isID`, `isALL`, `isLayers`, `isDHTML`) to 0 (false). The first three variables record the DOM type as detected; the fourth simply records whether any DOM is present—whether the browser is DHTML-capable (**Code 11.7**).

2. `if (document.getElementById)`
   `→ {isID = 1; isDHTML = 1;}`

   Detect for each DOM, and assign the corresponding variable to 1 (true) if that DOM works in this browser. Notice that if a DOM exists, the subsequent DOMs are not tested. This setup allows you to use the best DOM available to that browser.

3. `if (isID) {...}`

   You can use these variables to tailor the page for the available DOM. Netscape Layer Detection Bug

Although you can use feature sensing to detect the Layer DOM in Netscape 4, a bug in this browser prevents you from using feature sensing if you place your JavaScript detection in an external file (see "Using the Cross-Browser DOM" later in this chapter).

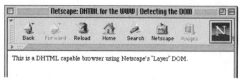

Figure 11.16 The message shows that this is a DHTML browser using the Netscape Layer DOM.

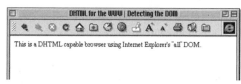

Figure 11.17 The message shows that this is a DHTML browser using Internet Explorer's All DOM.

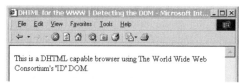

Figure 11.18 The message shows that this is a DHTML browser using the W3C's ID DOM.

Code 11.7 The code senses which DOM the browser uses and assigns the appropriate variable to have a value of 1 (true). If any DOM is detected, the isDHTML variable is also set to true.

```
                                    code
<html>
<head>
    <script>
var isDHTML = 0;
var isLayers = 0;
var isAll = 0;
var isID = 0;
if (document.getElementById) {isID = 1; isDHTML = 1;}
else {
if (document.layers) {isLayers = 1; isDHTML = 1;}
else {
if (document.all) {isAll = 1; isDHTML = 1;}
}}
    </script>
</head>
<body>
    <script>
if (isDHTML) {document.write('This is a DHTML capable browser using ');}
if (isID) {document.write('The World Wide Web Consortium\'s "ID" DOM.');}
else {
    if (isLayers) {document.write('Netscape\'s "Layer" DOM.');}
    else {
        if (isAll) {document.write('Internet Explorer\'s "all" DOM.');}
        else {document.write('This is not a DHTML capable browser...so what are you waiting for?');}
}}
    </script>
</body>
</html>
```

Building a Cross-Browser DOM

Like the Rosetta stone, the information returned from detecting the browser's DOM type can translate the DOM for a particular object in the Web page being displayed by the browser. The basic idea is to include methods for all three DOM types in a function called findDOM(), which uses if statements to determine which DOM type to use. A DHTML function then uses findDOM() to build the DOM for a particular object and access that object's properties (**Figure 11.19**).

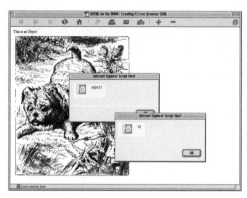

Figure 11.19 The first alert shows the object's ID. The second alert is the object's distance from the top of the screen, in pixels.

To create a cross-browser DOM:

1. var isDHTML = 0;

   In your JavaScript, type the JavaScript described in the previous section, "Detecting the DOM Type" (**Code 11.8**).

Code 11.8 The cross-browser DOM uses feature sensing to determine which DOM type is being used, and then a function to define the DOM for a particular object based on that information.

```
<html>
<head>
   <script>
var isDHTML = 0;
var isLayers = 0;
var isAll = 0;
var isID = 0;
if (document.getElementById) {isID = 1; isDHTML = 1;}
else {
   if (document.all) {isAll = 1; isDHTML = 1;}
   else {
        browserVersion = parseInt(navigator.appVersion);
      if ((navigator.appName.indexOf('Netscape') != -1) && (browserVersion == 4)) {isLayers = 1;
→ isDHTML = 1;}
}}

function findDOM(objectID,withStyle) {
   if (withStyle == 1) {
        if (isID) { return (document.getElementById(objectID).style) ; }
        else {
```

(code continues on next page)

Code 11.8 *continued*

```
                     code
         if (isAll) { return
      → (document.all
      → [objectID].style); }
   else {
         if (isLayers) { return
      → (document.layers[objectID]); }
   };}
}
else {
   if (isID) { return
   → (document.getElementById(objectID)
   ) ; }
   else {
         if (isAll) { return
      → (document.all[objectID]); }
   else {
         if (isLayers) { return
      → (document.layers[objectID]); }
   };}
}
}

function whoAmI(objectID) {
   domStyle = findDOM(objectID,1)
   dom = findDOM(objectID,0);

   if (domStyle.pixelTop != null)
   → { alert(domStyle.pixelTop); }
   else { alert(domStyle.top); }
   alert(dom.id);
}
</script>
   <style type="text/css">
#object1 {
      position: absolute;
      visibility: show;
      top: 10px;
      left: 10px;
       }
</style>
      </head>
   <body onLoad="whoAmI('object1')">
               <div id="object1">
               This is an Object<br>
               <img src="alice14.gif"
               → width="407" height="480"
               → border="0">
               </div>
</body>
</html>
```

2. `function findDOM(objectID,withStyle)`
   → `{...}`

   Add the findDOM() function to your JavaScript. This function takes the ID for the desired object and creates a DOM for the particular browser being used. Then you can use the function to change the object's style (`if withSTYLE=1`) or to change other properties associated with the object (`if withStyle=0`).

3. `if (isID) { return`
   → `(document.getElementById`
   → `(objectID).style) ; }`

   Each DOM type is tested to see whether it is the one used by this browser. If `isID` is true (`isID = 1`), the condition is met, and the W3C's ID DOM type is used to locate the object on the Web page.

   Now that you have translated the various DOMs into one common language, you are ready to use this language to control elements on the screen through a JavaScript function.

To access the cross-browser DOM:

1. `function whoAmI(objectID) {...}`

   In your JavaScript, set up a function that invokes the finDOM() function. In this example, I have set up two variables. This variable records the DOM with the style:

   `domStyle = findDOM(objectID,1)`

   This variable records the DOM without the style:

   `dom = findDOM(objectID,0);`

   These variables are used to find the object's ID and its position from the top of the screen (see "Finding an Object's Top and Left Positions" in Chapter 12).

2. `<body onLoad="whoAmI('object1')">`

   Use an event handler to trigger the function you set up in step 1. Remember that all DHTML functions have to be triggered from an event handler.

✔ Tip

- You can use any name you want for the `dom` variable, but I prefer to use `domStyle` if I'm going to use it to access an object's styles, or just plain `dom` if I'm accessing any other property of the object.

Alert! Results May Vary

Different browsers may show different results in these alerts. For example, Internet Explorer 5 for Windows will actually show `[object]` in both of these alerts. Rather than showing you the actual value, many browsers will display a variable that it is using to access the object in question. Don't worry, though: This variable contains the same information.

Code 11.9 You can import the findDOM.js file into any HTML document as needed to create DHTML functions. Remember this file; you will be using it often in this book.

```
                    code
var isDHTML = 0;

var isID = 0;

var isAll = 0;

var isLayers = 0;


if (document.getElementById) {isID = 1;
→ isDHTML = 1;}
else {
    if (document.all) {isAll = 1; isDHTML = 1;}
    else {
        browserVersion = parseInt
        → (navigator.appVersion);
    if ((navigator.appName.indexOf
    → ('Netscape') != -1) && (browserVersion
    → == 4)) {isLayers = 1; → isDHTML = 1;}
}}


function findDOM(objectID,withStyle) {
    if (withStyle == 1) {
        if (isID) { return
        → (document.getElementById
        → (objectID).style) ; }
        else {
            if (isAll) { return (document.all
            → [objectID].style); }
        else {
            if (isLayers) { return
            → (document.layers[objectID]); }
        };}
    }
    else {
        if (isID) { return
        → (document.getElementById
        → (objectID)) ; }
        else {
            if (isAll) { return → (docu-
            ment.all[objectID]); }
        else {
            if (isLayers) { return
            → (document.layers[objectID]);
            }
        };}
    }
}
```

Using the Cross-Browser DOM

Many of the dynamic functions presented in this book use the cross-browser DOM described in the preceding section. Rather than retype that code on every page where you need it, you can place all this code in an external text file and then import that file into the HTML pages as needed (see "Using an External JavaScript File" in Chapter 23).

To use the cross-browser DOM in a Web page:

1. findDOM.js

   Open a new text file, and type the cross-browser DOM code shown in Code 11.8. (See the previous section, "Building a Cross-Browser DOM," for a full explanation of how this code works.) Save this file as findDOM.js. Throughout the book, I will refer to this file as the *findDOM code* (**Code 11.9**).

2. index.html

   Start a new HTML page, and save it in the same folder as the findDOM.js file (**Code 11.10**).

3. <script src="findDOM.js"></script>

   In the <head> of the page, add a link to the external JavaScript file from step 1.

4. function moveObject (objectID) {...}

   In your JavaScript, set up your dynamic function, which has the object's ID passed as a variable.

   continues on next page

5. domStyle = findDOM(objectID,1);

In the function you created in step 4, include a call to the finDOM() function and pass it the objectID. Also include 1 if you will be accessing the object's styles or 0 if you are accessing any other properties. This code stores the value of the DOM (in this case, including the style) in a variable called domStyle.

6. domStyle.left = 120; domStyle.top = 200;

You can access any of the object's style properties by using the domStyle variable, a period (.), and then the style attribute. This example changes the top and left positions of the object.

7. onload="moveObject('object1')

Don't forget to trigger the function from an event. In this example, the function moveObject() will be run immediately after the page is loaded in the browser window (**Figure 11.20**).

✔ Tip

■ You can use any name you want for the dom variable, but I prefer to use domStyle if I'm going to use it to access an object's styles, or just plain dom if I'm accessing any other property of the object.

Code 11.10 index.html is an HTML file that is importing the findDOM.js file. This code then uses the finDOM() function to create a DOM to move the image of Alice by changing its top and left position style.

```
<html>
<head>
    <script src="findDOM.js"></script>
    <script>
    function moveObject (objectID) {
        domStyle = findDOM(objectID,1);
        domStyle.left = 120;
        domStyle.top = 200;
    }
    </script>
    <style type="text/css">
#object1 {
    position: absolute;
    visibility: show;
    top: 10px;
    left: 10px }
</style>
    </head>
<body onLoad="moveObject('object1')">
    <div id="object1">
    This script will run in any Netscape 4
 → and above, Internet Explorer 4 and
 → above, or W3C compatible browsers.<br>
    <img src="alice04.gif" width="200"
 → height="298" border="0">
    </div>
</body>
</html>
```

Figure 11.20 Alice moves on command.

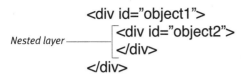

Figure 11.21 To access the CSS layer defined by object2 in this code...

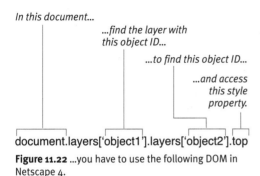

Figure 11.22 ...you have to use the following DOM in Netscape 4.

Netscape 4 and Nested Layers

When you are accessing layers nested within layers (Netscape layers or CSS layers), just having the ID of the final layer to be addressed is not enough. Netscape 4 requires that you include the IDs of *all* the objects.

Suppose that you have an object called object2 that is nested in another object called object1 (**Figure 11.21**). Internet Explorer 4/5 and Netscape 6 can address object2 directly by using the DOM, but Netscape 4 *has* to include object1 in the DOM path.

To get around this bug, you need to use a special version of the findDOM code (see the previous section, "Using the Cross-Browser DOM") rewritten for Netscape 4 (**Figure 11.22**).

Detecting Netscape 4 Layers

You will notice that the findDOM code I show you in this section uses browser detection (see "Detecting the Browser's Name and Version" in Chapter 12) rather than feature sensing (see "Detecting the DOM Type" earlier in this chapter) to detect Netscape 4's Layer DOM.

Theoretically, feature sensing should work to determine whether the browser is using the Layer DOM. Netscape 4, however, has a freaky bug that causes feature sensing to fail if— and only if—the feature sensing is being imported from an external JavaScript file *and* the document is the first one loaded into a new browser window. If the feature-sensing code is directly on the HTML page, it works every time. If the page with the external file is the second, third, fourth, or later page loaded into the browser window, it works every time.

Thus, to maintain an external file for DOM detection and creation, you have to resort to using browser detection (which works every time) to sense Netscape 4.

To set up a nested DOM for Netscape 4:

1. FindDOMNested.js

Open a new text file, and type the cross-browser DOM code shown in **Code 11.11**. This code is almost identical to the findDOM code in the previous section, except it allows Netscape 4 to access an object that is nested inside another object.

This version of the function findDOM() allows you to include two layer IDs. objectID1 is the parent of objectID2, which Netscape 4 uses to build the DOM. However, Internet Explorer 4/5 and Netscape 6 will need to use only objectID2.

Save this file as findDOMNested.js. Throughout the book, I will refer to this file as the *findDOMNested code*.

Code 11.11 This version of the findDOM code (findDOMNested.js) allows Netscape to see one level down into a nested CSS layer.

```
var isDHTML = 0;
var isID = 0;
var isAll = 0;
var isLayers = 0;

if (document.getElementById) {isID = 1; isDHTML = 1;}
else {
    if (document.all) {isAll = 1; isDHTML = 1;}
    else {
        browserVersion = parseInt(navigator.appVersion);
        if ((navigator.appName.indexOf('Netscape') != -1) && (browserVersion == 4)) {isLayers = 1;
        → isDHTML = 1;}
}}

function findDOM(objectID1,objectID2,withStyle) {
    if (withStyle == 1) {
        if (isID) { return (document.getElementById(objectID2).style) ; }
        else {
            if (isAll) { return (document.all[objectID2].style); }
            else {
```

(code continues on next page)

Code 11.11 *continued*

```
                    if (isLayers) {
                        if (objectID1) { return
                    → (document.layers[objectID
                    → 1].layers[objectID2]); }
                        else { return
                    → (document.layers
                    → [objectID2]); }
                    }
                };}
        }
        else {
            if (isID) { return
        → (document.getElementById
        → (objectID2)) ; }
            else {
                if (isAll) { return → (docu-
                ment.all[objectID2]); }
            else {
                if (isLayers) {
                    if (objectID1) { return
                → (document.layers[objectID
                → 1].layers[objectID2]); }
                    else { return
                → (document.layers
                → [objectID2]); }
                }
            };}
        }
```

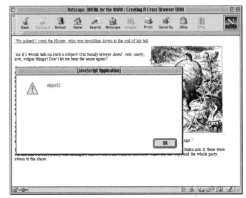

Figure 11.23 Clicking the link or the image reveals that object's ID.

2. `index.html`

Start a new HTML page, and save it in the same folder as the findDOM.js file (**Code 11.12**).

3. `function whoAmI(objectID1,objectID2)`
`→ {...}`

Create a function that invokes the revised findDOM() function. The function potentially needs to have two object IDs passed to it.

4. `onClick="whoAmI('object1',`
`→ 'object2');"`

Trigger the function from step 3, using an event handler, and pass the function the IDs of the object and its parent.

5. `onClick="whoAmI('','object1');`

Alternatively, if the object is not nested, you can leave the first object ID blank by placing nothing (not even a space) between the quotes in the function call (**Figure 11.23**).

✔ Tips

- For simplicity's sake, I recommend sticking with the non-nested version of the findDOM() function unless you *really* need to nest CSS layers.

- To add more nesting levels, simply add more if statements, as follows:

  ```
  if (objectID1) { return
  → (document.layers[objectID1].layers
  → [objectID2].layers[objectID3]); }
  if (objectID2) { return
  → (document.layers[objectID2].layers
  → [objectID3]); }
  else { return (document.layers
  → [objectID3]); }
  ```

Code 11.12 In this example, object2 is nested within object1, making it hard to reach for Netscape 4. So you have to alter the findDOM() function a bit to accommodate the browser.

```
                                  code
<html>
<head>
    <script src="findDOMNested.js"></script>
    <script>
function whoAmI(objectID1,objectID2) {
    dom = findDOM(objectID1,objectID2,0)
    alert(dom.id);
}
    </script>
    <style type="text/css">
#object1 {
        position: relative;
        visibility: show;}
#object2 {
        position: relative;
        visibility: show;
        float: right;}
    </style>
</head>
<body>
    <div id="object1">
        <a href="#" onClick="whoAmI('','object1');">'We indeed!' cried the Mouse, who was
        → trembling down to the end of his tail</a>.
        <div id="object2">
            <a href="#" onClick="whoAmI('object1','object2');">
                <img  src="alice14.gif" width="200" height="236" border="0">
            </a>
        </div>
        <p>'As if I would talk...</p>
        <p>'I won't indeed!'...</p>
        <p>So she called softly...</p>
        <p>It was high time to go...</p>
    </div>
</body>
</html>
```

LEARNING ABOUT YOUR ENVIRONMENT

12

"To change your world, you must first know yourself." I don't know whether this is an ancient proverb or whether I just made it up, but it definitely applies to DHTML. Many of the functions in the chapters that follow this one rely on knowing where something is, how big it is, and what it is doing.

The first half of this chapter deals with things that you can learn directly from the browser itself—things such as the screen size and browser-window size—and these things do not use the DOM. The second half of the chapter looks at things you can learn from the objects you will be changing—things such as position, height, and width—and these things do use the DOM.

Detecting the Browser's Name and Version

Although feature sensing is better for determining what a browser can and cannot do (see "Using Feature Sensing" in Chapter 11), sometimes you need to be able to tell your code what to do based on the browser type and browser version in which the Web page is running (**Figures 12.1**, **12.2**, and **12.3**).

Initially, this information comes in two big chunks (**Code 12.1**). The first chunk gives the full name of the browser (navigator.appName). The second chunk includes the version of the browser, along with compatibility information and the OS being used (navigator.appVersion). Although having the exact name and version of the browser is useful, that information can be a bit bulky when it comes time to code. You can use these chunks to get the data you require and store it in variables for later use.

To determine the browser type and version:

1. var isNS = 0;

   Type three variables (isIE, isNS, isOtherBrowser) in your JavaScript to record which browser is displaying the code. These variables are initially set to 0 (false) and are reassigned to 1 (true) if the browser in question is being used.

2. if (navigator.appName.indexOf
   → ('Netscape') != -1) {isNS = 1;}

   To reassign the variables from step 1, check for the name of the browser. This code looks for the word *Netscape* in the appName, and does the same for *Microsoft Internet Explorer*. If the browser is not Netscape or Internet Explorer, record it as being *other*.

Figure 12.1 The code is being run in Internet Explorer 5.5 on a Windows machine. Notice that the browser's designation includes (compatible; MSIE 5.5; Windows 95). It will show up, however, as being Internet Explorer 4 so that it can run older JavaScript code.

Figure 12.2 The code is being run in Netscape 6 on a Mac. Notice, though, that it claims to be Netscape 5.

Figure 12.3 The browser-sensing code is being run in Opera 5. Notice that Opera claims to be Internet Explorer. Most JavaScript code is designed to sense Internet Explorer or Netscape and may exclude other browsers. The Opera browser shows up as Internet Explorer so Opera users will not be left out in the cold.

Code 12.1 The code first writes the complete *appName* and *appVersion* on the page. It then uses that information to determine the browser name and version number so it can display the correct message.

```
code
<html>
<head>
<body>
    <script>
document.write('<b>This browser\'s
→ designation is:</b> ');
document.write(navigator.appName + ' ');
document.write(navigator.appVersion);
var isNS = 0;
var isIE = 0;
var isOtherBrower = 0;
if (navigator.appName.indexOf('Netscape')
→ != -1) {isNS = 1;}
else {
    if (navigator.appName.indexOf('Microsoft
    → Internet Explorer') != -1) {isIE = 1;}
    else {isOtherBrow = 1;}
}
browserVersion = parseInt
→ (navigator.appVersion);

document.write('<br><br>');
if (isNS) {document.write('This Browser is
→ compatible with Netscape version ');}
else {
    if (isIE) {document.write('This Browser
    → is compatible with Internet Explorer
    → version ');}
    else {
        if (isOtherBrowser) {document.write
        → ('I do not recognize this browser
        → type. Version = ');}
}}
document.write(browserVersion +'.');
    </script>
</body>
</html>
```

3. `parseInt(navigator.appVersion);`

The number of the browser version is assigned to the variable `browserVersion`.

4. `if (isNS) {...}`

Now you can use the variables you set up in steps 1, 2, and 3 for the particular browser and version.

✔ Tip

■ There are, of course, more than two browsers. But most non-Internet Explorer and non-Netscape browsers show up as one or the other, depending on which browser they are most compatible with. The Opera browser does this so it will not be excluded due to browser-sensing Web sites that allow their HTML to be viewed only by particular browsers.

Feature Sensing or Browser Sensing?

Browser sensing is often used instead of feature sensing to determine whether a DHTML function should be run in a particular browser. Using browser sensing, however, means that you have to know exactly what code will or will not run in the browsers you are including or excluding.

Using browser sensing to determine DHTML compatibility can cause problems, especially when newer browser versions either add new capabilities or fix bugs that prevented code from previously working. I recommend using feature sensing if at all possible.

Detecting the Operating System

The application version object (`appVersion`) not only includes the version number of the browser (see the previous section, "Detecting the Browser's Name and Version"), but also the operating system of the browser used to view the site (**Figures 12.4** and **12.5**). This information can be very useful, especially if you need to overcome font-size inconsistencies or other OS-related incompatibilities.

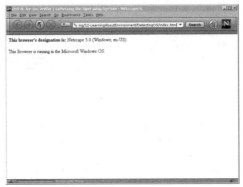

Figure 12.4 The code is being run in Windows 95.

To detect the operating system being used:

1. `var isMac = 0;`

   Set up three variables (`isMac`, `isWin`, `isOtherOS`) in your JavaScript to record which OS the browser is using. Each of these variables is initially set to `0` (false) and will be reassigned to `1` (true) if the applicable operating system is being used (**Code 12.2**).

2. `if (navigator.appVersion.indexOf`
   `→ ('Mac') != -1) {isMac = 1;}`

   To reassign the variables from step 1, check the name of the OS being used. This code looks for the word *Mac* in the `appVersion`, and does the same for *Win*. If the OS is not Macintosh or Windows, record it as being *other*.

3. `if (isMac) {...}`

   Now you can use the variables you set up in steps 1 and 2 for the OS that is being used.

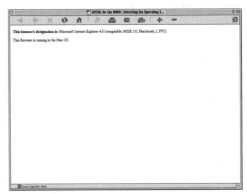

Figure 12.5 The same code is being run on a Mac.

✔ Tips

- One of the most common uses of OS detection is to help overcome the font-size and color incompatibilities between the Mac and Windows operating systems (see "Setting the CSS for the OS" in Chapter 22).

- There are, of course, more than two operating systems in the world. Linux is becoming increasingly popular but still accounts for less than 1% of the Web-viewing population.

Code 12.2 The code first writes the complete appName and appVersion on the page. It then uses that information to determine the operating system so that it can display the correct message.

```
<html>
<body>
   <script>
document.write('<b>This browser\'s designation is:</b> ');
document.write(navigator.appName + ' ');
document.write(navigator.appVersion);
var isMac = 0;
var isWin = 0;
var isOtherOS = 0;
if (navigator.appVersion.indexOf('Mac') != -1) {isMac = 1;}
else {
   if (navigator.appVersion.indexOf('Win') != -1) {isWin = 1;}
   else {isOtherOS = 1; }
}
document.write('<br><br>');
if (isMac) {document.write('This Browser is running in the Mac OS.');}
else {
   if (isWin) {document.write('This Browser is running in the Microsoft Windows OS.');}
   else {
      if (isOtherOS) {document.write('RESISTANCE IS FUTILE...YOU WILL BE ASSIMULATED');}
}}
   </script>
</body>
</html>
```

Finding the Screen Dimensions

The screen—that glowing, slightly rounded glass panel you stare at all day—is where all the windows that make up your Web site reside. You can try making Web sites with Morse code or punch cards, but trust me on this one: The cathode ray tube is currently the best medium for displaying Web sites (**Figures 12.6** and **12.7**).

One of the frustrations of Web design, however, is never knowing the size of the area in which your design will be placed or how much space is actually available.

So why don't you just ask the screen how big it is (**Figure 12.8**)?

Figure 12.6 The Windows screen dimensions. The live area includes everything but the bottom menu bar. In Windows, however, this bar may appear on any side of the screen at the user's discretion.

Figure 12.7 The Mac screen dimensions. The live area is everywhere but the top menu bar and approximately 6 pixels on the left and right sides. The Mac OS always displays a menu bar at the top of the screen.

Figure 12.8 The code displays the total and live dimensions of the screen for my computer.

Code 12.3 The code determines both the total and live dimensions of the window and assigns these values to variables, which write the values in the browser window.

```
code
<html>
<body>
    <script>
var screenHeight = screen.height;

var screenWidth = screen.width;

var liveScreenHeight = screen.availHeight;

var liveScreenWidth = screen.availWidth;

document.writeln('Your total screen height
→ is ' + screenHeight + 'px <br><br>');
document.writeln('Your total screen width
→ is ' + screenWidth + 'px <br><br>');
document.writeln('Your live screen height
→ is ' + liveScreenHeight + 'px <br><br>');
document.writeln('Your live screen width
→ is ' + liveScreenWidth + 'px <br><br>');
    </script>
</body>
</html>
```

To find the screen's dimensions:

1. var screenHeight = screen.height;

Add the variables screenHeight and screenWidth to your JavaScript, and assign to them the values screen.height and screen.width, respectively. These variables will now record the *total* height and width of the screen, in pixels (**Code 12.3**).

2. var liveScreenHeight =
→ screen.availHeight;

Add the variables liveScreenHeight and liveScreenWidth to your JavaScript, and assign to them the values screen.availHeight and screen.availWidth, respectively. These variables will now record the *live* (available) height and width of the screen, in pixels. This differs from the total in that it does not include any menu bars added by the OS—only the area in which windows can be displayed.

Finding the Number of Colors

Once upon a time, color was one of the biggest nightmares a Web designer could face. Not all computers are created equal, especially when it comes to color. On your high-end professional machine, you design a brilliant Web page with bold colors, deep drop shadows, antialiased text, and 3-D buttons (**Figure 12.9**). But on the machine across the hall, it looks like a grainy color photo that's been left out in the sun too long (**Figure 12.10**).

The problem was that some computers displayed millions of colors, while others displayed only a few thousand or (*gasp*) a few hundred or less.

So knowing the number of colors the person viewing your site can actually see might be useful. Over the past several years, however, as old machines have been thrown out and new machines brought in, the problem of color has diminished rapidly.

Still, older machines are in use, and you may need to be able to code around these machines' limitations (**Figures 12.11** and **12.12**).

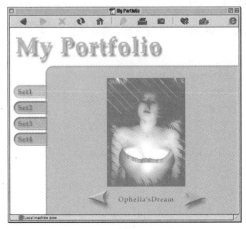

Figure 12.9 An image in all its 32-bit glory.

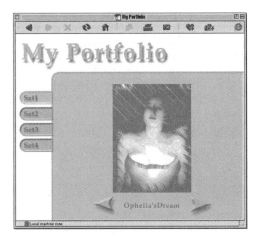

Figure 12.10 The same image in ho-hum 8-bit grayscale. Notice how much rougher the transitions are between areas of color than in the 32-bit version above.

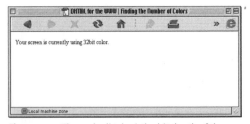

Figure 12.11 The code displays the bit depth of the monitor—in this case, 32-bit.

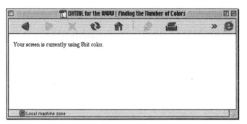

Figure 12.12 The code displays the bit depth of the monitor—in this case, 8-bit.

Code 12.4 The function findColors() returns one of the values in Table 12.1, depending on the number of colors available on the computer that is being used.

```
<html>
<body>
    <script>
function findColors() {
    return (screen.colorDepth);
}

document.write('Your screen is currently
→ using ' + findColors() + 'bit colour.');
    </script>
</body>
</html>
```

To detect the number of colors:

◆ `screen.colorDepth`

The number of colors that the visitor's screen can currently display is in the screen's color-depth object (**Code 12.4**). Using this code will return a Color-Bit Depth value as shown in **Table 12.1**.

Table 12.1

Pixel-Depth Values	
COLOR-BIT DEPTH	**NO. OF COLORS**
4	16
8	256
16	65,536
32	16.7 million

FINDING THE NUMBER OF COLORS

211

Finding the Browser Window's Dimensions

In Netscape, the browser window's current width and height can be determined. (Note: Internet Explorer does not support this JavaScript.) This information is the total width and height of the browser window, including all the controls around the display area (**Figure 12.13**).

To find the browser window's dimensions:

1. `window.outerHeight`

   Create a function that returns the value of the outer height of the window. This value is in pixels (**Code 12.5**).

2. `window.outerWidth`

   Create a function that returns the value of the outer width of the browser window. This value is in pixels.

✔ Tips

■ The total area of the browser window cannot be determined in Internet Explorer.

■ The live area of the browser window can be determined in both Internet Explorer and Netscape (see the following section, "Finding the Visible Page Dimensions").

Figure 12.13 The code displays the dimensions of the Netscape browser window.

Code 12.5 The functions findBrowserHeight() and findBrowserWidth() return the dimensions of the browser window, in pixels.

```
<html>
<head>
    <script>
function findBrowserHeight() {
    if (window.outerHeight != null)
        return window.outerHeight;
    return null;
}

function findBrowserWidth() {
    if (window.outerWidth != null)
        return window.outerWidth;
    return null;
}
    </script>
</head>
<body>
    <script>
browserHeight = findBrowserHeight() ;
browserWidth =  findBrowserWidth();

if (browserHeight!= null) {
document.writeln('Your total browser height
→ is ' + browserHeight + 'px <br><br>'); }
else {document.writeln ('The browser window\'s
→ height can not be determined.<br><br>'); }

if (browserWidth!= null) {
document.writeln('Your total browser width
→ is ' + browserWidth + 'px <br><br>'); }
else {document.writeln ('The browser window\'s
→ width can not be determined.'); }
    </script>
</body>
</html>
```

Figure 12.14 Clicking the image triggers an alert that returns the dimensions of the browser window's live area.

Finding the Visible Page Dimensions

Knowing the size of the browser window is nice (see the previous section, "Finding the Browser Window's Dimensions"), but a much more useful capability is finding the dimensions of the live area in which your content will be displayed (**Figure 12.14**).

To find the dimensions of the live area:

1. function findLivePageHeight() {...}

Add the function findLivePageHeight() to your JavaScript. This function uses feature sensing to determine which method the current browser uses to find the live window height; the function returns that value. Netscape uses window.innerHeight, and Internet Explorer uses document.body.clientHeight (**Code 12.6**).

continues on next page

Code 12.6 The functions findLivePageHeight() and findLivePageWidth() return the dimensions of the browser window's live area, in pixels.

```
<html>
<head>
    <script>
function findLivePageHeight() {
    if (window.innerHeight != null)
        return window.innerHeight;
    if (document.body.clientHeight != null)
        return document.body.clientHeight;
    return (null);
}

function findLivePageWidth() {
    if (window.innerWidth != null)
        return window.innerWidth;
    if (document.body.clientWidth != null)
        return document.body.clientWidth;
    return (null); }
```

(code continues on next page)

2. `function findLivePageWidth() {...}`

Add the function `findLivePageWidth()` to your JavaScript. This function uses feature sensing to determine the method the current browser uses to find the live window width; the function returns that value. Netscape uses `window.innerWidth`, and Internet Explorer uses `document.body.clientWidth`.

Code 12.6 *continued*

```
        </script>
    </head>
    <body>
        <script>

    function pageDim() {
        livePageHeight = findLivePageHeight();
        livePageWidth = findLivePageWidth();
        alert ('Visible Page Width: ' +
        livePageWidth + 'px; Visible Page
        Height: ' + livePageHeight + 'px');
    }

        </script>
        Click the image to find the windows live
        dimensions and the Web page's total
        size.
        <br>
        <a href="#" onClick="pageDim()">
            <img src="alice17.gif" width="640"
            height="480" border="0">
        </a>
    </body>
</html>
```

What Screen Size Should I Use for My Web Sites?

An 800x600-pixel screen size has become the design standard for most Web designers, but all sites should be usable in 640x480 even if it requires horizontal scrolling. Although the 640x480 screen size comprises less than 13% of Web site visitors and is falling (according to StatMarket, `www.statmarket.com`), it is important that any Web-site design be usable on smaller screens.

Significant content and design elements should be placed "above the fold" so that they are visible without vertical scrolling, and all important user-interface elements must be visible without horizontal scrolling within the 800x600 screen.

Keep in mind, however, that 800x600 is the maximum visible area available for the entire screen. In reality, an 800x600 screen will have a lot less live space available in which to display your Web site. The maximum live browser area varies, depending on the resolution of the monitor, the OS, the browser, and the actual size at which visitors set their browsers.

Figure 12.15 The linked title and page URL are displayed.

Code 12.7 The variables pageTitle and pageURI are defined and then displayed on the page. The URI is also used to create a link back to this page when the user clicks the title.

```
<html>
<body>
    <script>
var pageURI = self.location;

var pageTitle = document.title;

document.writeln('The location of the page
→ titled <i><a href="' + pageURI + '">' +
→ pageTitle + '</a></i> is: <br>');
document.writeln(pageURI);
    </script>
</body>
</html>
```

URI or URL?

Notice that I call the variable that stores the page's location **pageURI** instead of **pageURL**. *URL* stands for *Universal Resource Locator*, whereas *URI* stands for *Universal Resource Identifier*. What's the difference? Not much, really, but for some reason the World Wide Web Consortium (W3C) decided that the more commonly used URL was too specific a term and decided to switch to URI instead.

Does this really change your life? No.

Should you start using URI instead of URL when referring to a Web page's address? Only if you want to confuse your friends and impress your enemies.

Finding the Page's Location and Title

The URL (Universal Resource Locator) of a Web page is its unique address on the Web. The title is the designation you give that page between the <title> tags in the head of your document. You can easily display these two useful bits of information on a Web page (**Figure 12.15**).

To find the page's location and title:

1. var pageURI = self.location;

   Add the variable **pageURI** to your JavaScript, and assign to it the value self.location. This value is the address of your Web page (**Code 12.7**).

2. var pageTitle = document.title;

   Add the variable **pageTitle** to your JavaScript, and assign to it the value document.title. This value is the title of your document—that is, whatever you place between the <title> and </title> tags on the page.

You can now use these variables for a variety of purposes. The simplest is to write them out on the page, as this example does. In addition, I used the page's location to set up the title as a link back to this page.

✔ Tip

■ Netscape 4 for the Mac has trouble finding the actual title of the page. Instead of the title, it returns the filename or the DOM for the layer in which the code appears.

Finding the Page's Scroll Position

CSS positioning works on the basis of offsetting an object from the top and left corners of the page when it loads. If the page scrolls down, however, the origin (top-left corner) scrolls along with it. Fortunately, you can ask the browser how far down or over it has scrolled (**Figure 12.16**).

To find the page's scroll position:

1. function findScrollLeft() {...}

   Add the function findScrollLeft() to your JavaScript. This function uses feature sensing to determine which method the current browser uses to find the scroll-left position. Netscape uses window.pageXOffset, and Internet Explorer uses document.body. scrollLeft (**Code 12.8**).

Figure 12.16 An alert appears to tell you how the page has been scrolled, in pixels.

Code 12.8 The functions findScrollLeft() and FindScrollTop() determine the scroll position of the page. You can employ these functions in your Web page in a variety of ways. You can display the result of running the functions directly (as shown in this example) or assign the values to variables that you can use and change.

```
<html>
<head>
   <script>
function findScrollLeft() {
   if (window.pageXOffset != null)
       return window.pageXOffset;
   if (document.body.scrollHeight != null)
       return document.body.scrollLeft;
   return (null);
}

function findScrollTop() {
   if (window.pageYOffset != null)
       return window.pageYOffset;
   if (document.body.scrollWidth != null)
       return document.body.scrollTop;
   return (null);
}
```

(code continues on next page)

Code 12.8 *continued*

```
                    code
    </script>
</head>
<body>
    Scoll the window and then click the image
  → to find your current scroll
  → position.<br>
    <a href="javascript:alert ('Scrolled
  → From Top: ' + findScrollTop() + 'px;
  → Scrolled From Left: ' + findScrollLeft()
  → + 'px');">
        <img src="alice16.gif" width="640"
        → height="477" border="0">
    </a>
</body>
</html>
```

2. function findScrollTop() {...}

Add the function findScrollTop() to your JavaScript. This function uses feature sensing to determine which method the current browser uses to find the scroll-top position. Netscape uses window.pageYOffset, and Internet Explorer uses document.body. scrollTop.

✔ Tip

■ Netscape 4 (Windows) and Netscape 6 (all OSes) do something very silly when a frame's scrolling is set to no. They not only make the scrollbars disappear, but they also prevent the frame from scrolling at all—even when using the JavaScript code presented here.

Finding an Object's Dimensions

All the information gained about the environment so far in this chapter was derived from asking the browser questions, such as its type and screen size. The rest of this chapter deals with information gained by asking objects in the browser window about themselves. Finding an object's dimensions, position, visibility, and 3-D position requires the use of the cross-browser DOM.

All objects have a width and height that determine their dimensions (see "Understanding the Element's Box" in Chapter 7). Knowing the dimensions of an object (**Figure 12.17**) helps you move and position the object so that it does not go off the screen on the right or bottom, especially when you create scroll bars (see "Creating Your Own Scroll Bars" in Chapter 25).

To find the width and height of an object:

1. `<script src="findDOM.js"></script>`

   In any JavaScript function that addresses an object on the screen directly, you need to include the findDOM code. You do so by including it in an external text file and then importing that file into the page in which it will be used (see "Using the Cross-Browser DOM" in Chapter 11 and **Code 12.9**).

2. `function findWidth(objectID) {...}`

   Add the function findWidth() to your JavaScript. This function uses the ID for the object to be addressed—passed to it as the variable `objectID`—to build the DOM (see "Building a Cross-Browser DOM" in Chapter 11). It then uses feature sensing to determine which method the browser uses to find the height of the object. Internet Explorer 4/5

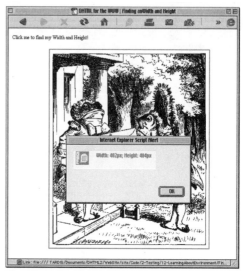

Figure 12.17 An alert appears to tell you the dimensions of the object—in this case, the object that has the image in it.

Code 12.9 The functions findWidth() and FindHeight() determine the dimensions of an individual object on the page. You can employ these functions in your Web page in a variety of ways. You can display the result of running the functions directly (as shown in this example) or assign the values to variables that you can use and change.

```
<html>
<head>
    <script src="findDOM.js"></script>
    <script>
function findWidth(objectID) {
    var dom = findDOM(objectID,0);
    if (dom.offsetWidth)
        return dom.offsetWidth;
    if (dom.clip.width)
        return dom.clip.width;
    return (null);
}

function findHeight(objectID) {
    var dom = findDOM(objectID,0);
    if (dom.offsetHeight)
```

(code continues on next page)

Code 12.9 *continued*

```
          return dom.offsetHeight;
      if (dom.clip.height)
          return dom.clip.height;
      return (null);
}
      </script>
      <style type="text/css">
#object1    {
      position: absolute;
      top: 50px;
      width: 402px;
      left: 100px;
      border: 2px gray solid;
      visibility: visible }
      </style>
</head>
<body>
      <script>
function showDim(objectID) {
      widthObj = findWidth(objectID);
      heightObj = findHeight(objectID);
      alert('Width: ' + widthObj + 'px;
      → Height: ' + heightObj + 'px' );
}
      </script>
      Click me to find my Width and
Height!<br><br>
      <div id="object1">
          <a href="#" onClick="showDim
          → ('object1')">
              <img src="alice20.gif"
              → width="398" height="480"
              → border="0">
          </a>
      </div>
</body>
</html>
```

and Netscape 6 use `offsetWidth`, and Netscape 4 uses `clip.width`.

3. `function findHeight(objectID) {...}`
   Add the function `findHeight()` to your JavaScript. This function uses the ID for the object to be addressed—passed to it as the variable `objectID`—to build the DOM. It then uses feature sensing to determine which method the browser uses to find the height of the object. Internet Explorer 4/5 and Netscape 6 use `offsetHeight`, and Netscape 4 uses `clip.height`.

4. `#object1 {...}`
   Set up the IDs for your object(s) with position, left, and top values.

5. `function showDim(objectID) {...]`
   Add a JavaScript function that uses the functions you created in steps 2 and 3. In this example, `showDim()` simply assigns the values returned by `findWidth()` and `findHeight()` to variables and then displays the values in an alert.

6. `onClick="showDim('object1')"`
   Add an event handler to trigger the function you created in step 5, and pass to it the ID of the object you want to address.

✔ Tip

■ If you test this code on several browsers, you will notice that the same object comes up with slightly different width and height values. This difference occurs because some browsers (such as Internet Explorer) include the border with the width and height, and others (such as Netscape 4) do not.

Finding an Object's Top and Left Positions

One major use of DHTML is to make objects move around on the page (see "Moving Objects from Point to Point" in Chapter 13). Often, though, to make something move, you need to know where it is currently located (**Figure 12.18**).

You can use CSS to set the top and left positions of positioned elements (see "Setting the Position from the Top and Left" in Chapter 8). Then you can use JavaScript to determine those positions (**Code 12.10**).

To find the top and left positions of an object:

1. `<script src="findDOM.js"></script>`

   In any JavaScript function that addresses an object on the screen directly, you need to include the findDOM code. You do so by including it in an external text file and then importing that file into the page in which it will be used (see "Using the Cross-Browser DOM" in Chapter 11).

2. `function findLeft(objectID) {...}`

   Add the function findLeft() to your JavaScript. This function uses the ID for the object to be addressed—passed to it as the variable objectID—to build the DOM (see "Building a Cross-Browser DOM" in Chapter 11). It uses feature sensing to determine which method the browser uses to find the left position of the object. Then the function returns that value. Internet Explorer 4/5 uses pixelLeft, Netscape 6 uses offsetLeft, and Netscape 4 uses left.

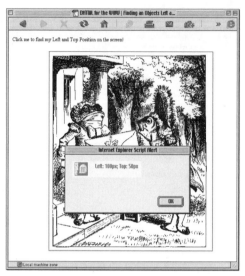

Figure 12.18 An alert appears to tell you the top and left positions of the object.

Code 12.10 The functions findLeft() and findTop() determine the position of an individual object on the page. You can employ these functions in your Web page in a variety of ways. You can display the result of running the functions directly (as shown in this example) or assign the values to variables that you can use and change.

```
                        code
<html>
    <script src="findDOM.js"></script>
    <script>
function findLeft(objectID) {
    var domStyle = findDOM(objectID,1);
    var dom = findDOM(objectID,0);
    if (domStyle.left)
        return domStyle.left;
    if (domStyle.pixelLeft)
        return domStyle.pixelLeft;
    if (dom.offsetLeft)
        return dom.offsetLeft;
    return (null);
}


function findTop(objectID) {
    var domStyle = findDOM(objectID,1);

                        (code continues on next page)
```

Code 12.10 *continued*

```
                   code
   var dom = findDOM(objectID,0);
   if (domStyle.top)
       return domStyle.top;
   if (domStyle.pixelTop)
       return domStyle.pixelTop;
   if (dom.offsetTop)
       return dom.offsetTop;
   return (null);
}
   </script>
   <style type="text/css">
#object1  {
   position: absolute;
   left: 100px;
   top: 50px;
   width: 410px;
   border: 2px gray solid;
   visibility: visible; }
</style>
</head>
<body>
   <script>
function showPos(objectID) {
   leftPos = findLeft(objectID);
   topPos = findTop(objectID);
   alert('Left: ' + leftPos + 'px;
→ Top: ' + topPos + 'px' );
}
   </script>
   Click me to find my Left and Top Position
→ on the screen!<br><br>
   <div id="object1">
       <a href="#" onClick="showPos
→ ('object1')">
           <img src="alice20.gif"
→ width="398" height="480"
→ border="0">
       </a>
   </div>
</body>
</html>
```

3. `function findTop(objectID) {...}`

   Add the function findTop() to your JavaScript. This function uses the ID for the object to be addressed—passed to it as the variable `objectID`—to build the DOM (see "Building a Cross-Browser DOM" in Chapter 11). It uses feature sensing to determine which method the browser uses to find the top position of the object. Then the function returns that value. Internet Explorer 4/5 uses `pixelTop`, Netscape 6 uses `offsetTop`, and Netscape 4 uses `top`.

4. `#object1 {...}`

   Set up the IDs for your object(s) with position, left, and top values.

5. `function showPos(objectID) {...]`

   Create a JavaScript function that uses the functions you created in steps 2 and 3. In this example, showPos() simply assigns the values returned by findLeft() and findTop() to variables and then displays the values in an alert.

6. `onClick="showPos('object1')"`

   Add an event handler to trigger the function you created in step 5, and pass to it the ID of the object you want to address.

✔ **Tip**

■ You may notice a slight disparity between the position found for the object in Internet Explorer and Netscape 4 and the one found in Netscape 6. Netscape 6 measures the position from inside the object's border; the other browsers measure from outside the border.

Finding an Object's Bottom and Right Positions

Like the top and bottom positions, the bottom and right positions can be determined with JavaScript (**Figure 12.19**). You do not do this directly, however. You find the left or top position of the object and the width or height of the object and add these values (**Code 12.11**).

To find the bottom and right positions of an object:

1. `<script src="findDOM.js"></script>`

   In any JavaScript function that addresses an object on the screen directly, you need to include the findDOM code. You do so by including it in an external text file and then importing that file into the page in which it will be used (see "Using the Cross-Browser DOM" in Chapter 11).

2. `function findRight(objectID) {...}`

   Add the function findRight() to your JavaScript. This function uses the ID for the object to be addressed—passed to it as the variable `objectID`—to build the DOM (see "Building a Cross-Browser DOM" in Chapter 11). It uses feature sensing to determine which method the browser uses to find the left position and width of the object. Then the function returns these values added together (see "Finding an Object's Dimensions" and "Finding an Object's Top and Left Position" earlier in this chapter).

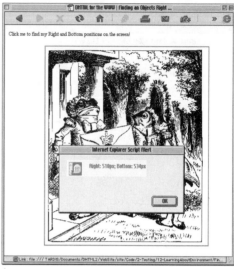

Figure 12.19 An alert pops up to tell you the bottom and right positions of the object.

Code 12.11 The functions findRight() and findBottom() are used to determine the position of an individual object. You can employ these functions in your Web page in a variety of ways. You can display the result of running the functions directly (as shown in this example) or assign the values to variables that you can use and change.

```
<html>
<head>
    <script src="findDOM.js"></script>
    <script>
function findRight(objectID) {
    var domStyle = findDOM(objectID,1);
    var dom = findDOM(objectID,0);
    if (dom.left)
        return (domStyle.left +
        → domStyle.clip.width);
    if (domStyle.pixelLeft)
        return (domStyle.pixelLeft +
        → dom.offsetWidth);
    if (dom.offsetLeft)
        return (dom.offsetLeft +
        → dom.offsetWidth);
    return (null);
}
```

(code continues on next page)

Code 12.11 *continued*

```
                    code
function findBottom(objectID) {
    var domStyle = findDOM(objectID,1);
    var dom = findDOM(objectID,0);
    if (domStyle.top)
        return (domStyle.top +
        → domStyle.clip.height);
    if (domStyle.pixelTop)
        return (domStyle.pixelTop +
        → dom.offsetHeight);
    if (dom.offsetTop)
        return (dom.offsetTop +
        → dom.offsetHeight);
    return (null);
}
    </script>
    <style type="text/css">
#object1 {
    position: absolute;
    left: 100px;
    top: 50px;
    width: 410px;
    border: 2px gray solid;
    visibility: visible; }
    </style>
</head>
<body>
    <script>
function showPos(objectID) {
    rightPos = findRight(objectID);
    bottomPos = findBottom(objectID);
    alert('Right: ' + rightPos + 'px;
    → Bottom: ' + bottomPos + 'px' );
}
    </script>
    Click me to find my Right and Bottom
    → positions on the screen!<br><br>
    <div id="object1">
        <a href="#"
onClick="showPos('object1')">
            <img src="alice20.gif"
            → width="398" height="480"
            → border="0"></a>
    </div>
</body>
</html>
```

3. `function findBottom(objectID) {...}`

Add the function findBottom() to your JavaScript. This function uses the ID for the object to be addressed—passed to it as the variable objectID—to build the DOM. It uses feature sensing to determine which method the browser uses to find the top position and height of the object. Then the function returns these values added together.

4. `#object1 {...}`

Set up the IDs for your object(s) with position, left, and top values.

5. `function showPos(objectID) {...]`

Create a JavaScript function that uses the functions you created in steps 2 and 3. In this example, showPos() simply assigns the values returned by findRight() and finBottom() to variables and then displays the values in an alert.

6. `onClick="showPos('object1')"`

Add an event handler to trigger the function you created in step 5, and pass to it the ID of the object you want to address.

✔ Tip

■ You may notice a slight disparity between the position found for the object in Internet Explorer and Netscape 4 and the one found in Netscape 6. Netscape 6 measures the position from inside the object's border; the other browsers measure from outside the border.

Finding an Object's 3-D Position

The CSS attribute z-index allows you to stack positioned elements in 3-D (see "Stacking Objects" in Chapter 8). Using JavaScript, you can determine the z-index of individual objects on the screen (**Figure 12.20**).

But there is a catch: Internet Explorer 4/5 and Netscape 6 can't see the z-index until it is set dynamically. To get around this little problem, you have to use JavaScript to set the z-index of each object when the page first loads (**Code 12.12**).

To find the z-index of an object:

1. `<script src="findDOM.js"></script>`

   In any JavaScript function that addresses an object on the screen directly, you need to include the findDOM code. You do so by including it in an external text file and then importing that file into the page in which it will be used (see "Using the Cross-Browser DOM" in Chapter 11).

2. `function setLayer(objectID,layerNum)` → `{...}`

   Add the `setLayer()` function to your JavaScript. This function sets the initial z-index of objects when the page first loads, to overcome the limitations of Internet Explorer 4/5 and Netscape 6.

3. `function findLayer(objectID) {...}`

   Add the function `findLayer()` to your JavaScript. This function uses the ID for the object to be addressed—passed to it as the variable `objectID`—to build the DOM (see "Building a Cross-Browser DOM" in Chapter 11). The function then uses this ID to access the z-index property and returns that value.

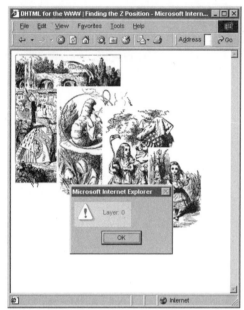

Figure 12.20 An alert appears to tell you the layer number of the object clicked.

Code 12.12 The function `findLayer()` determines the z-index of an individual object on the page.

```
<html>
<head>
    <script src="findDOM.js"></script>
    <script>
function setLayer(objectID,layerNum) {
    var domStyle = findDOM(objectID,1);
    domStyle.zIndex = layerNum;
}
function findLayer(objectID) {
    var domStyle = findDOM(objectID,1);
    if (domStyle.zIndex != null)
        return domStyle.zIndex;
    return (null);
}
    </script>
    <style type="text/css">
        #object1 { position: absolute;
        → z-index: 3; top: 175px; left: 255px }
        #object2 { position: absolute;
        → z-index: 2; top: 100px; left: 170px }
```

(code continues on next page)

Code 12.12 *continued*

```
          #object3 { position: absolute;
          → z-index: 1; top: 65px; left: 85px }
          #object4 { position: absolute;
          → z-index: 0; top: 5px; left: 5px }
     </style>
</head>
<body onLoad="setLayer('object1',3);
→ setLayer('object2',2);
→ setLayer('object3',1);
→ setLayer('object4',0);">
     <script>
function whichLayer(objectID) {
     layerNum = findLayer(objectID);
     alert('Layer: ' + layerNum );
}
     </script>
     <div id="object1">
          <a href="#" onCLick="whichLayer
          → ('object1')">
               <img src="alice22.gif"
               → width="100" height="147"
               → border="0"></a><br clear="all">
     </div>
     <div id="object2">
          <a href="#" onCLick="whichLayer
          → ('object2')">
               <img src="alice32.gif"
               → width="140" height="201"
               → border="0"></a><br clear="all">
     </div>
     <div id="object3">
          <a href="#" onCLick="whichLayer
          → ('object3')">
               <img src="alice15.gif"
               → width="150" height="198"
               → border="0"></a><br clear="all">
     </div>
     <div id="object4">
          <a href="#" onCLick="whichLayer
          → ('object4')">
               <img src="alice29.gif"
               → width="200" height="236"
               → border="0"></a><br clear="all">
     </div>
</body>
</html>
```

4. #object1 {...}

Set up the IDs for your objects with a position type and z-index.

5. onLoad="..."

In the <body> tag, use the setLayer() function to initialize the z-index of all the objects for which you need to know the initial z-index.

6. function whichLayer(objectID) {...]

Create a JavaScript function that uses the functions you created in steps 2 and 3. In this example, whichLayer() simply assigns the values returned by findLayer() and then displays those values in an alert.

7. onClick="whichLayer('object1')"

Add an event handler to trigger the function you created in step 6, and pass to it the ID of the object you want to address.

FINDING AN OBJECT'S 3-D POSITION

Finding an Object's Visibility State

All objects that have a position set also have a visibility state: `hidden` or `visible` (see "Setting the Visibility of an Element" in Chapter 9). This state defaults to visible (**Figure 12.21**), but you can use JavaScript to change that state (see "Making Objects Appear and Disappear" in Chapter 13).

Unfortunately, Netscape 6 and Internet Explorer 4/5 cannot access the visibility state that is initially set in the CSS; they are aware of the state only after it has been set dynamically (**Code 12.13**).

To find the visibility of an object:

1. `<script src="findDOM.js"></script>`

   In any JavaScript function that addresses an object on the screen directly, you need to include the findDOM code. You do so by including it in an external text file and then importing that file into the page in which it will be used (see "Using the Cross-Browser DOM" in Chapter 11).

2. `function setVisibility(objectID, → state) {...}`

   Add the `setVisibility()` function to your JavaScript. This function sets the initial visibility of objects when the page first loads, to overcome the limitations of Internet Explorer 4/5 and Netscape 6.

Figure 12.21 The Cheshire Cat is visible, but for how long?

Code 12.13 The function findVisibility() determines the current visibility state of an individual object in the window. This state is either visible or hidden.

```
<html>
<head>
    <script src="findDOM.js"></script>
    <script>
function setVisibility(objectID, state) {
    var dom = findDOM(objectID,1);
    dom.visibility = state;
}
function findVisibility(objectID) {
    var dom = findDOM(objectID,1);
    if ((dom.visibility == 'show') ||
 →  (dom.visibility == 'visible'))
        { return 'visible'; }
    return 'hidden';
}
    </script>
    <style type="text/css">
#object1   {
    position: relative;
    top: 5px;
    left: 5px;
    width: 640px;
    visibility: visible; }
    </style>
```

(code continues on next page)

Code 12.13 *continued*

```
                       code
</head>
<body
onLoad="setVisibility('object1','visible')">
    <script>
function showVisibility(objectID) {
    var thisVis = findVisibility(objectID);
    alert('Visibility Status: ' + thisVis );
}
    </script>
        <br><br>
    <a href="#" onClick="showVisibility
→ ('object1')">
    Where is the Cheshire Cat?
    </a>
    <div id="object1">
        <img src="alice24.gif" width="640"
→ height="435" border="0">
    </div>
</body>
</html>
```

3. `function findVisibility(objectID)`
   `→ {...}`

   Add the function findVisibility() to your JavaScript. This function uses the ID for the object to be addressed—passed to it as the variable objectID—to build the DOM (see "Building a Cross-Browser DOM" in Chapter 11). It then uses this ID to access the current visibility property set for the object. Based on that value, the function returns either visible or hidden.

4. `#object1 {...}`

   Set up the IDs for your objects with a position, type, and visibility.

5. `onLoad="..."`

   In the <body> tag, use the setVisibility() function to initialize the visibility of all the objects for which you need to know the initial visibility.

6. `function showVisibility(objectID)`
   `→ {...]`

   Create a JavaScript function that uses the function you created in step 3. In this example, showVisibility() simply assigns the values returned by findVisibility() and then displays those values in an alert.

7. `onClick="showVisibility('object1')"`

   Add an event handler to trigger the function you created in step 6, and pass to it the ID of the object you want to address.

✔ Tip

■ Although Netscape 4 can understand the visibility property if it is assigned to visible, it actually stores this value as show, which is the Netscape-layers equivalent. Thus, when detecting the visibility state of an object, you also have to look for show to be compatible across browsers.

Finding an Object's Visible Area

The width and height of an object tell you the maximum area of the element (see "Finding an Object's Dimensions" earlier in this chapter). When an object is clipped (see "Setting the Visible Area of an Element" in Chapter 9), the maximum area is cut down, and you can view only part of the total visible area. Using JavaScript, you can not only find the width and height of the visible area, but also the top, left, bottom, and right borders of the clipping region (**Figure 12.22**).

Like several other CSS visibility properties, however, Netscape 6 and Internet Explorer have a problem reading the clipping values until they have been set dynamically. You will use a relatively easy workaround for this problem when I show you how to change the clipping area (see "Changing an Object's Visible Area" in Chapter 13 and **Code 12.14**).

To find the visible area and borders of an object:

1. `<script src="findDOM.js"></script>`

In any JavaScript function that addresses an object on the screen directly, you need to include the findDOM code. You do so by including it in an external text file and then importing that file into the page in which it will be used (see "Using the Cross-Browser DOM" in Chapter 11).

2. `function setClip(objectID,state)`
`→ {...}`

Add the `setClip()` function to your JavaScript. This function sets the initial clip region of objects when the page first loads, to overcome the limitations of Internet Explorer 4/5 and Netscape 6.

Figure 12.22 An alert appears to tell us the location of the top border of the clip region.

Code 12.14 The functions findClipTop(), findClipRight(), findClipBottom(), findClipLeft(), findClipWidth(), and findClipHeight()find the clip region and borders of an individual object in the window.

```
<html>
<head>
    <script src="findDOM.js"></script>
    <script>
function setClip(objectID, clipTop,
→ clipRight, clipBottom, clipLeft) {
    var dom = findDOM(objectID,1);
    if (dom.clip.left) {
        dom.clip.top = clipTop;
        dom.clip.right = clipRight;
        dom.clip.bottom = clipBottom;
        dom.clip.left = clipLeft;
    }
    dom.clip = 'rect(' + clipTop + ' ' +
    → clipRight + ' ' + clipBottom + ' ' +
    → clipLeft +')';
}
function findClipTop(objectID) {
    var dom = findDOM(objectID,1);
    if (dom.clip.top)
        return dom.clip.top;
```

(code continues on next page)

Code **12.14** *continued*

```
                    code
    if (dom.clip !=null) {
        var clip = findClipArray(dom.clip);
        return (clip[0]) ;
    }
    return (null);
}


function findClipRight(objectID) {
    var dom = findDOM(objectID,1);
    if (dom.clip.right)
        return dom.clip.right;
    if (dom.clip !=null) {
        var clip = findClipArray(dom.clip);
        return (clip[1]);
    }
    return (null);
}
function findClipBottom(objectID) {
    var dom = findDOM(objectID,1);
    if (dom.clip.bottom)
        return dom.clip.bottom;
    if (dom.clip !=null) {
        var clip = findClipArray(dom.clip);
        return (clip[2]) ;
    }
    return (null);
}
function findClipLeft(objectID) {
    var dom = findDOM(objectID,1);
    if (dom.clip.left)
        return dom.clip.left;
    if (dom.clip !=null) {
        var clip = findClipArray(dom.clip);
        return (clip[3]) ;
                        }
    return (null);
}
function findClipWidth(objectID) {
    var dom = findDOM(objectID,1);
    if (dom.clip.width)
        return dom.clip.width;
    if (dom.clip !=null) {
```

(code continues on next page)

3. `function findClipArray(str) {...}`

Add the findClipArray() function to your JavaScript. This function is used by Internet Explorer, which stores the clipping dimensions as characters rather than numbers. This function translates this string of characters into an array of numbers, with each number in the array corresponding to a clip dimension.

4. `function findClipTop(objectID) {...}`

Add these functions:

findClipTop()

findClipRight()

findClipBottom()

findClipLeft()

All these functions do the same things on different sides of the object. The functions use the ID for the object to be addressed—passed to it as the variable `objectID`—to build the DOM (see "Building a Cross-Browser DOM" in Chapter 11). The functions then use the DOM to capture the clip borders, using `clip.top`, `clip.left`, `clip.bottom`, and `clip.right` for Netscape. Alternatively, the functions use findClipArray() to determine the clip array and then access that array by using 0, 1, 2, 3 for top, left, bottom, and right, respectively.

5. `function findClipWidth(objectID) {...}`

Add the functions findClipWidth() and findClipHeight() to your JavaScript. These functions use the ID for the object to be addressed—passed to it as the variable `objectID`—to build the DOM (see "Building a Cross-Browser DOM" in Chapter 11). The functions then use the DOM to capture the visible area's height and width through `clip.width` and `clip.height` for Netscape or by subtracting the clip-array values for Internet Explorer (see step 4).

continues on next page

6. #object1 {...}

Set up the IDs for your objects with a position, type, and visibility.

7. onLoad="..."

In the <body> tag, use the setClip() function to initialize the clip area of all the object(s).

8. onClick="alert(...)"

Trigger the functions in steps 4 and 5 from an event handler.

Code 12.14 *continued*

```
            var clip = findClipArray(dom.clip);
            return (clip[1] - clip[3]) ;
      }
      return (null);
}
function findClipHeight(objectID) {
      var dom = findDOM(objectID,1);
      if (dom.clip.height)
            return dom.clip.height;
      if (dom.clip !=null) {
            var clip = findClipArray(dom.clip);
            return (clip[2] - clip[0]) ;
      }
      return (null);
}
function findClipArray(clipStr) {
      var clip = new Array();
      var i;
      i = clipStr.indexOf('(');
      clip[0] = parseInt(clipStr.substring(i + 1, clipStr.length), 10);
      i = clipStr.indexOf(' ', i + 1);
      clip[1] = parseInt(clipStr.substring(i + 1, clipStr.length), 10);
      i = clipStr.indexOf(' ', i + 1);
      clip[2] = parseInt(clipStr.substring(i + 1 , clipStr.length), 10);
      i = clipStr.indexOf(' ', i + 1);
      clip[3] = parseInt(clipStr.substring(i + 1, clipStr.length), 10);
      return clip;
}
      </script>
```

(code continues on next page)

Code 12.14 *continued*

```
    <style type="text/css">
#object1    {
   position: absolute;
   top: 60px;
   left: 0px;
   overflow: hidden;
   clip: rect(15 350 195 50); }
        </style>
</head>
<body onLoad="setClip('object1',15,350,195,50)">
   <br><br>Clip Dimensions ||
   <a href="#" onClick="alert('Clip on Top: ' + findClipTop('object1') + 'px')">
       Top</a> |
   <a href="#" onClick="alert('Clip on Left: ' + findClipLeft('object1') + 'px')">
       Left</a> |
   <a href="#" onClick="alert('Clip on Bottom: ' + findClipBottom('object1') + 'px')">
       Bottom</a> |
   <a href="#" onClick="alert('Clip on Right: ' + findClipRight('object1') + 'px')">
       Right</a> ||
   <a href="#" onClick="alert('Clip Width: ' + findClipWidth('object1') + 'px')">
       Width</a> |
   <a href="#" onClick="alert('Clip Height: ' + findClipHeight('object1') + 'px')">
       Height
   </a>
   <div id="object1">
       <img src="alice31.gif" width="379" height="480" border="0">
   </div>
</body>
</html>
```

DYNAMIC TECHNIQUES: THE BASICS

Almost all of DHTML is based on a few basic tricks that allow you to hide and show objects, move them around, and make other changes. For the most part, these techniques are based on the ability to change the CSS positioning properties, which are the only common cross-browser CSS properties that can be changed. Netscape 4 does not allow you to address any other CSS properties.

So although Netscape 6 and Internet Explorer 4 allow you to change *any* CSS property (see Chapter 15), Netscape 4 limits cross-browser DHTML. The good news is that with the release of Netscape 6, Netscape 4 may soon be a distant memory.

Making Objects Appear and Disappear

The visibility property allows you to tell an object whether to appear (visible) or not (hidden) on the screen (see "Setting the Visibility of an Element" in Chapter 9). Using JavaScript, you can not only determine the current visibility state (see "Finding an Object's Visibility State" in Chapter 12), but also change the state back and forth (**Code 13.1** and **Figures 13.1** and **13.2**).

To change the visibility state of an object:

1. `<script src="findDOM.js"></script>`

   In any JavaScript function that addresses an object on the screen directly, you need to include the findDOM code. You do so by including it in an external text file and then importing that file into the page in which it will be used (see "Using the Cross-Browser DOM" in Chapter 11).

2. `function setVisibility(objectID,` → `state) {...}`

   Add the function `setVisibility()` to your JavaScript. This function uses the ID for the object to be addressed—passed to it as the variable `objectID`—to build the DOM (see "Building a Cross-Browser DOM" in Chapter 11). It then uses this ID to access the current visibility property set for the object and change it to whatever state you specify when you trigger it from an event handler (see step 6).

3. `function toggleVisibility(objectID)` → `{...}`

   Add the function `toggleVisibility()` to your JavaScript. This function uses the ID for the object to be addressed—passed to it as the variable `objectID`—to build the DOM. It then checks the current visibility state of the object and switches to its opposite.

Code 13.1 The setVisibility() and toggleVisibility() functions change the visibility state of a particular object in the browser window.

```
<html>
<head>
   <script src="findDOM.js"></script>
   <script>
function setVisibility(objectID,state) {
   var dom = findDOM(objectID,1);
   dom.visibility = state;
}


function toggleVisibility(objectID) {
   var dom = findDOM(objectID,1);
   state = dom.visibility;
   if (state == 'hidden' || state == 'hide' )
      dom.visibility = 'visible';
   else {
      if (state == 'visible' ||
      → state=='show')
         dom.visibility = 'hidden';
   else dom.visibility = 'visible';
   }
}
   </script>
   <style type="text/css">
#cheshireCat {
   position: absolute;
   top: 70px;
   left: 0px;
   visibility: visible;
}
   </style>
</head>
<body onLoad="setVisibility('cheshireCat',
→ 'visible');">
   <a href="javascript:void('')" onClick=
   → "setVisibility('cheshireCat',
   → 'hidden');">
      Hide The Cat</a>  |
   <a href="javascript:void('')" onClick=
   "setVisibility('cheshireCat',
   → 'visible');">
      Show the Cat</a>  |
```

(code continues on next page)

Code 13.1 *continued*

```
                    code
    <a href="javascript:void('')
    → "onClick="toggleVisibility
    → ('cheshireCat');">
        Change the Cat's Visibility</a>
    <div id="cheshireCat">
        <img src="alice24.gif" width="640"
        → height="435" border="0">
    </div>
</body>
</html>
```

Figure 13.1 Before the link is clicked, the cat is visible.

Figure 13.2 After the link is clicked, the Cheshire Cat does its vanishing act.

4. `#cheshireCat {...}`

Set up the IDs for your object(s) with a position, type, and visibility.

5. `onLoad="..."`

In the `<body>` tag, use the `setVisibility()` function to initialize the visibility of all the objects for which you need to know the initial visibility. For the `toggleVisibility()` function to work properly, the initial visibility has to be set.

6. `onClick="setVisibility('object1')"`

Add event handlers to trigger the functions you created in step 2, and pass to them the ID for the object you want to address.

7. `onClick="setVisibility('cheshireCat',`
`→ 'hidden');"`

Add event handlers to trigger the functions you created in step 2, and pass to them the ID for the object you want to address, as well as the visibility state you want it to have.

8. `<div id="cheshireCat">...</div>`

Set up your CSS layer(s).

✔ Tips

■ Notice that we not only check to see if the visibility state is set to `hidden` or `visible`, but also whether it is set to `hide` or `show`. Although Netscape 4 can accept the standard `hidden` and `visible` as input, it actually records these values as `hide` and `show`, and that's what it would output.

■ The ability to set the visibility of an object will be crucial to creating drop-down menus (Chapter 24), creating a slide show (Chapter 25), and fading HTML text (Chapter 26).

MAKING OBJECTS APPEAR AND DISAPPEAR

235

Moving Objects from Point to Point

Using CSS, you can position an object on the screen (see "Setting the Position from the Top and Left" in Chapter 8); then you can use JavaScript to find the object's position (see "Finding an Object's Top and Left Positions" in Chapter 12). But to make things really dynamic, you need to be able to move things around on the screen by changing the values for the object's position (**Code 13.2** and **Figure 13.3**).

To change the position of an object:

1. `<script src="findDOM.js"></script>`

   In any JavaScript function that addresses an object on the screen directly, you need to include the findDOM code. You do so by including it in an external text file and then importing that file into the page in which it will be used (see "Using the Cross-Browser DOM" in Chapter 11).

2. `function moveObjectTo(objectID,x,y)` → `{...}`

   Add the function moveObjectTo() to your JavaScript. This function uses the ID for the object to be addressed—passed to it as the variable objectID—to build the DOM (see "Building a Cross-Browser DOM" in Chapter 11). It then uses the x and y values to reset the left and top positions of the object.

3. `#madHatter {...}`

   Set up the IDs for your object(s) with a position, type, and top and left coordinates.

Code 13.2 The moveObjectTo() function changes the position of a particular object in the browser window.

```
code

<html>
<head>
   <script src="findDOM.js"></script>
   <script>
function moveObjectTo(objectID,x,y) {
var domStyle = findDOM(objectID,1);
→ domStyle.left = x; domStyle.top = y;
}
   </script>
   <style type="text/css">
#madHatter    {
      position: absolute;
      top: 30px;
      left: 30px; }
   </style>
</head>
<body>
   <a href="javascript:void('')"
→ onMouseOver="moveObjectTo('madHatter',
→ 200,200);"
   onMouseOut="moveObjectTo('madHatter',
→ 30,30);">I want a fresh cup...</a>
   <div id="madHatter">
       <img src="alice39.gif" width="200"
→ height="163" border="0">
   </div>
</body>
</html>
```

Figure 13.3 The Mad Hatter is dashing for a fresh cup of tea.

4. onMouseOver="moveObjectTo
→ ('madHatter',200,200);"

Add an event handler to trigger the function you created in step 2, and pass to it the ID for the object you want to address and the new coordinates for the object.

5. <div id="madHatter">...</div>

Set up your CSS layer(s).

✔ Tips

- Notice that to simply set the top and left positions, we use top and left. To find the value of these positions, however, each browser has its own keyword. Netscape 4 uses top and left, but Netscape 6 uses offsetLeft and offsetTop, while Internet Explorer 4/5 use pixelTop and pixelLeft. You can actually set the top and left values using these keywords as well, but it's easier to stick with the simple left and top.

- Moving objects will be the cornerstone of the DHTML in Part IV of this book, when I show you how to create a sliding menu (Chapter 24), your own scroll bars (Chapter 25), and floating objects (Chapter 26).

Moving Objects By a Certain Amount

Moving an object from one precise point to another is great, but you have to know exactly where you want to move the object. Often, though, you simply want the object to move by a certain amount from its current location (**Code 13.3** and **Figure 13.4**).

To change the position of an object by a certain amount:

1. `<script src="findDOM.js"></script>`

   In any JavaScript function that addresses an object on the screen directly, you need to include the findDOM code. You do so by including it in an external text file and then importing that file into the page in which it will be used (see "Using the Cross-Browser DOM" in Chapter 11).

2. `function moveObjectBy(objectID,`
   `→ deltaX,deltaY) {...}`

   Add the function moveObjectBy() to your JavaScript. This function uses the ID for the object to be addressed—passed to it as the variable objectID—to build the DOM (see "Building a Cross-Browser DOM" in Chapter 11). It then uses the deltaX and deltaY values to reset the left and top positions of the object by those amounts. For Internet Explorer 4/5 it sets the pixelTop and pixelLeft values. For Netscape 6, the top and left positions are set but have to be added to the object's current position. Netscape 4, rather than setting the positions directly, uses a built-in function called moveBy().

3. `#madHatter {...}`

   Set up the IDs for your object(s) with a position, type, and top and left coordinates.

Code 13.3 The moveObjectBy() function changes the position of a particular object in the browser window by a certain amount every time the mouse pointer rolls onto and then off the link.

```
<html>
<head>
    <script src="findDOM.js"></script>
    <script>
function moveObjectBy(objectID,deltaX,
→ deltaY) {
    var domStyle = findDOM(objectID,1);
    var dom = findDOM(objectID,0);
    if (domStyle.pixelLeft) {
        domStyle.pixelLeft += deltaX;
        domStyle.pixelTop += deltaY;
    }
    else {
        if (dom.offsetLeft != null) {
            var plusLeft = dom.offsetLeft;
            var plusTop = dom.offsetTop;
            domStyle.left = deltaX +
            → plusLeft;
            domStyle.top = deltaY + plusTop;
        }
        else dom.moveBy(deltaX,deltaY);
    }
}
    </script>
    <style type="text/css">
#madHatter    {
    position: absolute;
    top: 30px;
    left: 30px; }
    </style>
</head>
<body>
    <a href="javascript:void('')"
    → onMouseOver="moveObjectBy('madHatter',
    → 75,100); " onMouseOut="moveObjectBy
    → ('madHatter',-25,-55); ">I want a fresh
    → cup...</a>
    <div id="madHatter">
        <img src="alice39.gif" width="200"
        → height="163" border="0">
    </div>
</body>
</html>
```

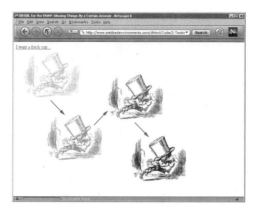

Figure 13.4 The Mad Hatter is now staggering for a new cup of tea.

4. onMouseOver="moveObjectBy
→ ('madHatter',75,100);"

Add an event handler to trigger the function you created in step 2, and to pass it the ID for the object you want to address and the number of pixels you want to move it from its current location. Positive numbers move the object down and to the right; negative amounts move it up and to the left.

5. <div id="madHatter">...</div>

Set up your CSS layer(s).

✔ Tips

- Netscape 6 does not like to have values added directly to the left and top properties. So whereas you can simply use += to add delta values to the current position in Internet Explorer 4/5, or use the layer moveBy() method for Netscape 4, you have to calculate the current position of the object in Netscape 6, add the delta values, and then assign the resulting value to the top. What a pain.

- Although it is much simpler to use the top and left properties to set an object's position, you have to resort back to pixelLeft and pixelTop when moving an object by a certain amount. Otherwise, Internet Explorer 4/5 muddle the values and the Mad Hatter goes flying off the screen.

MOVING OBJECTS BY A CERTAIN AMOUNT

Moving Objects in 3-D

All positioned objects can be stacked (see "Stacking Objects" in Chapter 8), and you can use JavaScript to find the object's order in the z-index (see "Finding an Object's 3-D Position" in Chapter 12), as well as to change that order (**Code 13.4** and **Figures 13.5** and **13.6**).

To set the 3-D position of an object:

1. `<script src="findDOM.js"></script>`

   In any JavaScript function that addresses an object on the screen directly, you need to include the findDOM code. You do so by including it in an external text file and then importing that file into the page in which it will be used (see "Using the Cross-Browser DOM" in Chapter 11).

2. `var prevObjectID = null;`
   → `var prevLayer = 0;`

   In your JavaScript, initialize two variables:

   ▲ `prevObjectID`, which stores the ID of the previously selected object

   ▲ `prevLayer`, which stores the z-index of the previously selected object

3. `function setLayer(objectID, layerNum)`
   → `{...}`

   Add the function `setLayer()` to your JavaScript. This function reassigns the z-index of an object to the indicated layer number.

4. `function findLayer(objectID) {...}`

   Add the function findLayer() to your JavaScript. This function uses the ID for the object to be addressed—passed to it as the variable objectID—to build the DOM. It then uses this ID to access the z-index property and returns that value.

Figure 13.5 The order when the page is first loaded.

Figure 13.6 The Queen and Alice now stand in the forefront.

5. `function swapLayer(objectID) {...}`

Add the function **swapLayer()** to your JavaScript. This function demotes the previously selected layer (if there is one) back to its preceding z-index and then promotes the selected layer (as indicated by the **objectID**) to the top.

6. `#object1 {...}`

Set up the IDs for your object(s) with a position, type, and z-index.

continues on next page

Code 13.4 The swapLayer() function works in conjunction with the findLayer() and swapLayer() functions to pop an object to the top of the stack.

```
code

<html>
<head>
    <script src="findDOM.js"></script>
    <script>
var prevObjectID = null;
var prevLayer = 0;
function setLayer(objectID,layerNum) {
    var dom = findDOM(objectID,1);
    dom.zIndex = layerNum;
}

function findLayer(objectID) {
    var dom = findDOM(objectID,1);
    if (dom.zIndex != null)
        return dom.zIndex;
    return (null);
}

function swapLayer(objectID) {
 if (prevObjectID != null)
   setLayer(prevObjectID,prevLayer);
 prevLayer = findLayer(objectID);
 prevObjectID = objectID;
 setLayer(objectID,1000);
}
    </script>
    <style type="text/css">
#object1 { position: absolute; border: gray solid 2px; z-index: 3; top: 175px; left: 255px }
```

(code continues on next page)

7. onLoad="..."

In the <body> tag, use the setLayer() function to initialize the z-index of all the objects for which you will need to know the initial z-index.

8. <div id="object1">...</div>

Set up your CSS layer(s).

9. onClick="swapLayer('object1')"

Add to the layer an event handler that triggers the swapLayer() function.

✔ Tips

■ Setting the z-indexes using the onload event handler in the <body> tag may seem repetitive since you already set the z-index in the CSS. A "feature" in Internet Explorer 5 and Netscape 6, however, prevents them from knowing the z-index until it is set by JavaScript.

■ The ability to set and reset the z-index is important for creating advanced drop shadows (Chapter 26).

Code 13.4 *continued*

```
                                    code
#object2 { position: absolute; border: gray solid 2px; z-index: 2; top: 100px; left: 170px }
#object3 { position: absolute; border: gray solid 2px; z-index: 1; top: 65px; left: 85px }
#object4 { position: absolute; border: gray solid 2px; z-index: 0; top: 5px; left: 5px }
    </style>
</head>
<body onLoad="setLayer('object1',3); setLayer('object2',2); setLayer('object3',1);
→ setLayer('object4',0);">
    <div id="object1">
        <a href="javascript:void('')" onCLick="swapLayer('object1')">
        <img src="alice22.gif" width="100" height="147" border="0"></a><br clear="all">
    </div>
    <div id="object2">
        <a href="javascript:void('')" onCLick="swapLayer('object2')">
            <img src="alice32.gif" width="140" height="201" border="0"></a><br clear="all">
    </div>
    <div id="object3">
        <a href="javascript:void('')" onCLick="swapLayer('object3')">
            <img src="alice15.gif" width="150" height="198" border="0"></a><br clear="all">
    </div>
    <div id="object4">
        <a href="javascript:void('')" onCLick="swapLayer('object4')">
            <img src="alice29.gif" width="200" height="236" border="0"></a><br clear="all">
    </div>
</body>
</html>
```

Figure 13.7 The controls down and over scroll the page to show different points on the Web page.

Figure 13.8 Now you have scrolled over to see the Mad Hatter singing and can use the Back to Left link to move back to the original scroll position. Notice that the bottom scrollbar has moved to the left.

Scrolling a Web Page

Normally, you think of scrolling the Web page as something that the visitor does by using the built-in scroll bars on the right or bottom side of the window or frame. You have seen how you can use JavaScript to determine the scroll position of a Web page (see "Finding the Page's Scroll Position" in Chapter 12). You can also force the page to scroll either horizontally or vertically by using a simple JavaScript trick (**Code 13.5** and **Figures 13.7** and **13.8**).

To scroll a Web page:

1. `var isIE = 0;`

   Use browser sensing to determine whether the browser is compatible with Internet Explorer.

2. `function scrollPageTo(x,y) {...}`

   Add the function `scrollPageTo()` to your JavaScript. This function uses the `scrollLeft` and `scrollRight` properties if the browser is determined to be compatible with Internet Explorer, or it uses Netscape's built-in `scrollTo()` function to scroll the page to the specified x and y coordinates.

continues on next page

Code 13.5 The `scrollPageTo()` function moves the entire Web page up, over, or both ways, depending on how you command it to behave.

```
<html>
<head>
    <script>
var isIE = 0;
if (navigator.appName.indexOf('Microsoft Internet Explorer') != -1) {isIE = 1;}

function scrollPageTo(x,y) {
    if (isIE) }
        document.body.scrollLeft = x;
        document.body.scrollTop = y;
```

(code continues on next page)

3. #overHere {...}

Set up the IDs for your object(s) with a position, type, and top and left positions. In this example, I've set up two objects: one set well below the top of the page and one set to the far-right side of the page. Now the scrollPageTo() function has somewhere to go.

4. <a href="javascript:scrollPageTo
→ (0,1990)">...</a>

Set up a link to trigger the scrollPageTo() function, and pass to the function the x and y coordinates to which you want to scroll. Keep in mind that because this function is not addressing a DOM, you do not have to trigger the function call by using an event handler.

✔ Tips

■ Although the example in this section still relies on the visitor to click something to cause the page to scroll, you could just as easily have used some other event handler to cause the page to scroll without the direct command of the visitor (by using onload, for example). Be careful when doing this, however. If the page suddenly starts jumping around, the effect can be confusing—not to mention unnerving—to the person viewing your Web page.

■ Netscape 4 (Windows) and Netscape 6 (all versions) have an unfortunate "feature" that prevents this technique from working in a frame where the scrollbars have been hidden (scrolling="no"). Rather than simply making the scrollbars disappear, setting scrolling to no in these browsers will prevent the frame from scrolling at all—even with JavaScript.

Code 13.5 *continued*

```
          return;
       }
       else {
          scrollTo(x,y)
          return;
       }
}
    </script>
    <style type="text/css">
#overHere    {
       position: absolute;
       top: 10px;
       left: 2000px;
       width: 1000px;
       z-index: 100;
       visibility: visible; }
#downHere    {
       position: absolute;
       top: 2000px;
       left: 10px;
       height: 1000px;
       z-index: 100;
       visibility: visible; }
    </style>
</head>
<body>
    <a href="javascript:scrollPageTo(0,1990)">
→ v Down</a> | <a href="javascript:
→ scrollPageTo(1990,0)">Over &gt;
→ <br style="clear:both"><img src=
→ "alice25.gif" width="300" height="228"
→ border="0"></a>
    <div id="downHere">
       <a href="javascript:scrollPageTo
→ (0,0)">^ Back to Top</a>
       <p><a href="javascript:scrollPageTo
→ (0,0)"><img src="alice27.gif"
→ width="200" height="180"
→ border="0"></a></p>
    </div>
    <div id="overHere">
       <a href="javascript:scrollPageTo
→ (0,0)">&lt; Back to Left</a>
→ <br style="clear:both">
       <p><img src="alice26.gif" width="179"
→ height="200" border="0"></p>
    </div>
    <br clear="all">
</body>
</html>
```

Changing an Object's Visible Area

The clipping region of an object defines how much of that object is visible in the window (see "Setting the Visible Area of an Element" in Chapter 9). If it is left alone, the entire object is visible. But if you clip the object, you can have as much or as little of it visible as you want, and you can use JavaScript to determine the clipping region (see "Finding an Object's Visible Area" in Chapter 12). In addition, DHTML allows you to change the clipping region on the fly (**Code 13.6** and **Figures 13.9** and **13.10**).

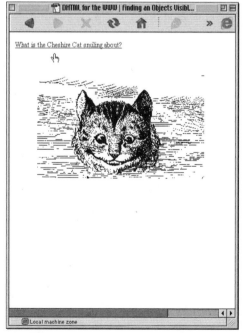

Figure 13.9 What is the Cheshire Cat smiling at? Roll over the link and find out.

Figure 13.10 The Cheshire Cat is smiling because the King can't order his executioner to chop off a head that has no body. This fact makes the Queen of Hearts very, very angry.

To change the visible area of an object:

1. `<script src="findDOM.js"></script>`

In any JavaScript function that addresses an object on the screen directly, you need to include the findDOM code. You do so by including it in an external text file and then importing that file into the page in which it will be used (see "Using the Cross-Browser DOM" in Chapter 11).

2. `function setClip(objectID, clipTop,`
`→ clipRight, clipBottom, clipLeft)`
`→ {...}`

Add the function setClip() to your JavaScript. This function uses the ID for the object to be addressed—passed to it as the variable objectID—to build the DOM. (see "Building a Cross-Browser DOM" in Chapter 11). It then changes the clipping region of the object to the new top, right, bottom, and left values. For Netscape 4 and 6, this is done by accessing the top, right, bottom, and left clip properties, while Internet Explorer 4/5 use the clip property directly.

3. `#cheshireCat {...}`

Set up the ID(s) for your object(s), and include the initial clipping region.

4. `<div id="cheshireCat">...</div>`

Set up your CSS layer(s).

5. `onMouseOver="setClip('cheshireCat',`
`→ 35,320,400,70)"`

Include an event handler to trigger the setClip() function. Remember that because this function will be using the DOM, it has to be triggered from an event.

Code 13.6 The setClip() function redraws the boundaries of the clipping region set around an object.

```
<html>
<head>
    <script src="findDOM.js"></script>
    <script>
function setClip(objectID, clipTop,
→ clipRight, clipBottom, clipLeft) {
    var dom = findDOM(objectID,1);
    if (dom.clip.left) {
        dom.clip.top = clipTop;
        dom.clip.right = clipRight;
        dom.clip.bottom = clipBottom;
        dom.clip.left = clipLeft;
    }
        dom.clip = 'rect(' + clipTop + ' ' +
        → clipRight + ' ' + clipBottom + ' ' +
        → clipLeft +')';
</script>
    <style type="text/css">
#cheshireCat    {
    position: absolute;
    top: 60px;
    left: 0px;
    overflow: hidden;
    clip: rect(15 350 195 50) }
    </style>
</head>
<body>
    <a href="javascript:void('')"
    → onMouseOver="setClip('cheshireCat',35,
    → 320,400,70)" onMouseOut="setClip
    → ('cheshireCat',15,350,195,50)">
        What is the Cheshire Cat smiling
        → about?</a>
    <div id="cheshireCat">
        <img src="alice31.gif" width="379"
        → height="480" border="0">
    </div>
</body>
</html>
```

Dynamic Techniques: Advanced

Beyond the basics, several techniques will help you create a dynamic interface for your Web site. Some of these techniques rely on the Document Object Model (DOM) presented in Chapter 11; others are JavaScript tricks that give you better control of the environment you present to your visitors.

Making a Function Run Again

To create a dynamic function, you often need to have that function run repeatedly until, well, until you don't want it to run anymore (**Code 14.1**). This *recursive* running of the function allows you to animate objects or allow objects to wait for a particular event to happen in the browser window before continuing (**Figure 14.1**).

To make a function recursive:

1. `theDelay = 1000;`

   Initialize the global variables:

   ▲ `theDelay`, which sets the amount of time between rerunning the function in milliseconds. The value 1,000 milliseconds equates to a one-second delay.

   ▲ `domStyle`, which records the DOM.

   ▲ `state`, which records the current visibility state of the object on which the function is acting.

   ▲ `toStop`, which records whether the function should be repeating (1) or not (0).

Code 14.1 The setUpAnnoyingFlash() function prepares the initial values of variables that are then run in the annoyingFlash() function. annoyingFlash() keeps running, and running, and running... causing the image to appear and disappear at 1-second intervals until the visitor clicks the image while it is showing.

```
code

<html>
<head>
    <script src="findDOM.js"></script>
    <script>
theDelay = 1000;
var domStyle = null;
var state = null;
var toStop = 0;

function setUpAnnoyingFlash(objectID,
→ onOffon) {
    if (onOffon == 1) {
        toStop = 1;
        domStyle = findDOM(objectID,1);
        domStyle.visibility = 'visible';
        state = 'visible';
        annoyingFlash();
```

(code continues on next page)

Figure 14.1 Click the image to stop the annoying flash. Please!

Code 14.1 *continued*

```
        }
        else toStop = 0;
}

function annoyingFlash() {
    if (toStop == 1) {
        if (state == 'hidden' || state ==
        → 'hide' )
            domStyle.visibility = 'visible';
        else {
            if (state == 'visible' ||
            → state=='show')
                domStyle.visibility =
                → 'hidden';
            else domStyle.visibility = 'visible';
        }
        state = domStyle.visibility;
        setTimeout ('annoyingFlash()',
        → theDelay);
    }
    else{
            domStyle.visibility = 'visible';
            return;
    }
}
    </script>
    <style type="text/css">
#cheshireCat {
    position: relative;
    visibility: visible }
    </style>
</head>
<body onLoad="setUpAnnoyingFlash
→ ('cheshireCat',1);">
    MAKE IT STOP!!!! MAKE IT STOP!!! (click
    → to make it stop)
    <div id="cheshireCat"><a href=
    → "javascript:void('')" onClick=
    → "setUpAnnoyingFlash('cheshireCat',0)" >
        <img src="alice24.gif" width="640"
        → height="435" border="0"></a>
    </div>
</body>
</html>
```

2. function setUpAnnoyingFlash(objectID,
→ onOffon) {...}

Add the function setUpAnnoyingFlash()
to your JavaScript. If the variable onOffon
is 1, the function sets toStop to 1 (the
function should keep repeating). It uses
the ID for the object to be addressed—
passed to it as the variable objectID—to
build the DOM (see "Building a Cross-
Browser DOM" in Chapter 11) and then
runs the function annoyingFlash().
If onOffon is 0, this function sets toStop
to 0, thus stopping the function
annoyingFlash() from running.

3. function annoyingFlash() {...}

Add the function annoyingFlash() to
your JavaScript. This function is started
by the setUpAnnoyingFlash() function in
step 2. If toStop is equal to 1, the visibility
is toggled (visible if hidden, hidden if
visible). Then the function runs itself
again, using the setTimeout() method.
The annoyingFlash() function keeps
running until toStop is equal to 0, in
which case the visibility is finally set to
visible and the function stops running.

continues on next page

MAKING A FUNCTION RUN AGAIN

4. `#cheshireCat {...}`

Set up the IDs for your object(s) with a position, type, and visibility.

5. `onLoad="setUpAnnoyingFlash`
`→ ('cheshireCat',1);"`

Add event handlers to trigger the function you created in step 2, and pass to it the ID for the object you want to have flashing, indicating whether you want the annoying flash to be activated (1) or not (0).

6. `<div id="cheshireCat">...</div>`

Set up your CSS layer(s).

✔ Tip

■ When you run this example code, notice that you can click the cat to stop the flash only while the image is visible. The link is on the page only if the object is visible.

Why setTimeOut()?

One common question I get about running a function repeatedly with the `setTimeout()` function is "Why not just call the function from within itself?" There are two reasons:

◆ Netscape 4 has a bug that causes the entire browser to crash when a function calls itself recursively. This can be very annoying.

◆ `setTimeout()` makes it easy to control a pause between the function's looping back and running again. This capability can come in handy if you need the function to run more slowly than the computer would run it automatically.

Passing an Event to a Function

All events (see "Detecting an Event" in Chapter 11) in the browser window generate certain information about what occurred, where it occurred, and how it occurred (**Figure 14.2**). You can pass this information directly to a JavaScript function so that it can access the object without having to create a cross-browser DOM (**Code 14.2**).

As is true of all things in Web design, Internet Explorer and Netscape have different methods for implementing event passing. The good news is that the two methods are easy to combine.

To pass an event to a JavaScript function:

1. `function passItOn(evt) {...}`

   Add the function **passItOn()** to your JavaScript. This function simply takes the variable **evt** and displays it in a JavaScript alert message. The **evt** variable represents the DOM for the object from which the event was triggered; it is generated automatically in Internet Explorer and created with **event** in Netscape (see step 2).

2. `onClick="passItOn(event)"`

   Add one or more event handlers to trigger the function. **event** has to be passed to the function for Netscape to access the event property.

✔ Tip

- Why not always use the **evt** variable instead of going through the machinations required to get a cross-browser DOM? My experience with the **evt** variable has been that it sometimes behaves in an unpredictable manner in different browsers, especially when trying to access CSS styles. In this chapter, I will present some of the best practices for using the **evt** variable.

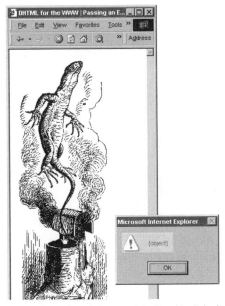

Figure 14.2 When the image of the lizard is clicked, an alert appears, letting you know that an [object] has been detected.

Code 14.2 The passItOn() function receives the event and then displays the result in an alert to show the type of event being generated.

```
<html>
<head>
   <script>
function passItOn(evt) {
   if (evt) {
       alert (evt);
       return;
   }
}
   </script>
</head>
<body>
   <div id="object1">
       <a href="javascript:void('')"
       → onClick="passItOn(event)">
           <img src="alice13.gif" width=
           → "174" height="480" border="0">
       </a>
   </div>
</body>
</html>
```

Creating a Global Event Handler

Events usually are for specific objects on a Web page (see "Understanding Event Handlers" in Chapter 11). But what if you want to set the results for a specific event, regardless of the object? Both Netscape and Internet Explorer are set to handle this situation (**Figure 14.3** and **Code 14.3**).

To add a global event handler to a Web page:

1. `<script src="findDOM.js"></script>`

   You will not be using the findDOM.js script to create a cross-browser DOM. Instead, you will take advantage of this script's capability to detect a DHTML browser (see "Using the Cross-Browser DOM" in Chapter 11).

2. `var isNS = 0;`

   Add browser sensing to your JavaScript (see "Detecting the Browser's Name and Version" in Chapter 12).

Figure 14.3 Don't click the image. I warned you.

Code 14.3 The defaultEvents() function sets up global events that will be run whenever the event is triggered anywhere in the browser window.

```
                                code
<html>
<head>
    <script src="findDOM.js"></script>
    <script>
var isNS = 0;
var isIE = 0;
if (navigator.appName.indexOf('Netscape') != -1) {isNS = 1;}
else {
if (navigator.appName.indexOf('Microsoft Internet Explorer') != -1) {isIE = 1;}
}
function defaultEvents() {
    if (isNS) {
        document.captureEvents(Event.CLICK || Event.MOUSEOUT)
    }
    if (isDHTML){
```

(code continues on next page)

Code 14.3 *continued*

```
                    code
  document.onclick = errorOn;

  document.onmouseout = validate;

  }

}


function errorOn() {

  alert ('Please do not click here again!')

}


function validate() {

  alert ('Where do you think you are going?')

}

  </script>

</head>

<body onLoad="defaultEvents()">

  <img src="alice34.gif" width="409"
→ height="480" border="2">

</body>

</html>
```

3. function defaultEvents() {...}

Add the function defaultEvents() to your JavaScript. This function prepares the global event handlers to be used in Netscape and then sets functions to be executed if those events are triggered anywhere in the browser window. You can use any event handler listed in "Understanding Event Handlers" in Chapter 11.

4. function errorOn() {...}

Add to your JavaScript the functions that will be run when the events in the function from step 2 are met. In this example, the functions errorOn() and validate() are triggered when the onClick and onMouseOut events, respectively, are triggered in the browser window.

5. onLoad="defaultEvents()"

Add an event handler in the <body> tag to trigger the function you created in step 3.

Animating an Object

When most people think about dynamic techniques, they don't think of simply moving objects from one point to another (see "Moving Objects from Point to Point" in Chapter 13), but of making objects slide across the screen from one point to another (**Figure 14.4**).

Using a function that runs recursively (refer to "Making a Function Run Again" earlier in this chapter), you can make any object that has been positioned (see "Setting the Positioning Type" in Chapter 8) seem to glide from one point to another (**Code 14.4**).

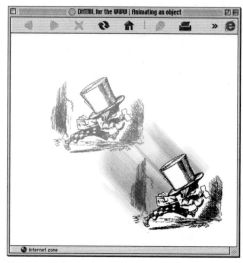

Figure 14.4 The Mad Hatter dashes across the screen.

Code 14.4 The startAnimate() function finds the initial left and top positions of the object. It also sets up the object's DOM and starts the animation function. animateObject() is a recursive function that keeps repositioning the object incrementally until the object reaches its finishing point.

```
<html>
<head>
<script src="findDOM.js"></script>
    <script>
var animaeDelay = 5;
var domStyle;
var fX = null;
var fY = null;

function findLeft(objectID) {
    var domStyle = findDOM(objectID,1);
    var dom = findDOM(objectID,0);
    if (domStyle.left)
        return domStyle.left;
    if (domStyle.pixelLeft)
        return domStyle.pixelLeft;
    if (dom.offsetLeft)
        return dom.offsetLeft;
    return (null);
}
```

(code continues on next page)

Code 14.4 *continued*

```
                    code
function findTop(objectID) {
   var domStyle = findDOM(objectID,1);
   var dom = findDOM(objectID,0);
   if (domStyle.top)
       return domStyle.top;
   if (domStyle.pixelTop)
       return domStyle.pixelTop;
   if (dom.offsetTop)
       return dom.offsetTop;
   return (null);
}


function startAnimate(objectID,x,y) {
   fX = x;
   fY = y;
   var cX = findLeft(objectID);
   var cY = findTop(objectID);
   domStyle = findDOM(objectID,1);
   animateObject(cX,cY)
}


function animateObject(cX,cY)  {
   if (cX != fX) {
       if (cX > fX) { cX -=1; }
       else { cX +=1; }
   }
   if (cY != fY) {
       if (cY > fY) { cY -=1; }
       else { cY +=1; }
   }
   if ((cX != fX)  || (cY != fY) ) {
           if (domStyle.pixelLeft) {
               domStyle.pixelLeft = cX;
               domStyle.pixelTop= cY;
           }
           else {domStyle.left = cX;
               domStyle.top = cY;}
       setTimeout ('animateObject(' + cX + ',
       → ' + cY + ')',animaeDelay);
   }
}
    </script>
```

(code continues on next page)

To animate an object:

1. `animaeDelay=5;`

   Initialize the global variables:

   ▲ `animaeDelay`, which sets the amount of delay in the recursive running of the function. The larger the number, the slower the object slides, but the choppier the animation looks.

   ▲ `domStyle`, which records the Document Object Model.

   ▲ `fX`, which records the final left position of the object.

   ▲ `fY`, which records the final top position of the object.

2. `function findLeft(objectID) {...}`

   Add the functions `findLeft()` and `findTop()` to your JavaScript (see "Finding an Object's Top and Left Positions" in Chapter 12).

3. `function startAnimate(objectID,x,y)`
   `→ {...}`

   Add the function `startAnimate()` to your JavaScript. This function sets the final x-y position of the object (`fX` and `fY`) and calculates the current x/y position of the object (`cX` and `cY`). Then the function uses the ID for the object to be addressed—passed to it as the variable `objectID`—to build the DOM (see "Building a Cross-Browser DOM" in Chapter 11). Finally, this function runs the `animateObject()` function, passing it the current x and y positions of the object (`cX` and `cY`).

   continues on next page

ANIMATING AN OBJECT

4. `function animateObject(cX,cY) {...}`

Add the function `animateObject()` to your JavaScript. This function is triggered from the `startAnimate()` function in step 3. This function subtracts or adds 1 from the current position of the object (depending on whether the final position is greater than or less than the current position) and sets the object to the new position. It then reruns itself and starts the process again (add/subtract move, add/subtract move, add/subtract move, and so on). The function keeps running until the current x and y values (`cX` and `cY`) are equal to the final x and final y values (`fX` and `fY`) that you set in step 2.

5. `#madHatter {...}`

Set up the IDs for your object(s) with a position, type, and top and left positions.

6. `onLoad="startAnimate('madHatter',`
   `→ 200,200)"`

Add event handlers to trigger the function you created in step 3, and pass it the ID for the object you want to animate and the final position to which you want that object to move.

7. `<div id="madHatter">...</div>`

Set up your CSS layer(s).

Code 14.4 *continued*

```
                    code
    <style type="text/css">
#madHatter    {
    position: absolute;
    top: 30px;
    left: 30px; }
    </style>
</head>
<body onLoad="startAnimate('madHatter',
→ 200,200)">
    <div id="madHatter">
        <img src="alice39.gif" width="200"
        → height="163" border="0">
    </div>
</body>
</html>
```

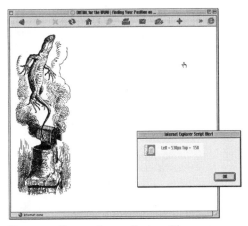

Figure 14.5 The x and y coordinates of the mouse pointer are displayed when the visitor clicks inside the browser window.

Finding Your Location on the Screen

Remember, no matter where you go, there you are. And if you want to know where you are in the browser window, this is the script for you.

All events in the browser window generate certain information about what occurred, where it occurred, and how it occurred (see "Passing an Event to a Function" earlier in this chapter). The most important piece of information is the screen location of the event (**Figure 14.5**).

To find the mouse pointer's position in the browser window:

1. function findXCoord(evt) {...}

   Add the functions findXCoord() and findYCoord() to your JavaScript. These functions return the value—in pixels—of the location of the mouse pointer when the event is triggered, using feature sensing to determine the appropriate method: Internet Explorer uses x and y, and Netscape uses pageX and pageY (**Code 14.5**).

continues on next page

Code 14.5 The findXCoord() and findYCoord() functions find the x and y positions of the mouse pointer when an event is triggered in the browser window.

```
<html>
<head>
   <script>
function findXCoord(evt) {
   if (evt.x)     return evt.x;
   if (evt.pageX) return evt.pageX;
}

function findYCoord(evt) {
   if (evt.y) return evt.y;
   if (evt.pageY) return evt.pageY;
}
```

(code continues on next page)

2. onClick="alert('Left = '
  → + findXCoord(event) + 'px Top = '
  → + findYCoord(event)) + 'px'"

Add an event handler to trigger the functions you set up in step 1. Where you place the event handler affects the area in which the functions will find the position of the mouse pointer. Placing the event handler in the **<body>** tag, for example, allows you to find the position of the mouse pointer anywhere on the screen. Placing the event handler in a link **<a>** allows you to find the mouse pointer's position only within the area defined for that link.

✔ Tip

- Netscape 4 can generate the onClick event only from a link **<a>**. Therefore, it ignores the onClick in the **<body>** tag and shows the position only if the visitor clicks the image in this example.

Code 14.5 *continued*

```
        </script>
    </head>
    <body onClick="alert('Left = ' +
  → findXCoord(event) + 'px Top =  ' +
  → findYCoord(event)) + 'px'">
        <div id="object1">
            <a href="javascript:void('')"
  → onClick="alert('Left = ' +
  → findXCoord(event) + 'px Top =  ' +
  → findYCoord(event)) + 'px'">
                <img src="alice13.gif"
  → width="174" height="480"
  → border="0">
            </a>
        </div>
    </body>
</html>
```

Figure 14.6 Pick an Alice, any Alice.

Identifying an Object on the Screen

In "Passing an Event to a Function" earlier in this chapter, I showed you how to use the **evt** value to find the object in which an event originated. Using DHTML, though, you can also have the browser determine the ID of the object in which the event occurred (**Figure 14.6**). In fact, with Internet Explorer and Netscape 6, this task is very easy, because the name of the element is part of the event object (**Code 14.6**).

Netscape 4 takes a good deal more work, and you have to rely on its layers capabilities (see Chapter 16) to make this function work.

Code 14.6 The findObject() function finds the ID or name of the object from which the event that triggered it came.

```
<html>
<head>
   <script>
var name = null;
function findObject(evt) {
   if (document.layers) {
        var testObj;
        var xPos = evt.pageX;
        var yPos = evt.pageY;
        for (var i = document.layers.length - 1; i >= 0; i--) {
             testObj = document.layers[i];
             if ((xPos > testObj.left) &&
             (xPos < testObj.left + testObj.clip.width) &&
             (yPos > testObj.top) &&
             (yPos < testObj.top + testObj.clip.height)) {
                  objectID = testObj.name;
                  alert('You clicked ' + objectID + '.');
                  return;
             }
        }
   }
   else {
        objectID = evt.target.name;
        alert('You clicked ' + objectID + '.');
        return;
        }
```

(code continues on next page)

To determine the element in which the event occurred:

1. `function findObject(evt) {...}`

Add the function `findObject()` to the JavaScript in the head of your document. This script determines the CSS element on the screen in which the event occurred and then displays an alert telling you which one it was. The function has two parts—one to be used in Netscape 4 and the other in Internet Explorer or Netscape 6:

▲ `if (document.layers) {...}`

If the code is running in Netscape 4, the function determines the position of the mouse and then checks each layer in the layer array (an automatic list of all the layers in the window that Netscape 4 keeps) to determine which one is under this position.

▲ `else {...}`

Otherwise (if it is running in Internet Explorer), the code simply finds the target object's name—which will be the name of the element from which the event comes.

2. `#alice1 {...}`

Set up your CSS elements, using whatever style properties you want. In this example, you set up three images (`alice1`, `alice2`, and `alice3`), each with a unique ID.

3. `onClick="findObject(event)"`

Add an event handler to trigger the function you created in step 1, and pass to it the event parameter for Netscape 4.

✔ Tip

■ Notice that you also specify a name in each image tag, as well as an ID in the `<div>` tag. Netscape uses the ID, and Internet Explorer uses the name of the actual image. Include both to remain cross-browser-compliant.

Code 14.6 *continued*

```
      return;
}

   </script>
   <style type="text/css">
#alice1 {
   position: absolute;
   top: 5px;
   left: 5px;
   visibility: visible }
#alice2 {
   position: absolute;
   top: 150px;
   left: 200px;
   visibility: visible }
#alice3 {
   position: absolute;
   top: 5px;
   left: 300px;
   visibility: visible }
   </style>
</head>
<body>
   <div id="alice1">
       <a href="javascript:void('')"
       → onClick="findObject(event)">
           <img src="alice04.gif"
           → width="301" height="448"
           → border="0"  name="alice1">
       </a>
   </div>

   <div id="alice2">
       <a href="javascript:void('')"
       → onClick="findObject(event)">
           <img src="alice22.gif"
           → width="329" height="482"
           → border="0"  name="alice2">
       </a>
   </div>

   <div id="alice3">
       <a href="javascript:void('')"
       → onClick="findObject(event)">
           <img src="alice30.gif"
           → width="353" height="480"
           → border="0"  name="alice3">
       </a>
   </div>
</body>
</html>
```

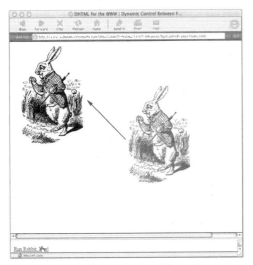

Figure 14.7 The rabbit may be in a different frame, but the DOM hunts him down and makes him run.

Code 14.7 This alternate version of the cross-browser DOM script, findDOMFrame.js, allows you to pass a frame name to the function, which then creates the DOM for an object in the specified frame.

```
var isDHTML = 0;
var isLayers = 0;
var isAll = 0;
var isID = 0;

if (document.getElementById) {isID = 1;
→ isDHTML = 1;}
else {
if (document.all) {isAll = 1; isDHTML = 1;}
else {
browserVersion = parseInt
→ (navigator.appVersion);
if ((navigator.appName.indexOf('Netscape') !=
→ -1) && (browserVersion == 4)) {isLayers =
→ 1; isDHTML = 1;}
}}


function findDOMFrame(objectID,frameName,
→ withStyle) {if (document.getElementById)
→ {isID = 1; isDHTML = 1;}else {if
→ (document.layers) {isLayers = 1; isDHTML =
→ 1;}else {if (document.all) {isAll = 1;
→ isDHTML = 1;}}}
```

(code continues on next page)

Dynamic Content Between Frames

You can use JavaScript to control objects in one frame without much trouble (**Figure 14.7**). The challenge comes in the way you construct your cross-browser DOM, which now needs to find a path to an element in another frame. In effect, this is like adding the country code to your address (see "Understanding the DOM" in Chapter 11). You need to set up a different version of the findDOM code, called findDOMFrame.js, rather than addressing an object in the same document, the function has to find an object in a document in a different frame. This means that rather than just passing the function the name of the object you want to change, you also have to pass the function the name of the frame the object is in.

To control elements in other frames:

1. findDOMFrame.js

   Create a new version of the findDOM external file with an alternative version of the findDOM() function:

   findDOMFrame(objectID,frameName,
   → withStyle)

   This version includes the capability to pass the function a frame name, which is then included in the cross-browser DOM that is generated to address an object in a specific frame (**Code 14.7**). Use this code instead of the one you set up in "Using the Cross-Browser DOM" in Chapter 11.

2. index.html

   Set up your frames document, making sure to name the frames that will have dynamic content (**Figure 14.8**). These names will be used by the DOM in step 1 (**Code 14.8**).

   continues on next page

3. `content.html`

Now set up an HTML document with the objects to be controlled from the other frame. Include positioned objects with IDs that can be controlled with JavaScript (**Code 14.9**).

4. `controls.html`

Set up the HTML document that will control the element in the other frame. You need to import the findDOMFrame.js code from step 1 and then add the DHTML function you want to use. You have to change this function slightly to allow it to pass the function the `frameName`—which, along with the `objectID` and `withStyle` variables, creates the DOM (**Code 14.10**).

✔ Tips

- This example shows you how to move an object across frames, but you can use any of the dynamic functions described in this book.

- For all intents and purposes, a window is like another frame. If you have two windows open, you can use this technique to communicate between two windows as long as they are named.

Code 14.7 *continued*

```
                        code
 if (withStyle == 1) {
     if (isID) { return (top
     → [frameName].document.getElementById
     (objectID).style) ; }
     else {
         if (isAll) { return (top
         → [frameName].document.all
         → [objectID].style); }
     else {
         if (isLayers) {  return (top
         → [frameName].document.layers
         → [objectID]); }
     };}
 }
 else {
     if (isID) { return (top
     → [frameName].document.getElementById
     → (objectID)) ; }
     else {
         if (isAll) { return (top
         [frameName].document.all
         → [objectID]); }
     else {
         if (isLayers) { return (top
         [frameName].document.layers
         → [objectID]); }
     };}
   }
 }
```

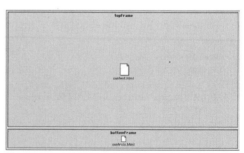

Figure 14.8 The frameset that is set up from index.html.

Code 14.8 In this example (index.html), I have set up a frame document with two frames named content and controls. The frames' sources are content.html and controls.html, respectively.

```
<html>
<frameset rows="*,50">
    <frame src="content.html" name="topFrame"
    → noresize scrolling="no">
    <frame src="controls.html" name=
    → "bottomFrame" noresize scrolling="no">
</frameset>
</html>
```

Code 14.9 The object whiteRabbit has been set up and can now be controlled from this frame or any other frame using its DOM.

```
<html>
<head>
    <style type="text/css">
#whiteRabbit { position: absolute; top:
→ 125px; left: 350px }
    </style>
</head>
<body>
    <div id="whiteRabbit">
            <img src="alice02.gif" width=
            → "200" height="300" border="0">
    <div>
</body>
</html>
```

Code 14.10 controls.html uses a variation on moveObject() (see "Moving Objects from Point to Point" in Chapter 13). The main difference is that I pass the function not only the ID of the object to moved, but also its frame. The moveObject() function then uses the findDOMFrame() function that has been imported from findDOMFrame.js to locate the object in the browser window.

```
<html>
<head>
    <script src="findDOMFrame.js"></script>
    <script>
function moveObject(objectID,frameName,x,y){
    var domStyle = findDOMFrame(objectID,
    → frameName,1);
    if (domStyle.pixelLeft) {
        domStyle.pixelLeft = x;
        domStyle.pixelTop= y;
    }
    else {
        domStyle.left = x;
        domStyle.top= y;
    }
}
    </script>
</head>
<body>
    <a href="#" onMouseOver="moveObject
    → ('whiteRabbit','topFrame',10,10)"
    → ONMOUSEOUT="moveObject('whiteRabbit',
    → 'topFrame',350,125)">Run Rabbit,
    → Run!</A>
</body>
</html>
```

Moving the Browser Window

When you create a user interface on the Web, it often is helpful to position the browser window on the visitor's computer screen (**Figure 14.9**). This is especially useful if your site will be opening multiple windows and you want to set an initial position so that the windows do not crowd one another (see the following section, "Opening a New Browser Window").

In addition, you can have a window move from its current position by a certain amount (**Code 14.11**).

Figure 14.9 The initial position of the browser window on the screen.

Code 14.11 The JavaScript methods moveTo(x,y) and moveBy(dx,dy) move the entire browser window to a certain position on the screen or by a specific amount.

```
<html>
<body>
    <b>Window Controls</b> ||
    <a href="javascript:moveTo(10,15)">
        Move to 10, 15
    </a> |
    <a href="javascript:moveBy(10,15)">
        Move By 10, 15<br><br>
    <img src="alice42.gif" width="360"
 → height="480" border="0"></a>
</body>
</html>
```

Figure 14.10 After the window has been moved to 10 pixels from the left edge of the screen and 15 pixels from the top.

Figure 14.11 After the browser window has been moved an additional 10 pixels over and 15 pixels down.

To set the position of a window on the screen:

1. moveTo(10,15)

Add the moveTo(x,y) method to your JavaScript. This built-in JavaScript function tells the browser window to move its top-left corner to the indicated x-y coordinates in relation to the top-left corner of the live screen area (see "Finding the Screen Dimensions" in Chapter 12 and **Figure 14.10**).

2. moveBy(10,15)

Add the moveBy(dx,dy) method to your JavaScript. This built-in JavaScript function moves the browser window by the x and y amounts (dx,dy) indicated (**Figure 14.11**).

✔ Tip

■ These methods are best used to move a window when it first opens. You do so by placing the moveTo() or moveBy() method in an onLoad event handler in the <body> tag, as shown in the following section, "Opening a New Browser Window."

Opening a New Browser Window

An often-used interface trick on the Web is opening a new browser window (**Figure 14.12**). These pop-up windows are useful for a variety of purposes, including navigation controls, advertisements, and other content that supplements what is in the main window.

When dealing with pop-up windows, consider three basic functions:

- **Open the window.** This function opens a new window and brings it to the front of the screen.

- **Close the window.** This function closes the window.

- **Toggle the window.** This function can both open and close the window. If the window is not open (closed), the function opens a new window and brings it to the front of the screen. If the window is open, the function closes the window.

To open and close a new browser window:

1. `index.html`

   Start a new file, and save it as something like index.html. This file will contain the controls that open and close the pop-up window (**Code 14.12**).

2. `var newWindow = null;`

   Initialize the variable `newWindow`. This variable will record the current state (open or closed) of the window. `null` means that the window is closed.

3. `function openWindow(contentURL,`
   `→ windowName,windowWidth,`
   `→ windowHeight) {...}`

   Add the function `openWindow()` to your JavaScript. This function opens a new window, using these variables:

Figure 14.12 The screen with a pop-up window.

Code 14.12 The openWindow(), closeWindow() and toggleWindow() functions open and close a pop-up window.

```
<html>
<head>
   <script>
var newWindow = null;

function openWindow(contentURL,windowName,
→ windowWidth,windowHeight) {
    widthHeight = 'height=' + windowHeight + ',
    → width=' + windowWidth;
    newWindow = window.open(contentURL,
    → windowName,widthHeight);
    newWindow.focus()
}


function closeWindow() {
    if (newWindow != null)  {
        newWindow.close();
        newWindow = null;
    }
}


function toggleWindow(contentURL,windowName,
→ windowWidth,windowHeight) {
    if (newWindow == null) {
        widthHeight = 'HEIGHT=' +
        → windowHeight + ',WIDTH=' +
        → windowWidth;
        newWindow = window.open(contentURL,
        → windowName,widthHeight);
```

(code continues on next page)

Code 14.12 *continued*

```
          newWindow.focus()
  }
  else {
          newWindow.close();
          newWindow = null;
  }
}
  </script>
</head>
<body onUnload="closeWindow()">
  <b>Window Open Controls</b> ||
  <a href="javascript:openWindow
→ ('newWindow.html','myNewWindow',
→ 150,50)">
  Open</a> |
  <a href="javascript:closeWindow()">
  Close</a> |
  <a href="javascript:toggleWindow
→ ('newWindow.html','myNewWindow',
→ 150,50)">
  Toggle</a>
</body>
</html>
```

▲ `contentURL` for the name of the HTML file to be placed in the new window

▲ `windowName` for the name of the new window

▲ `windowWidth` and `windowHeight` for the width and height of the new window

The new window is forced to the front of the screen by `newWindow.focus()`.

4. `function closeWindow() {...}`

Add the function `closeWindow()` to your JavaScript. This function checks to see whether the pop-up window is, in fact, open. If so, the function tells the window to close and sets the `newWindow` variable to `null` (closed).

5. `function toggleWindow(contentURL,windowName, windowWidth,windowHeight) {...}`

Add the function `toggleWindow()` to your JavaScript. This function combines the functions presented in steps 3 and 4 but allows the window to open only if `newWindow` is equal to `null` (closed); otherwise, it closes the window.

6. `onUnload="closeWindow()"`

Optionally, you can add an `onUnload` event handler to force the new window to close when this page (the opening page) is left. This event handler keeps the pop-up window from hanging around when the user moves on.

7. `openWindow('newWindow.html', → 'myNewWindow',150,50)`

Add a function call to your HTML. This function call can be part of an event handler (as shown in step 6) or part of the JavaScript in the HREF.

To set up the content for the pop-up window:

1. `newWindow.html`

   Open the file, and save it as something like newWindow.html. This file will be loaded into the pop-up window (**Code 14.13**). You can add anything to this document that you normally would have in a Web page.

2. `function closeWindow() {...}`

   Add the function `closeWindow()` to the JavaScript in this file. When triggered, this function closes the pop-up window.

3. `onUnload="opener.newWindow=null;"`

   In the <body> tag, include an onUnload event handler that sets the variable newWindow in the opening window to null if this window is closed. This variable tells the opening window when the pop-up window closes.

4. `onLoad="window.moveTo(100,100)"`

   Add an **onLoad** event handler to the <body> tag to move the window to a particular position on the screen when it first opens (refer to "Moving the Browser Window" earlier in this chapter).

5. `<a href="javascript:closeWindow()">` `→ C...</a>`

   Set up a link to trigger `closeWindow()` so that the visitor can close this window when she doesn't need it anymore.

Code 14.13 newWindow.html is the Web page that will be used in the pop-up window.

```
                        code
<html>
<head>
    <script>
function closeWindow() {
    self.close();
}
    </script>
</head>
<body onLoad="window.moveTo(100,100)"
→ onUnload="opener.newWindow = null;">
    New Window<br>
    <a href="javascript:closeWindow()">
    → Close Window</a>
</body>
</html>
```

✔ Tips

- Why not always use the toggle version of the function? Generally, toggling the open/close state of the window is preferable, but sometimes it's useful to have the other two functions, in case you need to make sure the window is either open or closed.

- I especially like using step 4 if I am using a frame to create my Web site. I place the `onUnload` event in the `<frameset>`. When the visitor leaves the site and the frame document unloads, the pop-up window also disappears.

- Opening multiple pop-up windows can be a bit problematic, because you can't use a variable in place of `newWindow`. Instead, you need to include a separate function for each window (`openWindow1()`, `openWindow2()`, and so on), using a different name for each window (`newWindow1`, `newWindow2`, and so on).

Modal Problems with Pop-Up Windows

Many of the site developers who use pop-up windows complain about what mode the window is in when it is being used.

Suppose that you use a pop-up window to allow a visitor to enter information in a form that is then used to update information in the main window. What happens if the visitor does not enter the information in the pop-up window, does not close the window, and returns to the main page? The system is waiting for information that may never come. The visitor might make other changes and return to the pop-up window, enter the information, and really mess up the system.

My advice is simple. If the pop-up window can cause trouble if it is left open, place the following code in the `<body>` of the document in the pop-up window:

```
onblur="self.close();"
```

This code forces the window to close whenever the visitor leaves it. He can always open it again from the main page but cannot return directly to this window.

Changing a Window's Size

In Netscape, when you open a new window, you can set the initial size of that window (see the previous section, "Opening a New Browser Window"). After that, you can resize the window dynamically (**Code 14.14**). Note: This section applies only to Netscape; Internet Explorer does not support this function. **Figure 14.13** shows the initial position of the window before this exercise starts.

Figure 14.13 The initial size of the browser window.

Code 14.14 The changeWindowSize(), magnifyWindow(), and fillScreen() functions control the browser window's size.

```
<html>
<head>
    <script>
function changeWindowSize(windowWidth,windowHeight) {
    if (window.outerWidth) {
        resizeTo(windowWidth,windowHeight);
    }
}

function magnifyWindow(dWindowWidth,dWindowHeight) {
    if (window.outerWidth) {
        resizeBy(dWindowWidth,dWindowHeight);
    }
}

function fillScreen() {
    if (window.outerWidth) {
        windowWidth = screen.width;
        windowHeight = screen.height;
        moveTo(0,0);
        resizeTo(windowWidth,windowHeight);
    }
}
    </script>
</head>
<body>
    Window Size ||
    <a href="javascript:changeWindowSize(300,300)">
```

(code continues on next page)

Code 14.14 *continued*

```
                    code
  Resize to 300 by 300</a> |

  → <a href="javascript:
  magnifyWindow(30,30)">

  Increase</a> |

  <a href="javascript:
  → magnifyWindow(-30,-30)">

  Decrease</a> |

  <a href="javascript:fillScreen()">

  Fill Screen</a>

  <br><br><img src="alice04.gif"
  → width="301" height="448" border="0">

</body>

</html>
```

Figure 14.14 After the window has been resized to 300x300 pixels.

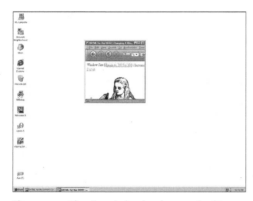

Figure 14.15 The window's size has been increased by 30 pixels in both dimensions.

To change a window's size:

1. `function changeWindowSize`
    `→ (windowWidth,windowHeight) {...}`

    Add the function `changeWindowSize()` to your JavaScript. This function first uses feature sensing to determine whether it can determine the outer width of the browser window. If so, this browser is a Netscape browser (see "Finding the Browser Window's Dimensions" in Chapter 12). Then the function uses the `resizeTo()`method to change the size of the window to `windowWidth` and `windowHeight` (**Figure 14.14**).

2. `function magnifyWindow(dWindowWidth,`
    `→ dWindowHeight) {...}`

    Add the function `magnifyWindow()` to your JavaScript. This function first uses feature sensing to see whether it can determine the outer width of the browser window. If so, this browser is a Netscape browser. Then the function uses the JavaScript method `resizeBy()` to add or subtract `dWindowWidth` and `dWindowHeight` to or from the window (**Figure 14.15**).

    continues on next page

CHANGING A WINDOW'S SIZE

3. `function fillScreen() {...}`

Add the function `fillScreen()` to your JavaScript. This function first uses feature sensing to see whether it can determine the outer width of the browser window. If so, this browser is a Netscape browser. Then the function finds the width and height of the live screen area, moves the top-left corner of the window to the top-left corner of the screen, and resizes the window to the size of the live area of the screen (**Figure 14.16**).

4. `changeWindowSize(300,300)`

Add a function call to whichever function you want to use, passing it the appropriate parameters. This function call can be associated with an event handler or can be included in the `HREF` of a link.

Figure 14.16 The browser window fills the entire screen.

DYNAMIC TECHNIQUES: CSS

The Document Object Model (DOM) for Internet Explorer 4/5 and Netscape 6 allows for some interesting effects when you create dynamic HTML with CSS. In contrast to Netscape 4, which allows you to change only the CSS position properties, Internet Explorer 4/5 and Netscape 6 recognize changes in *any* of the CSS properties available to them (see Appendix B). As a result, you can dynamically control your CSS in the browser window by making changes in styles, and these changes are visible immediately—dynamic CSS.

In this chapter, I will show you how to add and remove CSS rules and definitions dynamically by learning how to treat style sheets as objects.

Changing a Definition

CSS allows you to set up definitions (**Figure 15.1**); JavaScript allows you to change those definitions on the fly (**Figure 15.2**). You can change or add to any CSS property defined for any object on the screen—at least in Internet Explorer and Netscape 6 (**Code 15.1**).

To change the definition of an object:

1. `<script src="findDOM.js"></script>`

   In any JavaScript function that addresses an object on the screen directly, you need to include the findDOM code. You do so by including it in an external text file and then importing that file into the page in which it will be used (see "Using the Cross-Browser DOM" in Chapter 11).

2. `function changeStyle(objectID,`
   `→ styleName,newVal) {...}`

   Add the function changeStyle() to your JavaScript. This function uses the ID for the object to be addressed—passed to it as the variable objectID—to build the DOM (see "Building a Cross-Browser DOM" in Chapter 11). It then uses that DOM to change the style passed to it as styleName to the new value (newVal).

3. `#object1 {...}`

   Set up the IDs for your object(s) with whatever CSS properties you want to change.

4. `<div id="object1">...</div>`

   Set up your CSS layer(s).

5. `onClick="changeStyle('object1',`
   `→ 'fontSize','18px')`

   Add event handlers to trigger the function you created in step 2. Pass the function the ID for the object you want to address, as well as the style property you want to change and its new value.

Figure 15.1 Before *Eat Me* is moused over, the text is microscopically small.

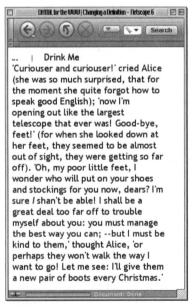

Figure 15.2 After *Eat Me* is moused over, the text has grown from 4 pixels to 18 pixels.

Code 15.1 The `changeStyle()` function changes or adds styles to the definition of a particular object in the browser window. In this code, the visitor can roll over the words *Eat Me* or *Drink Me* to make the text below grow or shrink.

```
code
<html>
<head>
    <script src="findDOM.js"></script>
    <script>
function changeStyle(objectID,styleName,
→ newVal) {
    var dom = findDOM(objectID,1);
    dom [styleName] = newVal;
}
    </script>
    <style type="text/css">
#object1 {
    font-size: 4px;
    position: relative;
    width: 300px }
#eatMe {
    font-size: 18px;
    position: relative;
    margin-right: 20px;}
#drinkMe {
    font-size: 4px;
    position: relative;
    margin-left: 20px;}
    </style>
</head>
<body>
    <span id="eatMe" onmouseover=
    "changeStyle('object1','fontSize','18px');
    → changeStyle('drinkMe','fontSize','18px');
    → this.style.fontSize = '4px';">
        Eat Me</span> |
    <span id="drinkMe" onmouseover=
    → "changeStyle('object1','fontSize','4px');
    → changeStyle('eatMe','fontSize','18px');
    → this.style.fontSize = '4px';">
        Drink Me</span>
    <div id="object1">'Curiouser and
curiouser!' cried Alice...</div>
</body>
</html>
```

✔ Tips

- Notice that because I'm concerned about running this code only in Internet Explorer 4/5 and Netscape 6, I've placed the event handler inside the `<div>` tag. Remember that Netscape 4 is currently the only popular browser that does not support events for all objects in the window.

- Style names that are composed of two or more words are separated by hyphens for CSS (`font-size`). To use them for dynamic CSS, you need to translate style names into the JavaScript naming style (`fontSize`).

JavaScript Naming Convention

JavaScript has a very particular naming convention. Words cannot include periods, hyphens, spaces, or any other separators. Instead, multiple words are expressed in the following manner:

All letters are lowercase except for the first letter of any words after the first word.

The CSS property `font-size`, for example, would be expressed as `fontSize`.

I recommend sticking to this naming convention for JavaScript function names and variables, as well as CSS class and ID names, just to make things easier.

CHANGING A DEFINITION

275

Changing an Object's Class

Although being able to add or change an individual definition is great (see the previous section, "Changing a Definition"), doing this for more than one definition at a time is time-consuming. Instead, you need the ability to change multiple definitions at once (**Figures 15.3** and **15.4**). You can accomplish this task simply by changing the entire CSS class assigned to an object (**Code 15.2**).

To change the CSS class of an object:

1. `<script src="finDOM.js"></script>`

   In any JavaScript function that addresses an object on the screen directly, you need to include the findDOM code. You do so by including it in an external text file and then importing that file into the page in which it will be used (see "Using the Cross-Browser DOM" in Chapter 11).

2. `function setClass(objectID,newClass)`
   `→ {...}`

   Add the function setClass() to your JavaScript. This function uses the ID for the object to be addressed—passed to it as the variable objectID—to build the DOM (see "Building a Cross-Browser DOM" in Chapter 11). Then this function uses the DOM to change the class name being applied to this object to the new class name (newClass).

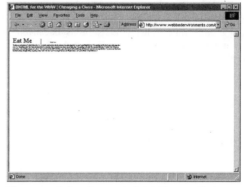

Figure 15.3 Before the words *Drink Me* are rolled over, the text is very small and black, because its class has been set to copyTiny.

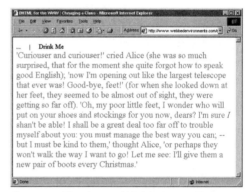

Figure 15.4 After the words *Drink Me* are rolled over, the text is much larger and red, because the class has been reassigned to copyHuge.

Code 15.2 The setClass() function reassigns the CSS class assigned to a particular object in the browser window.

```
                         code
<html>
<head>
    <script src="finDOM.js"></script>
    <script>
function setClass(objectID,newClass) {
    var dom = findDOM(objectID,0);
    dom.className = newClass;
}
    </script>
```

(code continues on next page)

Code 15.2 *continued*

```
              code
   <style type="text/css">
#object1 {   position: relative; }
#eatMe {
   position: relative;
   margin-right: 20px; }
#drinkMe {
   position: relative;
   margin-left: 20px;}
.copyTiny {
      font-size: 4px;
      position: relative;
      color: black;
      width: 300px; }
.copyHuge {
      font-size: 24px;
      position: relative;
      color: red;
      width: 600px; }
.tiny {
      font-size: 4px;
      position: relative;
      color: red;}
.huge {
      font-size: 18px;
      position: relative;
      color: black;}
   </style>
</head>
<body>
   <span class="huge" id="eatMe" onmouseover=
   → "setClass('object1','copyHuge');
   → setClass('drinkMe','huge');
   → this.className = 'tiny';">

   Eat Me</span> |

   <span class="tiny" id="drinkMe"
   → onmouseover="setClass('object1',
   → 'copyTiny');setClass('eatMe','huge');
   → this.className = 'tiny';">

   Drink Me</span>

   <div id="object1" class="copyTiny">
   → 'Curiouser and curiouser!' cried
   → Alice...</div>
</body>
</html>
```

3. #object1 {...}

Set up the IDs for your layer(s) with whatever styles you desire.

4. copyTiny {...}

Set up the classes that you will be applying to your objects.

5. onmouseover="setClass('object1',
→ 'copyHuge');

Add event handlers to trigger the function you created in step 2, and pass it the ID for the object you want to address and the name of the class you want to apply to that object.

6. <div id="object1">...</div>

Set up your CSS layer(s).

Adding a New Rule

Note that this section applies only to Internet Explorer.

Changing a class is great (see the previous section "Changing an Object's Class"), but what if you want to add a rule that does not currently exist, or replace an existing rule (**Figures 15.5** and **15.6**)?

First, you must give the `<style>` tag an ID that turns it into an object (**Code 15.3**). Then you can use JavaScript to access the style sheet.

Figure 15.5 Before the link is clicked, the page's default values are used in the window (black text on a white background).

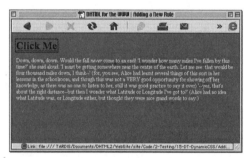

Figure 15.6 After the link is clicked, the page uses the rule set up for the <body> tag (white text on a red background).

Code 15.3 The `addARule()` function adds a new CSS rule to the style sheet called `myStyles`.

```
                          code
<html>
<head>
    <script>
function addARule(selector,definition) {

document.styleSheets.MyStyles.addRule
→ (selector,definition)
}
    </script>
    <style id="MyStyles">
h1 {
    font-size: 24pt}
    body { color: gray; }
    </style>
</head>
<body>
    <h1>
        <a href="javascript:void('')"
        → onclick="addARule('body',
        → 'background-color:red; color:
        → white')">
            Click Me</a>
</h1>
    <p>Down, down, down. Would the fall
    → <i>never</i> come to an end!...</p>
</body>
</html>
```

To add a new rule
to a Web page dynamically:

1. `function addARule(selector,definition)`
   `→ {...}`

   Add the function `addARule()` to your JavaScript. This function adds the new rule to the style sheet that you identify in step 2, using the name of the selector for which you want to add a rule (see "Kinds of HTML Tags" in Chapter 1) and the definition(s) you want to apply to that selector.

2. `<style id="MyStyles">...</style>`

   Add a `<style>` container in the head of your document—even if you do not set any initial rules—and give it a unique ID that can be used by the function in step 1 to address this style sheet.

3. `onclick="addARule('body',`
   `→ 'background-color:red; color:`
   `→ white;')"`

   Add an event handler to trigger the `addARule()` function from step 1. Pass this function the name of the selector for which you want to add a new rule and the definitions you want to assign for this new rule.

Disabling a Style Sheet

Note that this section applies only to Internet Explorer.

What if you want to eliminate a CSS rule—not change it or add to it, but get rid of it and revert to the browser's default values (**Figures 15.7** and **15.8**)?

As you can when you add a rule (see the previous section, "Adding a New Rule"), you can access a style that has been given an ID. But instead of adding a new rule, you disable it (**Code 15.4**).

Sometimes, your visitors might want to see just the text without all those fancy styles. Their loss—but everyone has his own taste. Internet Explorer allows you to disable a particular style and then turn it on again to suit your needs.

This function does not work in Netscape 6.

Figure 15.7 Before the link is clicked, the text is very large, light-colored, and hard to read.

Figure 15.8 After the link is clicked, the text is displayed in the browser's default style (black text at 12-point font size).

Code 15.4 When the word *here* is clicked, the `disabled` property of the `strangeStyle` style sheet is set to true. This value turns the style sheet off, and any elements on the screen that use this style sheet revert to their original condition. I also set the display property for this element—the one with the `onClick` event in it—to none, so that the element disappears along with the style and will not confuse the visitor, because the style is already turned off.

```
                      code
<html>
<head>
   <style id="strangeStyle">
.bizzaro {
   color: #eeeeee;
   font: italic 100px fantasy; }
   </style>
</head>
<body>
   <span class="bizzaro"> 'What a curious
   → feeling!'</span><br>
   <span id="styleOff">If you can not read
   → the above, click --&gt;
   → <span onclick="document.styleSheets.
   → strangeStyle.disabled=true; document.
   → all.styleOff.style.display='none';">
   → here</span> &lt;--- </span>
</body>
</html>
```

To disable a style sheet:

1. `<style id="strangeStyle">...</style>`

   Set up a style sheet in the head of your document. Give the `<style>` tag the ID attribute and a name. In this example, I created a style sheet called `strangeStyle`.

2. `onclick= "document.styleSheets.`
   `→ strangeStyle.disabled=true;"`

   Set up an event handler that sets the `disabled` property of the style sheet identified in step 1 to `true`.

✔ Tip

■ Rather than set the `disabled` property to `true`, you can set it to `false` to enable a style sheet that was inactive.

16

NETSCAPE LAYERS

Netscape layers are a way to create independent objects in the browser window—objects that can be positioned, repositioned, shown or hidden, and stacked at will. They sound a lot like CSS layers, don't they? Netscape layers and CSS layers do basically the same thing but are set up differently. In fact, a Netscape layer is just another object on the screen created with a slightly different method (see "Creating an Object" in Chapter 11).

The biggest difference is that Netscape layers are supported by only one browser: Netscape 4. Although Netscape the company promised to continue to support layers in future iterations of its browser, this turned out not to be the case; Netscape 6 (Netscape 4's successor) has no support for Netscape layers.

Still, layers are used in Netscape 4 and have to be used for certain cross-browser DHTML solutions in conjunction with Internet Explorer-specific technologies.

In this chapter, I'll show you how to use the `<layer>` and `<ilayer>` tags, as well as how to add external content and change that content on demand.

What Is a Netscape Layer?

A *Netscape layer* is an independent chunk of Web content within an HTML document, set off with one of the two layer-tag pairs:

- `<layer>`: the CSS equivalent is `<div style="position:absolute;">`
- `<ilayer>`: the CSS equivalent is `<span style="position:relative">`

You can place as many Netscape layers in a Web page as you want. Each layer can have its own properties, which you can control dynamically by using JavaScript.

Generally speaking, whatever you can do with a CSS layer, you can do with Netscape layers. Like CSS layers, Netscape layers can be stacked and shuffled around as desired. They can be made transparent (with `hide`) or opaque (with `show`). In addition, you can specify background images and colors.

The greatest advantage layers offer is that they allow you to include content from an external URL and to change that content dynamically. But you can approximate even that capability with CSS, using ilayers for Netscape and iframes for Internet Explorer (see "Combining iLayers and iFrames" in Chapter 23).

Aside from that, the other advantage of Netscape layers is that you can associate them with JavaScript event handlers—something CSS layers cannot do for Netscape 4 (see "Understanding Event Handlers" in Chapter 11). Although Internet Explorer and Netscape 6 allow mouse-based event handlers to be placed in any HTML tag, Netscape 4 can trigger mouse events only in a link (`<a>`) or layer tag.

Netscape Layers vs. CSS Layers

The really big difference between Netscape's layers and the World Wide Web Consortium's (W3C) CSS layers is their philosophies about positioning elements on the screen. Netscape, continuing a popular trend started with its first browser, added new tags, hoping to extend the capabilities of HTML.

Conversely, the W3C, in an attempt to preserve HTML as a true markup language, added new properties to its style-sheet standard.

Both Netscape and Internet Explorer, however, have pledged to follow the W3C's lead in future versions of their browsers. Thus, CSS layers are the future of dynamic content on the Web.

Table 16.1

Layer Tags	
TAG NAME	WHAT IT DOES
<layer>...</layer>	Creates a discrete area of HTML code in Netscape 4 that can be positioned anywhere on the page and that can be defined with the layer attributes
<ilayer>...</ilayer>	Creates a discrete area of HTML code in Netscape 4 that can be positioned in context to the other elements around it and that can be defined with the layer attributes
<nolayer>...</nolayer>	Hides content intended for non-layers-capable browsers from layers-capable browsers

Creating a Layer

Unlike CSS layers, Netscape layers (**Figure 16.1**) require the use of one of two HTML tags (Netscape extensions of HTML) that specify whether the layer's content is to be positioned freely on the screen (**Table 16.1**). Absolutely positioned layers use the <layer>...</layer> tags (like position: absolute). Relative layers use the <ilayer>...</ilayer> tags (like position: relative).

Like most HTML tags, the <layer> tag has a bevy of attributes that control the layer's appearance and behavior. These attributes are listed in Table 16.1.

continues on next page

The first layer is positioned absolutely.
The third layer is positioned absolutely within the second layer.

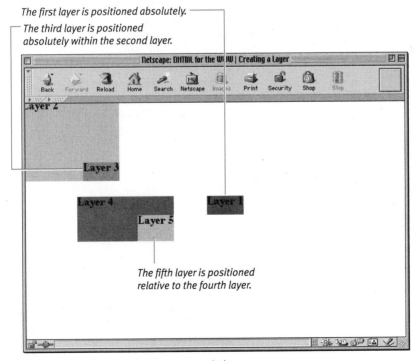

The fifth layer is positioned relative to the fourth layer.

Figure 16.1 The five layers in a Netscape 4 window.

CREATING A LAYER

285

For the most part, the layer attributes are identical to those used with CSS, with a few exceptions:

- pageX and pageY. These attributes allow you to position any absolutely positioned layer in the window with the top-left corner of the document as the origin, even when the layer is nested in other layers.

- src. This attribute allows you to specify an external file to be included within the document (see the next section, "Importing External Content with Netscape Layers").

- above and below. These attributes specify which layers should be above or below the current layer in the z-index.

Table 16.2

Netscape Layer-Tag Attributes		
ATTRIBUTE NAME	**VALUES**	**WHAT IT DOES**
id	<alphanumeric>	Identifies the layer for use in JavaScript
name	<alphanumeric>	Identical to ID; ID is preferred
left	<length>	Horizontal position relative to parent
top	<length>	Vertical position relative to parent
pageX*	<length>	Horizontal position; always relative to window
pageY*	<length>	Vertical position; always relative to window
z-index	<number>	Stacking order for this layer in relation to others
above*	<alphanumeric>	Name of the layer to appear above this one
below*	<alphanumeric>	Name of the layer to appear below this one
width	<length> <percentage>	Horizontal length
height	<length> <percentage>	Vertical length
clip	<length, length>	Visible area
visibility	show hide inherit	Visibility status
bgcolor	<color>	Color that appears behind the layer's contents
backgroundD-Ccolor	<color>	Same as bgcolor
background	<url>	Image (GIF or JPEG) that appears behind the layer's contents.
background-image	<url>	Same as background
src*	<url>	URL of external content to be included in layer

*No CSS equivalent

Code 16.1 Five layers, five locations.

```
                    code
<html>
<body>
    <layer top="150" left="300"
    → bgcolor="#666666">
        <h2>Layer 1</h2>
    </layer>

<layer top="-5" left="-5" bgcolor="#CCCCCC">
        <h2>Layer 2</h2>
<layer top="100" left="100"
→ bgcolor="#999999">
        <h2>Layer 3</h2>
        </layer>
    </layer>

    <layer top="150" left="85"
    → bgcolor="#666666">
        <h2>Layer 4</h2>
        <ilayer top="0" left="100"
        → bgcolor="#CCCCCC">
            <h2>Layer 5</h2>
        </ilayer>
    </layer>
</body>
</html>
```

To set up a layer:

1. `<layer top="150" left="300" bgcolor=`
   `→ "#666666">`

   Within your HTML, open your layer with the `<layer>` or `<ilayer>` tag. **Table 16.2** shows the attributes you can add to the layer tags and what effects they have (**Code 16.1**).

2. `<h2>Layer 1</h2>`

   Within the layer container, include content for this layer. Content in a layer can be anything that normally might appear in an HTML document.

3. `</layer>`

   Close the layer with the appropriate closing tag (`</layer>` or `</ilayer>`).

✔ Tip

■ The inline layer tag (`<ilayer>`) is set up identically to the `<layer>` tag described in this section.

CREATING A LAYER

Importing External Content with Netscape Layers

One of the most useful capabilities of Netscape layers is that they allow you to import content from other HTML files—that is, you can draw the content of a layer from another HTML file.

To add attributes to a layer:

1. `layer1.html`

   Set up the external file that you will be importing into index.html. This file can contain any standard HTML that you would find between the <body> tags of an HTML document, but it should not include <html>, <head>, or <body> tags (**Code 16.2**).

2. `index.html`

   Set up your HTML file into which you want to import the external file from step 1, and save it as something like index.html. Steps 3 and 4 apply to this file (**Code 16.3**).

3. `<layer id="layer1" src="layer1.html"`
   `→ bgcolor="#CCCCCC">`

   Open your layer tag. In the layer tag from step 1, type the attributes you want to use to define this layer. In this example, an external source document is being loaded into the layer. The layer is identified with a name (`layer1`) as well as a background color.

Code 16.2 layer1.html includes the external content to be used by index.html. Notice that there are no <html>, <head>, or <body> tags.

```
code
<h2>Layer 1</h2>
<img src="alice26.gif" width="134"
→ height="150">
```

Code 16.3 index.html contains four Netscape layers. The first layer pulls its source from a file called layer1.html.

```
code
<html>
<body>
    <layer id="layer1" src="layer1.html"
    → bgcolor="#CCCCCC"></layer>
    <layer id="layer2" above="layer1"
    → width="100" height="100" top="125"
    → left="125" bgcolor="#666666">
        <h2>Layer 2</h2>
    </layer>
    <layer id="layer3" top="10" left="350"
    → bgcolor="#CCCCCC">
        <h2>Layer 3</h2>
        <layer id="layer4" pagey="125"
        → pagex="250" bgcolor="#666666"
        → width="100" height="100">
        <h2>Layer 4</h2>
        </layer>
    </layer>
</body>
</html>
```

4. `</layer>`

Close your layer container. If you define an external source by using the SRC attribute for a layer, you cannot include any other content within the layer-container tags.

The result is that layer 1 pulls in an external file with the Mad Hatter and, despite being defined before layer 2, layer 1 appears on top of layer 2 because of the *above* attribute set in layer 2 (**Figure 16.2**). Layer 4 has been nested in layer 3, but because it has been positioned with pageX and pageY, it is still positioned absolutely in relation to the document, not in relation to layer 3.

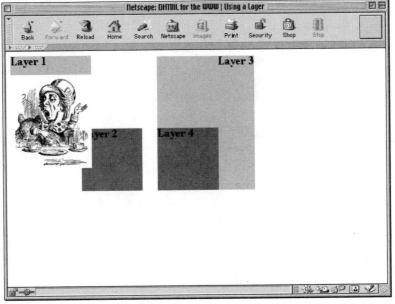

Figure 16.2 Four layers have been set up. Layer 1 is importing a picture of the Mad Hatter from an external file.

Accessing Layers with JavaScript

In addition to a layer's attributes, the <layer> tag can include the event handlers onMouseOver, onMouseOut, onFocus, onBlur, and onLoad. You can associate these event handlers with the layer to access JavaScript functions (see "Understanding Event Handlers" in Chapter 11), which CSS layers cannot do directly in Netscape 4 (**Figures 16.3** and **16.4**).

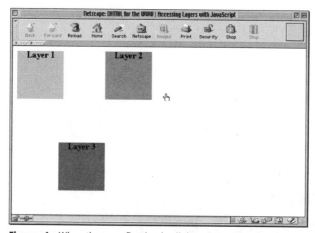

Figure 16.3 When the page first loads all three layers are showing.

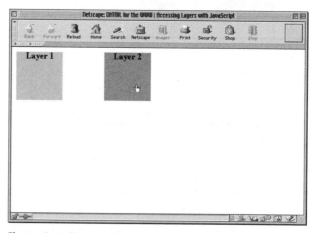

Figure 16.4 Rolling over layer 2 causes layer 3 to disappear.

Table 16.3 shows all the properties associated with the layer object and indicates whether they can be modified by the user.

Table 16.3

Netscape Layer Object Properties

Property Name	Modifiable with JavaScript?	What It Does
document	No	Every layer can be treated as an independent document used to access its images, applets, embeds, links, anchors, and embedded layers.
name	No	The NAME or ID given to the layer.
left	Yes	The horizontal position of the element. For <LAYER>, this will be absolutely within the page or relative to surrounding layers. For <ilayer>, this will be relative to its natural position within the document or a surrounding layer.
top	Yes	The vertical position of the element. For <ilayer>, this will be absolutely within the page or relative to its surrounding layer. For <ilayer>, this will be relative to its natural position within the document or a surrounding layer.
pageX	Yes	The horizontal position of the element relative to the document, regardless of what type of layer it is.
pageY	Yes	The vertical position of the element relative to the document, regardless of what type of layer it is.
zIndex	Yes	The layer's position in the stacking order relative to its siblings.
visibility	Yes	Whether the layer can be seen.
clip.width	Yes	The horizontal visible area of the layer.
clip.height	Yes	The vertical visible area of the layer.
bgcolor	Yes	The background color to appear behind the layer's content.
background	Yes	The background image to appear behind the layer's content.
siblingAbove	No	The NAME or ID of the sibling layer that appears above this layer in the stacking order.
siblingBelow	No	The NAME or ID of the sibling layer that appears below this layer in the stacking order.
above	No	The NAME or ID of the layer in z-index that appears above this layer in the stacking order.
below	No	The NAME or ID of the layer in z-index that appears below this layer in the stacking order.
parentLayer	No	The name of this layer's parent. Defaults to the window's name if there is no parent.
src	Yes	The URL of the layer's external source.

To access layers through JavaScript:

1. function toggleLayerViz(objectID,
   → state){...}

   Add a function in your JavaScript that
   will change a Netscape layer's property
   or properties (**Code 16.4**). Do this by
   accessing the layer using the ID for the
   layer in the layer array:

   document.layers[objectID].visibility=
   → state;

   This example changes the visibility
   property, but you can access any of the
   properties in the same way.

2. <layer id="layer1"...>

   Create a layer with an id attribute.
   In the <layer> tag, add an event handler
   to trigger the function from step 1:

   onmouseover="toggleLayerViz
   → ('layer2','hide')"

   In this case, when the mouse passes over
   the layer, it runs the toggleLayerViz()
   function and passes to the function the
   layer's ID for the layer you want to act on
   and the change (state) you want to make.

Code 16.4 Three layers have been created in the
window, each with onmouseover to hide the layer after
it and onmouseout to show the layer before it.

```
<html>
<head>
    <script language="JavaScript">
function toggleLayerViz(objectID,state){
    document.layers[objectID].visibility=
    → state;}
}
    </script>
</head>
<body>
    <layer id="layer1" bgcolor="#CCCCCC"
    → width="100" height="100" top="10"
    → left="10" onmouseover="toggleLayerViz
    → ('layer2','hide')" onmouseout=
    → "toggleLayerViz('layer3','show')"
    → visibility="show">
        <center><h2>Layer 1</h2></center>
    </layer>
    <layer id="layer2" bgcolor="#999999"
    → width="100" height="100" top="10"
    → left="200" onmouseover="toggleLayerViz
    → ('layer3','hide')" onmouseout=
    → "toggleLayerViz('layer1','show')"
    → visibility="show">
        <center><h2>Layer 2</h2></center>
    </layer>
    <layer id="layer3" bgcolor="#666666"
    → width="100" height="100" top="200"
    → left="100" onmouseover="toggleLayerViz
    → ('layer1','hide')" onmouseout=
    → "toggleLayerViz('layer2','show')"
    → visibility="show">
        <center><h2>Layer 3</h2></center>
    </layer>
</body>
</html>
```

✔ Tips

- One of the most interesting things that you can change is the source file (`src`) of a layer. This change gives you dynamic control of what external HTML file is being displayed (see Chapter 23). If only you had that type of control with CSS!

- Whether you are using Netscape layers or CSS layers to position your content, Navigator 4 uses the layer's Document Object Model (DOM) to access the elements. With CSS layers, Navigator 4 treats the various IDs as though they are layers, which can be accessed through its DOM (see "How the DOM Works" in Chapter 11).

- In the Netscape layers array, as in all arrays, the first layer is always `0`; so the third layer defined in any document is actually second (`0,1,2`) in the array.

- Unlike most elements that can have event handlers associated with them, events that are associated with layers can call only JavaScript functions and methods. You cannot place JavaScript in the quotes after the event handler.

- Notice that I used the variable name `objectID` rather than something like `layerID` in the function `toggleLayerViz()`. I did this for consistency's sake because, within some limitations, it doesn't matter what the variable is called. For all intents and purposes, a layer is just another object on the screen.

Modifying Layers with JavaScript

In addition to the various properties that can be changed through the layer object, several layer object methods can perform a variety of tasks on a layer (**Figure 16.5**). These methods are listed in **Table 16.4**.

A *method* is a predefined JavaScript function that can save you a lot of time and make simple tasks, such as moving the layer on the screen, much easier.

Figure 16.5 Here, kitty, kitty, kitty. Moving the mouse over the layer reveals the Cheshire Cat. Move the mouse away, and the cat disappears.

Table 16.4

Netscape Layer Object Methods	
METHOD NAME	**WHAT IT DOES**
moveBy(x,y)	Moves the layer x pixels to the right and y pixels down from its current position.
moveTo(x,y)	Moves the layer to the specified x,y coordinates within its containing layer or within the document.
moveToAbsolute(x,y)	Moves the layer to the specified x,y coordinates within the document.
resizeBy(x,y)	Resizes the layer x pixels to the right and y pixels down from its current size.
resizeTo(x,y)	Resizes the layer to a width of x pixels and a height of y pixels.
moveAbove(layer)	Moves this layer above the specified layer.
moveBelow(layer)	Moves this layer below the specified layer.
load(URL,width)	Loads the URL specified as the source of the layer with the specified width. You can omit the width to leave that value unchanged.

Code 16.5 The `clipLayer()` function resizes the layer. When the page first loads, the layer is clipped down to 200x175 pixels. When the mouse moves over the layer (the visible part), the layer grows to 400x271 pixels. When the mouse moves out of the layer, it shrinks back to 200x175.

```
                    code
<html>
<head>
    <script language="JavaScript">
function clipLayer(objectID,x,y){
document.layers[objectID].resizeTo(x,y);
}
    </script>
</head>
<body>
    <layer id="cheshireCat" clip="200,175"
    → onmouseover="clipLayer('cheshireCat',
    → 400,271)" onmouseout="clipLayer
    → ('cheshireCat',200,175)" top="0"
    → left="0" visibility="show">
        <img src="alice24.gif" width="400"
        → height="271">
    </layer>
</body>
</html>
```

To expand the layer:

1. `function clipLayer(objectID,x,y)`
   `→ {...}`

   Set up a function that uses the layer object and the method you want to perform on it (**Code 16.5**).

   In this example, the `resizeTo` method is being used to change the size of `layer1`:

   `document.layers[objectID].resizeTo`
   `→ (x,y)`

   You can use any of the methods listed in Table 16.4 in a similar fashion.

2. `<layer id="cheshireCat">`

   Create your layer with an `id` to identify it. Add an event handler to the layer tag to trigger the function you set up in step 1:

   `onmouseover="clipLayer('cheshireCat',`
   `→ 400,271)"`

   Pass that function the layer's ID and the parameters for the method to be used in the function.

✔ Tip

■ Netscape 6 does not support the layer object methods—a shame, because that support would save us a lot of time.

Providing Content for Nonlayer Browsers

As the `<noframes>` tag allows a frame document's content to be displayed in browsers that do not understand frames, a special `<nolayers>` tag allows a layer document's content to be displayed by browsers that do not support layers (**Figures 16.6** and **16.7**).

To add nonlayer content:

1. `<ilayer id="special" top="10"`
   → `height="10" src="daily_special.html">`
   → `</ilayer>`

   Add the Netscape layer content that you want to include in your Web page. In this example (**Code 16.6**), an external file called daily_special.html (**Code 16.7**) is being imported (see "Importing External Content with Netscape Layers" earlier in this chapter).

2. `<nolayer>`

   Open the nonlayers area of your document with the `<nolayer>` tag.

3. `<a href="daily_special.html">The Daily`
   → `Specials are available here! </a>`

   Add the content you want to display in browsers that cannot handle layers. Here, I have added a link to the file being imported in step 1.

4. `</nolayer>`

   Close the nonlayer content.

Figure 16.7 Netscape 6 does not support the `<ilayer>` tag, so the link is available here.

Code 16.6 The `<ilayer>` tag imports the file daily_special.html, but also includes a link to the page in the `<nolayer>` tag.

```
<html>
<body>
    <h1>Mad Tea-Party Menu</h1>
    <h3>DAILY SPECIAL</h3>
    <p>
    <ilayer id="special" top="10" height="10"
    → src="daily_special.html">
    </ilayer>
    <nolayer>
    <a href="daily_special.html">The Daily
    → Specials are available here! </a>
    </nolayer>
</body>
</html>
```

Code 16.7 This code is imported into the layer in index.html if the browser being used is Netscape 4. Otherwise, the page is linked to and includes a link back to the menu in the `<nolayers>` tag.

```
<nolayer>
    <a href="index.html">&lt;&lt;
    → Return to Menu</a>
</nolayer>

<!-HTML CONTENT GOES HERE ->
```

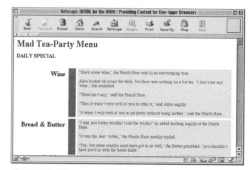

Figure 16.6 The page displayed in Netscape 4, with a layer that has a daily special for the Mad Tea-Party being pulled in from an external file.

INTERNET EXPLORER FOR WINDOWS

17

Internet Explorer for Windows has several built-in special effects that you can use to add dynamism to your Web pages. These filters allow you to create a variety of special effects, especially for transitions between objects or pages.

Note: The special effects described in this chapter are supported only by the Windows version of Internet Explorer 4/5. They may be pretty cool, but you should use them sparingly because they do not work in the Netscape browsers—or in the Macintosh and Unix versions of Internet Explorer. These capabilities are based on a proprietary technology called ActiveX, which is controlled solely by Microsoft.

Unlike JavaScript or other Web technologies, ActiveX controls are not open standards. Still, they will not interfere with other browsers, so they are all right to use—even in cross-browser situations—to add a bit of spice for your Internet Explorer for Windows users.

Fading Between Objects

By far the most popular way to show a transition between two elements is the fade. For Internet Explorer for Windows, you can set up two images (or a pair of any screen elements, for that matter) and fade one out as the other fades in (**Figure 17.1**).

To fade elements:

1. `function fadeElement(){...}`

   Add the function `fadeElement()` to the JavaScript in the head of your document. This function applies the `blendTrans` filter between the current source image for `image1` (alice04.gif, in the example) and its replacement, alice05.gif (**Code 17.1**).

2. `<img id="alice" src="alice04.gif"`

   Set up the initial image to be displayed when the screen first loads.

3. `style="filter:blendTrans(duration=3)"`
   `→ onclick="fadeElement()">`

   In the `style` attribute for `image1`, add a call to Internet Explorer's `blendTrans` filter, and set its fade duration to 3 (seconds). This filter will not be acted upon until the image is clicked and the `fadeElement()` function is executed.

Figure 17.1 One image fades in as the other fades out.

Code 17.1 The `fadeElement()`function, when activated, causes `image1` to fade from its initial source (alice04.gif) to its new source (alice05.gif).

```
<html>
<head>
    <script>
var isFade = 0;

function fadeElement() {
    if (document.all && isFade == 0) {
        isFade = 1;
        alice.filters.blendTrans.Apply();
        alice.src = "alice05.gif";
        alice.filters.blendTrans.Play();
    }
}
    </script>
</head>
<body>
    This fade will only work in Internet
    → Explorer 4 and above on Windows.
    <img id="alice" src="alice04.gif"
    → style="filter:blendTrans(duration=3)"
    → onClick="fadeElement()"><br>
</body>
</html>
```

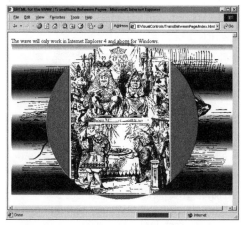

Figure 17.2 The page is shown in mid-transition as the new page with the King and Queen spins in.

Transitions Between Pages

When you're jumping between Web pages, it's always a bit disconcerting when the first page blinks out and is slowly replaced by the next page piece by piece. Using the `RevealTrans()` filters, however, you can produce transitions between Web pages that are more cinematic (**Figure 17.2**).

Table 17.1 lists the transition-filter effects that are available.

Table 17.1

IE Transition Filters	
TRANSITION	REFERENCE #
Box In	0
Box Out	1
Circle In	2
Circle Out	3
Wipe Up	4
Wipe Down	5
Wipe Right	6
Wipe Left	7
Vertical Blinds	8
Horizontal Blinds	9
Checkerboard Across	10
Checkerboard Down	11
Random Dissolve	12
Split Vertical In	13
Split Vertical Out	14
Split Horizontal In	15
Split Horizontal Out	16
Strips Left Down	17
Strips Left Up	18
Strips Right Down	19
Strips Right Up	20
Random Bars Horizontal	21
Random Bars Vertical	22
Random	23

To set up a transition between Web pages:

1. <meta http-equiv="Page-Enter"

Set up a <meta> tag in the head of your document (**Code 17.2**). Set the http-equiv attribute to Page-Enter.

2. content = "RevealTrans (Duration=20,
→ Transition=3)>

Set the content attribute for the <meta> tag in step 1 to execute the RevealTrans() filter, and set its duration to 2 (seconds). Then add the name of a transition from Table 17.1. For this example, I chose the Circle In effect, to have the page spiral in.

3. <meta http-equiv="Page-Exit"
→ content = "RevealTrans
→ (Duration=20, Transition=3)>

To set a filter to run when the visitor leaves this page, type another <meta> tag for Page-Exit. For this one, I selected the Circle Out filter.

Code 17.2 Here, the <meta> tag is used to execute transition filters when the document is opened and when it is closed.

```
<html>
<head>
    <meta HTTP-EQUIV="Page-Enter"
    → CONTENT="RevealTrans(Duration=20,
    → Transition=3)">
    <meta HTTP-EQUIV="Page-Exit"
    → CONTENT="RevealTrans(Duration=20,
    → Transition=3)">
</head>
<body style="background-color:red">
    This transition will only work in
    → Internet Explorer 4 and above for
    → Windows.
    <center>
    <a href="page2.html">
        <img src="alice01.gif" height="90%">
        <br>
        Next Picture --&gt;
    </a>
    </center>
</body>
</html>
```

Figure 17.3 The griffin blurs across the screen.

Code 17.3 The blurOn() function causes the image to blur across the screen slowly.

```
                        code
<html>
<head>
   <script>
function blurOn(currStrength,currDirection){
    if (document.all && currStrength < 360) {
        currStrength += 1;
        currDirection += 1;
        document.all.blurMe.style.filter =
        → "blur(strength= " + currStrength + ",
        → " + currDirection + ")";
        setTimeout("blurOn(" + currStrength + ",
        → " + currDirection + ")",100);
    }
  }
  </script>
</head>
<body onLoad="blurOn(15,15)">
    The blur will only work in Internet
    → Explorer 4 and above for Windows.
    <img id="blurMe" src="alice33.gif"
    → height="95%" style="FILTER:blur
    → (strength=0, direction=5)">
</body>
</html>
```

Making an Element Blur

Blurring can make an element—text or graphic—look as though it is moving by simulating the blurring caused by motion (**Figure 17.3**).

To blur an element:

1. `function blurOn(currStrength,` `→ currDirection) {...}`

   Add the `blurOn()` function to the JavaScript in the head of your document. This function recursively applies the blur filter to the image named `blurMe` until it reaches a `strength` of 360. The `strength` attribute specifies how far the element should be blurred (**Code 17.3**).

2. `<body onLoad="blurOn(15,15)">`

   Add an `onLoad` event handler that runs the `blurOn()` function from step 1.

3. `<img id="blurMe" src="alice33.gif"` `→ height="95%" style="FILTER:blur` `→ (strength=0, direction=5)">`

   In the body of your document, add the image you want to blur. In the `<img>` tag, add the `style` attribute with the blur filter. Set its initial `strength` to 0; set `direction` to 0 as well.

MAKING AN ELEMENT BLUR

Making an Object Wave

The wave filter causes an image or other element to distort in a rippling effect, like a flag undulating in the wind (**Figure 17.4**).

To make an element look wavy:

1. `<img src="alice08.gif" height="90%"`

   Set up an image in the body of your document (**Code 17.4**).

2. `style="FILTER:wave(freq=3,`
   `→ strength=6)">`

   Add the `style` property to your image, using the wave filter with the frequency set to 3. (This number controls the number of ridges in the wave.) Set `strength` to 6 (this controls the size of the ripples).

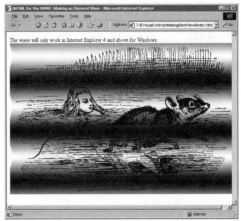

Figure 17.4 The image appears to be rippled as Alice swims across the page.

Code 17.4 The wave filter is applied to the image aliceo8.gif.

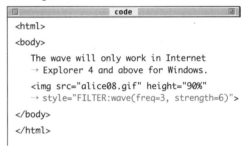

```
<html>
<body>
    The wave will only work in Internet
    → Explorer 4 and above for Windows.
    <img src="alice08.gif" height="90%"
    → style="FILTER:wave(freq=3, strength=6)">
</body>
</html>
```

PART 3

USING DHTML AND CSS TOOLS

Chapter 18:   GoLive Primer   305

Chapter 19:   Dreamweaver Primer   319

GoLive Primer

GoLive is a complete HTML-creation package that bundles together *WYSIWYG* (What You See Is What You Get) and HTML code editors. It started life as CyberStudio and was created by a company called GoLive. Both the software and the company were eventually purchased by Adobe Systems Inc., which has made the program a shining star in its Web-development software lineup.

GoLive has evolved over the years to encompass JavaScript editing, CSS, and dynamic HTML tools. It includes these tools in an easy-to-use environment. The tags are located conveniently and can be altered from various palettes, allowing you to see your changes as you make them.

In this chapter, I'll show you how to create DHTML and CSS in GoLive, including how to add external style sheets and animate multiple objects through complex paths.

The GoLive Interface

Although GoLive was not created by Adobe, recent versions of the program have benefited from the influence of Adobe's interface standards. Adobe included additional functionality while keeping the interface well organized and simple to use.

While GoLive's WYSIWYG interface allows even novice Web designers to create Web pages, this program also includes some of the best code-editing tools (for HTML, JavaScript, and CSS) available to professionals.

The GoLive interface can be broken into five main areas: the document window, toolbar, palettes, site controls, and other tools (**Figure 18.1**).

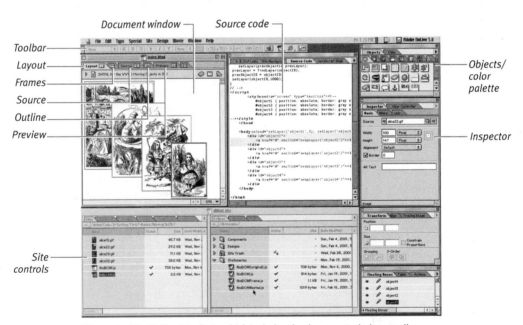

Figure 18.1 The GoLive interface, which includes the document window, toolbar, site controls, and various palettes.

THE GOLIVE INTERFACE

Figure 18.2 The document window in layout mode. You can add, change, and move elements without having to know a single HTML tag.

Document window

The document window is where the code for an individual Web page can be viewed and changed in a variety of modes, each supporting a different way of interacting with the page's content. To switch among these various modes, simply click on the tabs at the top of the window.

- ◆ **Layout mode** is the most like working in a word processor. Rather than deal with HTML tags, you see what the page should look like (**Figure 18.2**).

- ◆ **Frames mode** allows you to view and edit the frame layout of a page.

- ◆ **Source mode** allows you to edit the raw HTML, CSS, and JavaScript source code (**Figure 18.3**).

- ◆ **Outline mode** is useful for viewing the structure of a Web page (**Figure 18.4**).

- ◆ **Preview mode** allows you to view the page as it should appear in a browser. It also lets you play around with different variables, such as CSS support, to see how the page might appear in a variety of environments. If the page includes framesets, frames-preview mode is also available.

Figure 18.3 The document window in source mode. All the code for the Web page (including the JavaScript and CSS) can be edited directly in this window.

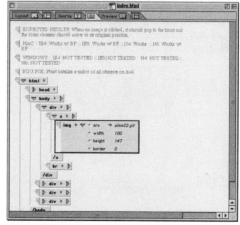

Figure 18.4 Outline mode also allows you to edit the code in a Web page, but it shows the code in a hierarchical structure. This feature is especially valuable for validating your code.

Toolbar

The toolbar provides shortcuts to the most common styles and tasks in a thin ribbon across the top of the screen (although you can move it anywhere you want).

The toolbar is contextual, meaning that its tools change depending on what is displayed and selected in the document window. If you are editing text in layout mode, for example, you'll see text tools that control header level, alignment, and font size (**Figure 18.5**). If you select a layer (called a *floating box* in GoLive), the toolbar changes to allow you to control the layer's size, position, and alignment (**Figure 18.6**).

Text controls   Universal controls

Figure 18.5 The toolbar changes many of its options depending on the element that is selected in the document window. This figure shows what the bar looks like when text is selected.

Box controls   Universal controls

Figure 18.6 This figure shows what the toolbar looks like when a layer is selected. Notice that certain elements (document selection, browser preview, and online help) stay consistent.

Palettes

More than a dozen palettes give you access to a multitude of features and functions. You can show or hide palettes by choosing them from the Window menu. The most important palettes for CSS and DHTML are:

◆ **Objects.** This palette provides access to the myriad HTML and other object tags you may use in your Web page.

◆ **Color.** This palette allows you to select foreground and background colors.

◆ **Inspector.** This palette allows you to set attributes for the selected object in the document window. The inspector is a contextual palette, so the options depend on what objects are selected in the document window.

◆ **Source Code.** This palette allows you to view and change the source code while you are in the document window's layout mode.

Site controls

GoLive includes an excellent FTP client and site-management tools. Various options allow you to manage your site and even selectively upload only those files that have changed since the last upload.

Other tools

GoLive includes a robust spelling checker, as well as tools that predict download times, alert you to potential problems in various browsers, and check all your links to ensure that they are valid.

In addition, GoLive provides several editors for new Web technologies, including CSS and JavaScript.

Adding CSS

Part I of this book deals with style sheets. GoLive includes an assortment of tools that helps you add and control the CSS in a Web page (see "Adding CSS to a Web Page" in Chapter 2) or an entire Web site (see "Adding CSS to a Web Site" in Chapter 2).

To add CSS to a Web page:

1. Open a new or existing HTML file by choosing File > New or File > Open.

2. With the document window in layout mode (see the previous section, "Interface Overview"), click the CSS button in the top-right corner of the window (**Figure 18.7**) to open the page-styles window (**Figure 18.8**).

3. In the toolbar (**Figure 18.9**), click the button for the CSS selector type you want to use: HTML, class, or ID (see "The Parts of a CSS Rule" in Chapter 1).

   A new style element appears in the page-styles window.

4. In the Inspector palette, set the CSS definitions you want to use (see "CSS in the Inspector" in this section).

5. After you define all the CSS definitions and rules you want to use, return to the document window.

6. If you set up any classes, put the document window in layout mode and use the Style tab of the Inspector palette to set that class (**Figure 18.10**).

You can also set up external CSS files and then use GoLive to create a link to your Web page.

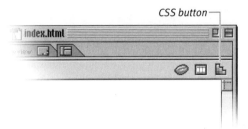

CSS button

Figure 18.7 The CSS button opens the page-styles window.

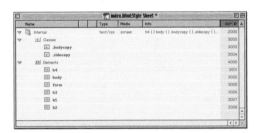

Figure 18.8 The page-styles window shows all the styles that are available for this Web page.

Figure 18.9 When the page-styles window is open, the toolbar allows you to add styles, link to external files, or duplicate the selected styles.

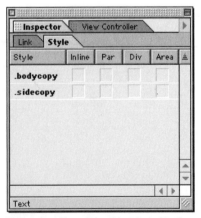

Figure 18.10 If an element is selected in the layout window, you can use the Inspector palette to apply class styles.

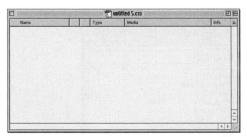

Figure 18.11 The external-style-sheet window looks pretty much like the page-styles window (refer to Figure 18.9). This one is blank, because nothing has been entered yet.

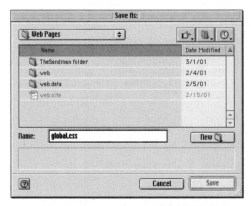

Figure 18.12 Saving your external style sheet.

Figure 18.13 If a link to an external style sheet is selected, the Inspector palette allows you to type the URL for the style sheet.

Setting up and linking to an external CSS file:

1. Choose File > New Special > Style Sheet Document to start a new external CSS file (**Figure 18.11**).

2. Use the toolbar to choose a CSS selector type: HTML, class, or ID.

   A new style element appears in the page-styles window.

3. Use the Inspector palette to set CSS definitions.

4. Save the file (**Figure 18.12**).

5. Open a new or existing HTML document.

6. With the document window in layout mode, click the CSS button.

7. In the toolbar, click the CSS button to add a link to an external file.

   A blank link reference appears in the page-styles window.

8. With the new external-style-sheet reference selected in the page-styles window, change the reference in the Inspector palette to point to the external file's URL (**Figure 18.13**).

   Now the HTML file can access the styles in the external file.

9. Repeat steps 1 through 8 for as many external style sheets as you want to add.

✔ Tip

■ Older versions of GoLive had a problem with uppercase letters. Although the program accepted uppercase letters in classes and IDs, it put the CSS in lowercase. Yet when the style was applied, it used the correct case. In many browsers, this situation causes the rules to fail.

ADDING CSS

CSS in the Inspector

When you are adding or editing a CSS rule, the Inspector palette displays eight tabs that allow you to access the following CSS controls:

◆ **Overview.** This tab shows the complete CSS rule being edited but does not allow you to change the definitions (**Figure 18.14**).

◆ **Font Controls.** These controls are described in Chapter 3 (**Figure 18.15**).

◆ **Text Controls.** These controls are described in Chapter 4 (**Figure 18.16**).

◆ **Block (Border and Margin) Controls.** These controls are described in Chapter 7 (**Figure 18.17**).

◆ **Position Controls.** These controls are described in Chapter 8 (**Figure 18.18**).

◆ **Border Controls.** These controls are described in Chapter 7 (**Figure 18.19**).

◆ **Background Controls.** These controls are described in Chapter 6 (**Figure 18.20**).

◆ **List and Other Controls.** These controls are described in Chapter 5 (**Figure 18.21**). In addition, this tab allows you to enter CSS properties that GoLive does not include (such as cursor).

Figure 18.14 Overview tab.

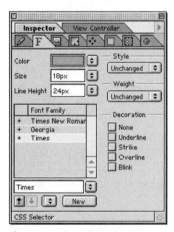

Figure 18.15 Font Controls tab.

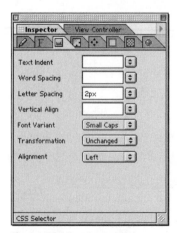

Figure 18.16 Text Controls tab.

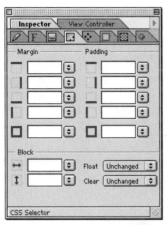

Figure 18.17 Block Controls tab (border and margin).

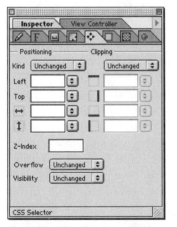

Figure 18.18 Position Controls tab.

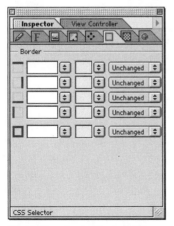

Figure 18.19 Border Controls tab.

Figure 18.20 Background Controls tab.

Figure 18.21 List and Other Controls tab.

ADDING CSS

Adding a Layer (Floating Box)

Earlier in this book, I showed you how to set up a CSS layer by turning an element into an object (see "Creating an Object" in Chapter 11). GoLive refers to a CSS layer as a *floating box*, but they are virtually identical, and anything you can do to one, you can do to the other.

To add a CSS layer to a Web page:

1. With the document window open in layout mode, double-click the Floating Box button (**Figure 18.22**) in the Objects palette.

    The layer (Floating Box) now appears in the document window as a numbered rectangle. The numbers correspond to the order in which the layers were created.

2. Move the mouse pointer to any edge of the layer so that the I-beam pointer changes to a hand (**Figure 18.23**). Then click to select the object or drag the layer anywhere you want in the window.

3. To change the size of the box after you have selected it, drag one of the handles on any side or corner of the layer (**Figure 18.24**).

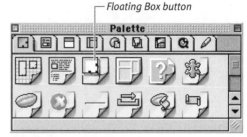

Floating Box button

Figure 18.22 The Floating Box button is located in the Objects palette. It allows you to add a layer to your Web page.

Figure 18.23 When a layer has been added to the page, you can select the entire layer by clicking one of its borders.

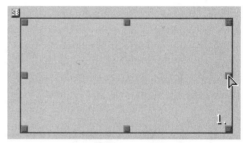

Figure 18.24 When a layer is selected, you can change its width or height by dragging one of the handles.

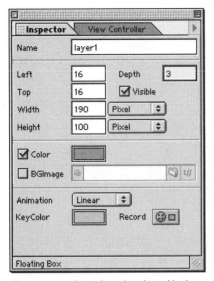

Figure 18.25 When a layer is selected in the document window in layout mode, the Inspector palette allows you to change that layer's properties.

To change the CSS layer's properties:

1. With the layer selected in the document window, use the Inspector palette to adjust the layer's properties (**Figure 18.25**).

   The properties are separate from the properties you can set for this object in the Position Controls tab (see the previous section, "Adding CSS"). The Inspector palette also includes animation controls, which are discussed in "Adding DHTML Animation" later in this chapter.

2. Type a name for this layer.

   This name will be used as the layer's unique ID in the CSS.

3. Type top and left positions (see "Setting the Position from the Top and Left" in Chapter 8) for the layer.

4. Type a width and height for the layer (see "Setting the Width and Height of an Element" in Chapter 7).

5. Type the depth of the layer, which will be used for the object's z-index (see "Stacking Objects" in Chapter 8).

6. Specify whether you want the layer to be visible (see "Setting the Visibility of an Element" in Chapter 9).

7. Set the background color or image (see Chapter 6).

✔ Tips

■ Remember that a CSS layer is an object that has a unique ID, has a position type, and usually is in a `<div>` or `<span>` tag.

■ GoLive assumes that the CSS layer will be positioned absolutely (see "Setting the Positioning Type" in Chapter 8). You can use the Inspector palette to set up relatively positioned layers.

ADDING A LAYER (FLOATING BOX)

Adding DHTML Animation

Earlier in this book, I showed you how to create simple point-to-point animation (see "Animating an Object" in Chapter 14). Although this technique is highly effective for moving a single object in a straight line, more complex animations are better created with a program such as GoLive, because the calculation and timing involved are difficult to hand-code.

In the following example, I have set up five layers, each with a different letter of Alice's name (**Figure 18.26**). After the animation runs, the letters have moved around the page to spell *ALICE*.

To create an animation with GoLive:

1. Set up a CSS layer (see the previous section, "Adding a Layer [Floating Box]"), and add any content you want (**Figure 18.27**).

2. With the layer selected, click the Timeline button in the top-right corner of the document window, between the CSS and JavaScript buttons (**Figure 18.28**). The Timeline Editor window opens (**Figure 18.29**).

3. With the layer still selected in the document window, in the Inspector, choose curve from the Animation drop-down menu; then click the Record button (**Figure 18.30**).

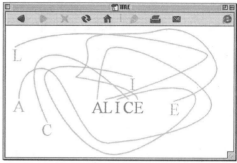

Figure 18.26 The letters start out scattered across the screen but gradually move through curved paths to form the word *ALICE*.

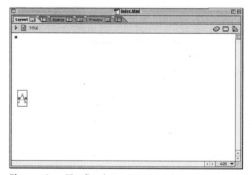

Figure 18.27 The first layer in its initial position.

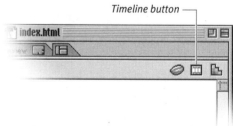

Timeline button —

Figure 18.28 The Timeline button opens the Timeline Editor window.

Figure 18.29 When it first opens, the Timeline Editor window is empty, awaiting your commands.

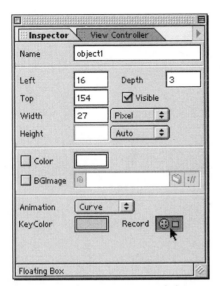

Figure 18.30 With the layer selected, the Inspector palette allows you to record the path of the layer as you move it around on the screen.

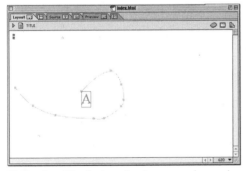

Figure 18.31 After the layer has been moved around on the screen, the line shows its animation path.

4. Move the object along the path you want it to follow (**Figure 18.31**).

In the Timeline Editor window, you see a rectangle with a dot for each point in the animation (**Figure 18.32**). These points are called *keyframes*.

5. Repeat steps 1 through 4 for each layer you want to animate.

When this page is loaded into a Web browser, the layers should move around as programmed (**Figure 18.33**).

Keyframe

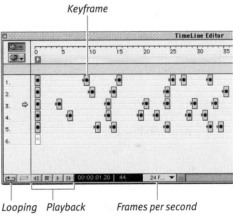

Looping   Playback   Frames per second

Figure 18.32 The Timeline Editor window after all five letters have been added.

Figure 18.33 In this version, the image appears only after the letters have moved into position.

19

DREAMWEAVER PRIMER

Dreamweaver started its life as a DHTML development tool and has integrated more and more HTML tools. It was usually thought of as a WYSIWYG layout program that relied on third-party software to provide rigorous HTML-editing capabilities. But this situation has changed. With the most recent release, Version 4, Dreamweaver now stands on its own.

Dreamweaver includes a bevy of other tools and utilities, such as FTP and site management, and it allows you to create templates that separate content from design. In addition, because Macromedia is also the developer of Flash, Dreamweaver includes several tools that allow you to add Flash text and buttons even if you do not own Macromedia Flash (see "Flash vs. DHTML" in Chapter 10).

In this chapter, I'll show you how to set up CSS using Dreamweaver's tools and how to use Dreamweaver to animate multiple objects along complex paths.

The Dreamweaver Interface

Macromedia worked hard between each release to develop Dreamweaver from a simple DHTML generator into a full-featured Web-design program, and the results are impressive. Although early releases of this software suffered due to a lack of integration between the code and WYSIWYG editors, the most recent release has real-time integration between the two editing modes so that changes made in one mode are reflected in the other instantly.

Dreamweaver provides an easy-to-use layout mode that allows you to add, move, and delete objects directly on the page while it generates the HTML code in the background (**Figure 19.1**). You can edit the HTML code directly, however, if you feel more comfortable doing things that way.

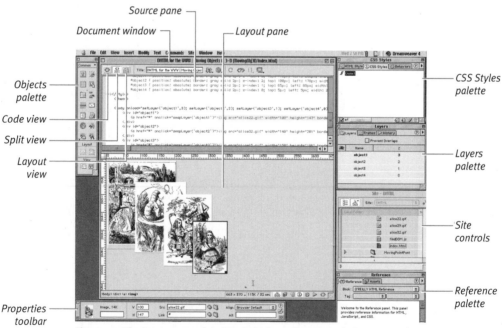

Figure 19.1 The Dreamweaver interface includes a document window, properties toolbar, site controls, and various palettes.

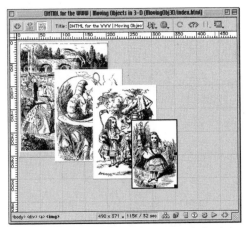

Figure 19.2 The Dreamweaver document window in Layout view. This mode allows you to add and move elements around on the page much like in a word processor.

Figure 19.3 The Dreamweaver document window in Code view. You can edit all of the code for the page (HTML, JavaScript, and CSS) directly in this mode.

Document window

You create individual Web pages in the document window, interacting with the pages' code in a variety of ways, depending on your needs and preferences. You can switch among the following views by using the buttons at the top of the document window.

◆ **Layout view** is the most like working with a word processor. It shows how the page should look when it is displayed in a browser window. You can move and change elements around on the screen as desired (**Figure 19.2**).

◆ **Source view** allows you to interact directly with the HTML tags used to generate your Web pages (**Figure 19.3**).

◆ **Source and Layout view** splits the document window into two panes, allowing you to work in both code and layout mode simultaneously. Changes you make in one area affect the other when you switch from one pane to the other.

Properties toolbar

The properties toolbar allows you to control all the attributes of the selected object in the document window. This includes shortcuts to common tags and styles that might be used with the selected object, as well as to input fields that allow you to define the element's properties.

Because these options vary, depending on the element that is selected, the properties toolbar displays options contextually. If you are editing text, for example, you see options for setting the header level, alignment, font size, and other text attributes (**Figure 19.4**). If you select a layer in the document window, the properties toolbar changes to allow you to control the size, position, and visibility of the layer (**Figure 19.5**).

Text controls

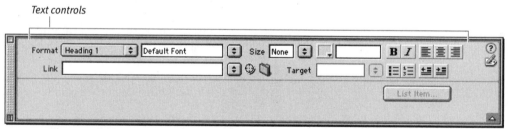

Figure 19.4 The properties toolbar changes its options depending on the element selected in the document window. This figure shows the toolbar when text is selected.

Layer controls

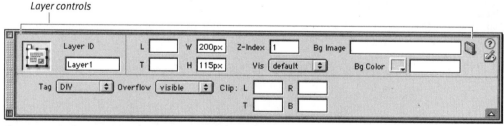

Figure 19.5 This version shows the toolbar when a layer is selected.

Palettes

You can access Dreamweaver's 12 palettes from the Window menu. These palettes add features and functionality to the program but can be closed when they are not needed (which, for many of them, is most of the time). The most important of these palettes for CSS and DHTML are:

- **Objects.** This palette provides quick access to a variety of HTML tags and objects that can be inserted into your Web page.

- **Reference.** The contents of several Web reference books are available within the program for quick reference.

- **CSS Styles.** This palette provides access to all class and ID styles set for this page, including linked styles in external style sheets. In addition, the palette links to a CSS-creation wizard that steps you through the process of setting up your own styles.

- **Layers.** As new CSS layers are added to the page, they can become hard to manage. This palette lists all the layers on the page. You can select layers from a list and even change their names.

Site controls

Dreamweaver offers an excellent selection of tools to help manage your entire Web site. The most impressive of these tools allows you to check files into and out of a common server, so that two parties working on the same file do not overwrite each other's changes.

Other tools

Dreamweaver provides all the tools you would expect in a robust Web-editing package, including a spelling checker, code-validation checker, and link checker. In addition, Dreamweaver can import a variety of formats into HTML.

Adding CSS

In Part I of this book, I showed you how to add style sheets to your Web pages. Dreamweaver includes an assortment of tools that take some of the drudgery out of creating and maintaining well-formed style sheets. You can use Dreamweaver to add CSS to a single Web page (see "Adding CSS to a Web Page" in Chapter 2) or to an entire Web site (see "Adding CSS to a Web Site" in Chapter 2).

To add CSS to a Web page:

1. Open a new or existing HTML file by choosing File > New or File > Open.

2. In the CSS Styles palette, click the New Style button (**Figure 19.6**).

   If the palette is not open, choose Window > CSS Styles.

   The New Style dialog box appears (**Figure 19.7**).

3. Choose the CSS selector types you want to use (see "The Parts of a CSS Rule" in Chapter 1).

   Choose Make Custom Style (Class) if you want to add a class; choose Redefine HTML Tag or Use CSS Selector for an ID.

4. Click the radio button labeled "This Document Only" to include your new style in the <style> tag on this page, and then click OK.

5. In the Style Definition window, specify the CSS definitions you want to use (see "The CSS Editor" in this section).

   You can click Apply at any time to view the document window and see the changes you are making.

6. After you define all the CSS rules you want to use, click OK to return to the document window.

7. If you set up any classes, use the CSS Styles palette to set the class for a selected object in the document window (**Figure 19.8**).

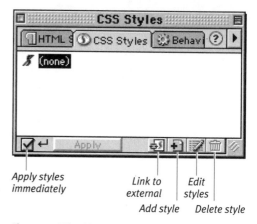

Apply styles immediately   Link to external   Edit styles

Add style   Delete style

Figure 19.6 The CSS Styles palette shows all the classes that are available in this document (in this figure, none).

Figure 19.7 The New Style dialog box allows you to select the type of style you are adding and if you want the style in an external style sheet or not.

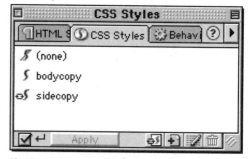

Figure 19.8 Two styles have been added. The first (bodycopy) is embedded in the file, and the second (sidecopy) is in an external file, as shown by the small chain link next to it.

ADDING CSS

Adding a new external style sheet is very much like adding a style directly to the page. Dreamweaver takes care of all the linking in the background.

Setting up and linking to an external CSS file:

1. Open a new or existing HTML file.

2. In the CSS Styles palette, click the New Style button.

   The New Style dialog box opens.

3. Choose the CSS selector types you want to use.

   Choose Make Custom Style (Class) if you want to add a class; choose Redefine HTML Tag or Use CSS Selector for an ID.

4. Make sure that the radio button next to (New Style Sheet File) is selected, and then click OK.

   This will create a new external CSS file to be linked to the current Web page. Alternatively, you can select a style sheet to edit that is already linked to this page from the drop-down menu.

5. Set the CSS definitions you want to use.

   You can click Apply at any time to view the document window and see the changes you are making.

6. After you define all the CSS rules you want to use, click OK to return to the document window.

7. If you set up any classes, use the CSS Styles palette to set that class for the selected object in the document window.

✔ Tip

■ Dreamweaver does not allow you to add styles, so you are stuck with using the styles it knows. You can add style rules directly in the code editor, however.

The CSS Editor

When you are adding or editing a CSS rule, Dreamweaver requires that you use the CSS editor to enter your values for each rule. The CSS Editor is made up of the following parts:

◆ **Type.** These controls are described in chapters 3 and 4 (**Figure 19.9**).

◆ **Background.** These controls are described in Chapter 6 (**Figure 19.10**).

◆ **Block (Border and Margin).** These controls are described in Chapter 4 (**Figure 19.11**).

◆ **Box.** These controls are described in Chapter 7 (**Figure 19.12**).

◆ **Border,** These controls are described in Chapter 7 (**Figure 19.13**).

◆ **List.** These controls are described in Chapter 5 (**Figure 19.14**).

◆ **Positioning.** These controls are described in Chapters 8 (**Figure 19.15**).

◆ **Extensions.** These controls include new or browser-specific CSS such as cursor (**Figure 19.16**).

Figure 19.9 Type.

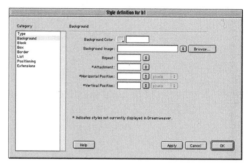

Figure 19.10 Background.

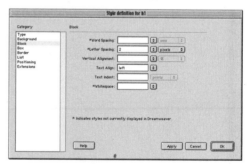

Figure 19.11 Block (Border and Margin).

ADDING CSS

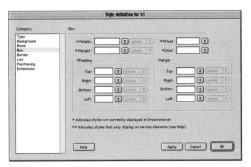

Figure 19.12 Box.

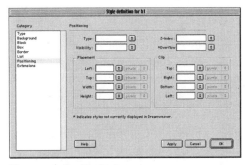

Figure 19.15 Positioning.

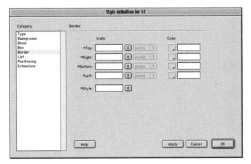

Figure 19.13 Border.

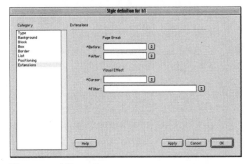

Figure 19.16 Extensions.

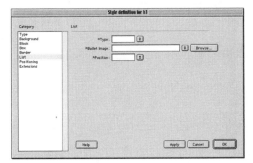

Figure 19.14 List.

ADDING CSS

Adding a Layer

You create a CSS layer when you define an object with a unique ID and give it a position type (absolute or relative), usually associated with a `<div>` tag (see "Creating an Object" in Chapter 11). Dreamweaver gives you easy access to controls for layers.

To add a CSS layer to a Web page:

1. With the document window open in layout mode, or layout and source mode, drag the Draw Layer icon from the Objects palette and drop it in the document window's layout pane (**Figure 19.17**).

   The layer now appears as a rectangle in the document window.

2. Move the mouse pointer to any edge of the layer so that the I-beam pointer changes to a hand (**Figure 19.18**). Then click to select the layer, or drag and position the layer anywhere you want in the window.

3. To change the size of the box after you have selected it, drag one of the handles on any side or corner of the layer (**Figure 19.19**).

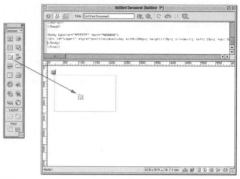

Figure 19.17 Add a new layer to your Web page by dragging the Draw Layer icon from the Objects palette to the document window.

Figure 19.18 To select the entire layer, click any edge.

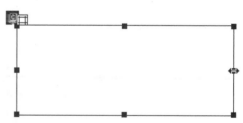

Figure 19.19 You can change the width and/or height of a layer directly by dragging the handle on its side.

Figure 19.20 The properties toolbar gives you access to all the layer properties that are controlled by CSS.

To change the CSS layer's properties:

1. With the layer selected in the document window, use the properties toolbar to adjust the layer's properties (**Figure 19.20**).

2. Type a name for this layer.

   This name will be used as the object's unique ID in the CSS.

3. Type top and left positions (see "Setting the Position from the Top and Left" in Chapter 8) for the layer.

4. Type a width and height for the layer (see "Setting the Width and Height of an Element" in Chapter 7).

5. Type the layer's z-index (see "Stacking Objects [3-D Positioning]" in Chapter 8).

6. Specify whether you want the layer to be visible (see "Setting the Visibility of an Element" in Chapter 9).

7. Set the background color and/or image (see Chapter 6).

8. Specify the tag type that the layer should use.

   This tag type usually is <span> or <div>, but you can use Netscape 4's <layer> or <ilayer> tag (see Chapter 16). This type defaults to ,div>, which usually is preferable.

9. Set the left, top, right, and bottom edges of the clipping region, if applicable; then specify how the overflow should be treated (see "Setting the Visible Area of an Element (Clipping)" and "Setting Where the Overflow Goes" in Chapter 9).

✔ Tip

■ Dreamweaver places all the layer's CSS in the <div> tag, rather than setting up an ID in the <style> tag. I like to have the ID definition in the <style> tag or in an external CSS file, but Dreamweaver's method works.

ADDING A LAYER

Adding Animation

Earlier in this book, I showed you how to create a simple point-to-point animation (see "Animating an Object" in Chapter 14). Animating a layer through a curved path or animating multiple layers, however, is better done with a program such as Dreamweaver. Imagine having to plot every pixel in an image individually, setting the position and color of every dot. Not much fun, is it? Image-editing programs take the drudgery out of the work. The same is true of DHTML animation. You can do it by hand, but it's time-consuming, more subject to error, and much harder to update quickly.

In the following example, I have set up five layers, each with a different letter (**Figure 19.21**). The letters will float around the screen for a few seconds and then come together to spell *ALICE*.

To create an animation with Dreamweaver:

1. Set up a CSS layer (see the previous section, "Adding a Layer"), and add any content you want (**Figure 19.22**).

2. Choose Window >Timelines.
   The Timelines window opens (**Figure 19.23**).

3. With the layer you added in step 1 selected in the document window, choose Record Path of Layer from the drop-down menu in the top-right corner of the Timelines window (**Figure 19.24**).

4. Move the object across the screen in the path you want it to follow (**Figure 19.25**).
   In the Timelines window, you should see a circle for each point in the animation (**Figure 19.26**). These points are called *keyframes*.

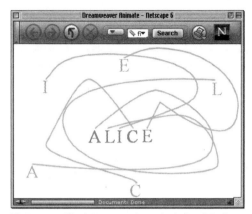

Figure 19.21 The letters are shown in their original positions. When the document loads in the Web page, the letters will follow paths to spell *Alice*.

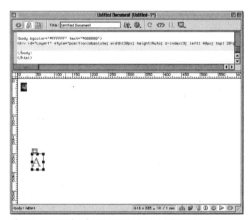

Figure 19.22 The first layer in its initial position.

Figure 19.23 The Timelines window as it appears before any objects have been animated.

5. Repeat steps 1 through 4 for each layer you want to animate.

6. Check the Autoplay checkbox in the Timelines window to have the animation start playing as soon as it loads in a browser window.

When this page is loaded into a DHTML-capable Web browser, the layers should move around as programmed.

continues on next page

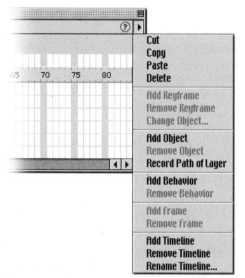

Figure 19.24 Choose Record Path of Layer from the drop-down menu to begin recording the animation.

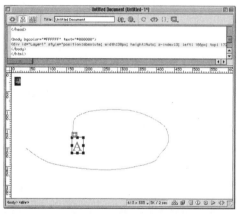

Figure 19.25 The layer has been moved around on the screen, and Dreamweaver has plotted the points of the path to use to animate the object.

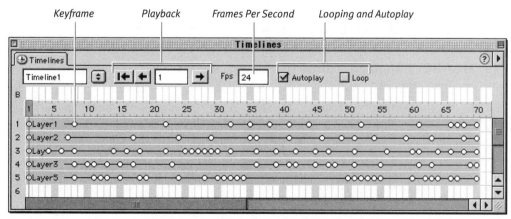

Figure 19.26 The Timelines window now includes all five letters to be animated.

ADDING ANIMATION

✔ Tip

- You can also use keyframes to change the visibility of objects and their z-index. In the preceding example, after all the letters have moved into place, the image of Alice—previously hidden—can become visible (**Figure 19.27**). To do this, simply select the keyframe where you want the layer to appear or disappear; then uncheck the Visible checkbox in the properties toolbar. The object remains invisible until you select another keyframe and check the Visible checkbox.

Figure 19.27 Only after the letters have assembled does the image appear.

Understanding the Timelines Window

Animators have long used timelines to produce and control their creations. Most commercial animation and video programs use them, and Dreamweaver has also applied this methodology to creating animation.

The Timelines window allows you not only to move objects around on the screen, but also to control when they move and how long it takes for them to move.

Although it may look intimidating at first, the Timelines window is easy to use once you get the hang of it. It is composed of the following primary parts:

- ◆ **Playback controls.** These controls allow you to jump to the beginning of the timeline or advance through it one frame at a time.

- ◆ **Keyframe editing.** Each keyframe can be controlled individually for position and visibility of the object at any moment during the animation.

- ◆ **FPS controls.** By setting the number of frames per second, you can control the quality of the animation playback.

- ◆ **Autoplay and looping controls.** You can have the animation start immediately after the page loads and run once or repeat *ad infinitum*.

PART 4

DYNAMIC WEB SITES

Chapter 20:   Understanding the Dynamic Web   335

Chapter 21:   Creating a Dynamic Web Site   347

Chapter 22:   Web Page Layout   359

Chapter 23:   Importing External Content   385

Chapter 24:   Web Site Navigation   393

Chapter 25:   Controls   425

Chapter 26:   Special Effects   459

Chapter 27:   Multimedia   485

Chapter 28:   Debugging Your Code   507

Chapter 29:   The Future of the Dynamic Web   519

Understanding the Dynamic Web

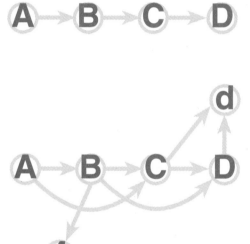

Figure 20.1 The first model shows a linear path from A to B to C to D. This model is fairly typical of how traditional media work. You watch a movie from beginning to end, for example. The dynamic model (bottom) lets you jump between any point without passing through the intervening points, and can offer alternative versions (d) or link to outside information (4).

A line is defined by two points; call them A and B. The direct path between these two points is a line. All you can do with a line is travel straight from point A to point B, following a linear path without deviation or interruption. Most media that communicate information are linear. You may be able to fast-forward through a video or flip through a book, but these media are best suited for presenting ideas in a linear order that is set by the author.

Human beings, however, tend to reason in far more chaotic, intricate, and cryptic ways than mere lines can ever describe. We learn by exploring, searching, and finding, by making mistakes and trying again. We often learn completely by accident. We rarely think in a straight line; we think dynamically (**Figure 20.1**).

The Web has already begun to change the way we look at information and how we structure knowledge. Despite the great leap forward that hypertext presents, we still have a way to go before mastering this new media. Before we can take the next step, the Web must become far more dynamic.

In this chapter, I'll introduce some of the issues you need to consider when designing a dynamic Web site. This information prepares you for Chapter 21, which shows you how to define, design, and build a dynamic Web site.

What Makes a Web Site Dynamic?

Dynamic can mean many things, and the meaning varies depending on whom you ask (and maybe even on when you ask them). The term can be applied liberally to mean animation on the screen or multimedia.

The Web itself is a highly dynamic medium through the use of hypertext. With hypertext, Web designers can link information and facilitate a more natural human learning environment. But with CSS, JavaScript, and the Document Object Model (DOM), designers can make a dynamic Web site.

Most Web sites today are relatively static. Once a Web page loads, very little on it changes. DHTML lets Web designers transform their designs by creating Web pages that adapt and change to meet visitors' needs as they explore the page. A dynamic Web page should meet one or more of the following criteria (**Figure 20.2**):

◆ **Interactivity.** A dynamic Web site should adapt and react to the visitor's actions as quickly as possible.

◆ **Synchronicity.** A dynamic Web site should bring together relevant information and activities from a variety of sources— either directly or through linking—with a minimal amount of searching on the visitor's part.

◆ **Flexibility.** A dynamic Web site should give the visitor a variety of ways to find information or accomplish tasks so that they can choose the method that best suits their needs.

◆ **Adaptability.** A dynamic Web site adjusts to cater to individual visitors' needs. Sometimes, this adjustment is made on the server through customization of content, but much can be done by Web designers to accommodate visitors without requiring them to load a new Web page.

◆ **Activity.** A dynamic Web site uses motion and sound to draw attention to changes on the screen.

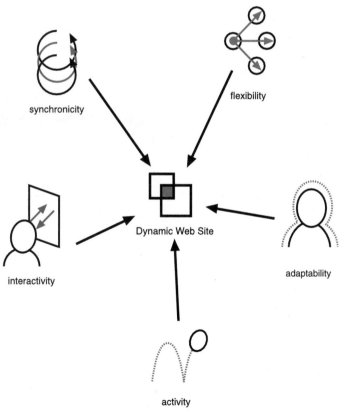

Figure 20.2 What does the term *dynamic* mean? Here are a few ideas.

What Is Hypertext?

Many people confuse the term *hypertext* with *navigation links*. This mistake is not hard to make, because on the Web, hypertext and navigation links are both created with the same HTML code: `<a>...</a>`. But navigation links are what you use to move from topic to topic in a linear fashion on the Web. Hypertext, on the other hand, allows you to click a word, a phrase, or an image in a Web page and receive a more detailed explanation of that thing. In theory, hypertext allows a single page to include an infinite amount of information (**Figures 20.3** and **20.4**).

In practice, including infinite information is not feasible, but you can include a great deal of information for the visitor to explore. Authors (the ones who provide the content) control what is and what is not referenced through a hypertext link, and they have to consider every link they create.

The Web designer has two goals: to help visitors find the information they are looking for as quickly and efficiently as possible, and to enable visitors to explore, define, and discuss that information through hypertext.

Rather than being a medium for discourse—such as a book, through which one person speaks to many people—the best Web sites use the Web as a medium for intercourse (no, I'm not talking about the porn sites). Using the Web, many people can learn from and speak to one another. Otherwise, what is the point of the Web? Conversation, video, audio, and text can all be provided on the Web but can be provided better via telephone, TV, radio, and magazines.

Through hypertext, the Web can break the mold of linear thought and work with natural learning processes. But this potential will remain only potential until the people who design for the Web use hypertext's unique features.

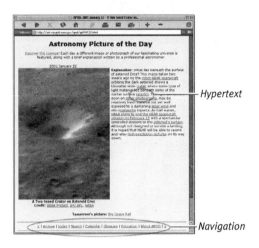

Hypertext

Navigation

Figure 20.3 The Astronomy Picture of the Day site provides a good example of the difference between navigation and hypertext. The links in the main text offer access to a more detailed description of the term (hypertext), and the navigation links move the visitor to another item on the site.

Figure 20.4 Clicking the hypertext link takes you to a page that defines the term *regolith*.

Dynamic by Design

People probably are not coming to your Web site to see cool special effects; they are coming to your site for information. Your design, dynamic or not, needs to support their information needs. But a dynamic Web site, if properly designed, is always better than a static one.

Here are some pointers to keep in mind while designing your dynamic Web site:

♦ **Keep it simple.** For many people, dynamic content means added complexity—more options, more functions, more to learn, and more to remember. Generally speaking, people do not want more options; they want what they want. You should use dynamic features to simplify the use of your site, not to add complexity.

♦ **Show only relevant information.** Information becomes knowledge when its relevance is understood. But information that is not immediately relevant can be distracting, and too much information can be just as confusing as too little. Use DHTML to show and hide relevant information as necessary.

♦ **Make changes clear.** We often do not notice changes in our environment, even when they occur right in front of our faces. Changes in the content of a Web page generally should be initiated by the visitor, should occur almost instantly, and should be easy to recognize.

♦ **Direct, don't dictate.** The point of a Web site is to allow visitors to move freely within the content. As the author and designer, you want to direct visitors to the information you want them to see but simultaneously allow them to follow their own paths. In terms of what you are communicating to your audience, the links that you do or do not include in a Web page are as important as the words and graphics you put there. Think of yourself as a guide, not a tyrant.

♦ **Provide a sense of location and direction.** One common complaint about the Web is that it's easy to get lost. Compared with the real world, where we can turn to see where we came from and look ahead to see what is next, most Web pages seem to be very insular. Use DHTML to let visitors know where they came from and where they are going.

Understanding Layout on the Web

Because of the Web's expandable windows, unpredictable screen resolutions, and variable font sizes, you have a better chance of predicting the price of Internet stocks than the final appearance of your Web design. You know that your design must fit into a rectangle (the browser window), but will that rectangle be wide and long enough?

All Web designers must start their designs by deciding which of the four main layout styles they will use.

All Web layouts have two basic parts. The first part is the content area, which features navigation, titles, graphics, and text—in other words, the stuff visitors are interested in. The other part is filler. Whether the filler is just empty space or a design that fills the void, it is there simply to absorb extra space in the browser window. The balance between content and filler is crucial to creating an attractive Web layout.

Based on this balance, there are four broad categories of Web layout:

◆ **Unrestrained.** The content is allowed to stretch horizontally from the left edge to the right edge of the window and vertically down to the bottom edge of the window (**Figure 20.5**). This design eliminates the need for filler. But wide columns of text, which can be a symptom of unrestrained layout, can be difficult to read. *Wired* (**Figure 20.6**) uses unrestrained layout on its news site (www.wired.com/news), allowing the content in the center column to grow as wide as necessary to fill the empty space.

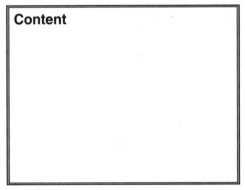

Figure 20.5 The unrestrained Web-page layout.

Figure 20.6 Wired News uses an unrestrained layout that stretches to fill the entire browser window.

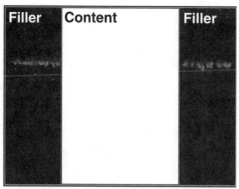

Figure 20.7 The fixed Web-page layout.

Figure 20.8 Salon uses a fixed-width layout to keep the content in one central column with filler on either side.

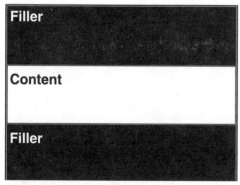

Figure 20.9 The fixed-height Web-page layout.

- ◆ **Fixed width.** The content is given a set margin on the left side, the right side, or both, restraining the horizontal length of the content to a fixed width (**Figure 20.7**). Salon (`www.salon.com`) restrains the width of its content area, centering it in the window with a fixed width of 736 pixels (roughly the size that a 800-pixels-wide monitor can display without horizontal scrolling if the window fills the entire screen) and white space filling additional areas to the left and right (**Figure 20.8**).

- ◆ **Fixed height.** The content area is given a set margin on the top, the bottom, or both sides, restraining its vertical length to a fixed height (**Figure 20.9**). Therefore, the content is forced to scroll horizontally. This design is rarely used, however, because it usually is advantageous to maximize the height in which the content can appear. I used this method to set up a small site for my daughter's birthday pictures—www.webbedenvironments.com/jocelynstory (**Figure 20.10**).

continues on next page

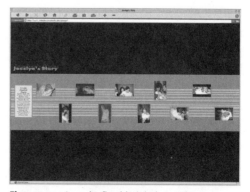

Figure 20.10 I used a fixed-height layout for my daughter's Web site to create a cinematic experience.

◆ **Fixed size.** Both the height and width of the display area are restrained to a fixed size (**Figure 20.11**). You can create this layout in two ways. The first way is to surround one central frame with other frames that expand around it. The Portishead Web site—www.portishead.co.uk—uses this method (**Figure 20.12**). The other method is to open a new browser window to a fixed size (see "Opening a New Browser Window" in Chapter 14).

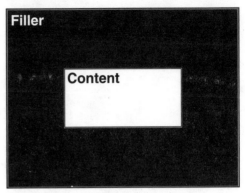

Figure 20.11 The fixed-size Web-page layout.

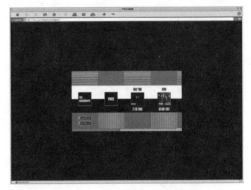

Figure 20.12 The Portishead Web site uses a fixed-size layout. This provides the greatest control of the dimensions that the design will fill, but means the page displays at the same size regardless of the size of the visitor's screen.

Navigation
Do's and Don'ts

A great deal is wrong with Web design. This fact is especially evident when I see the way Web designers throw together the navigation links for their sites. However, this medium is very young, and Web designers are still experimenting with new ideas and new techniques. After six years of my own experimentation, I have learned a few do's and don'ts.

Do's

Some of these points may seem obvious, but when you are in the midst of a project, it is easy to lose sight of even the most obvious considerations.

◆ **Keep navigation consistent.** This point is fairly straightforward: After you establish the general navigation structure of your site, don't move it around or radically alter it on each page. If the main navigation is on the left side of the screen, do not suddenly move it to the right on the next screen. If you placed the auxiliary navigation on the bottom of the screen, do not suddenly start placing banner ads in that area. Too many sites create a "Where's Waldo?" situation with their navigation.

The consistency rule has some exceptions, however. Home pages can have a different navigational layout from the rest of the site, just as the cover of a magazine has a different layout from the pages inside.

continues on next page

◆ **Let visitors know where they are and how they got there.** Remember Hansel and Gretel following their breadcrumbs back home from the witch's gingerbread house? Marking your path can keep you from getting lost and help you find your way back to where you started.

The most common method way to do this is to list the pages (usually starting with the home page) that visitors traveled through to get where they are, as follows:

```
Home > Forest> More forest >
Witch's house
```

The path shows a logical progression, and each title actually is a link back to that page. Like Theseus following the thread back through the Minotaur's maze, visitors to your site can retrace their paths and go in other directions (see "Creating a Breadcrumb Menu" in Chapter 24).

◆ **Show and tell if the navigation is vague.** It's nice to know where you are and how you got there. It's also nice to know where you are going. Visitors who are new to a site, however, may not understand some of the vague terms you use to describe the navigation.

One of the chief frustrations of many Web surfers is following the wrong path when they are looking for particular information. This frustration is compounded by having to wait to load pages that were not what they really wanted. Providing a sentence or two of explanation to tell visitors what they can expect to find behind the link helps lessen this problem. You may not have the screen space to provide a thorough explanation, but DHTML can come in handy for this purpose (see "Creating Pop-Up Hypertext" in Chapter 25).

◆ **Give the visitor control and flexibility.** Not everyone works the same way. Most software these days allows users to move control palettes around on the screen, add and subtract tools, and generally tailor the interface to their needs.

The Web limits what you can do to give visitors control of the interface, but I like to do a few things. The most important is providing a site map displayed in a small remote-control window. Visitors can use the site-map palette to move around in the site quickly, just as they use a TV remote control (see "Creating a Remote Control" in Chapter 24). Some visitors want to stick with the navigation provided in the main window; others enjoy the freedom of surfing with the remote. The important thing is to let the visitor decide.

◆ **Give visitors somewhere to go next.** Recently, I was reading an article in a popular Web magazine for information architects. When I reached the end of the article, I found that I could go backward and forward through the pages of the article, but there was no link back to the actual magazine or to any other part of the site.

Nothing on a Web site is more irritating than a dead end. This situation occurs with alarming regularity when you fill out forms online: You enter all your information and click Submit; a page comes up with a message thanking you for entering your information, and nothing more happens. Often, these pages don't even include the site's standard navigation.

Don'ts

Now that you know what to do, here are some things you should avoid when designing your Web site navigation.

- **Don't waste space with navigation.**
  Any link on a page that visitors are not interested in clicking is wasted space on the screen. Yet many Web designers fill the pages of their sites with links that visitors did not click on the home page and are unlikely to click at all.

  Consider a banking site that offers services to individuals, small businesses, and corporations. The front page presents all three options as starting points that take visitors to the diverse services available in each category. But links to all three areas remain on subsequent pages. Can you think of any reason why someone who is interested in an individual banking account would want to switch over to the corporate services? I can't, and even if this rare case existed, that person could always return to the home page, which should never be more than a click away.

  One common way of giving visitors the maximum number of links without wasting space is to use clamshell menus, which allow you to organize your links in main topics listed in a single menu. When one of the topics is selected, a submenu of topics appears below the main topic, but the full menu of topics is still available (see "Creating a Clamshell Menu" in Chapter 24).

- **Don't lose the navigation.** Imagine that you are typing a letter in your word processor. When you reach the bottom of the typing area, the menu bar scrolls off the top of the screen as you continue to type. Every time you need to access the menu bar, you have to scroll back up to the top of the page. This situation would

make for a frustrating user interface, but this is exactly what most Web designers expect visitors to do.

One way around this problem is to include ubiquitous *Return to top* links, but this solution gets clunky. I prefer to put my navigation in frames so that it is always available and in a consistent position on the screen. Visitors do not have to monkey around searching the page and wasting their valuable time. It is important, of course, to minimize the size of these frames to maximize the area available for the content (see "Opening and Closing Frames" in Chapter 22).

- **Don't confuse navigation types.** Not all navigation is created equal. Web pages can contain many types of navigation, depending on a variety of factors. Visitors use the main navigation to travel among the most important areas of the site.

  One convenient way to differentiate navigation types is appearance (see "Setting Multiple Link Styles" in Chapter 24).

- **Don't rely on the browser's controls for navigation.** Many visitors depend on the built-in browser controls. They are comfortable with the way these controls work, and they know what to expect when they click the Back or Forward arrow. But at least as many visitors never think to touch the controls at the top of the browser, and if they can't get where they want to go on your site, guess who gets the blame?

continues on next page

Make sure visitors can always get back to where they were in your Web site with a minimum of fuss. Never lead them down a dead end and then tell them to use the browser's back arrow. Instead, include a link back to the page they just came from (see "Creating Your Own Back Button" in Chapter 25).

◆ **Don't put every link on every page.** One of the most common mistakes that Web designers make is placing every possible link on every page of the site, in the mistaken belief that visitors will want to go anywhere at any time. Not only does this waste space, but, more importantly, it may make it harder for visitors to find what they are looking for. (See the sidebar "Snowflake in a Blizzard".)

Any link that visitors are not going to click is wasted space. If visitors did not select the link on the home page of the site, the chance that they will click it on subsequent pages goes way down. This is not to say that visitors always follow a linear path through the site to their goal; you can expect visitors to skip around looking for what they want. But you should organize the site so that visitors can move among subjects quickly and then move to more-detailed subjects without having to see all the detailed links at the same time (see "Creating Drop-Down Menus" in Chapter 24).

Snowflake in a Blizzard

The feature that distinguishes the Web from other media is its capability to link fragments of information so that visitors can understand the relationships among them. This feature is called hypertext, and it's what separates the Web from books, TV, radio, cinema, telephony, CDs, and even from CD-ROMs.

So why do so many Web pages and Web sites seem to have been designed for one of these older media? Some designers use vague index-like menus that give visitors no clear idea of where they are going; page after page of information that readers have to plod through to find what they really want; and screens crammed full of graphics, banner ads, and buttons that take forever to download.

Even worse are pages on which every possible link to every other point in the Web site is crammed into a narrow sidebar. Finding the link you are looking for becomes similar to finding a snowflake in a blizzard.

One reason why so many Web sites present all this information is that the only way to change the content of a Web page used to be to load a new Web page with the additional content. While the new page loaded, visitors had to wait...and wait...and wait. Rather than forcing visitors to wait while they drilled down through several pages to find the information they wanted, designers saved time by placing all this content on the same page.

DHTML changes all that. Because DHTML allows you to show and change objects dynamically, you can tailor the content of the Web page for visitors based on their immediate needs. A variety of content can be loaded and then revealed without the long wait involved in loading new Web pages.

CREATING A DYNAMIC WEB SITE

Figure 21.1 To show you how to create a dynamic site, I'll be using the work I've done for the site that supports this book.

All Web sites need a plan before they can be built. This plan works as a blueprint for the site, to help you define the structure around which all the fixtures of the site (graphics, text, and code) will be placed.

A large Web site built without the benefit of a blueprint will fail as surely as a skyscraper built without the benefit of a blueprint. But even if you are building only a garden-shed-size Web site, a good plan will save you time and aggravation in the long run.

Including dynamic content in this equation makes a good plan even more necessary. Because dynamic content adds more options, it adds more possibilities and more variables that can go wrong. A little fore-thought can go a long way.

In this chapter, I'll show you the steps to take to define, design, and build your Web site (**Figure 21.1**).

Step 1: Define

The Web is about information, and before you can begin your Web design, you have to collect, identify, and distill the information that will make up your site.

Designing a dynamic Web site requires a good deal more effort than simply stringing together a series of Web pages with links, but the rewards will be worth it.

Whether you are designing a Web site for your daughter's class play, for photographs, or for an intranet that allows insurance underwriters to process claims, you need to define what you are doing before you turn on your computer and begin coding.

Collect and review your content

This step may seem obvious, but you would be surprised how many sites begin their lives before the designers know what is going into them (**Figure 21.2**). What is your site's message?

You also need to break the content down and consider how visitors will navigate all the information you will be presenting. How can similar chunks of information be grouped to create the different sections of the Web site? What should those sections be called, and how should they be represented? This decision will play an important role when you map out the site and determine its structure.

Example:

◆ Text for introduction
◆ Sample chapter
◆ Code examples and downloads

Figure 21.2 Collect your content.

Figure 21.3 Know your audience.

Know your audience

The type of content will determine the type of visitor who wants to view it (**Figure 21.3**). This factor probably is most important in determining a demographic for your site visitors. The more accurately you can define the content, the more accurately you can define the demographic. In addition, the content will help determine the site's look and feel. The audience for a computer store's Web site, for example, probably will not expect to see a floral pattern in the background.

After you determine the general audience for your site based on content, try to answer the following questions, based on your experience or direct observation:

◆ What type of equipment is the visitor using, and where?

◆ What type of browser and software is the visitor using?

◆ What do you hope the visitor will achieve at this site?

A single site might—and probably will—have many purposes. Set up different scenarios for several potential visitors who have different reasons for coming to your Web site. Map out how visitors might get from their entry point (probably the home page) to their goal, and use this information to optimize the navigation for your site.

Example:

◆ Web Design Professionals

◆ Web Design Amateurs

◆ Web Project Managers

User or Visitor?

Most Web designers commonly refer to the audience of a Web site as users. I have never been terribly fond of this term, for several reasons. First, *user* often implies a negative and unhealthy relationship (as in *drug user*), and I really don't want to think of the people who come to my site in such a manner. Second, *user* sounds like something a marketer came up with to describe human beings, much like using the term *resources* to describe workers. To me, *user* dehumanizes the very real people for whom I am designing.

Instead, I refer to the audience of my sites as *visitors*. Yes, the difference may simply be semantics, but language is a powerful tool that shapes our concepts of the people and things with which we interact. I would rather think of myself as a host to visitors than as a supplier to users.

Always remember that the visitor is the person for whom you are designing. Whether you are creating a personal site or a multimillion-dollar Web application, you should consider your visitors at all times, from conception to design, implementation, and production.

STEP 1: DEFINE

Establish your goals

Now that you know who will be visiting your little corner of the Internet, it's time to solidify your goals (**Figure 21.4**). What do you expect to achieve? Why do you want to add your voice to the throng?

For some Web sites, clients dictate the goals; for others, the goals may be selfish. Regardless, you must know what you are trying to accomplish with all your hard work.

Example:

◆ Provide place to view examples
◆ Provide place to download code
◆ Provide updates and corrections

Figure 21.4 Establish your goals.

Plan the features and interactivity

Now it's time to identify the features you will be using to accomplish your goals (**Figure 21.5**). Will this site need video or sound? DHTML? Interactive navigation? CGI forms? Java? Back-end databases? Flash? Always try to find the simplest solution to get the job done.

Example:

◆ Navigation: Sliding menu
◆ Special Effects: Fading text
◆ Controls: Pop-up hypertext

Figure 21.5 Plan features and interactivity.

Consider the design style

Consider the most effective design for your Web site, based on the audience's expectations, your goals, and the site's features. Consider the colors, fonts, and other graphics you will be using (**Figure 21.6**).

Example:

◆ Layout: Restricted height
◆ Color: Purple, silver, green, and red
◆ Fonts: Arial, Arial Black, Trebuchet MS

Figure 21.6 Consider the design style.

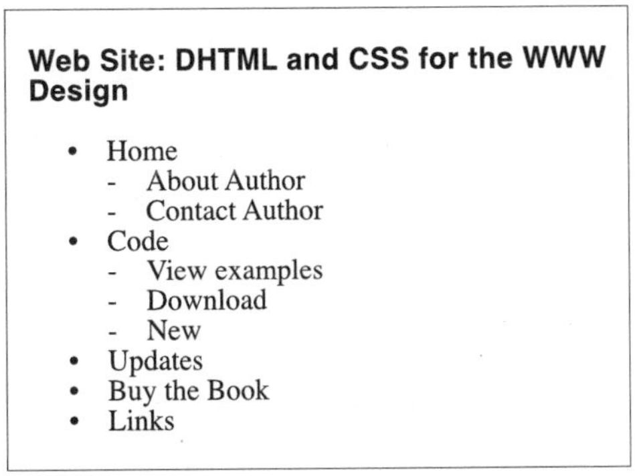

Web Site: DHTML and CSS for the WWW Design

- Home
  - About Author
  - Contact Author
- Code
  - View examples
  - Download
  - New
- Updates
- Buy the Book
- Links

Figure 21.7 The outline helps you organize your site in a logical order, placing the most important concepts at the top and the detailed ideas below them.

Step 2: Design

Different people have different ideas when they think of the design of the site. For someone with an arts background, *design* means the way the site will look, what colors will be used, and how the page will be laid out. For someone with a technology background, *design* implies how the various programming components will act and work together.

The design of a Web site must address both of these factors, and more.

During the design phase, you need to consider many aspects of your site to make sure all of them will work coherently.

Outline the site

An outline treats the Web site as a linear object, with each section of the site being a top level in the outline, and each Web page fitting in subcategories (**Figure 21.7**). A site outline probably will mirror the file structure of the site. One warning, though: Because of their linear nature, outlines can be highly misleading when they are applied to a Web site that has links among its sections.

Create a site map

A site map allows other people (clients, artists, programmers, project managers, and so on) to see the site structure. It gives them a common blueprint to work with and reference (**Figure 21.8**).

Flowcharts show how various pages and functions within the site fit and work together. Generally, pages are represented by rectangles and links by lines, but you can add other symbols to the flowchart to indicate decision paths, external links, or other code (such as Java applets). The advantage of a flowchart over a simple outline is that the former can show the relationships among pages more accurately.

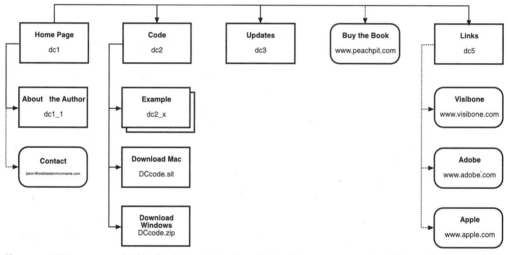

Figure 21.8 Site maps are a highly visual way to show the relationships among pages in a Web site. In this example, each box represents a Web page; lines represent links. Rounded boxes with dotted lines represent pages outside this Web site.

Sketch the layout grid

Select the Web layout style you want to use (see "Understanding Layout on the Web" in Chapter 20). Then, on paper or in an drawing program, sketch the basic structure of a Web page in your site (**Figure 21.9**). You don't have to draw a detailed diagram of every page you plan to create. Instead, identify what goes where on your pages.

In addition, you can use notes to describe the interactive components that will go in a particular area of a Web site.

Play with different concepts, and don't be afraid to experiment. It will be easier to try new things now than when you have the design in HTML.

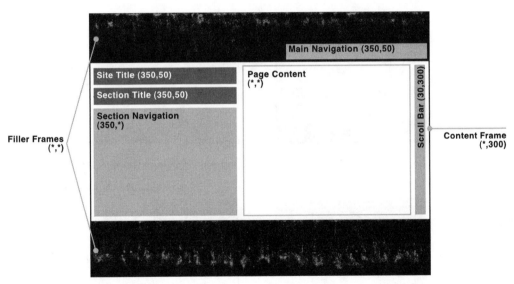

Filler Frames (*,*)

Site Title (350,50)

Section Title (350,50)

Section Navigation (350,*)

Main Navigation (350,50)

Page Content (*,*)

Scroll Bar (30,300)

Content Frame (*,300)

Figure 21.9 The layout-grid sketch allows you to plan where the various elements in the Web site will go and how they will interact.

Create a storyboard

A storyboard (**Figure 21.10**) works like a flowchart, but provides a visual representation of the page and its content. A flowchart represents a page with a symbol (such as a rectangle) and gives no indication of its content.

A storyboard may also indicate the layout of each page, making it indispensable for narrating how the site works to people who may have a hard time imagining it without some visual representation. It is especially useful for describing interactive processes that occur on a single page.

Storyboards generally take up a lot of space and need to be laid out on large paper to accommodate all their information.

Figure 21.10 A storyboard is extremely effective for describing how a visitor will accomplish a particular task in a Web site. In this storyboard, the visitor is trying to view a code example. The storyboard shows what links the visitor would select and what each screen would look like. Create a storyboard for all the major processes in your Web site.

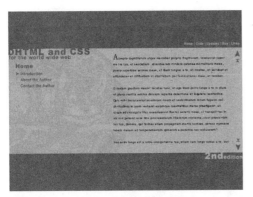

Figure 21.11 The look and feel of the Web site composed in Photoshop. Elements, such as the text links, will be created with HTML text and CSS in the final version, but it helps to plan what those elements will look like. This example uses dummy text where real text will appear in the final version.

Define the look and feel

In a graphics program such as Adobe Photoshop, create a mockup of your Web site, based on the layout grid from step 3 (**Figure 21.11**). Programs such as Photoshop and Macromedia Fireworks allow you to design interactive graphics and help you prepare them for use on the Web.

Again, you can play around with design ideas more easily at this stage of the game.

The Layout Grid

One tool at your disposal is the layout grid. Simply stated, the layout grid defines what type of content should be placed where on the page. The layout grid organizes the content on a Web page into specific rectangular areas. If your grid is well defined, it allows you the flexibility to create a variety of layouts along a similar theme.

If used properly, a layout grid identifies where specific types of content will be placed on the page and provides continuity between different pages. This format works to visitors' advantage, because it creates consistent areas on the page where visitors know to look for particular kinds of content (titles, illustrations, text, page numbers, and so on).

You can create a layout grid for any Web-layout category. Each format has its own strengths and weaknesses, depending on the size of the browser window.

With an unrestrained layout, for example, you may find that the columns of text stretch uncomfortably wide for reading purposes. Restraining the width of the content area can create uncomfortably large areas of negative space in the design, and restraining the height of the content area discriminates against visitors who have large monitors.

Step 3: Build

Now the tire hits the pavement, as you create the Web site that you have been planning.

Before you start, make sure you review the information you gathered when defining your Web site (audience, goals, content, and features).

This is where all of your hard planning pays off. If you have properly prepared, creating the code and placing the content should be relatively simple.

Prepare the content

Gather the content you will be using in the site—all the text, video, animations, and audio that will appear on the pages. Check all content thoroughly, and prepare it for use in the Web site. This preparation may simply mean having the text available in a word processing file (**Figure 21.12**). Or you may want to go ahead and place the basic tags (`<p>`, `<br>`, `<h1>`) in the files.

Create the code

Even if you are copying JavaScript, DHTML, or CSS from this book or another source, you need to adapt it for your own design (**Figure 21.13**).

Create a template

In an HTML editor (or whatever program you use to create HTML), set up a generic version of your Web page. Add the DHTML and CSS that you plan to use on every page as the basic navigation. Test this page in a variety of browsers, under a variety of conditions, and refine it until you are satisfied.

Now that you have a full working prototype of your Web page, strip out anything that is not needed on every page, and use what remains as the template. You can use this template to build the rest of the pages in a program such as Dreamweaver or GoLive.

Figure 21.12 Check your content for spelling and grammar mistakes.

Figure 21.13 Before you create your Web site, test your code, and make any tweaks required for your Web site.

Figure 21.14 Assemble all the components.

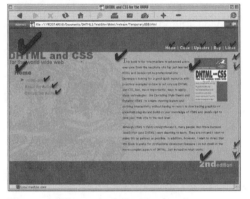

Figure 21.15 The result of all my hard work (www.webbedenvironments.com/dhtml).

Assemble the pages

Using your template as a starting point for each page, add the rest of the content (**Figure 21.14**). Make sure you keep a clean copy of the template for creating each new Web page.

Test your site

Always test your work before putting it online. Small mistakes can lead to great headaches if they are not caught and corrected at this stage. You should test your pages in a wide variety of browsers and operating systems (**Figure 21.15**).

Layout with CSS vs. Tables

Before tables, Web layout consisted of wide pages of text stretching from the left side of the window to the right. Designers had no way to break up this single column of content. Yet most designers came from a print background, and they were used to breaking text into two or more columns.

Tables allow designers to create a layout grid with multiple columns. Although tables were never meant to be the workhorses of Web layout, nothing better has come along.

I would like to tell you that CSS changes this situation—you can use it to create stunning layouts for the Web without relying on tables. Unfortunately, that is not the case.

CSS does offer Web designers many options for the exact placement of content in the window, via positioning. But it falls flat for creating column-intensive layouts. That said, CSS positioning is still young, and many people are still playing around with the possibilities.

I managed to avoid using tables on my own Web site. But I had to settle for a relatively simple layout, with only one row and two columns (the left for navigation and the right for content), and some floating side elements (such as the "This Week" area).

If you design a great layout using CSS without tables, send me the URL. I'd love to check it out.

22

WEB PAGE LAYOUT

There are as many ways to use CSS and DHTML as there are Web designers to use them. Yet these design tools are still relatively new, and designers are still discovering their capabilities and limitations. In addition, some designers who were initially captivated by the "gee-whiz" aspects of CSS to create dynamic HTML neglected its many layout strengths.

In the rush to experiment with the dynamic aspects of CSS, many designers overlooked some of the nuts-and-bolts problems that CSS solves: It facilitates solid, compelling page layout on the Web.

This chapter explores some of the valuable solutions CSS offers for everyday design issues and the best ways to integrate DHTML into the layout.

Netscape CSS Bug Fix

Netscape has an obvious, and often-complained-about CSS bug. When visitors resize their browsers, all CSS formatting that comes from an external CSS file (one that was imported via the `<link>` tag) mysteriously disappears, as though the linked style sheet never existed. If the visitor reloads the page, however, the CSS reappears (**Figures 22.1** and **22.2**). This bug can be a big turnoff for visitors to your site, especially if they don't know that reloading the page solves the problem.

How do you make sure the page is reloaded after the page is resized? Just tell the browser to stay on the lookout (**Code 22.1**).

To force the browser to reload the page after resizing:

1. `if (document.layers) {...}`

    In the `<script>` tag in the `<head>` of your HTML page, add code that detects whether the browser uses the layer's Document Object Model (see "Using Feature Sensing" in Chapter 11). If it does, the code records the current width (`innerWidth`) and height (`innerHeight`) of the visible page area (see "Finding the Visible Page Dimensions" in Chapter 12).

Figure 22.1 How the page should look in Netscape.

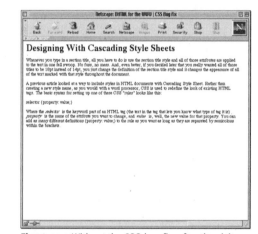

Figure 22.2 Without the CSS-bug fix, after the visitor resizes the screen, the browser's default settings are used to display the page.

Code 22.1 If this browser uses layers (which would mean that it is Netscape 4), the JavaScript records the initial values of the width and height of the live window area. If the window is resized, this code compares the original dimensions with the new dimensions and, if they are different, reloads the page, restoring the CSS.

```
<html>
<head>
    <script>
if (document.layers) {
    origWidth = innerWidth;
    origHeight = innerHeight;
    }
function reloadPage() {
    if (innerWidth != origWidth ||
    ⇨ innerHeight != origHeight)
    location.reload();
    }
if (document.layers) onresize = reloadPage;
    </script>
    <link rel="stylesheet" href="styles.css">
</head>
<body>
    <h1>Designing With Cascading Style
    ⇨ Sheets</h1>
    <p class="copy">Whenever you type in a
    ⇨ section title...</p>
    <p class="copy">A previous article looked
    ⇨ at a ...</p>
    <div class="code">
        selector {property: value;}<BR>
    </div>
    <p class="copy">Where the <I>selector</I>
    ⇨ is the keyword part of an HTML...</p>
</body>
</html>
```

2. `function reloadPage() {...}`

Add the function `reloadPage()` to your JavaScript. When triggered, this function compares the current width and height of the visible page area with the values recorded in step 1. If the values are different, the page reloads.

3. `onresize = reloadPage;`

Set the **onresize** event to trigger the **reloadPage** function from step 2. If the user resizes the page, changing the visible area of the Web page, the browser reloads the page, restoring the CSS to its rightful place.

✔ Tip

■ It's a good idea to stick this code in an external .js file that you import into every page in your site that uses CSS (see "Using an External JavaScript File" in Chapter 23).

Setting the CSS for the OS

Several inconsistencies between the Mac and Windows operating systems frustrate Web designers who use CSS to design their Web pages, especially when it comes to matching font sizes and colors. Actually, the problem is not with CSS itself, but with the way in which the OSes define font sizes and colors on the screen.

Without getting into the history and technical details, the basic problem is that Windows displays the same size font larger than a Mac does and displays the same colors a bit darker. This situation can lead to a design that may look great on the Mac but may have huge text and dark colors on a PC.

The answer? Using JavaScript and multiple CSS files tailored to the operating systems, you can deliver the right font sizes and colors for the OS in which your audience is viewing your site (**Figures 22.3, 22.4**, and **22.5**).

To set the CSS for the visitor's OS:

1. `default.css`

   Create an external CSS file with the styles to be used in the Web site, and save this file as default.css (**Code 22.2**). This file is directly linked to the Web pages in step 3.

2. `mac.css`

   Create a second CSS file, and save it as mac.css (**Code 22.3**). This version should be used to tweak the definitions set up in default.css and make them more palatable for Mac users by making the font larger and the color lighter. You do not have to reenter every definition in default.css, because the ones you want from that style sheet cascade down.

3. `<link href="default.css"`
   `→ rel="styleSheet" type="text/css">`

   In the <head> of the HTML document—index.html, in this example (**Code 22.4**)—link to the default version of the style sheet.

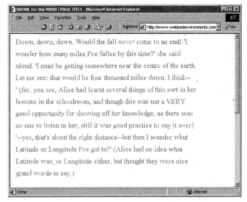

Figure 22.3 A Web page displayed in Internet Explorer 5 for Windows.

Figure 22.4 The same Web page displayed in Internet Explorer 5 for the Mac without correction. The text is smaller and much too light.

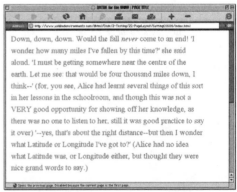

Figure 22.5 The same Web page displayed in Internet Explorer 5 for the Mac *with* correction. Notice that the text is slightly larger and darker to compensate.

Code 22.2 The default.css file contains the default styles to be used for the Web page.

```
.copy   {
    color: #cc3;
    font: 20px/32px "Times New Roman",
    → Georgia, Times, serif;
    width: 500px
    }


body    {
    background-color: #fff
    }
```

Code 22.3 The styles in mac.css override the ones set in default.css.

```
.copy    {
    color: #bb2;
    font: 23px/35px;
    width: 600px
    }
```

Code 22.4 The JavaScript detects whether the computer is a Mac. If it is, another style sheet is added to the page to make corrections.

```
<html>
<head>
    <link href="default.css" rel="styleSheet"
    → type="text/css">
    <script language="JavaScript">
if ((navigator.appVersion.indexOf
→ ('Mac') != -1)) {
document.write('<link href="mac.css"
→ rel="styleSheet" type="text/css">'); }
    </script>
</head>
<body>
    <p class="copy">Down, down, down...</p>
    <p class="copy">Presently she began
    → again...</p>
</body>
</html>
```

4. if ((navigator.appVersion.indexOf
→ ('Mac') != -1)) {...}

After the <link> tag, place JavaScript that checks whether the browser being used is on a Mac. If it is, the <link> tag to the Mac version of the CSS is "written" into the page via JavaScript. This second style sheet adjusts the definitions, making them more suitable for the Mac.

✔ Tips

■ Notice that although the version of the class **copy** in the Mac version of the CSS does not include a font face, the text still displays in Times. Why doesn't the definition of the class **copy** in the Mac CSS file replace the definition in the default CSS file? The term *cascading* in *cascading style sheets* refers to the capability to blend definitions, even if they come from different sources.

■ Operating systems are not the only problem. Browsers, even running in the same operating system, have idiosyncrasies for font size and the positioning of elements on the screen. You can use the same technique to detect the browser (see "Detecting the Browser's Name and Version" in Chapter 12) and use that information to deliver style sheets tailored to the browser.

■ You can use the JavaScript trick shown in this section for many purposes. If you want to deliver a different style sheet depending on a preference expressed by the visitor, for example, you could use a cookie variable to control which style sheet is loaded. This script gives the Web designer and the site visitor much more control over how the page is displayed, and the designer doesn't have to make a new page for each version.

Creating Headlines

One hassle in Web design is headlines created from a graphic, which usually means creating a new graphic for every headline. Using the CSS background property, however, you can create as many different title graphics as you want—without having to create new graphics and without incurring the additional download time involved with using text in graphics.

To create a headline with a graphic background:

1. `background_headline.gif`

    Create and save your background in a graphics program. Call the graphic something like background_headline.gif (**Figure 22.6**).

2. `h3.graphic {...}`

    Add a CSS rule for the <h3> tag (**Code 22.5**) with an associated class of `graphic` (see "Defining Classes to Create Your Own Tags" in Chapter 2). Include the background attribute, and point to the graphic you created in step 1 (see "Setting the Background" in Chapter 6).

    Note: You do not have to call the class created in step 2 `graphic`; you may call it anything you want.

Figure 22.6 The background graphic that will be tiled behind headlines.

Code 22.5 Applying a background graphic to a header is fairly straightforward, but the possibilities are infinite.

```
<html>
<head>
    <style type="text/css">
h3.offset {
    color: #000000;
    font-weight: bold;
    font-size: 14px;
    font-family: Verdana, Arial, Helvetica,
    → sans-serif;
    background-color: #ccc;
    padding: 3px;
    border: solid 1pt #000000;
    position: relative;
    width: 440px; }
h3.graphic {
    background: black url
    → (background_headline.gif) no-repeat;
    font: bold 16px helvetica,sans-serif;
    color: white;
    width: 400px;
    padding:10px; }
p {
    font: normal 10pt/14pt times,serif;
    left-margin: 25px;
    width: 400; }
    </style>
</head>
<body>
    <h3 class="offset">CHAPTER VII<br>
    A Mad Tea-Party</h3>
    <p>The table was a large one...</p>

    <h3 class="graphic">CHAPTER VII<br>
    A Mad Tea-Party</h3>
    <p>There was a table set out under a tree
    → in front of the house...</p>
</body>
</html>
```

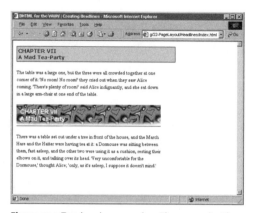

Figure 22.7 Two header examples. Play around with other graphics, different borders, and even different padding in the titles for other effects.

Figure 22.8 The headers About the Site and Reading the Code are both HTML text on a background graphic.

3. `<h3 class="graphic">CHAPTER VII<br>`
→ ` A Mad Tea-Party </h3>`

Whenever you use level-3 headings in your document, your background graphic will appear behind them as long as you include the **class** attribute and set it to the class you added in step 2 (**Figure 22.7**).

✔ Tips

- You can set the other heading levels the same way. You can use different graphics or use the same graphic by grouping the selectors (see "Defining Tags with the Same Rules" in Chapter 2).

- Play around with different graphics in the background. One background that I set up for a Web site used a gradient that started with a color on the left side and faded into the background on the right (**Figure 22.8**).

Creating a Fixed Header

One principle of good Web design is letting people know where they are at all times. Unfortunately, Web pages scroll, and important information about the page being viewed, such as the page title, can scroll off the top.

Using CSS, you can fix the title at the top of the Web page so that no matter how far visitors scroll, they always know where they are in the Web site (**Figure 22.9**).

You should know up front, however, that Internet Explorer 4 (Mac and Windows) and 5 (Windows) and Netscape 4/6 (Mac and Windows) do not support fixed positioning. The only browser that seems to support fixed positioning is Internet Explorer 5 for the Mac.

To set a fixed header:

1. `#header {`

Open a definition list with either a class or an ID. In this example, create an ID called header (**Code 22.6**).

2. `position: fixed;`

Type the `position` attribute, and give it the `fixed` value.

3. `color: red;`

Add any other definitions to the list that you want to use to create the header. This example displays the header in red on a gray background.

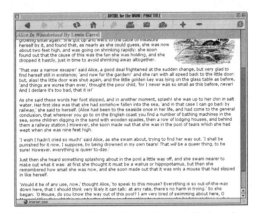

Figure 22.9 Even though the text has scrolled up, the header stays at the top of the browser window.

Code 22.6 The fixed header style is set as an ID that is then applied to a `<div>` tag.

```
                        code
<html>
<head>
    <style type="text/css">
#header   {
    color: red;
    font-weight: bold;
    font-size: 16px;
    font-family: "Times New Roman", Georgia,
    → Times, serif;
    background-color: #aaa;
    padding: 5px;
    position: fixed;
    z-index: 1000;
    top: 0px;
    left: 0px;
    width: 110%;
    visibility: visible; }
    </style>
</head>
<body>
    <div id="header">
        <i>Alice In Wonderland</i> By Lewis
        → Carrol
    </div>
    <br>
    <p>'I'm sure those are not the right
    → words,...</p>
    <p><img src="alice08.gif" width="200"
    → height="131" border="0" align="right">
    → As she said this she looked down at her
    → hands...</p>
    <p>'That <i>was</i> a narrow
    → escape!...</p>
    <p>As she said these words her foot
    → slipped...</p>
</body>
</html>
```

4. }

Close the definition list with a curly bracket (}).

5. `<div id="header"> <i>Alice In Wonderland → </i> By Lewis Carroll</div>`

Add the ID to the desired element. In this case, use a `<div>` tag to set off the title of the page.

✔ Tips

■ Remember that this technique will not work in all browsers. Browsers that do not recognize the fixed position treat the header as a static element, and it scrolls with the rest of the page. The rest of the CSS formatting will work, however.

■ Although it would be great if you could also place links in this fixed header, a bug in Internet Explorer 5 for the Mac makes links in a fixed element almost useless (see the sidebar "Is It Fixed?" in Chapter 8).

CREATING A FIXED HEADER

367

Creating a Sidebar

Sidebars are possibly the most common method used to set off navigation tools. The traditional method is to create a long, horizontal background graphic that includes the sidebar and the background color for the content area. Using CSS, though, you can create a much smaller graphic that is just the width of the sidebar and use the repeat-y property to tile the sidebar image down the left side. This technique saves download time by reducing the size of the background graphic.

To create a sidebar:

1. `background_side.gif`

   Create a graphic of a thin strip the width that you want your sidebar to be (**Figure 22.10**).

2. `body {`

   `background: #cccccc url`

   `→ (background_side.gif) repeat-y;}`.

   Set up the body selector in the document to use the graphic you created in step 1, but repeat it only in the y direction (see "Setting Individual Background Properties" in Chapter 6). You'll also want to set the background color for the rest of the page (**Code 22.7**).

3. Use tables or CSS positioning to set up a left column for the sidebar's content and a right column for everything else.

   In this example, I've set up two absolutely positioned columns: one for the sidebar and the other for the content (**Figure 22.11**).

✔ Tip

■ Play around with different graphics and different effects. Try running the graphic across the top of the page (repeat-x) to set up a header instead of a sidebar. The possibilities are endless.

Figure 22.10 The background graphic used to create a sidebar 160 pixels wide.

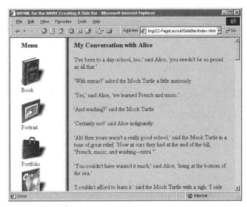

Figure 22.11 The sidebar runs down the left side of the screen, and the background color will fill the rest of the screen to the right.

Code 22.7 Create the sidebar by using a background graphic and setting up two columns over it.

```
<html>
<head>
    <style type="text/css">
body {
    background: #cccccc url(background_side.gif) repeat-y;          }
#sidebar {
    position: absolute;
    top: 10px;
    left: 30px;
    width: 150px; }
#content {
    position: absolute;
    top: 10px;
    left: 175px }
    </style>
</head>
<body>
    <div id="sidebar">
        <h3>Menu</h3>
        <img src="b_book.gif" width="69" height="81"><br>Book<br>
        <img src="b_portrait.gif" width="69" height="81"><br>Portrait<br>
        <img src="b_portfolio.gif" width="72" height="79"><br>Portfolio<br>
        <img src="b_painting.gif" width="69" height="81"><br>Painting<br>
        <img src="b_letter.gif" width="72" height="79"><br>Letter<br>
        <img src="b_hammer.gif" width="72" height="81"> <br>Tools
    </div>
    <div id="content">
        <H3>My Conversation with Alice</H3>
        <p>'I've been to a day-school, too,' said Alice; 'you needn't be so proud as all that.'</p>
        <p>'With extras?' asked the Mock Turtle a little anxiously.</p>
        <p>'Yes,' said Alice, 'we learned French and music.'</p>
        <p>'And washing?' said the Mock Turtle.</p>
        <p>'Certainly not!' said Alice indignantly. </p>
    </div>
</body>
</html>
```

CREATING A SIDEBAR

Setting a Dynamic Header and Footer

One problem with designing a large Web site is that it's hard to change the design once you get started.

On my own Web site, I maintain close to a hundred articles that I have written over the years. I'm not a database guru, so I keep them in static HTML pages. But I like to tweak my designs every now and then. Rather than place the header and footers directly on the pages, I use JavaScript to "write" them onto the page. I use a JavaScript variable on the page to tell the imported JavaScript the title, date, and other information about the article (see "Using an External JavaScript File" in Chapter 23).

To set up a dynamic header and footer:

1. `header.js`

   Create an external JavaScript file, and save it as `header.js`. This file will be imported into the top of index.html in step 4. Include `document.writeln(...)` statements to write all the HTML for the header for the page. In addition, this header will use variables (`index.html`) to add the title, subtitle, teaser, and date (**Code 22.8**).

2. `footer.js`

   Create an external JavaScript file, and save it as `footer.js`. This file will be imported at the bottom of index.html in step 4. Include `document.writeln(...)` statements to write all the HTML for the footer for the page. In this example, the footer will display the page title—the one between the `<title>` tags, not the JavaScript variable `title`—and the URL for the page, as well as a link to a copyright page and a `mailto` link (**Code 22.9**).

Code 22.8 This JavaScript is imported into the top of index.html to create the header for the document.

```
document.writeln ('<h1>')
document.writeln (title)
document.writeln ('</h1>')
document.writeln ('<h3>')
document.writeln (subTitle)
document.writeln ('</h3>')
document.writeln ('<i>')
document.writeln (teaser)
document.writeln ('</i><br><br> <span
→ style="font: 10pt arial">')
document.writeln (dDate + ' ' + mDate + ' ' +
→ yDate)
document.writeln ('</span>')
```

Code 22.9 This code is imported into the bottom of index.html to create the footer for the document.

```
document.writeln('<br><hr><br clear="all">')
document.writeln('<span class="copyright">')
document.writeln('<b>Title:</b> ' +
→ self.document.title)
document.writeln('</br>')
document.writeln('<b>URL:</b> <a href="' +
→ self.location + '">' + self.location +
→ '</a>' )
document.writeln('</br>')
document.writeln
→ ('<a href="../aux/copyright.html">
Copyright &copy;</a> 1998-2000 <A HREF=
→ "mailto:jason@webbedenvironments.com">
→ Jason Cranford Teague</A>. All rights
→ reserved.' )
document.writeln('</span></br>')
```

Code 22.10 This sample Web page (index.html) imports the header and footer. It also includes several JavaScript variables that add the title, subtitle, teaser, and date to the header of the document.

```
code

<html>
<head>
    <script>
title = 'The Begining of the End';
subTitle= 'Why I went to the Store';
teaser = 'The day started like any other, but
→ little did I know that it would soon turn
→ into the worst day of my life!'
dDate = '01'
mDate = 'January'
yDate = '2001'
    </script>
    <link rel="stylesheet" href="default.css">
</head>
<body>
    <script src="header.js"></script>
<!-- Begin Content -->
    <p>Et quid erat, quod me delectabat, nisi
→ amare et amari? </p>
<!-- End Content -->
    <script src="footer.js"></script>
</body>
</html>
```

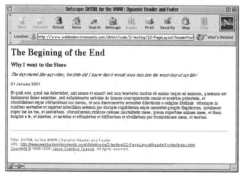

Figure 22.12 The final output with the dynamically generated header and footer. Because you do not embed the header and footer code in the page, you can change the layout in the JavaScript files, and those changes will affect every HTML page that uses them.

3. `title = 'The Beginning of the End';`

   In a `<script>` tag in the `<head>` of the document in which you want to include the header and footer, include the following variables: `title`, `subTitle`, `teaser`, `dDate`, `mDate`, and `yDate`. JavaScript will use these values when writing the header (**Code 22.10**).

4. `<script src="header.js"></script>`

   In the `<body>` of the HTML page, add `<script>` tags, with the sources set to the URLs of the header and footer JavaScript files (**Figure 22.12**).

✔ Tips

- You can place any HTML code in the header and footer. On my Web site, for example, I place all the navigation for the page in external JavaScript files such as these. This practice allows me to add or delete navigation elements without having to change every page on my Web site.

- The variables in step 3 are just examples of the kinds of information you could include on an individual HTML page for use by a global JavaScript page that is being imported. You can include any type of data about the article, such as volume number, issue number, or its location within the Web site.

Making Your Own Frame Borders

One of the most frustrating aspects of using frames is the clunky-looking borders that standard HTML puts between them (**Figure 22.13**). When you use the background property, however, you can use any border design you can dream up (**Figure 22.14**).

Although these borders can be placed only along the left side or top of an individual frame, they are still very useful for showing boundaries between frames.

To create a frame border:

1. `border.gif`

   Create the frame-border graphic. For this example, I'm using an ornate design that I saved as border.gif (**Figure 22.15**). You can use anything you want for this graphic.

2. `index.html`

   Create a frame document, making sure that you turn off the default border:

   `border="0" framespacing="0"`
   `→ frameborder="no"`

   Save this frameset as index.html (**Code 22.11**).

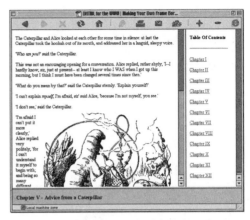

Figure 22.13 A frameset with the default frame borders.

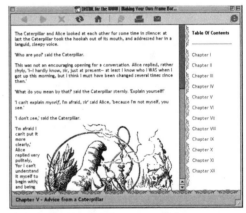

Figure 22.14 A frameset created with CSS, with an ornate red border separating the frames.

Figure 22.15 The two graphics used to create the borders for the right and bottom frames. Remember, you can use anything you want for these. Go wild.

Code 22.11 The frameset document.

```
                    code
<html>
<frameset rows="*,40" border="0"
→ framespacing="0" frameborder="no">
    <frameset cols="*,150" border="0"
    → framespacing="0" frameborder="no">
        <frame src="center_frame.html"
        → name="center" noresize>
        <frame src="right_frame.html"
        → name="right" noresize>
    </frameset>
    <frame src="bottom_frame.html"
    → name="bottom" noresize scrolling="no">
</frameset>
</html>
```

Code 22.12 A frame with a vertical border set.

```
                    code
<html>
<head>
    <style type="text/css">
body    {
        background: white url(border.gif)
        → repeat-y }
    </style>
</head>
<body>
    <h4>Table Of Contents</h4>
    <hr width="90%" align="left">
    <p><a href="#">Chapter I</a></p>
</body>
</html>
```

Code 22.13 A frame with a horizontal border set.

```
                    code
<html>
<head>
    <style type="text/css">
body    {
background: silver url(border.gif) repeat-x
→ 0px 0; }
    </style>
</head>
<body>
    <h3>Chapter V - Advice from a
    → Caterpillar</h3>
</body>
</html>
```

3. `right_frame.html`

Use the background property in the `<body>` tag of an HTML document (**Code 22.12** and **22.13**) to place the border graphic from step 1 in the background of the desired frame(s) (refer to Figure 22.14). Repeat this graphic either horizontally (`repeat-x`) or vertically (`repeat-y`) (see "Setting the Background" in Chapter 6).

✔ Tips

■ This technique works only for setting the border on the top of the frame or the left side. You cannot use it to set both of those sides at the same time or to set the bottom or right border.

■ The design of the border can be anything you want, and it can be as thick or thin as you want. Just remember that the image repeats along whichever axis you specify.

■ These borders have one big drawback compared with the default frame-border style: Neither you nor the visitor can use these borders to resize the frame.

MAKING YOUR OWN FRAME BORDERS

Opening and Closing Frames

One complaint about frames is that they monopolize screen space by placing menus and titles permanently on the screen. Although this arrangement may be fine if you have a large monitor with plenty of room, people who have smaller monitors can be turned off by the experience.

Here is a technique I developed that uses nested framesets and some JavaScript to open and close a menu in a frame (**Figures 22.16** and **22.17**). When the menu is closed, the content area of the window can use as much space as needed.

Figure 22.16 The menu is closed.

Figure 22.17 The menu is open.

Code 22.14 The frameset document used to create the layout of the Web site.

```
<html>

<frameset  rows="35,*" border="0"
framespacing="0" frameborder="no">

    <frame name="header" src="header.html"
    → scrolling="no" frameborder="no" noresize
    → marginHeight="2px" marginWidth="2px">

    <frame name="content"
    → src="nomenu_frames.html" marginwidth="10"
    → marginheight="10" frameborder="no">

</frameset>

</html>
```

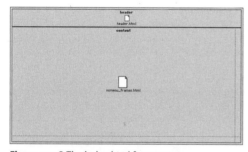

Figure 22.18 The index.html frameset.

Code 22.15 The frameset that will be loaded into the content frame of index.html when the menu is closed.

```
<html>

<frameset  cols="25,*" border="0"
framespacing="0" frameborder="no">

    <frame name="control" src="control.html"
    → marginwidth="0" marginheight="0"
    → scrolling="no" frameborder="no"
noresize>

    <frame name="content2" src="content.html"
    → marginwidth="10" marginheight="10"
    → scrolling="auto" frameborder="no">

</frameset>

</html>
```

To set up collapsible frames:

1. `index.html`

   Set up the main frameset. In this example, I've set up two frames: header and content (**Code 22.14** and **Figure 22.18**). The frame called header will stay static (not change its source) and contain the file header.html, which contains most of the JavaScript needed to pull off this trick. The frame content starts with a nested frameset called nomenu_frames.html, but then switches to the frameset menu_frames.html to toggle the menu open.

2. `nomenu_frames.html`

   Create a frameset with two columns, and save it as nomenu_frames.html (**Code 22.15** and **Figure 22.19**). The first frame, called control, will house the file control.html; the second column, called content2, initially contains content.html.

   continues on next page

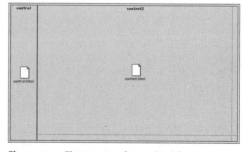

Figure 22.19 The nomenu_frames.html frameset, which will be loaded into the frame content of index.html when the menu is closed.

3. menu_frames.html

Create a frameset with three columns, and save it as menu_frames.html (**Code 22.16** and **Figure 22.20**). The second two frames in this frameset are identical to nomenu_frames.html. The first frame, however, is 150 pixels wide and displays the file menu.html. Visitors will be switching back and forth between the two framesets you set up in steps 2 and 3, depending on whether they want the menu to be open.

Code 22.16 The frameset document that is loaded into the content frame of index.html when the menu is open.

```
<html>

<frameset  cols="100,25,*" border="0"
→ framespacing="0" frameborder="no">

<frame name="menu" src="menu.html"
→ marginwidth="10" marginheight="10"
→ scrolling="no" frameborder="no" noresize>

<frame name="control" src="control.html"
→ marginwidth="0" marginheight="o"
→ scrolling="no" frameborder="no"
noresize>

<frame name="content2" src="content.html"
→ marginwidth="10" marginheight="10"
→ scrolling="auto" frameborder="no">

</frameset>

</html>
```

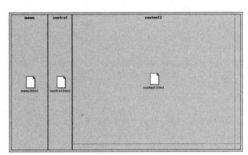

Figure 22.20 The menu_frames.html frameset, which will be loaded into the frame content of index.html when the menu is open.

Code 22.17 The HTML document used in the header frame of index.html. It contains the function menuToggle(). When triggered, that function opens or closes the frame menu.

```
                      code
<html>
<head>
   <script language="JavaScript">
var frameState = 0;
var contentSRC = null;
function menuToggle() {
   if (frameState == 0) {
       contentSRC = parent.content.
       → content2.location.href;
       top.content.location =
       → 'menu_frames.html';
       frameState = 1;
       return;
   }
   else {
       contentSRC = parent.content.
       → content2.location.href;
       top.content.location =
       → 'nomenu_frames.html';
       frameState = 0;
       return;
   }
}
   </script>
   <style type="text/css">
h2 { color: gray; font-weight: bold;
→ font-size: 24px; font-family: "Trebuchet MS",
→ Arial, Helvetica, Geneva, sans-serif; }
body { background-color: #333; }
   </style>
</head>
<body>
   <h2>webbedENVIRONMENTS</h2>
</body>
</html>
```

4. `header.html`

Create the HTML file that will be used in the frame header from step 1, and save it as header.html (**Code 22.17**). The function **menuToggle()** is the meat of this page; it is executed when a visitor clicks the Menu link in control.html. The function first checks to see what HTML document is loaded into the **content2** frame and stores that URL in the variable **contentSRC**. It then checks to see whether the menu is visible and switches the frameset to either nomenu_frames.html or menu_frames.html. The variable **frameState** records the current state of the menu: **0** (closed) or **1** (open).

continues on next page

5. menu.html

Create an HTML file to be displayed when the menu is open, and save it as menu.html (**Code 22.18**). Although I've used HTML links in this example, you can place any Web content in this file. You should target all links to the frame content2.

6. control.html

Create the HTML file that will be used in the frame control, and save it as control.html (**Code 22.19**). This file contains a link that, when clicked, triggers the menuToggle() function from step 4.

Code 22.18 The HTML document that contains the menu to be displayed in the menu frame of menu_frames.html. This document can include any HTML content.

```
                       code
<html>
<head>
    <style type="text/css">
body { color: gray; font: bold 12px/24px
→ "Trebuchet MS", Arial, Helvetica, Geneva,
→ sans-serif; background-color: black }
a:link { color: white; text-decoration:
→ none; }
a:hover { color: white; text-decoration:
→ underline }
a:active { color: silver; text-decoration:
→ underline }
a:visited { color: white; text-decoration:
→ none }
    </style>
</head>
<body>
    <a href="home.html"
    → target="content2">Home</a><br>
    <a href="page1.html"
    → target="content2">Page 1</a><br>
    <a href="page2.html"
    → target="content2">Page 2</a><br>
    <a href="page3.html"
    → target="content2">Page 3</a><br>
</body>
</html>
```

Code 22.19 The HTML document used in the control frame of menu_frames.html and nomenuframes.html. This file contains a link that triggers the menuToggle() function in header.html.

```
                       code
<html>
<head>
<body>
    <div id="tabs">
        <a href="javascript:top.header.
        → menuToggle();">
            <img src="images/tabMenu.gif"
            → width="20" height="100"
            → border="0">
        </a>
    </div>
</body>
</html>
```

Code 22.20 The initial file that loads into the content2 frame of menu_frames.html and nomenuframes.html. The JavaScript in this file finds the URL of the current page before the menu was changed (recorded in contentSRC in header.html) and reloads that page into this frame.

```
<html>
<head>
    <script language="JavaScript">
var contentSRC;
function replaceContent() {
    contentSRC = top.header.contentSRC;
    if (contentSRC == null) self.location =
→ 'home.html';
    else self.location = contentSRC;
}
    </script>
</head>
<body onload="replaceContent();">
</body>
</html>
```

Code 22.21 A typical content page on the site.

```
<html>
<head>
    <style media="screen" type="text/css">
body {
    background-color: white }
h2 { color: silver; font-weight: bold;
→ font-size: 36px; font-family: "Trebuchet MS",
→ Arial, Helvetica, Geneva, sans-serif; }
    </style>
</head>
<body>
    <h2>Home</h2>
</body>
</html>
```

7. content.html

Create an HTML page that contains **Code 22.20**. This document is an intermediary step and never stays on the screen long. It checks what document was loaded into the content2 frame by accessing the variable in the header frame that recorded it (contentSRC); then it reloads that document. If no previous source exists (when the file first loads, for example), it loads home.html.

8. home.html

Create the Web pages for your site (**Code 22.21**). All these pages will be in the content2 frame.

✔ Tips

■ This technique lets a site visitor open or close the navigation menu without losing her place within the site.

■ You do not have to use a menu in the collapsible frame. I created an intranet for an organization that used this technique to provide a calendar of events that could be popped out at any time.

■ Due to a security restriction in both Netscape and Internet Explorer, you cannot open or close the menu when the content2 frame contains a document from a server other than the one that hosts your Web pages, so you cannot use content from different Web sites.

OPENING AND CLOSING FRAMES

Keeping Pages Framed

Imagine that you are reading a book. You finish for the night, place a bookmark on the last page you read, and put down the book. The next night, you pick up the book to resume reading where you left off. Through some strange shift in reality, however, the bookmark returns you to the cover, and you have to flip through all the intervening pages again to get back to where you were. If you are creating a Web site with frames, that is how the site may appear to your visitors: They want to bookmark an interior page but end up bookmarking the cover.

This situation is not the only problem with referencing framed Web pages. What if you want to refer visitors to a specific page within the site from an e-mail or from another Web site? Sure, you can give them the URL for that single page, but if you send them directly to that page without the frames, it's like giving them the book without the rest of the pages or the spine. You could create a different frameset document for every page, but this process is problematic and unwieldy.

There is an easier method. You can't change the way that frames work, and for some reason, browser manufacturers have ignored these major usability problems. But you can implement a workaround in your Web site to help visitors overcome these problems (**Figures 22.21** and **22.22**).

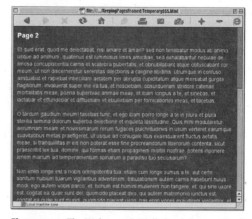

Figure 22.21 The Web page initially loads into a naked screen, but almost instantly...

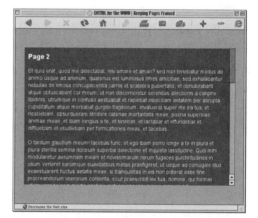

Figure 22.22 ...the screen blinks, and the page you were viewing is now in the appropriate frameset.

Code 22.22 This small external JavaScript file makes sure that your framed pages stay framed. As soon as a page containing this code loads, it will reload into the appropriate frameset file.

```
                    code
myPage = self.location;
thisPage = top.location;

if (thisPage == myPage) {
    contentSRC = escape(myPage);
    frameURL = 'index.html?' + contentSRC;
    top.location.href = frameURL;
}
```

Code 22.23 The frameset is not coded directly in HTML, but is coded with JavaScript document.write so that you can add variables to the HTML.

```
                    code
<html>
    <script language="JavaScript">
    contentSRC = (location.search.
    → substring(1)) ? location.search.
    → substring(1) : 'defaultContent.html';
    contentSRC = unescape(contentSRC);
    var writeFrame = ''
    writeFrame += '<FRAMESET COLS="*,575,*"
    → BORDER="0" FRAMESPACING="0"
    → FRAMEBORDER="NO">';
    writeFrame += '<FRAME SRC="filler.html">';
    writeFrame += '<FRAMESET ROWS="50,*,
    → 50">';
    writeFrame += '<FRAME SRC="filler.html">';
    writeFrame += '<FRAME SRC=
    → "' + ( contentSRC ) + '" NAME="content"
    → NORESIZE>';
    writeFrame += '<FRAME SRC="filler.html">';
    writeFrame += '</FRAMESET>';
    writeFrame += '<FRAME SRC="filler.html">';
    writeFrame += '</FRAMESET>';
    document.write(writeFrame);
    </script>
</html>
```

To place an HTML page in a frameset automatically:

1. `framed.js`

   Create an external JavaScript file (see "Using an External JavaScript File" in Chapter 23), and save it as framed.js (**Code 22.22**). Add script that first determines whether the document is loaded into a frameset by comparing the document's URL with the URL of the entire window. If the document is in a frameset, the URLs are different, and nothing happens. If the URLs are the same (no surrounding frameset exists), the script combines the URL for the frameset the document should be in (in this case, index.html) with its own URL (myPage), separating these two URLs with a question mark (?). The function finishes by resetting the location of the window to this new frameURL.

2. `index.html`

   Set up a frameset document, using JavaScript to write the HTML code into the page, and save it as index.html (**Code 22.23**). This JavaScript extracts the URL for the page to be loaded into the content frame from the URL of the page currently loaded. If a question mark (?) appears in the main URL for the page, the script uses whatever is after that question mark for the URL of the content frame saved in the variable contentSRC. Otherwise, the script uses a default URL—in this case, defaultContent.html—which you can set to be any file that you want.

   continues on next page

3. `content.html`

Create the Web pages for your site
(**Code 22.24** and **22.25**). In the <head>
of all the documents that you want to
place dynamically in the **content** frame
of the frameset, link to the external
JavaScript file you created in step 1:

`<script src="framed.js"></script>`

✔ Tips

■ If you want to point someone directly to
a page within your site, just send him the
URL for the document created in step 2
(`index.html`). Any HTML page will place
itself in the frameset automatically as
long as you import the file **framed.js** into
that page, as shown in step 3.

■ When visitors follow a link to one of these
pages and then bookmark it, they return
to that page with the frameset intact.

■ Netscape for Windows and Internet
Explorer for both the Mac and Windows
allow you to bookmark a page in a frame
by clicking and holding (Mac) or right-
clicking (Windows) and then choosing
the appropriate option from the pop-up
menu. If a visitor bookmarks a page in a
frameset that was created with the technique described in this section, when she
returns to that page via the bookmark,
the page frames itself automatically.

■ This technique does not solve all the
problems involved with bookmarking
frames, but until the browser makers get
their acts together, it will help make your
framed Web sites much more usable.

Code 22.24 This page is loaded if no question mark
(?) is used in the URL. It includes the `frames.js` link
to force the page into a frameset, if necessary.

```
<html>
<head>
    <script src="framed.js"></script>
    <link rel="stylesheet"
    → href="default.css">
    </head>
<body>
    <h2>Page 1</h2>
</body>
</html>
```

Code 22.25 This page includes a link to the `frames.js`
code.

```
<html>
<head>
    <script src="framed.js"></script>
    <link rel="stylesheet"
    → href="default.css">
    </head>
<body>
    <h2>Page 2</h2>
</body>
</html>
```

Looking Good in Print (on the Web)

I have never seen a paperless office and would be quite surprised if I ever did. But the big promise that came along with the computer was the elimination of paper from our lives—no more filing cabinets, clutter, or dead trees, just an entropy-free utopia in which electrons were constantly recycled and reused, just like in "Star Trek."

But something tells me that we'll have the technology to fly between the most distant stars before we eliminate paper from our lives.

With the advent of laser and inkjet printers, we seem to be buried under mounds of perfectly printed paper. Even the Web seems to increase the amount of paper we use. If a Web page is longer than a couple of scrolls, most people print it.

But the Web was created to display information on the screen, not on paper. Web graphics look blocky when printed, and straight HTML lacks much in the way of layout controls. That said, you can take steps to improve the appearance of printed Web pages. Looking good in print on the Web may take a little extra effort, but your audience will thank you in the long run.

continues on next page

Here are eight simple things you can do to improve the appearance of your Web page when it gets printed:

◆ **Use CSS.** Cascading style sheets are the future of Web design. CSS allows you to create documents that look as good printed as anything spit out of a word processor.

◆ **Define your media.** CSS allows you to define different style sheets to be used depending on the way the page is displayed—usually on a screen or on paper (see "Setting the CSS for Printing" in Chapter 2).

◆ **Use page breaks to keep headers with their text.** Although the page-break attribute is not widely supported at this time (see "Setting Page Breaks for Printing" in Chapter 4), it may be a universal standard before long.

◆ **Use frames to separate content from navigation.** Try to keep the main content—the part your audience is interested in reading—in a frame by itself. You can then place all the navigation, titles, and advertisements for the site in other frames. This practice allows visitors to print the frame with the good stuff in it and leave the rest (refer to "Opening and Closing Frames" earlier in this chapter).

◆ **Avoid using background colors or background graphics with light-colored text.** Although they can add flavor in the window, background colors and graphics turn into noise when printed. Some browsers allow you to print documents without backgrounds, but light-colored text will not show up against the white background of the paper.

◆ **Avoid using transparent colors in graphics,** especially if the graphic is on a background color or a graphic other than white. The transparent area of a GIF image usually prints as white regardless of the color behind it in the window. This situation is not a problem if the graphic is on a white background to begin with, but the result is messy if the graphic is supposed to be on a dark background.

◆ **Avoid using text in graphics.** The irony of printing stuff off the Web is that text in graphics, which look smooth in the window, look blocky when printed, but regular HTML text, which may look blocky on the screen, prints smoothly in any decent printer. Try to stick with HTML text as much as possible.

◆ **Provide a separate print-ready version of the Web site.** Rather than force visitors to follow every link on your site and print each page along the way, provide a single document for your Web site that visitors can download and print. Adobe Acrobat is a great way to provide this content in a more-or-less universal file format that retains most formatting, fonts, and graphics for delivery over the Web. Find out more about Acrobat at the Adobe Web site (www.adobe.com).

Importing External Content

Imagine you are designing a large Web site with the same menu on every page. Every time you need to change the menu, you must change every page. Not only is this process time-consuming, but the possibility of making mistakes is high. Wouldn't it be nice to have that menu in one file and import it into each page as the visitor uses the Web site? Then you can correct one file and have the changes reflected throughout the site.

To do this, you need a way to import external content into HTML files. You can use any of three methods, each of which has strengths and weaknesses.

Combining ilayers and iframes

The `<ilayer>` tag is the easiest way to place external content in an HTML document, at least in Netscape 4. When you set a source for this tag, it imports an HTML file and uses that content as though it were part of the document itself (**Figure 23.1**). Unfortunately, this tag is available only with Netscape 4, so you have to use something else to import content if the document is being viewed in Internet Explorer or Netscape 6.

The `<iframe>` tag can place external content in an HTML document. This content is treated as though it is in a separate frame, however, so it interacts differently with surrounding content (**Figure 23.2**). In addition, you need to include some contingency method for visitors who are not using a browser that supports Netscape layers (see Chapter 16) or iframes.

To import external content with iframes and ilayers:

1. `<ilayer></ilayer>`

   In the `<body>` of your HTML document (**Code 23.1**), add an `<ilayer>` tag, and set it to import external.html (see "Importing External Content with Netscape Layers" in Chapter 16).

2. `<nolayer>...</nolayer>`

   Add the `<nolayer>` tag. This tag hides the code inside it from Netscape 4 (see "Providing Content for Nonlayers Browsers" in Chapter 16).

3. `<iframe>...</iframe>`

   Inside the `<nolayer>` tag, add the `<iframe>`, and set it to import.

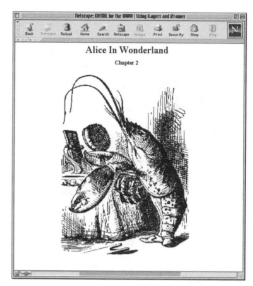

Figure 23.1 Netscape 4 imports the content via the `<ilayer>`.

Figure 23.2 Netscape 6 supports `<iframes>` instead. Both browser versions, however, see the same content.

Code 23.1 The HTML file uses ilayers and iframes to import content regardless of whether the browser is Netscape or Internet Explorer.

```
                    code
<html>
<body>
    <ilayer id="htNAV"
src="external.html"></ilayer>
    <nolayer>
        <iframe id="htIE" src="external.html"
    → frameborder="0" marginheight="0"
    → marginwidth="0" width="100%"
    → height="100%">
            <a href="external.html">
            → External Content</a>
        </iframe>
    </nolayer>
</body>
</html>
```

Code 23.2 The external content being imported into index.html.

```
                    code
<div style="text-align:center">
    <h1>Alice In Wonderland</h1>
    <h3>Chapter 2</h3>
    <img src="alice36.gif" width="360"
    → height="480" border="0">
```

4. `<a href="external.html">`
  `→ External Content</a>`

Inside the `<iframe>` tag, add a link to external.html for browsers that do not support ilayers or iframes.

5. `external.html`

Create a new HTML file, and save it as external.html (**Code 23.2**). This file does not contain the regular `<html>` open and close tags, which are supplied by the main document—only the `<body>` tag and whatever HTML you want to use.

✔ Tips

- Note: Because the `<iframe>` acts like an independent frame, you have to target all links in external.html to `top` or to the frame in which you want the content to be displayed. Otherwise, these links will appear in the `<iframe>`.

- I once used this method on my Web site to place at the bottom of the page a list of articles related to the one the visitor was reading. I maintained 14 related-articles files, each on a different topic. Each article imported the relevant related article's file by using ilayers or iframes. When I placed a new article on my site, I simply linked it to the appropriate related-articles file: Every article in the site that imported that file was updated automatically.

COMBINING ILAYERS AND IFRAMES

Using Server-Side Includes

The easiest way to import external content into a Web page is to use a *server-side include*. This is not an HTML tag, but a tag that tells the computer that serves your Web pages to the Internet (called a *server*) to add the referenced file to the page. Although this method's success depends on whether your server understands this tag, almost all servers do these days.

To add a server-side include:

1. `<!--#include virtual="external.html"-->`

   Add the include tag anywhere in the `<body>` of your HTML document, and set it to import external.html (**Code 23.3**).

2. `<!-- #echo var="DATE_LOCAL" -->`
   `<!-- #echo var="DATE_GMT" -->`

   Another useful server side tag is the `#echo` tag in which the server includes either its local time and date or Greenwich Mean Time (GMT) on the page.

3. `external.html`

   Create a new HTML file, and save it as external.html. This file does not contain the regular `<html>` open and close tags, which are supplied by the main document—only the `<body>` tag and any HTML that could be included in a regular HTML document (**Code 23.4**). The results are shown in **Figure 23.3**.

✔ Tips

- The disadvantage of this method is that you cannot see the external content unless it is coming off a server. If you try to view this file on your local hard disk, you will see a whole lot of nothing.

- You can also add a clock that shows visitors their local time (see "Creating a Clock" in Chapter 26).

Code 23.3 The server-side include tags allow you to import external content, but only if the page is being delivered from a Web server.

```
<html>
<body>
    <!-- #include virtual="external.html" -->
    <br><br>
    <!-- #echo var="DATE_LOCAL" -->
    <br><br>
    <!-- #echo var="DATE_GMT" -->
    <br><br>
</body>
</html>
```

Code 23.4 The external content being imported into index.html. This content can be any standard HTML code; just don't use `<html>` or `<body>` tags.

```
<div style="text-align:center">
    <h1>Alice In Wonderland</h1>
    <h3>Chapter 1</h3>
    <img src="alice28.gif" width="358"
→ height="481" border="0">
```

Figure 23.3 The external content has been imported successfully.

Code 23.5 You can place the `<script>` tag anywhere in your HTML document, but to add visible content, you need to place it in the `<body>` of the document. This practice allows you to write HTML into the page with JavaScript.

```
code

<html>
<body>
    <script src="external.js"></script>
</body>
</html>
```

Code 23.6 The external JavaScript file can include any JavaScript, but if you want to include HTML content, use document.write for each line of HTML code.

```
code

document.writeln('<div style="text-align:
→ center">')
document.writeln('<h1>Alice In Wonderland
→ </h1>')
document.writeln('<h3>Chapter 3</h3>')
```

Figure 23.4 The imported JavaScript writes the title and adds an image to the Web page.

- Remember, the content to be written using JavaScript has to be inside single quotes ('). If you need to include a single quote in the content you are writing out with JavaScript, it has to be proceeded by a backslash (\). So `document.write ('How's it going?');` will not work. Instead use: `document.write ('How\'s it going?');`

Using an External JavaScript File

You can use the `<script>` tag to import an external JavaScript file into an HTML document. In turn, you can use the JavaScript file to write HTML code onto the page. The advantage of using this method is that you can use the JavaScript to tailor the content as needed (see "Setting a Dynamic Header and Footer" in Chapter 22).

1. `<script src="external.js"></script>`

   Importing an external JavaScript file is relatively straightforward. Simply add the `src` attribute to the `<script>` tag, and don't place anything between the `<script>` tags (**Code 23.5**). This method places the external JavaScript in the HTML file at this exact location. If the JavaScript will add HTML tags to the page, those tags will be added to the page in this location.

2. `external.js`

   Create an external JavaScript file, and save it as external.js (**Code 23.6**). This file can contain any standard JavaScript, but to deliver content, you need to have the code write the HTML tags and other content. Each line of HTML code gets its own `document.write`. The results of importing the code are shown in **Figure 23.4**.

✔ Tips

- The drawback of this method is that you have to place every line of HTML code in JavaScript. This practice can be labor-intensive, and it makes the file harder to debug and fix in most WYSIWYG programs.

- If you do place anything between the `<script>` tags, that content is ignored.

Viewing Someone Else's External Content

The best way to learn about DHTML and CSS (other than reading this book) is to look at other Web sites and dissect their code. Unfortunately, Web designers sometimes hide their code by placing it in external files that don't show up when you attempt to view the source in the usual way.

Never fear—you can view the code if you are willing to dig a bit deeper.

To view hidden code:

1. Open the Web page for which you want to find the code (**Figure 23.5**).

2. View the source code.

   Different browsers have different ways of providing access to the source code, but you typically will find a View Source or Source command in the View menu (**Figures 23.6** and **23.7**).

3. In the source code, find the reference to the external code you want to view (**Figure 23.8**).

   You may have to do some hunting, but the <script> (for JavaScript) or <link> (for CSS) tag will be in the <head> of the document.

4. Piece together the URL to the external content.

   <script> tags have an src attribute for the URL, whereas <link> tags use href. If the URL is an absolute path (begins with http://), use that path in step 5. Otherwise, use the current URL (the one in the browser's location/address bar), and add the relative path to it.

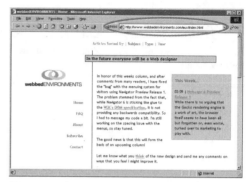

Figure 23.5 The page with the external code you want to see. The absolute path is at the top.

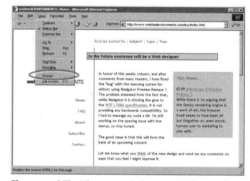

Figure 23.6 The View menu in Internet Explorer 5 for Windows.

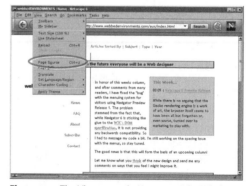

Figure 23.7 The View menu in Netscape 6 for Windows.

Figure 23.8 The source code for the Web page. Many of the links to external files use a relative path (an URL that is relative to the current page's URL).

Figure 23.9 A simple equation that finds the absolute URL for the external content.

Figure 23.10 The external code's URL typed in the browser's location bar.

Figure 23.11 Some browsers require you to download the file rather than view it in your browser.

Remove the final level of the current page's URL, and for every `../` in the referenced URL, remove an additional level from the end of the current page's URL. Then add the remainder of the page's URL to the relative path without `../` (**Figure 23.9**).

5. Open the URL for the external content that you found in step 4 (**Figure 23.10**).

Again, different browsers have different methods, but the File menu typically contains the Open Location option. A shortcut is to type the URL in the browser's address/location bar. Some browsers open the code directly in the browser window; others require you to download the code file first (**Figure 23.11**) and then open it in a program such as Notepad or SimpleText (**Figure 23.12**).

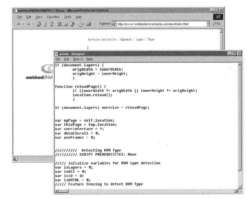

Figure 23.12 The external source code you seek.

WEB SITE NAVIGATION

Navigation is what makes the Web run. Navigation can come in many flavors: main menus, submenus, auxiliary menus, image maps, hypertext links, and other schemes that allow visitors to move from page to page. A well-planned navigation scheme lets visitors get to the information they want with minimal fuss. Poorly planned navigation leads to blindness, low sex appeal, and sometimes death. Even worse, poor navigation may upset site visitors enough that they will never return.

In this chapter, I'll look at some effective ways to create dynamic navigation that gives visitors maximum flexibility and allows you to maximize the impact of your content.

Setting Link Styles

Most browsers allow you to specify link colors for different states (a link, a visited link, and an active link) in the <body> tag of the document. With CSS, you can define not only color, but also any other CSS properties that you want the links to have.

Although a link is a tag (<a>), its individual attributes are not. To set these properties, you have to use the pseudo-classes associated with each one (**Code 24.1**). See the sidebar "Not Really a Class" on the next page.

Code 24.1 The four link states. You can set one or more of these states; they will affect all <a> tags on the page.

```
<html>
<head>
    <style type="text/css">
a:link {
    color: #cc0000;
    font-weight: bold;
    }
a:active {
    color: #990000;
    background-color: #ff0000;
    text-decoration: none;
    }

a:visited {
    color: #990000;
    text-decoration: none;
    font-weight: normal;
    }

a:hover {
    text-decoration: none;
    color: #ff0000;
    cursor: nw-resize;
    }
    </style>
</head>
<body>
    <h3>CHAPTER XI<br>
        Who Stole the Tarts?</h3>
    <p><a href="index.html">The King</a> and
    → <a href="#">Queen of Hearts</a> were
    → seated on their throne when they arrived,
    → with a great crowd assembled...</p>
</body>
</html>
```

Queen of Hearts

Figure 24.1 The style for a hypertext link.

Figure 24.2 The style for a hypertext link that has just been clicked (active).

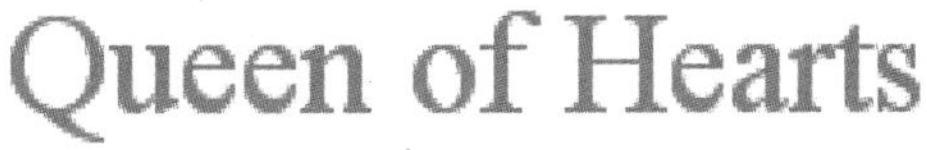

Queen of Hearts

Figure 24.3 The style for a hypertext link that has already been visited.

Queen of Hearts

Figure 24.4 The style for a hypertext link that the mouse pointer is over (hovering).

To set contrasting link appearances:

1. `a:link {...}`

   The `link` pseudo-class allows you to define the appearance of hypertext links that have not yet been selected (**Figure 24.1**).

2. `a:active {...}`

   The `active` pseudo-class allows you to set the appearance of the link when the visitor clicks it (**Figure 24.2**).

3. `a:visited {...}`

   The `visited` pseudo-class allows you to set the appearance of links that the visitor selected previously (**Figure 24.3**).

4. `a:hover{...}`

   The `hover` pseudo-class allows you to set the appearance of the link that the mouse pointer is over (**Figure 24.4**).

✔ Tips

- The `hover` and `visited` pseudo-classes do not work in Netscape 4.

- The order in which you define your styles makes a difference in certain browsers. In Internet Explorer 5 for Windows, for example, placing the `hover` pseudo-class before the `visited` pseudo-class keeps `hover` from working after a link has been visited. Due to the cascade order, `active` is defined after `hover`, so, in case of a tie, the `active` pseudo-class wins.

- The link styles should be inherited by the different states. (Setting the font for the link appearance, for example, should be inherited by the `active`, `visited`, and `hover` states.) But some inconsistencies exist among browsers. To play it safe, I recommend defining all attributes for each link style.

continues on next page

Not Really a Class

CSS-supporting browsers automatically recognize certain special classes: *pseudo-classes*. Pseudo-classes represent tags with unique attributes that can be defined separately. The anchor tag (`<a>`), for example, includes several link states: `active`, `visited`, `hover`, and the default `link` state. You can define these pseudo-classes individually, as if they were HTML selectors.

SETTING LINK STYLES

- The Web is a hypertext medium, so it is important that users be able to distinguish among text, links, and visited links. Because you can't count on users having their underline-links option turned on, it's a good idea to set the link appearance for every document.

- Although CSS allows you to change more than just the color of a link, I recommend caution when you change other attributes with hover. Changing things such as font face, font size, and weight often cause the text to grow larger than the space reserved for it in the layout. The entire page has to refresh to adjust, which can be highly annoying to site visitors.

Picking Link Colors

Most browsers default to blue and either red or purple for link colors, using blue for unvisited links and red or purple for visited ones. The problem with using two different colors for visited and unvisited links is that visitors may not remember which color is for which type of link. The colors you choose need to distinguish links from other text on the screen and to distinguish among the different states (visited, hover, active, and link) without dominating the screen and becoming distracting.

I recommend using a color for unvisited links that contrasts with both the page's background color and the text color. For visited links, use a darker or lighter version of the same color (depending on how light or dark the background color is) that contrasts with the background but is dimmer than the unvisited-link color. Brighter unfollowed links stand out dramatically from dimmer followed links.

If I were designing a page with a white background and black text, I might use bright red for my links (#ff0000) and pale red (#ff6666) for visited links. The brighter version stands out; the paler version is less distinctive, but still obviously a link.

<Previous Chapter

Figure 24.5 The style for menu links.

Queen of Hearts

Figure 24.6 The style for links in a paragraph. (In reality, these links should be green.)

Code 24.2 Two link styles have been added. The first style sets up a class called menu that can be applied to links. The second style defines how links should look when they are in a <p> tag.

```
                    code
<html>
<head>
   <style media="screen" type="text/css">
a.menu:link {
    color: #cc0000;
    font-weight: bold;
    text-decoration: none; }
a.menu:active {
    color: #666666;
    font-weight: bold;
    text-decoration: none; }
a.menu:visited {
    color: #cc0000;
    font-weight: bold;
    text-decoration: none; }
a.menu:hover {
    text-decoration: none;
```

(code continues on next page)

Setting Multiple Link Styles

When you set up rules, you can treat link styles just as you do any other HTML tag selectors. You can associate a class with the appearance of a link pseudo-class or define the pseudo-class contextually within other HTML tags. You are free to set up as many link styles on a single page as you need.

If you want the links in your navigation menus to be a different color from the hypertext links in a paragraph, for example, you can set up two independent link styles (**Figures 24.5** and **24.6**).

To set up multiple links:

◆ a.menu:link{...}

You can set up link styles as part of a true class if you place a period (.) and the name of the class before the colon (:). In this example (**Code 24.2**), link styles have been set up for a class called menu that is applied as a class to the link tag (<a>) (see "Defining Classes to Create Your Own Tags" in Chapter 2).

or

◆ p a:link{...}

You can also set link styles contextually so they have a certain appearance if their parent is a particular tag. In this example, the link tag (<a>) has the defined appearance if it is within a paragraph tag (<p>). (See "Defining Tags in Context" in Chapter 2.)

continues on next page

The Missing Link Style?

Although the four link states provided by CSS are very useful, I recommend that a fifth state—current—be added to the standard to help Web designers create more versatile pages. A current attribute would allow Web designers to set the appearance of a link if it is the same as the page that is currently being displayed (the URL for the Web page is the same as the href, for example). This attribute would allow designers to use CSS to show which page a visitor is on without having to hard-code a special link style into every page.

✔ Tips

- Setting multiple link colors can be useful for showing different kinds of links. In this example, the menu has one appearance, whereas links in the text have a different appearance. You might want links that go outside your site to be a particular color.

- If you use too many colors, your visitors may not be able to tell which words are links and which are not.

Text Decoration: To Underline or Not

Underlining has been the standard way of indicating a hypertext link on the Web since its inception. I have seen many sites on which both the link and text colors are set to black. Apparently, the designers assumed that people would know links because they were underlined. If visitors have underlining turned off, however, they cannot see links on the page.

The problem with underlining links is that if you have many links on a page, the page becomes an impenetrable mass of lines, and the text is difficult to read.

CSS allows you to turn off underlining for links, overriding the visitor's preference. I recommend this practice and prefer to rely on clear color choices to highlight hypertext links. You can use underlining with the hover state, so when visitors place the mouse over a link, they see a clear visual change.

Code 24.2 continued

```
      color: #ff0000;
      cursor: move; }
  p a:link {
      color: #00cc00;
      font-weight: bold;      }
  p a:active {
      color: #666666;
      text-decoration: none; }
  p a:visited {
      color: #00cc00;
      text-decoration: none;
      font-weight: normal; }
  p a:hover {
      text-decoration: none;
      color: #00ff00;
      cursor: nw-resize;}
      </style>
  </head>
  <body>
      <h3>
          <a class="menu" href="#">&lt;Previous
→ Chapter</a> |
          <a class="menu" href="#">Next Chapter
→ &gt;</a>
      </h3>
      <h3>CHAPTER XI<br>
          Who Stole the Tarts?
      </h3>
      <p><a href="index.html">The King</a> and
→ <a href="#">Queen of Hearts</a> were
→ seated on their throne when they
→ arrived, with a great crowd assembled
→ about them...</p>
  </body>
  </html>
```

Figure 24.7 The menu headers.

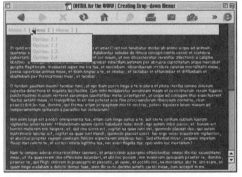

Figure 24.8 After a menu header has been rolled over.

Code 24.3 The popMenu() function shows the menu; the delayHide() function keeps it from disappearing before you can choose an option.

```
<html>
<head>
    <script src="findDOM.js"></script>
    <script>
var menuTop = 45;
var menuLeft = 400;

var domSMenu = null;
var oldDomSMenu = null;
var t = 0;
var lDelay = 3;
var lCount = 0;
var pause = 100;
```

(code continues on next page)

Creating Drop-Down Menus

Drop-down menus have been a favorite GUI (graphical user interface) device for years. The menu header appears as a single word at the top of the window or screen that, when clicked, displays a list of further options. In a File menu, for example, you might find Save, Close, and Print.

Now you can achieve the same effect on the Web with DHTML (**Figures 24.7** and **24.8**).

To add drop-down menus:

1. `<script src="findDOM.js"></script>`

   In any JavaScript function that addresses an object on the screen directly, you need to include the findDOM code (see "Using the Cross-Browser DOM" in Chapter 11). To do so, include it in an external text file and then import that file into the page in which it will be used (**Code 24.3**).

2. `var menuTop = 45;`

   Initialize the variables. Several variables in this code control and record various things:

   ▲ **menuTop.** Records the position of the top edge of a drop-down menu (to be reassigned later).

   ▲ **menuLeft.** Records the position of the left edge of a drop-down menu (to be reassigned later).

   ▲ **domSMenu.** Records the DOM for the menu.

   ▲ **oldDomSMenu.** Records the DOM for the last menu opened.

   ▲ **t:** Records whether the menu is waiting to close (1) or not (2).

   ▲ **lDelay.** Records how long a menu should wait before closing.

   ▲ **lCount.** Records how long the menu has waited before closing. When lCount = lDelay, the menu closes.

continues on next page

The one variable you may want to change is **lDelay**, which controls how long the menu pauses on the screen before disappearing if the mouse pointer is not hovering over it. The higher the number, the longer the delay.

3. **function popMenu(menuNum){...}**

   Add **popMenu()** to your JavaScript. This function first closes any other menus that are open and then calculates the left edge and bottom edge of the menu header, placing the appropriate drop-down menu in that position and then making it visible.

4. **function delayHide() {...}**

   Add **delayHide()** to your JavaScript. This function hides the visible menu after a slight delay, based on the size of **lDelay**.

5. **.menuStyle {...}**

   Create a class style for the menus. This style defines the appearance of the menus and headers.

6. **#menuHead1 {...}**

   Create an ID for each menu head. These IDs define the menu headers and should be positioned relatively.

7. **#menu2 {...}**

   Create an ID for each menu. These IDs define the individual menus and should be positioned absolutely.

8. **a.menulink:link {...}**

   Create a link style for the menus. Although this step is optional, it makes for much more attractive menus.

9. **<div id="menuHead"class= → "menuStyle">...</div>**

   Create a CSS layer for the menu headers. The links to all the menu headers in step 10 will be in this layer.

Code 24.3 *continued*

```
function popMenu(menuNum){
   if (isDHTML) {
      t = 2;
      if (oldDomSMenu) {
         oldDomSMenu.visibility =
         → 'hidden';
         oldDomSMenu.zIndex = '0';
         t = 2;
         lCount = 0;
      }
      var idMenu = 'menuHead';
      var domMenu = findDOM(idMenu,0);
      var idMenuOpt = 'menuHead' + menuNum;
      var domMenuOpt = findDOM(idMenuOpt,0);

      var idSMenu = 'menu' + menuNum;
      var domSMenu = findDOM(idSMenu,1);
   if (isID || isAll) {
         var menuLeft =
         → (domMenu.offsetLeft) +
         → (domMenuOpt.offsetLeft) + 5;
         var menuTop =
         → (domMenu.offsetTop) +
         → (domMenu.offsetHeight) + 5;
      }
      if (isLayers) {
         var menuLeft = document.layers
         → [idMenu].layers[idMenuOpt].
         → pageX - 5;
         var menuTop = domMenu.pageY +
         → domMenu.clip.height - 5;
      }
      if (oldDomSMenu != domSMenu) {
         domSMenu.left = menuLeft;
         domSMenu.top = menuTop;
         domSMenu.visibility = 'visible';
      domSMenu.zIndex = '100';
         oldDomSMenu = domSMenu;
      }
      else { oldDomSMenu = null; }
   }
   else { return null; }
}

function delayHide() {
   if ((oldDomSMenu) && (t == 0)) {
```

(code continues on next page)

Code 24.3 *continued*

```
                    code
      oldDomSMenu.visibility = 'hidden';
      oldDomSMenu.zIndex = '0';
      oldDomSMenu = null;
      lCount = 0;
      return false;
   }
   if (t == 2) { lCount = 0; return false; }
   if (t == 1) {
      lCount = lCount + 1;
      if (lDelay <= lCount) { t = 0; }
      if (lDelay >= lCount) { setTimeout
      → ('delayHide(' + t + ')',pause); }
   }
}

   </script>
   <style type="text/css">
body  { color: white; font-family:
→ "Trebuchet MS", Arial, Helvetica, Geneva,
→ sans-serif; background-color: #333; }
#content { margin-top: 35px;          }
.menuStyle  { color: #000000; font-size:
→ 12px; font-family: "Trebuchet MS",
→ Verdana, Arial, Helvetica, sans-serif;
→ background-color: #ccc; padding: 5px;
→ width: 100%; border: solid 1px #000000; }
#menuHead { background-color: #ccc;
→ position: absolute; z-index: 50; top: 0px;
→ left: 0px; }
#menuHead1, #menuHead2, #menuHead3 {
→ position: relative; }
#menu1,#menu2,#menu3 { position: absolute;
→ z-index: 100; visibility: hidden; width:
→ 150px; }
a.menulink:link { font-weight: bold;
→ text-decoration: none; }
a.menulink:visited { font-weight: bold;
→ text-decoration: none; }
a:menulink:active { color: #666; font-family:
→ "Trebuchet MS", Verdana, Arial, Helvetica,
→ sans-serif; text-decoration: underline; }
a.menulink:hover { color: #900; font-family:
→ "Trebuchet MS", Verdana, Arial, Helvetica,
→ sans-serif; font-weight: bold;
→ text-decoration: none; cursor: ne-resize; }
   </style>
</head>
<body>
   <div id="menuHead"class="menuStyle">
<b>
```

(code continues on next page)

10. `<a id="menuHead1" class="menuLink"`
`→ href="#" onMouseOver="popMenu(1)"`
`→ onMouseOut="t = 1; delayHide()">`
`→ Menu 1</a> |`

For each menu header, add a link. The menu headers are links that trigger the popMenu() function onMouseOver and trigger the delayHide() function onMouseOut.

11. `<div id="menu1" class="menuStyle">`
`→ ...<div>`

Add a CSS layer for each menu. Each menu is just a CSS layer with HTML links that you set in step 12.

12. `<a class="menuLink" onMouseOut="`
`→ t = 1; delayHide()" onMouseOver="`
`→ t = 2;" onClick="t = 0; delayHide();"`
`→ href="#">Option 1.1</a><br>`

Add a link for each menu option. Whenever the mouse pointer hovers over a link, the menu is visible. As soon as the pointer moves away from the link, the menu disappears after a slight delay unless the pointer moves back over a link.

continues on next page

CREATING DROP-DOWN MENUS

✔ Tips

- You can turn the menus on their side—having the menu headers running down instead of across—by placing the drop-down menus on the right top instead of the bottom left.

- This script is one of my favorites. I use it to create the drop-down menus on my own Web site (**Figure 24.9**).

- Most operating systems require you to click a menu header before the menu appears. You can change the event that triggers the menus to onClick if you think that would be easier for your site visitors.

Figure 24.9 The menus used in webbedENVIRONMENTS.

Code 24.3 *continued*

```
        <a  id="menuHead1" class="menuLink" href="#" onMouseOut="t = 1; delayHide()"
    → onMouseOver="popMenu(1)">Menu 1</a> |

        <a  id="menuHead2" class="menuLink" href="#" onMouseOut="t = 1; delayHide()"
    → onMouseOver="popMenu(2)">Menu 2</a> |

        <a  id="menuHead3" class="menuLink" href="#" onMouseOut="t = 1; delayHide()"
    → onMouseOver="popMenu(3)">Menu 3</a> |

        </b>

</div>
<div id="menu1" class="menuStyle">

    <b>

    <a class="menuLink" onMouseOut="t = 1; delayHide()" onMouseOver="t = 2;"  onClick="t = 0;
    → delayHide();"  href="#">Option 1.1</a><br>

    <a class="menuLink" onMouseOut="t = 1; delayHide()" onMouseOver="t = 2;"  onClick="t = 0;
    → delayHide();"  href="#">Option 1.2</a><br>

    <a class="menuLink" onMouseOut="t = 1; delayHide()" onMouseOver="t = 2;"  onClick="t = 0;
    → delayHide();"  href="#">Option 1.3</a><br>

    </b>

</div>
<div id="menu2" class="menuStyle">

    <b>

    <a class="menuLink" onMouseOut="t = 1; delayHide()" onMouseOver="t = 2;"  onClick="t = 0;
    → delayHide();"  href="#">Option 2.1</a><br>

    <a class="menuLink" onMouseOut="t = 1; delayHide()" onMouseOver="t = 2;"  onClick="t = 0;
    → delayHide();"  href="#">Option 2.2</a><br>

    <a class="menuLink" onMouseOut="t = 1; delayHide()" onMouseOver="t = 2;"  onClick="t = 0;
    → delayHide();"  href="#">Option 2.3</a><br>

    <a class="menuLink" onMouseOut="t = 1; delayHide()" onMouseOver="t = 2;"  onClick="t = 0;
    → delayHide();"  href="#">Option 2.4</a><br>

    </b>
```

(code continues on next page)

Code 24.3 *continued*

```
                                      code
      </div>
      <div id="menu3" class="menuStyle">
          <b>
          <a class="menuLink" onMouseOut="t = 1; delayHide()" onMouseOver="t = 2;" onClick="t = 0;
          → delayHide();" href="#">Option 3.1</a><br>
          <a class="menuLink" onMouseOut="t = 1; delayHide()" onMouseOver="t = 2;" onClick="t = 0;
          → delayHide();" href="#">Option 3.2</a><br>
          <a class="menuLink" onMouseOut="t = 1; delayHide()" onMouseOver="t = 2;" onClick="t = 0;
          → delayHide();" href="#">Option 3.3</a><br>
          <a class="menuLink" onMouseOut="t = 1; delayHide()" onMouseOver="t = 2;" onClick="t = 0;
          → delayHide();" href="#">Option 3.4</a><br>
          <a class="menuLink" onMouseOut="t = 1; delayHide()" onMouseOver="t = 2;" onClick="t = 0;
          → delayHide();" href="#">Option 3.5</a><br>
          <a class="menuLink" onMouseOut="t = 1; delayHide()" onMouseOver="t = 2;" onClick="t = 0;
          → delayHide();" href="#">Option 3.6</a><br>
          </b>
      </div>
    <div id="content">
          <p>Et quid erat, quod me delectabat, nisi amare et amari?</p>
    </div>
  </body>
  </html>
```

CREATING DROP-DOWN MENUS

Preventing Navigation Noise

One of my chief gripes about most Web sites is the overabundance of unorganized links. You've probably seen sites with long lists of links that stretch off the window. These links add visual noise to the design and waste precious screen space without assisting navigation.

Web surfers rarely take the time to read an entire Web page. Instead, they scan for relevant information. But human beings can process only so much information at a time. If a Web page is cluttered, visitors must wade through dozens or hundreds of links to find the one path to the information they desire. Anything designers can do to aid visitors' ability to scan a page, such as organizing links in lists, will improve the usability of Web sites. Drop-down menus area a great way to organize your page to prevent navigation noise.

Creating a Sliding Menu

Are you tired of sites that have the same old sidebar navigation? Are your menus taking more and more valuable screen real estate from the content? Are your pages cluttered with links that visitors need only when they are navigating, not when they are focusing on the content?

If you answered "yes" to any of these questions, I have a simple solution: Allow visitors to pull out menus or put them away as needed (**Figures 24.10**, **24.11**, and **24.12**).

To set up a sliding menu:

1. `<script src="findDOM.js"></script>`

   In any JavaScript function that addresses an object on the screen directly, you need to include the findDOM code. To do so, include it in an external text file and then import that file into the page in which it will be used (**Code 24.4**).

2. `var open = 0;`

   Initialize the variables:

   ▲ **open.** Records whether the menu is open or closed.

   ▲ `slideDelay`. Records the delay in animating the slide. A larger number means a slower delay, but may look more choppy.

   ▲ `domStyle`. Records the DOM for the menu.

3. `function setMenu (objectID) {...}`

   Add `setMenu()` to your JavaScript. This function sets the starting (`cX`) and final (`fX`) points for the sliding menu, based on whether the menu is open or not. `cX` defines the current location of the left edge of the menu and ranges between −80 and 0. The low value depends on the width of your menu minus the width of the tab.

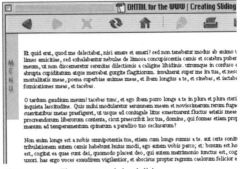

Figure 24.10 The menu tab is visible.

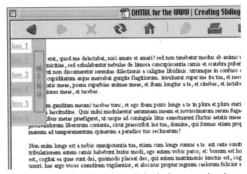

Figure 24.11 After the tab is clicked, the menu begins to slide out.

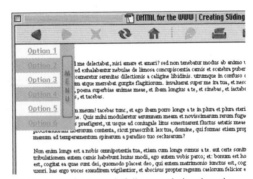

Figure 24.12 The menu is fully extended and can be used to navigate the site.

Code 24.4 The setMenu() function prepares the menu for the slideMenu() function, which slides out the menu.

```
                        code
<html>
<head>
    <script src="findDOM.js"></script>
    <script language="JavaScript">
var open = 0;
var slideDelay = 0;
var domStyle = null;
function setMenu (objectID) {
    if (isDHTML){
        domStyle = findDOM(objectID,1);
        if (open) { fX = -80; cX = 0; open =
        → 0; }
        else { fX = 0; cX = -80; open = 1; }
        slideMenu(cX,fX);
    }
}
function slideMenu (cX,fX) {
    if (cX != fX) {
        if (cX > fX) { cX -= 2; }
        else { cX += 2; }
        domStyle.left = cX;
        setTimeout('slideMenu(' + cX + ',' +
        → fX + ')', slideDelay);
        }
    return;
}
    </script>
    <style type="text/css">
body  { margin-left: 30px; }
#mainMenu { left: -80px; top: 0px; }
.menu{ position:absolute; }
a:link { color: red; font: bold 12px
→ "Trebuchet MS", Arial, Helvetica, Geneva,
→ sans-serif ;}
    </style>
</head>
<body>
    <span id="mainMenu" class="menu">
    <table border="0" cellpadding="5"
    → cellspacing="0" frame width="100"
    → bgcolor="#999999">
        <tr>
```

(code continues on next page)

When cX is −80, for example, the first 80 pixels of the menu are off the screen to the left. Only the menu tab, which is about another 20 pixels, is visible on the screen, and the menu is closed.

When cX is 0, the left edge of the menu is against the left edge of the window, and the menu is open. This function also resets the open variable to 0 (closed) if it was open or 1 (open) if it was closed. The last thing it does is start the slideMenu() function.

4. function slideMenu (cX,fX) {...}

   Add slideMenu() to your JavaScript. This function first checks to see whether the current position (cX) is equal to the final position (fX). If so, the function stops running. If the positions are not the same, the function subtracts 2 pixels from or adds 2 pixels to cX, depending on whether the menu is opening or closing. It also sets the left edge of the menu to this new position. The function then starts over with the new cX value. slideMenu() continues to loop this way until cX increases or decreases to equal fX, thereby creating the illusion that the menu is sliding across the screen.

5. .menu {...}
   #mainMenu {...}

   In the <head> of the document, set up a style sheet with one general class that collects all the common properties of the menus (.menu) and an ID for each menu you will be setting up. In this example, I'm setting up a single menu and calling it mainMenu. Notice that the left margin in .menu, which will change when the slideMenu() function is run, has an initial position of −80. This setting does not hide the menu; it leaves a small tab visible.

continues on next page

6. `<span id="mainMenu" class="menu">`
`→ ...</span>`

In the `<body>` of the page, create the menu. In this example, the menu is made from a table that is used to control the layout. One of the `<td>` cells contains a link that, when clicked, runs the `setMenu()`function, causing the menu to slide out or slide back.

✔ Tips

■ You can set up as many menus as you want, each between its own `<span>` tags and each with a different ID name. Make sure to move the top margin down for each menu so that it does not overlap the menu above it. You can use any type of content between the `<span>` tags—graphics, hypertext links, forms, and so on—to create your menus.

■ What happens in older browsers that do not support DHTML depends on how you construct the menu. In this example, the menu would simply appear on the left side of the page. If you nested the menu in a table with content on the right, it would look like a normal (non-dynamic) sidebar.

Code 24.4 *continued*

```
                                    code
        <td bgcolor="#cccccc" width="80" align="right"><a href="#">Option 1</a></td>
        → <td rowspan="6" width="10">
        <div align="left">
        <a href="javascript:setMenu('mainMenu')"><img src="menuTab.gif" width="15" height="100"
        → border="0">
</a>
        </div>
        </td>
        </tr><tr>
        <td width="80" align="right"><a href="#">Option 2</a></td>
        </tr><tr>
        <td bgcolor="#cccccc" width="80" align="right"><a href="#">Option 3</a></td>
        </tr><tr>
        <td width="80" align="right"><a href="#">Option 4</a></td>
        </tr><tr>
        <td bgcolor="#cccccc" width="80" align="right"><a href="#">Option 5</a></td>
        </tr><tr>
        <td width="80" align="right"><a href="#">Option 6</a></td>
        </tr></table>
    </span>
    <p>Et quid erat, quod me delectabat, nisi amare et amari?</p>
</body>
</html>
```

Figure 24.13 The links in the remote-control window target the main window.

Code 24.5 The openRemote() function can open an external window with a variety of sizes and uses.

```
<html>
<head>
    <script>
var remote = null;
window.name = "content";
function
openRemote(contentURL,windowName,x,y) {
    widthHeight = 'height=' + y + ',
    → width=' + x;
    remote = window.open(contentURL,
    → windowName,widthHeight);
    remote.focus()
}
    </script>
    <style type="text/css">
h1 { color: silver; font-size: 36px;
→ font-family: Palatino, "Times New Roman",
→ Georgia, Times, serif; }
    </style>
</head>
```

(code continues on next page)

Creating a Remote Control

Whether you are channel-surfing or Web-surfing, a remote control can make the experience more convenient and comfortable. On the Web, a remote control is a small browser window with links that change the content in the main browser window (**Figure 24.13**).

To set up remote control, open a new browser window (see "Opening a New Browser Window" in Chapter 14) and place in it an HTML file with links that target the main browser window.

To create a remote control:

1. `var remote = null;`

   In the Web page in which you will be opening the remote control, initialize the variable remote to null, indicating that the remote is not open (**Code 24.5**).

2. `window.name = "content";`

   To target content back to this window, the window has to have a name. In this example, the main window is called content.

3. `function openRemote(contentURL,`
   `→ windowName,x,y) {...}`

   Add openRemote() to the JavaScript. This function opens a new browser window that is x wide by y tall. This window is called windowName. The source is contentURL. In addition, to make sure that even if the remote window is already open it will appear in the front of the screen, the window is given *focus*, meaning it is placed on top of all other windows.

continues on next page

CREATING A REMOTE CONTROL

4. openRemote('remote.html',
→ 'remote',150,300)

The function in step 3 that opens the remote has to be triggered, either by an event handler or through a link. The source file, window name, and dimensions of the new window need to be passed to the function.

5. remote.html

The source file for the remote can be anything you want, but I recommend using a frameset with the controls in the top frame and a thin frame at the bottom with a link to close the remote (**Code 24.6**). In this example, I use onLoad in the frameset to move the new remote window to a set position on the screen. When the frame closes, the function tells the main window that the frame has closed by resetting the remote variable to null.

6. controls.html

All links in the control page should target the main frame (content, in this example), as follows (**Code 24.7**):

target = "content"

7. close.html

The close.html file contains a simple function, closeWindow(), that closes the window when a link is clicked (**Code 24.8**).

Code 24.5 continued

```
                    code
<body onload="openRemote('remote.html',
→ 'remote',150,300)">
    <b><a href="javascript:openRemote
    → ('remote.html','remote',150,300)">
    Open Remote Control </a>
    <h1>Home</h1>
</body>
</html>
```

Code 24.6 The frameset holds the controls in the top frame and a link to close the window in the bottom frame.

```
                    code
<html>
<frameset rows="*,20" border="0"
→ framespacing="0" frameborder="no"
→ onLoad="window.moveTo(100,100)"
→ onUnload="opener.remote = null;">
    <frame src="controls.html"
    → name="controls" noresize>
    <frame src="close.html" name="close"
    → noresize scrolling="no"
    → marginHeight="0" marginWidth="0">
</frameset>
</html>
```

Code 24.7 The controls.html file is where the action is. The controls change the content of the main window.

```
                    code
<html>
<body>
    <h2>Menu </h2>
    <p><a href="index.html"
 → target="content">Home</a></p>
    <p><a href="page1.html"
 → target="content">Page 1</a></p>
    <p><a href="page2.html"
 → target="content">Page 2</a></p>
    <p><a href="page3.html"
 → target="content">Page 3</a></p>
</body>
</html>
```

Code 24.8 The closeWindow() function allows visitors to hide the remote if they don't want to see it.

```
                    code
<html>
<head>
    <script>
function closeWindow() { top.self.close(); }
    </script>
    <style type="text/css">
body { background-color: #366; }
a:Link { color: #6ff; font-size: 12px
 → "Courier New", Courier, Monaco, monospace;
 → text-decoration: none; }
    </style>
</head>
<body>
    <div style="align: center">
    <a href="javascript:closeWindow()">
 → &lt;Close&gt;</a>
    </div>
</body>
</html>
```

✔ Tips

■ A remote control can contain anything you can put in an HTML document, but keep in mind that it has to fit into the dimensions you defined in the openRemote() function. If you want links from the remote to appear in the main window, simply target the links to the content frame.

■ Unlike a standard window, a remote window does not display menus, browser navigation (back and forward arrows), the current URL, or anything other than the basic border around the window. This border (called the *chrome*) does include the standard Close button in the top-right corner, allowing the visitor to close the remote at any time.

■ To open the remote, you have to run the openRemote() function. You can do this in several ways, such as having it open automatically when the main browser window opens (onload). It is a good idea, however, to include a link that allows visitors to reopen the remote if they close it or to bring the remote to the front if it disappears behind another window.

■ Notice that the openRemote() function gives the remote focus—that is, places it on top of any other windows on the screen. Otherwise, if the remote window were already open but covered by another window, the window would simply reload without coming to the front. Visitors to your site could be confused if they clicked the link to reopen the remote and nothing appeared.

Ideas for the Remote Control

The universal remote is good for much, much, more. Try these exciting ideas on your site:

- **Web tour.** If you have a page of your favorite Web sites, consider placing it in a remote control. Without a remote, visitors have to keep going back to your page; with a remote, they can keep the links in one window while surfing in another. Check out the winners in the interactive section of the Communication Arts Web tour (www.commarts.com/interactive/ia_home.html) for an example of how this feature works (**Figure 24.14**).

- **Spotlight.** Many sites use a remote-control window to draw attention to particular areas. News, special offers, and other information can be placed in the remote control. Unfortunately, some sites (such as Netscape, www.netscape.com) use this technique to drop down annoying advertisements every time you visit a new page (**Figure 24.15**).

- **Control pad.** You can add functionality to a site by making the remote a control pad. Kairos (english.ttu.edu/kairos/3.2; **Figure 24.16**), an academic-journal site, uses a remote control with two frames. The left frame contains the links; the right frame displays information about the journal, links to search engines, and links to other reference materials.

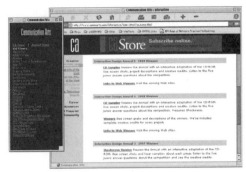

Figure 24.14 Communication Arts uses the remote as a tour guide to the best the Web has to offer.

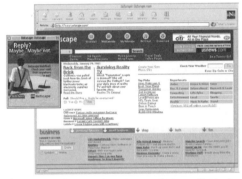

Figure 24.15 Netscape uses the remote to spotlight ads.

Figure 24.16 Kairos uses the remote not only for navigation, but also for links to other resources inside and outside the Web site.

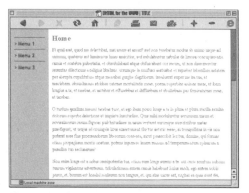

Figure 24.17 The list of menu options is in the left frame, and the content is in the right.

Figure 24.18 The submenus of Menu 1 and Menu 3 contain links that target the right frame.

Creating a Clamshell Menu

Anyone who has used a GUI— Mac-, Windows-, or UNIX-based—has watched menus in a window collapse and expand. Click a folder, and its contents are displayed below the folder; the other files and directories move down to accommodate the expanded content. In Windows, you click plus and minus signs. On the Mac, you click triangles. You can achieve a similar effect on the Web by using the display property (**Figures 24.17** and **24.18**).

To create a collapsing/expanding menu:

1. `<script src="findDOM.js"></script>`

   In any JavaScript function that addresses an object on the screen directly, you need to include the findDOM code. To do so, include it in an external text file and then import that file into the page in which it will be used (**Code 24.9**).

   continues on next page

CREATING A CLAMSHELL MENU

Code 24.9 The `toggleClamShellMenu()` function shows or hides submenus.

```
<html>
<head>
    <script src="findDOM.js"></script>
    <script>
function toggleClamShellMenu(objectID) {
    if (isAll || isID) {
        domStyle = findDOM(objectID,1);
        if (domStyle.display =='block')  domStyle.display='none';
        else domStyle.display='block';
    }
    else {
```

(code continues on next page)

2. function toggleClamShellMenu
→ (objectID) {...}

Add toggleClamShellMenu() to your
JavaScript. If this function is being run in
a browser that understands the ID or All
DOM, the function uses the ID for the
object to be addressed—passed to it as
the variable objectID—to build the DOM
(see "Building a Cross-Browser DOM" in
Chapter 11). It then sets the display of
that object to none if it is already block
or block if it is already none. The effect
is that the menu seems to appear and
pushes everything after it down.

Alternatively, if the browser is *not* compatible with the All or ID DOM, the
function loads a version of the menu that
shows the options for the menu selected.

Code 24.9 *continued*

```
        destination = objectID + '.html';
        self.location = destination;
    }
    return;
}
    </script>
    <style type="text/css">
.menuHead  { color: blue; font-weight: bold; font-size: 14px; font-family: "Trebuchet MS", Arial,
→ Helvetica, Geneva, sans-serif; text-decoration: none }
.menuOption { color: blue; font-size: 12px; font-family: "Trebuchet MS", Arial, Helvetica, Geneva,
→ sans-serif;margin-left: 10px; }
#menu1,#menu2,menu3 { display: none; }
body { font-family: "Trebuchet MS", Arial, Helvetica, Geneva, sans-serif; background-color:
→ silver; }
    </style>
</head>
<body>
    <hr width="90" align="left">
    <a class="menuHead" href="javascript:toggleClamShellMenu('menu1')"><b>&gt; Menu 1 </b></a>
    <span id="menu1">
        <a class="menuOption" href="option1.html" target="content">Option 1</a><br>
        <a class="menuOption" href="option2.html" target="content">Option 2</a><br>
        <a class="menuOption" href="option3.html" target="content">Option 3</a><br>
```

(code continues on next page)

3. #menu1 {...}

Create an ID rule for each of your collapsible menus, setting the display property to none (see "Telling an Element How to Display (or Not)" in Chapter 7). This way, the menus do not appear when the document first loads.

4. toggleClamShellMenu('menu1')

Set up links for each menu that will be used to trigger the function you created in step 2. The function should be passed the ID for the menu that is to be shown.

5. <span id="menu1">...</span>

Set up a <span> tag surrounding the element (graphic or text) that will make up the menu, and assign it an ID.

continues on next page

Code 24.9 *continued*

```
        <a class="menuOption" href="option4.html" target="content">Option 4</a><br>
    </span><br>
    <hr width="90" align="left">
    <a class="menuHead" href="javascript:toggleClamShellMenu('menu2')"><b>&gt; Menu 2</b></a>
    <span id="menu2">
        <a class="menuOption" href="option1.html" target="content">Option 1</a><br>
        <a class="menuOption" href="option2.html" target="content">Option 2</a><br>
        <a class="menuOption" href="option3.html" target="content">Option 3</a><br>
        <a class="menuOption" href="option4.html" target="content">Option 4</a><br>
    </span><br>
    <hr width="90" align="left">
    <a class="menuHead" href="javascript:toggleClamShellMenu('menu3')"><b>&gt; Menu 3</b></a>
    <span id="menu3">
        <a class="menuOption" href="option1.html" target="content">Option 1</a><br>
        <a class="menuOption" href="option2.html" target="content">Option 2</a><br>
        <a class="menuOption" href="option3.html" target="content">Option 3</a><br>
        <a class="menuOption" href="option4.html" target="content">Option 4</a><br>
    </span>
</body>
</html>
```

CREATING A CLAMSHELL MENU

6. `menu1.html`

If you need this function to be compatible with Netscape 4, set up a backup version of each menu option. Browsers that do not understand the `display` property will use these editions.

✔ Tips

- You can use any elements in these menus, including graphics, forms, and lists. The design is up to you.

- The Mac version of Internet Explorer 4 has problems using CSS in a function. Therefore, this technique may not work.

- This expanding/collapsing menu technique does not work in Netscape 4. Moreover, because the `display` property of the menus is set to `none`, the menus do not appear. That's why I included the backup plan. If you don't need to support Netscape 4, you can remove that part of the function.

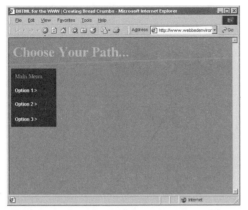

Figure 24.19 The main menu is just the beginning of the journey.

Creating a Breadcrumb Menu

I mentioned breadcrumb navigation in "Web Site Navigation Do's and Don'ts" in Chapter 20. The basic idea is that when visitors select a link, they not only see where they can go next, but also where they have been.

This version of that concept allows visitors to select a path through several menus to find the option they want. If they change their minds along the path, they can always choose a different option from a previous menu (**Figures 24.19** through **24.23**).

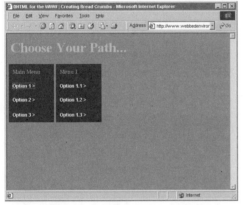

Figure 24.20 The level-1 menu presents additional options. > indicates that further options are available.

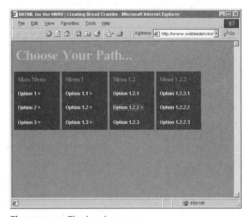

Figure 24.22 The level-3 menu.

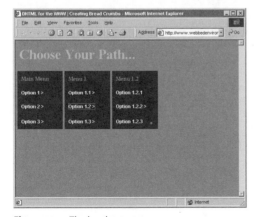

Figure 24.21 The level-2 menu.

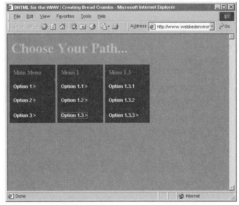

Figure 24.23 At any time, the visitor can choose a different path from a previous menu.

To add breadcrumb navigation:

1. `<script src="findDOM.js"></script>`

In any JavaScript function that addresses an object on the screen directly, you need to include the findDOM code. To do so, include it in an external text file and then import that file into the page in which it will be used (**Code 24.10**).

2. `var domLevel1 = null;`

For each level you will be drilling down, initialize a variable called **domLevel#**.

Code 24.10 The showMenu() function reveals the next menu level when an option is selected.

```
<html>
<head>
    <script src="findDOM.js"></script>
    <script>
var domLevel1 = null;
var domLevel2 = null;
var domLevel3 = null;
function showMenu(level1,level2,level3) {
    if (domLevel1 != null){
        if (level2 == null) { domLevel1.visibility =  "hidden"; }
        if (domLevel2 != null){
            if (level3 == null)  { domLevel2.visibility =  "hidden"; }
            if (domLevel3 != null)  { domLevel3.visibility =  "hidden"; }
        }
    }
    if (level2 == null) { objectID = 'menu' + level1; domLevel2 = null; }
    else {
        if (level3 == null) { objectID = 'menu' + level1 + '--' + level2; domLevel3 = null; }
        else   { objectID = 'menu' + level1 + '--' + level2 + '--' + level3  }
    }
    var domStyle = findDOM(objectID,1);
    domStyle.visibility =  "visible";
    if (level2 == null) { domLevel1 = domStyle; }
    else  {
        if (level3 == null) { domLevel2 = domStyle; }
        else { domLevel3 = domStyle; }
    }
}
    </script>
```

(code continues on next page)

3. `function showMenu(level1,level2,`
`→ level3) {...}`

Add **showMenu()** to your JavaScript. This function first hides any menus that are at a lower level than the one selected and then shows the selected menu, regardless of its level.

4. `.menu {...}`

Set up a **menu** class that will be applied to all the menus. Among other things, this class defines all the menus as being absolutely positioned, 75 pixels from the top of the page, and 115 pixels wide.

continues on next page

Code 24.10 *continued*

```
                              code
    <style type="text/css">
a:link   { color: white; font-weight: bold; width:100%; font-size: 12px; font-family: Arial,
→ Helvetica, Geneva, sans-serif; text-decoration: none; }
a:visited    { color: white; font-weight: bold; font-size: 12px; font-family: Arial, Helvetica,
→ Geneva, sans-serif; text-decoration: none; }
a:hover    { background-color: #666666; color: white; font-weight: bold; font-size: 12px;
→ font-family: Arial, Helvetica, Geneva, sans-serif; text-decoration: none; }
h3 { color: #777; font-size: 14px; font-family: "Times New Roman", Georgia, Times; }
h1 { color: #bbb; font-size: 34px; font-family: "Times New Roman", Georgia, Times; }
.menu { background-color: #000; layer-background-color: #000; padding: 10px; position: absolute;
→ width: 115px; top: 75px; }

#menuMain  { left: 5px; visibility: visible; }
#menu1,#menu2,#menu3  { left: 125px; visibility: hidden; }
#menu1--1,#menu1--2,#menu1--3,#menu2--1,#menu2--2,#menu3--1  { left: 245px; visibility: hidden; }
#menu1--1--1,#menu1--2--2,#menu1--3--3,#menu2--2--2 { left: 365px; visibility: hidden; }
body { background-color: #777; }
    </style>
</head>
<body>
    <h1> Choose Your Path...</h1>
    <div id="menuMain" class="menu">
        <h3>Main Menu</h3>
        <a href="javascript:showMenu(1,null,null)">Option 1 ></a><br><br>
        <a href="javascript:showMenu(2,null,null)">Option 2 ></a><br><br>
        <a href="javascript:showMenu(3,null,null)">Option 3 ></a>
    </div>
    <div id="menu1" class="menu">
```

(code continues on next page)

5. #menuMain {...}

Set up an ID for the main menu. Set its left position to 5 pixels, and make sure that it is visible initially.

6. #menu1,#menu2,#menu3 {...}

For each menu on the page, set up an ID. Each menu at the same level should have the same left value, which should be 125 pixels over from the preceding level's menus. All these menus should be hidden.

7. <div id="menuMain" class="menu">
→ ...</div>

Set up the main menu as a CSS layer (see "Creating an Object" in Chapter 11). All the links in step 8 will be within this layer.

Code 24.10 *continued*

```
                                        code

        <h3>Menu 1</h3>
        <a href="javascript:showMenu(1,1,null)">Option 1.1 ></a><br><br>
        <a href="javascript:showMenu(1,2,null)">Option 1.2 ></a><br><br>
        <a href="javascript:showMenu(1,3,null)">Option 1.3 ></a>
    </div>
    <div id="menu2" class="menu">
        <h3>Menu 2</h3>
        <a href="javascript:showMenu(2,1,null)">Option 2.1 ></a><br><br>
        <a href="javascript:showMenu(2,2,null)">Option 2.2 ></a><br><br>
            <a href="#">Option 2.3</a>
    </div>
    <div id="menu3" class="menu">
        <h3>Menu 3</h3>
        <a href="javascript:showMenu(3,1,null)">Option 3.1 ></a><br><br>
        <a href="#">Option 3.2</a><br><br>
            <a href="#">Option 3.3</a>
    </div>
    <div id="menu1--1" class="menu">
        <h3>Menu 1.1</h3>
        <a href="javascript:showMenu(1,1,1)">Option 1.1.1 ></a><br><br>
        <a href="#">Option 1.1.2</a><br><br>
            <a href="#">Option 1.1.3</a>
    </div>
    <div id="menu1--2" class="menu">
        <h3>Menu 1.2</h3>
```

(code continues on next page)

8. `<a href="javascript:showMenu`
   → `(1,null,null)">Option 1 ></a>`

For each option in the menu, set up a link. If the link goes to a new page, use that URL for the `href`. If the link reveals another menu level, use the `showMenu()` function, passing it the number of the menu to be shown at the first level.

9. `<div id="menu1" class="menu">`
   → `...</div>`

Set up the level-1 menus as CSS layers, using a separate layer for each menu. All the links in step 10 will be within these layers.

continues on next page

Code 24.10 *continued*

```
     <a href="#">Option 1.2.1</a><br><br>
     <a href="javascript:showMenu(1,2,2)">Option 1.2.2 ></a><br><br>
     <a href="#">Option 1.2.3</a>
</div>
<div id="menu1--3" class="menu">
     <h3>Menu 1.3</h3>
     <a href="#">Option 1.3.1</a><br><br>
     <a href="#">Option 1.3.2</a><br><br>
     <a href="javascript:showMenu(1,3,3)">Option 1.3.3 ></a>
</div>
<div id="menu2--1" class="menu">
     <h3>Menu 2.1</h3>
     <a href="#">Option 2.1.1</a><br><br>
     <a href="#">Option 2.1.2</a><br><br>
     <a href="#">Option 2.1.3</a>
</div>
<div id="menu2--2" class="menu">
     <h3>Menu 2.2</h3>
     <a href="#">Option 2.2.1</a><br><br>
     <a href="javascript:showMenu(2,2,2)">Option 2.2.2 ></a><br><br>
     <a href="#">Option 2.2.3</a>
</div>
<div id="menu3--1" class="menu">
     <h3>Menu 3.1</h3>
     <a href="#">Option 3.1.1</a><br><br>
     <a href="#">Option 3.1.2</a><br><br>
```

(code continues on next page)

CREATING A BREADCRUMB MENU

10. `<a href="javascript:showMenu`
    `→ (1,1,null)">Option 1.1></a>`

As you did in step 8, set up a link for each menu option. This time, however, you need to pass the **showMenu()** function the menu number for levels 1 and 2.

11. `<div id="menu1–1" class="menu">`

Set up the level-2 menus as CSS layers, using a separate layer for each menu. All the links in step 12 will be within these layers.

12. `<a href="javascript:showMenu`
    `→ (1,1,1)">Option 1.1.1></a>`

Set up a link for each menu option. This time, however, you need to pass the **showMenu()** function the menu number for levels 1, 2, and 3.

13. `<div id="menu1–1–1" class="menu">`
    `→ ...</div>`

Set up the level-3 menus as CSS layers, using a separate layer for each menu. All the links in step 14 will be within these layers.

14. `<a href="#">Option 1.1.1.1</a>`

Set up a link for each menu option. Because the breadcrumb trail has no more levels, all these links should point to URLs.

✔ Tip

- This version of the script allows for only four levels, but you could have as many menu levels as you want.

Code 24.10 *continued*

```
                <a href="#">Option 3.1.3</a>
        </div>
            <div id="menu1--1--1" class="menu">
            <h3>Menu 1.1.1</h3>
            <a href="#">Option 1.1.1.1</a><br><br>
            <a href="#">Option 1.1.1.2</a><br><br>
            <a href="#">Option 1.1.1.3</a>
        </div>
        <div id="menu1--2--2" class="menu">
            <h3>Menu 1.2.2</h3>
            <a href="#">Option 1.2.2.1</a><br><br>
            <a href="#">Option 1.2.2.2</a><br><br>
            <a href="#">Option 1.2.2.3</a>
        </div>
        <div id="menu1--3--3" class="menu">
            <h3>Menu 1.3.3</h3>
            <a href="#">Option 1.3.3.1</a><br><br>
            <a href="#">Option 1.3.3.2</a><br><br>
            <a href="#">Option 1.3.3.3</a>
        </div>
        <div id="menu2--2--2" class="menu">
            <h3>Menu 2.2.2</h3>
            <a href="#">Option 2.2.2.1</a><br><br>
            <a href="#">Option 2.2.2.2</a><br><br>
            <a href="#">Option 2.2.2.3</a>
        </div>
    </body>
</html>
```

Figure 24.24 The page in a browser that understands JavaScript (Internet Explorer).

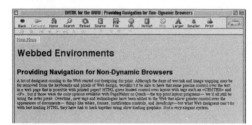

Figure 24.25 The same code in a browser in which JavaScript is disabled. Although the pages look pretty much the same, the navigation and title at the top come from different sources.

Code 24.11 The <noscript> tags hide content from browsers that understand JavaScript.

```
code
<html>
<head>
   <script language="JavaScript">
aNum=0;
pageTitle="Providing Navigation for
 → Non-Dynamic Browsers"
   </script>
</head>
<body>
   <noscript>
       <a href="menu.html">
           Main Menu
       </a>
       <h1>Webbed Environments</h1><br>
       <h2>Providing Navigation for
       → Non-Dynamic Browsers</h2>
   </noscript>
   <script language="JavaScript"
   → src="javascript/header.js"></script>
   <!--<content>-->
   <p class="copy">A lot of designers coming
   → to the Web started out designing for
   → print...</p>
</body>
</html>
```

Navigation for Nondynamic Browsers

Almost everyone surfing the Web today uses a browser that supports JavaScript. But some browsers do not support JavaScript, and some people have turned JavaScript off in their browsers.

You still need to provide these Web surfers some basic navigation and possibly some content that you otherwise would include dynamically (**Figures 24.24** and **24.25**).

To use the <noscript> tag:

◆ <noscript>...</noscript>

The <noscript> tag works by not displaying its content in browsers that *do* support scripting technology (**Code 24.11**). The upshot is that browsers that *do not* support scripting languages ignore the <noscript> tags and display whatever is between them. Thus, if you want to include content to be used in non-JavaScript browsers, simply place it between <noscript> tags.

✔ Tip

■ It's a good idea to include <noscript> tags any time you import external content that uses JavaScript (see "Using an External JavaScript File" in Chapter 23). Doing so provides some backup for non-JavaScript browsers.

Educating the Browser

When you get right down to it, computers and browsers are stupid. All they know is what we tell them. A Web browser has no idea what a Web page is about, what came before it, and what comes next.

Meta data can help fill in some of the blanks, providing information such as copyright data, keywords, and descriptions. The `<meta>` tag goes in the `<head>` of your document and is used to describe the nature of the Web page. Some of these tags will be used directly by the browser if the visitor views information about the HTML file. However, meta data is most frequently used by search engines to help categorize Web pages.

Link relationships tell the browser about the current page's relationship to other pages within a Web site (**Figure 24.26**). These link relationships are the same `<link>` tags you use to import a style sheet (see "Adding CSS to a Web Site" in Chapter 2). The browser, in turn, can use this information to set up site navigation outside of what appears on the actual Web page.

Unfortunately, only iCab, a relatively obscure Mac browser (`www.icab.de`), supports this use of the link tag. But there is always the future.

To set up a `<link>` tag:

◆ `<link rel="home" href="index.html">`
   In the `<head>` of your document, include the `<link>` tag. Include a `rel` (relationship) from the list in **Table 24.1** in quotes; then list the `href` (URL) to which this link should point (**Code 24.12**).

Figure 24.26 iCab link controls allow you to navigate a Web site without using the links on the Web page, but only if the author set up those relationships. The links include home, start of site, previous page, next page, end of site, index, help, copyright, and contact information.

Table 24.1

Important Link Relationships

REL	WHERE IT SHOULD LINK
home	Home page
start	First page of the Web site
next	Following page of the Web site
prev	Preceding page of the Web site
contents	Table of contents or site map
index	Table of contents or site map
glossary	Glossary
help	Help page
chapter	Beginning of a chapter
section	Beginning of a section
subsection	Beginning of a subsection
appendix	Appendixes
copyright	Copyright information
made	About page or mailto link for the author

Code 24.12 The <meta> and <link> tags tell the browser what this page is about and describe its relationship to other pages on the Web site.

```
                                    code
<html>
<head>
    <meta name="Author" content="Jason Cranford Teague">
    <meta name="copyright" content="1998-2000 Jason Cranford Teague">
    <meta name="keywords" content="Jason Cranford Teague,Webbed Environments,CSS,DHTML,
 → JavaScript,HTML,Search Engines, Information Architecture,World Wide Web,
 → Web Art,GIF,JPEG,PNG, Macromedia Flash">
    <meta name="description" content="In the Future Everyone will be a Web Designer.">
    <link rel="home" href="index.html">
    <link rel="index" href="index.html">
    <link rel="first" href="index.html">
    <link rel="last" href="copyright.html">
    <link rel="next" href="siteMap.html">
    <link rel="prev" href="index.html">
    <link rel="glossary" href="glossary.html">
    <link rel="chapter" href="index.html">
    <link rel="section" href="index.html">
    <link rel="subsection" href="index.html">
    <link rel="appendix" href="appendix.html">
    <link rel="help" href="help.html">
    <link rel="copyright" href="copyright.html">
    <link rel="made" href="mailto:question@webbedenvironments.com">
    <style type="text/css">
h1 { color: silver; font-size: 36px; font-family: Arial, Helvetica, Geneva, Sans-Serif; }
    </style>
</head>
<body>
    <h1>Home</h1>
    <p>Et quid erat, quod me delectabat...</p>
</body>
</html>
```

To set up a <meta> tag:

◆ <meta name="Author" content=
→ "Jason Cranford Teague">

In the <head> of the document, include the <meta> tag with the name of the content you are providing, as listed in **Table 24.2**, followed by the content of that <meta> tag in quotes. The name defines the type of content being provided.

✔ Tips

■ The major browsers may never embrace <link> tags, but I still think they are a neat idea. Are they worth adding to all your old Web pages? No. But if you have a template for your Web site, you may want to include these tags in the future.

■ Keep in mind that these tags can link to anything. The Web police will not come knocking down your door if you link the home relationship to help.html, but you may end up with very confused visitors.

■ Despite popular belief, <meta> tags are not the magic solution to search-engine woes. In fact, not all search engines use these tags, and those that do generally consider them to be a small part of the relevancy equation. This is not to say that you should not include them or that they don't help, but don't rely on them to propel you to the top of the search-engine charts.

■ That said, you should always include two <meta> tags in the <head> of a document to catch a search engine's eye. The <description> tag is a sentence or two that tells the search engine what is on the page; the search engine may use its content to describe the page in the results. More important than the <description> tag is the <keywords> tag. This is a list of words, provided by the author, that are relevant to the page.

Table 24.2

Important Meta Names	
NAME	**WHAT IT DESCRIBES**
author	Who created these pages
copyright	Copyright information
keywords	List of words that are relevant to the subject of this page
description	Brief description of the page

CONTROLS

With straight HTML, your visitors' ability to control what happens on the screen is fairly limited. They have scroll bars but no means of changing the content on the screen to meet their needs.

A truly dynamic Web site, however, allows visitors to interact with the pages. You must provide controls that permit that interaction.

In this chapter, I'll show you how to add interactive functions that give visitors greater control of the way the Web page is presented to them.

Creating Your Own Scroll Bars

Without scroll bars, a GUI (graphical user interface) would be about as useful as a car without a steering wheel. Scroll bars allow you to place an infinite amount of information in a finite space and move that information around as needed. Because the computer's operating system defines the look and feel of the scroll bars, however, they often limit the design of Web interfaces.

In "Scrolling a Web Page" in Chapter 13, I showed you how to force a page to scroll. You can also use DHTML to scroll an individual layer in a window or frame (**Figures 25.1** and **25.2**).

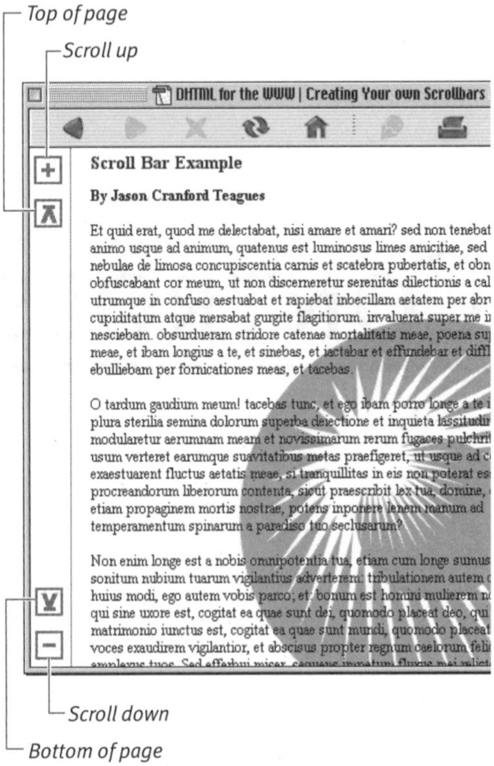

Figure 25.1 The controls allow the visitor to scroll up or down the page, jump to the bottom, or jump back to the top.

Figure 25.2 I used this technique in a Web site I designed for the independent film *The Sandman* (www.sandmanfilm.org).

Code 25.1 This code sets up two frame columns: a narrow column on the left is for the scroll bar; the content takes up the rest of the space.

```
                   code
<html>

</head>

<frameset cols="35,*" border="0"
framespacing="0" frameborder="NO">

    <frame src="scrollBar.html"
name="scrollBar" scrolling="NO" noresize
marginheight="0" marginwidth="0">

    <frame src="content.html" name="content"
scrolling="NO" noresize>

</frameset>

</html>
```

Code 25.2 All the JavaScript that controls the content page goes in scrollBar.html. The scroll() function animates the scrollArea in the content frame, and URT() and URB() take it to the top or bottom.

```
                   code
<html>

<head>

    <script src="findDOMFrame.js"></script>

    <script language="JavaScript">

var scrolling = 0;

var yT = 5;

var lT = 5;

var yI = 5;

var yH = 0;

var domStyle;

var dom;

if (document.images){

    imag = new Array();

    imag[0] = "up_off.gif";

    imag[1] = "up_on.gif";

    imag[2] = "down_off.gif";

    imag[3] = "down_on.gif";

    imag[4] = "top_off.gif";

    imag[5] = "top_on.gif";

    imag[6] = "bottom_off.gif";

    imag[7] = "bottom_on.gif";

    im = new Array();

    for (var i = 0; i < imag.length; i++) {
```

(code continues on next page)

To set up scroll bars:

1. `index.html`

   Create a frameset file, and save it as index.html (**Code 25.1**). Set up two frame columns. The first column (named `scrollBar`) is a narrow frame containing the source, scrollBar.html; the second (named `content`) contains the file content.html.

2. `scrollBar.html`

   Create an HTML file, and save it as scrollBar.html (**Code 25.2**). This file will contain the scroll-bar controls. Steps 3 through 14 apply to this file.

3. `<script src="findDOMFrame.js">` → `</script>`

   In any JavaScript function that addresses an object on the screen directly, you need to include the findDOM code. Because you are using frames, you need to use the frames version of this code (see "Dynamic Content Between Frames" in Chapter 14).

4. `var scrolling = 0;`

   In the `<script>` of scrollBar.html, initialize the following variables:

   ▲ `scrolling`. Sets whether the layer is currently scrolling.

   ▲ `yT`. Records the current top position of the scrolling layer.

   ▲ `lT`. Sets the initial position of the top of the layer.

   ▲ `yI`. Sets the increment by which the scrolling layer should move. You can change this number as desired. The higher the number, the faster the layer scrolls, but the choppier its movement.

   ▲ `yH`. Records the height of the layer.

   continues on next page

▲ domStyle. Records the generic Document Object Model (DOM) for the scrolling layer to access style properties.

▲ dom. Records the generic DOM for the scrolling layer to access other properties.

5. function startScroll(objectID,
→ frameName,direction) {...}

Add startScroll() to the JavaScript. This function sets scrolling to 1 (on), identifies the current location of the top of the layer (yT), the height of the layer (–25, to leave a margin at the bottom), and then triggers the scroll() function.

Code 25.2 *continued*

```
                code
        im[i] = new Image();
        im[i].src = imag[i];
        }
    }

function startScroll(objectID,frameName,direction) {
    domStyle = findDOMFrame(objectID,frameName,1);
    dom = findDOMFrame(objectID,frameName,0);
    scrolling = 1;
    yT = domStyle.top;
    if (document.getElementById) {
        pxLoc = yT.indexOf('px');
        if (pxLoc >= 1) yT = yT.substring(0,pxLoc);
    }
    if (window.innerHeight != null)
        yH = window.innerHeight - 25;
    else
        yH = document.body.clientHeight - 25;
    if (dom.offsetHeight != null)
        yH = yH - dom.offsetHeight;
    else
        yH = yH - dom.clip.height;
    scroll(direction);
}
function scroll(direction) {
    if (scrolling == 1) {
```

(code continues on next page)

6. `function scroll(direction) {...}`

Add `scroll()` to the JavaScript. This function (`yI`) moves the layer up or down incrementally; the direction depends on the `direction` variable. 1 is for up; 0 is for down. The function will continue to run while `scrolling` is equal to 1.

7. `function stopScroll() {...}`

Add `stopScroll()`to the JavaScript. The function sets the variable `scrolling` to 0 (off), stopping the layer from scrolling.

8. `function URB(objectID,frameName) {...}`

continues on next page

Code 25.2 *continued*

```
                                        code
        if ((direction == 1) && (yT <= lT)) {
            yT = (yT/1) + yI;
        if (yT > lT) yT = lT;
        domStyle.top = yT; }
    else {
        if ((direction == 0) && (yT >= yH)) {
            yT -= yI;
        if (yT < yH) yT = yH;
            domStyle.top = yT; }
        }
        if (document.getElementById) {
            yT = domStyle.top;
            pxLoc = yT.indexOf('px');
            if (pxLoc >= 1) yT = yT.substring(0,pxLoc);
        }
        code2run = 'scroll('+ direction + ')';
        setTimeout(code2run,0);
    }
    return false;
}
function stopScroll() {
    scrolling = 0;
    return false;
}

function URB(objectID,frameName) {
```

(code continues on next page)

Add URB() to the JavaScript. This function moves the bottom of the layer to the bottom of the window.

9. `function URT(objectID, frameName) {...}`

   Add URT() to the JavaScript. This function moves the top of the layer to the top of the window.

10. `startScroll('scrollArea',`
    `→ 'content',1); return false;`

    The controls have to be set up as links with event handlers. To add a scroll-up event, trigger startScroll() with an event handler such as onMouseDown. Pass the function the ID of the object to be scrolled, the name of the frame that contains the object, and a 1 (up).

Code 25.2 *continued*

```
                                      code

    domStyle = findDOMFrame(objectID,frameName,1);
    dom = findDOMFrame(objectID,frameName,0);
    if (window.innerHeight != null)
        yH = window.innerHeight - 25;
    else
        yH = document.body.clientHeight - 25;
    if (dom.offsetHeight != null)
        yH = yH - dom.offsetHeight;
    else
        yH = yH - dom.clip.height;
    domStyle.top = yH;
}
function URT(objectID,frameName) {
    domStyle = findDOMFrame(objectID,frameName,1);
    domStyle.top = lT;
}
function toggle(imgName,num){
    if (document.images && imgName){
        imgName.src = im[num].src;
    }
    return false; }
    </script>
    <style type="text/css">
body  { background: white url(bg_scroll.gif) repeat-y 33px 30px; margin-left: 3px; }
```

(code continues on next page)

11. startScroll('scrollArea','content',0)

Trigger **startScroll()** with an event handler such as **onmousedown**. Pass the function the ID of the object to be scrolled, the name of the frame that contains the object, and a **0** (down).

12. stopScroll()

To stop the layer from scrolling, use the **stopScroll()** function with an event handler such as **onMouseUp**.

13. URT('scrollArea','content')

To get to the top of the layer, trigger the URT() function, and pass it the ID of the object and the name of the frame that contains the object.

continues on next page

Code 25.2 *continued*

```
</style>
</head>
<body>
    <table border="0" cellpadding="0" cellspacing="0" width="25" height="100%">
    <tr>
    <td align="center" valign="top">
        <a href="javascript:void('');" onmouseover="window.status='Up'; return true;"
        → onmousedown="toggle(up,1); startScroll('scrollArea','content',1); return false;"
        → onmouseup="stopScroll(); toggle(up,0);"><img height="25" width="25" src="up_off.gif"
        → border="0" vspace="5" name="up"></a>

        <a href="javascript:void('');" onmouseover="window.status='Return To Top'; return true;"
        → onmousedown="toggle(top,5); URT('scrollArea','content');return false;"
        → onmouseup="toggle(top,4);"><img height="25" width="25" src="top_off.gif" border="0"
        → vspace="5" name="top"> </a>
    </td></tr>

    <tr><td align="center" valign="bottom">
        <a href="javascript:void('');" onmouseover="window.status='Go To Bottom'; return true;"
        → onmousedown="toggle(bottom,7); URB('scrollArea','content'); return false;"
        → onmouseup="toggle(bottom,6);"><img height="25" width="25" src="bottom_off.gif"
        → border="0" vspace="5" name="bottom"> </a>

        <a href="javascript:void('');" onmouseover="window.status='Down'; return true;"
        → onmousedown="toggle(down,3); startScroll('scrollArea','content',0); return false;"
        → onmouseup="stopScroll(); toggle(down,2);"><img height="25" width="25"
        → src="down_off.gif" border="0" vspace="5" name="down"></a>
    </td></tr></table>
</body>
</html>
```

14. `1URB('scrollArea','content')`

To get to the bottom of the layer, use the URB() function, and pass it the ID of the object and the name of the frame that contains the object.

15. `content.html`

Create an HTML file, and save it as content.html (**Code 25.3**). This file will contain the layer that is being scrolled. Steps 16 and 17 apply to this file.

16. `#scrollArea {...}`

Set up an ID called `scrollArea` in content.html. This ID should be positioned absolutely.

17. `<span id="scrollArea">...</span>`

Set up the `scrollArea` layer in either a `<div>` or `<span>` tag (see "Creating an Object" in Chapter 11).

✔ Tips

- I added a simple graphic-toggling function to this example so the controls will appear to light up when clicked.

- Use `return false;` in the event handlers for the scroll controls to prevent the pop-up menu from appearing on the Mac.

- You can also place the controls in the same HTML file as the layer (content.html). To do this, take out all the references to `frameName`, and use `findDOM.js` instead of `findDOMFrame.js`.

- *URT* stands for *ubiquitous return to top*, and *URB* stands for—you guessed it—*ubiquitous return to bottom*. Unlike most return-to-top buttons on most Web pages, these controls are always available.

Code 25.3 The content frame contains the scrollArea layer, which JavaScript scrolls in the scrollBar frame.

```
code
<html>
<head>
    <style type="text/css">
#scrollArea  {
    position: absolute;
    top: 5px;
    left: 15px;
    }
body {
    color: black;
    font-size: 12px;
    line-height: 14px;
    font-family: "Times New Roman", Georgia,
    → Times, serif;
    background: white url(bg_content.gif)
    }
    </style>
</head>
<body>
    <span id="scrollArea">
        <h2>Scroll Bar Example</h2>
        <h3>By Jason Cranford Teagues</h3>
        <p>Et quid erat, quod me delectabat,
        → nisi amare et amari?
    </span>
</body>
</html>
```

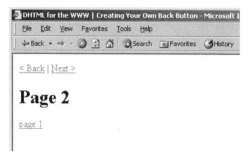

Figure 25.3 Click the Back button on page 2...

Figure 25.4 ...to return to page 1 (if that is where you came from).

Code 25.4 To create your own Back button, use JavaScript to access the browser's history object.

```
<html>
<body>
  <p>
  <a href = "javascript:history.go(-1);">
  Back</a> |
  <a href = "javascript:history.go(1)">
  Next </a>
  </p>
  <h1>Page 1</h1>
  <p><a href="index2.html">page 2</a></p>
</body>
</html>
```

Creating Your Own Back Button

When you create a Web-based application, you may want to remove browser controls to keep visitors from going back or forward inadvertently during an important part of the procedure.

Taking away the ability to go back, however, can frustrate visitors. Therefore, you need a way to return a Back button (and a Next button) to the interface as needed (**Figures 25.3** and **25.4**).

To add Next and Back buttons:

1. `history.go(-1)`

   Add the `history.go()` method with a value of –1 to go back one level in the browser's history (**Code 25.4**).

2. `history.go(1)`

   Add the `history.go()` method with a value of 1 to go forward one level in the browser's history.

✔ Tip

■ Although you can use the history element to move up and down in the history tree, you cannot access the actual URLs or even detect whether the tree contains URLs before or after the current one. This situation severely limits your ability to display or hide the back and forward links dynamically.

Creating a Slide Show

If you want to show a series of photos (or other content) in order, presenting them in slide-show format may be useful. You may even want to run two or more slide shows simultaneously to display different aspects of your work (**Figure 25.5**).

A slide show hides and shows objects (see "Making Objects Appear and Disappear" in Chapter 13), and nests absolutely positioned elements in a relative flow (see "Nesting an Absolute Element in a Relative Element" in Chapter 8).

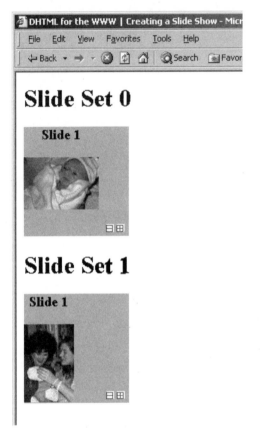

Figure 25.5 The slide-show controls allow you to move forward or backward in a particular slide show.

Removing the Browser Controls

There is a lot of debate about whether you should *ever* remove the browser controls from a browser window. Some studies conclude that visitors do not like having control taken away from them. But your decision to remove browser controls should be balanced against whether the controls may cause catastrophic usability problems.

I have visited Web sites that require visitors to fill out a multiple-page application. If you click the Back button to return to a previous page in the application to make a correction, the entire process fails. You not only have to start over, but also have to restart the browser. This is one example where it makes sense to remove the browser controls.

Code 25.5 The slide-show code allows you to move forward or backward through a stack of slides.

```
                      code
<html>
<head>
    <script src="findDOMNested.js"></script>
        <script>
slideT = new Array();
slideC = new Array();

slideT[0] = 5;
slideC[0] = 1;

slideT[1] = 3;
slideC[1] = 1;

function nextSlide(setNum) {
    var objectID1 = 'slideSet' + setNum;
    var objectID2 = 'slide' + setNum +
 → slideC[setNum];
    var domStyle = findDOM(objectID1,
 → objectID2,1);
    domStyle.visibility = 'hidden';
    if (slideT[setNum] == slideC[setNum])
 → slideC[setNum] = 1;
    else slideC[setNum]++;
    var objectID1 = 'slideSet' + setNum;
    var objectID2 = 'slide' + setNum +
 → slideC[setNum];
    var domStyle = findDOM(objectID1,
 → objectID2,1);
    domStyle.visibility = 'visible';
}

function previousSlide(setNum) {
    var objectID1 = 'slideSet' + setNum;
    var objectID2 = 'slide' + setNum +
 → slideC[setNum];
    var domStyle = findDOM(objectID1,
 → objectID2,1);
    domStyle.visibility = 'hidden';
    if (slideC[setNum] == 1) slideC[setNum] =
 → slideT[setNum];
    else slideC[setNum]--;
    var objectID1 = 'slideSet' + setNum;
    var objectID2 = 'slide' + setNum +
 → slideC[setNum];
```

(code continues on next page)

To set up a slide show:

1. `<script src="findDOMNested.js">`
 → `</script>`

   In any JavaScript function that addresses an object on the screen directly, you need to include the findDOM code (**Code 25.5**). Because this code uses nested layers, you have to use the special version of the findDOM code that allows Netscape 4 to work (see "Netscape 4 and Nested Layers" in Chapter 11).

2. `slideT = new Array();`

   Initialize two new arrays. The first array, `slideT[]`, records the number of slides in a slide show; the second array, `slideC[]`, records the current slide being displayed.

3. `slideT[0] = 5;`

   For each slide show, initialize the `slideT[]` array with the total number of slides.

4. `slideC[0] = 1;`

   For each slide show, initialize the `slideC[]` array to 1 (the first slide in the show).

5. `function nextSlide(setNum) {...}`

   Add `nextSlide()` to the JavaScript. This function hides the currently displayed slide and shows the following slide in order. If the current slide is the last slide in the show, the function loops to the first slide.

6. `function previousSlide(setNum) {...}`

   Add `previousSlide()` to the JavaScript. This function hides the currently displayed slide and shows the preceding slide in order. If this slide is the first slide in the show, the function loops to the last slide.

continues on next page

7. `#slideSet0,#slideSet1 {...}`

Set up an ID for each slide set, and call it `slideSet#`. This layer will hold all the slides, allowing them to be absolutely positioned in a relative flow.

8. `.slides {...}`

Set up a class that will be applied to all the slides; this class is called (oddly enough) `slides`. This class sets the general style for all slides and should be positioned absolutely.

9. `#slide01,#slide11 {...}`

Set up IDs for all the slides, naming each `slide##`. The slides are numbered, with the first digit representing the slide set and the second digit representing the slide number. So `slide01` is the first slide in slide set zero.

10. `<div id="slideSet0">...</div>`

Set up a CSS layer, and define it with the `slideSet#` class.

11. `<div class="slides" id="slide01">`
`→ ...</div>`

For each slide in the show, set up a nested layer inside the layer you created in step 10, using the `slide##` ID. Place the content of the slide in that layer.

12. `onclick="previousSlide(0)"`

Add a link to trigger the `previousSlide()` function for this slide set.

13. `onclick="nextSlide(0)"`

Add a link to trigger the `nextSlide()` function for this slide set.

✔ Tip

■ DHTML slide shows can contain any HTML code you want, not just images.

Code 25.5 *continued*

```
                     code
    var domStyle = findDOM(objectID1,
    → objectID2,1);
    domStyle.visibility = 'visible';
}
    </script>
    <style type="text/css">
#slideSet0,#slideSet1 {
    position: relative;
    background-color: silver;
    layer-background-color: silver;
    width: 140px;
    height: 140px;
    text-align: center;
    }

.slides {
    position: absolute;
    top: 0px;
    left: 0px;
    z-index: 1;
    }
.controls {
    position: absolute;
    top: 120px;
    left: 110px;
    z-index: 10;
    }
#slide01,#slide11 {
    visibility: visible;
    }
#slide02,#slide03,#slide04,#slide05,
→ #slide12,#slide13{
    visibility: hidden;
    }
    </style>
</head>
<body>
    <h1>Slide Set 0</h1>
    <div id="slideSet0">
        <div class="slides" id="slide01">
            <h3>Slide 1</h3>
            <img src="0010s.gif" width="100"
            → height="67" border="0">
```

(code continues on next page)

Code 25.5 *continued*

```
                                    code
</div>
        <div class="slides" id="slide02">
        <h3>Slide 2</h3>
        <img src="0016s.gif" width="100" height="67" border="0"></div>
        <div class="slides" id="slide03">
        <h3>Slide 3</h3>
        <img src="0021s.gif" width="100" height="67" border="0"></div>
        <div class="slides" id="slide04">
        <h3>Slide 4</h3>
            <img src="0022s.gif" width="100" height="67" border="0"></div>
            <div class="slides" id="slide05">
            <h3>Slide 5</h3>
            <img src="0023s.gif" width="100" height="67" border="0"></div>
    <div class="controls">
        <a href="javascript: void('');" onclick="previousSlide(0)">
        <img src="back.gif" width="10" height="10" border="0"></a>
        <a href="javascript: void('');"      onclick="nextSlide(0)">
        <img src="next.gif" width="10" height="10" border="0"></a>
    </div>
    </div>
    <script>
////// Extra breaks are required to seperate the slide shows in Netscape 4
    if (isLayers) { document.write ('<br><br><br><br><br><br><br><br><br><br><br><br>') }
    </script>
        <h1>Slide Set 1</h1>
        <div id="slideSet1">
            <div class="slides" id="slide11">
                <h3>Slide 1</h3>
                <img src="0007s.gif" width="67" height="100" border="0"></div>
            <div class="slides" id="slide12">
                <h3>Slide 2</h3>
                <img src="0012s.gif" width="67" height="100" border="0"></div>
            <div class="slides" id="slide13">
                <h3>Slide 3</h3>
                <img src="0014s.gif" width="67" height="100" border="0"></div>
        <div class="controls">
            <a href="javascript: void('');" onclick="previousSlide(1)"><img src="back.gif"
            → width="10" height="10" border="0"></a> <a href="javascript: void('');"
            → onclick="nextSlide(1)"><img src="next.gif" width="10" height="10" border="0"></a>
            </div>
    </div>
</body>
</html>
```

CREATING A SLIDE SHOW

Creating Pop-Up Hypertext

Hypertext promises site visitors extra information as needed. But to access that information, you have to click a link, which opens a new document and replaces what you were reading with the new material. This setup can be highly distracting, not to mention frustrating on slow modem connections. Wouldn't it be better if that information—written or visual—simply appeared below the link upon mouseover? That arrangement would truly be hypertext (**Figures 25.6** and **25.7**).

To add pop-up hypertext:

1. `<script src="findDOM.js"></script>`

   In any JavaScript function that addresses an object on the screen directly, you need to include the findDOM code. To do so, include it in an external text file and then import that file into the page in which it will be used (**Code 25.6**).

2. `function findLivePageWidth() {...}`

   Add the findLivePageWidth() function to the JavaScript (see "Finding the Visible Page Dimensions" in Chapter 12).

3. `function popUp(evt,objectID){...}`

   Add popUp() to the JavaScript. This function checks the width of the browser window and then—based on the variable objectID—builds the basic DOM and style DOM for the hypertext object to be displayed. Then the function hides the object (if it is visible) or positions it below the triggering link (adjusting it if it is too close to the edge of the screen), and displays the object.

4. `.hyperText {...}`

   Add the hypertext class to the CSS. This class will be applied to all hypertext objects and sets their basic appearance.

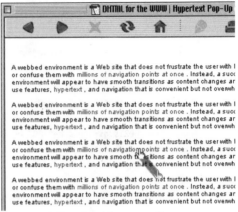

Figure 25.6 When the visitor moves the mouse pointer over the link...

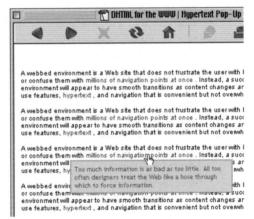

Figure 25.7 ...text appears below the link.

Code 25.6 The pop-up code uses information from the event to place an object below the link that triggered it.

```
<html>
<head>
<script src="findDOM.js"></script>
    <script>
function findLivePageWidth() {
    if (window.innerWidth != null)
        return window.innerWidth;
    if (document.body.clientWidth != null)
        return document.body.clientWidth;
```

(code continues on next page)

Code 25.6 *continued*

```
                    code
    return (null);
}
function popUp(evt,objectID){
    if (isDHTML) {
        var livePageWidth =
        → findLivePageWidth();
        domStyle = findDOM(objectID,1);
        dom = findDOM(objectID,0);
        state = domStyle.visibility;
        if (dom.offsetWidth) elemWidth =
        → dom.offsetWidth;
        else { if (dom.clip.width)
        → elemWidth = dom.clip.width; }
        if (state == "visible" || state ==
        → "show") { domStyle.visibility =
        → "hidden"; }
        else {
            if (evt.pageY) {
                topVal = evt.pageY + 4;
                leftVal = evt.pageX -
                → (elemWidth / 2);
            }
            else {
                if (evt.y) {
                    topVal = evt.y + 4 +
                    → document.body.
                    → scrollTop;
                    leftVal = evt.x -
                    → (elemWidth / 2) +
                    → document.body.
                    → scrollLeft;
                }
            }
            if(leftVal < 2) { leftVal = 2; }
            else {
                if ((leftVal + elemWidth) >
                → livePageWidth) { leftVal =
                → leftVal - (elemWidth / 2);
                → }
            }
            domStyle.top = topVal; //
            → Positions the element from the
            → top
            domStyle.left = leftVal; //
            → Positions the element from the
            → left
```

(code continues on next page)

5. **#ht1,#ht2 {...}**

   For each hypertext pop-up object you will be using, set up an ID called ht#. Define each ID as absolutely positioned, hidden, and with a z-index that sets it above all other layers. These objects will be repositioned when they are needed.

6. **<span id="ht1" class="hyperText">**
   → ...</span>

   For each hypertext pop-up object, create a layer with the class set to hyperText and an ID from step 5. You can place any content you want within the <span> tags.

7. **<a href="#" onmouseover="popUp**
   → (event,'ht1')" onmouseout=
   → "popUp(event,'ht1')">...</a>

   Add a link around the text or other element that you want to trigger the pop-up object. In the link, include onMouseOver and onMouseOut event handlers that trigger the popUp() function. Feed the function the event (see "Passing an Event to a Function" in Chapter 14) and the ID of the hypertext pop-up object.

✔ Tips

- Notice that the links associated with the pop-up text go nowhere (actually, they link to the top of the page). You could, however, link to documents that elaborate on the concepts presented in the pop-up text or to anything else you want to use. Or you could use a simple function that returns no value, to have the links do nothing when clicked. You decide.

- You can also pop-up text as ToolTips that explain the purpose of a particular link in the navigation.

- You can include pop-up text in an image map. This technique is nice if you have a large graphic with areas that need explanation.

Code 25.6 *continued*

```
                    domStyle.visibility = "visible"; // Makes the element visable
         }
    }
}
   </script>
   <style type="text/css">
#ht1,#ht2 {
   position: absolute;
   z-index: 100;
   top: 0px;
   left: 10px;
   visibility: hidden; }
.hyperText  {
   color: #333333;
   font: 10px/12px "Trebuchet MS", Arial, Helvetica, Geneva, sans-serif;
   background-color: #cccccc;
   padding: 5px;
   border: solid 2px #ff6666;
   width: 250px;
   layer-background-color: #CCCCCC
   }
   </style>
</head>
<body>
   <span id="ht1" class="hyperText">
   Too much information is as bad as too little. All too often designers treat the Web like a hose
   → through which to force information.
   </span>
   <span id="ht2" class="hyperText">
       Hypertext allows you to include &quot;meta-textual&quot; information for readers who want
          → to know more.
   </span>
   <p>A webbed environment is a Web site that does not frustrate the user with long download
   → times, or confuse them with
   <a href="#" ONMOUSEOUT=" popUp(event,'ht1')"
onmouseover="popUp(event,'ht1')">
   millions of navigation points at once
   </a>
   . Instead, a successful webbed environment will appear to have smooth transitions as content
   → changes and provide easy to use features,
   <a href="#" onmouseout="popUp(event,'ht2')"
onmouseover="popUp(event,'ht2')">
   hypertext
   </a>
   , and navigation that is convenient but not overwhelming.
   </p>
</body>
</html>
```

Code 25.7 Enter the coordinates to move Coco the Cat around on the screen (Figure 25.8).

```
<html>
<head>
    <script src="findDOM.js"></script>
    <script language="JavaScript">
var theForm = null;
function moveObjectTo(objectID,formNum) {
    x = document.forms[formNum].xVal.value;
    y = document.forms[formNum].yVal.value;
    var domStyle = findDOM(objectID,1);
    if (domStyle.pixelLeft != null) {
        domStyle.pixelLeft = x;
        domStyle.pixelTop= y;
    }
    else {
        domStyle.left = x;
        domStyle.top= y;
    }
}
    </script>
</head>
<body>
    <div id="object1" style=" position:
    → absolute; top: 60px; left: 60px;
    → visibility: visible">
        <img src="coco.jpg" width="138"
        → height="168" border="0">
        <h2>meep</h2>
    </div>
    <form action="#" name="form1"
    → method="get">
        x:<input type="TEXT" name="xVal"
        → size="3"><br>
        y:<input type="TEXT" name="yVal"
        → size="3"><br>
        <input type="button" value="Move"
        → onclick="moveObjectTo('object1',0)">
    </form>
</body>
</html>
```

Using Form Input for Dynamic Actions

The most common way users interact with a Web page is via the mouse. You can also use forms to receive input from visitors and then perform a specific action. In Chapter 13, I showed you how to move objects from point to point, but you defined those points. Now, it's the visitors' turn.

To receive visitor input through a form:

1. `<script src="findDOM.js"></script>`

   In any JavaScript function that addresses an object on the screen directly, you need to include the findDOM code. To do so, include it in an external text file and then import that file into the page in which it will be used (**Code 25.7**).

2. `function moveObjectTo(objectID,x,y)` → `{...}`

   Add moveObjectTo() to the JavaScript at the head of your document. This function moves the element from its current position to a new position (see "Moving Objects from Point to Point" in Chapter 13), based on the xVal and yVal values of the specified form.

3. `<div id="object1" style=" position:` → `absolute; top: 60px; left: 60px;` → `visibility: visible">...</div>`

   Set up a CSS layer positioned with the top and left properties.

4. `<form action="#" name="form1"` → `method="get">...</form>`

   Set up a simple form, and give it a name.

continues on next page

5. `<input type="TEXT" name="xVal"`
`→ size="3">`

Add form fields that allow visitors to enter the x and y coordinates of the position to which they want to move the object.

6. `<input type="button" value="Move"`
`→ onclick="moveObjectTo`
`→ ('object1',0)">`

Add a form button that triggers moveObjectTo(). Pass the function the ID of the object you want to move and the number of the form you created in step 5. Clicking this button causes the element to move to the specified coordinates (**Figure 25.8**).

Figure 25.8 The cat has moved to the indicated coordinates. Good kitty!

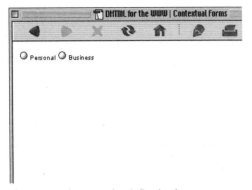

Figure 25.9 The page when it first loads.

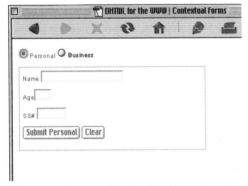

Figure 25.10 The page after the visitor has selected the personal form.

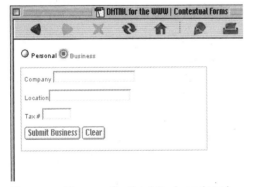

Figure 25.11 The page after the visitor has selected the business form.

Creating Contextual Forms

Forms are used to enter information on a Web page. This information is sent back to the Web server for a multitude of purposes. Often, however, the form's creator does not know exactly what information a particular visitor must enter.

If I am registering a product (**Figure 25.9**), I may be registering it for my own use (**Figure 25.10**) or for business (**Figure 25.11**). Both options may require different forms. The traditional solutions to this problem are to put both forms on a common page and tell the visitor to fill out the appropriate one, or to use a different page for each form. With DHTML, you can fit both forms on a common page and simply have one or the other appear, depending on the visitor's input.

To create contextual forms:

1. `<script src="findDOMNested.js">`
   `→ </script>`

   In any JavaScript function that addresses an object on the screen directly, you need to include the findDOM code (**Code 25.8**). To do so, include it in an external text file and then import that file into the page in which it will be used. Because this script uses nested layers, you have to adjust the code for Netscape 4 (see "Netscape 4 and Nested Layers" in Chapter 11).

2. `var oldDom = null;`

   Initialize the variable oldDOM to null. This step allows the swapForm() function to run the first time without an error.

3. `function swapForm(objectID){...}`

   Add swapForm() to the JavaScript. This function hides the form that is currently displayed and displays the form selected by the visitor.

4. `#formStack {...}`

   Set up an ID for the stack of forms. This ID is a relatively positioned object that contains a stack of absolutely positioned forms.

5. `#personal, #business {...}`

   Set up IDs for all forms, making them absolutely positioned and hidden. Because all the forms have the same definitions, you can include them in a common list (see "Defining Tags with the Same Rules" in Chapter 2).

6. `<input type="radio" onclick="swapForm`
   `→ ('personal')" name="context">`

   In the <body> of your document, set up a form with no action and a radio <input> for each form in the stack. Include in each button an onClick event handler that executes swapForm() and passes it the name of the form to be revealed.

Code 25.8 The code sets up radio buttons that allow the visitor to select the personal or business form.

```
<html>
<head>
    <script src="findDOMNested.js"></script>
    <script language="JavaScript">
var oldDom = null;
function swapForm(objectID){
    dom = findDOM('formStack',objectID,1);
    if (oldDom) oldDom.visibility = 'hidden';
    dom.visibility = 'visible';
    oldDom = dom;
    oldObjectID = objectID;
}
    </script>
    <style type="text/css">
#formStack {
    position: relative;
    width: 300px;
    visibility: visible
    }
#personal,#business { padding: 5px; border:
→ solid 1px gray; position: absolute; top:
→ 0px; left: 0px; visibility: hidden }
    </style>
</head>
<body>
    <form name="myForm" method="get">
        <input type="radio"
        → onclick="swapForm('personal')"
        → name="context">Personal <input
        → type="radio"
        → onclick="swapForm('business')"
        → name="context">Business
    </form>
    <div id="formStack">
        <div id="personal">
    <form name="personalForm"
    → action="submit.html" method="get">
        Name <input type="text" name="name"
        → size="24"><br><br>
        Age<input type="text" name="age"
        → size="3"><br><br>
        SS# <input type="password" name="ss#"
        → size="7"><br><br>
```

(code continues on next page)

Code 25.8 *continued*

```
                      code
      <input type="submit"
   → name="submitPeronal" value="Submit
   → Peronal"> <input type="reset"
   → name="clearPersonal"
   → value="Clear">
   </form>
   </div>
   <div id="business">
   <form name="businessForm"
→ action="submit.html" method="get">
      Company <input type="text"
   → name="company" size="24"><br><br>
      Location<input type="text"
   → name="location" size="24"><br><br>
      Tax # <input type="password"
   → name="tax#" size="7"><br><br>
      <input type="submit"
   → name="submitBusiness"
   → value="Submit Business"> <input
   → type="reset" name="clearBusiness"
   → value="Clear">
      </form>
      </div>
   </div>
</body>
</html>
```

7. `<div id="formStack">...</div>`

Add a layer for the stack of forms. This layer will have the form layers nested within it and allows you to position the forms on the page easily.

8. `<div id="personal">...</div>`

Within the layer you added in step 7, add a separate layer for each form to be used.

9. `<form name="personalForm"`
`→ action="submit.html"`
`→ method="get">...</form>`

Within the layer you added in step 8, add the form code. This form stands apart from other forms on the page and includes its own Submit and Clear buttons.

✔ Tip

■ This version of contextual forms is fairly simple, partly because of limitations in Netscape 4. It would be nice to have a single Submit button and allow the contextual forms to be integrated into a larger form, for example, but Netscape 4 does not allow the `<form>` tag to penetrate tables or CSS layers.

CREATING CONTEXTUAL FORMS

Drag-and-Drop Objects

Another staple of GUIs is drag and drop: the capability to drag windows, files, and whatnot across the screen and drop them into a new element or location.

As an example of this technique, you will create a refrigerator magnetic poetry kit for a Web page (**Figure 25.12**). You may have one of these games on your own refrigerator right now: Each word is on a magnetic chip, which can be moved around and combined with other chips to make sentences.

To set up element dragging:

1. `<script src="findDOM.js"></script>`

   In any JavaScript function that addresses an object on the screen directly, you need to include the findDOM code (**Code 25.9**). To do so, include it in an external text file and then import that file into the page in which it will be used.

2. `var domStyle = null;`

   Initialize domStyle to record the DOM style.

3. `function pickIt(evt) {...}`

   Add pickIt() to the JavaScript. This function—which is very much like the findObject() function (see "Identifying an Object on the Screen" in Chapter 14)—finds the ID of the object that the visitor has clicked in both Netscape 4 and Internet Explorer. If the visitor clicked one of the objects that contains the word *chip* in its ID, the function sets the z-index of that object to 100, which should place it well above all other objects on the page. Otherwise, the function does nothing.

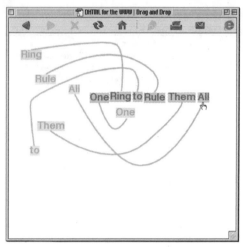

Figure 25.12 Can you figure out the word jumble?

Code 25.9 Pick it, drag it, and drop it. Three functions allow the visitor to move an object around on the screen.

```
<html>
<head>
    <script language="JavaScript"
    → src="findDOM.js"></script>
    <script language="JavaScript">
var domStyle = null;

function pickIt(evt) {
    if (isLayers) {
        var testObject;
        var xPos = evt.pageX;
        var yPos = evt.pageY;
        for (var i = document.layers.
        → length - 1; i >= 0; i--) {
            testObject = document.layers[i]
            if ((xPos > testObject.left) &&
            (xPos < testObject.left +
            → testObject.clip.width) &&
            (yPos > testObject.top) &&
            (yPos < testObject.top +
            → testObject.clip.height)) {
                domStyle = testObject;
```

(code continues on next page)

Code 25.9 *continued*

```
              }
          }
      }
  else {
      objectID = event.srcElement.id;
      if (objectID.indexOf('chip') != -1){
          domStyle = findDOM(objectID,1);
      }
  }
  if (domStyle) {
      domStyle.zIndex = 100;
      return false;
  }
  else {
      domStyle = null;
      return;
  }
}
function dragIt(evt) {
  if (domStyle) {
      if (isLayers) {
          domStyle.left = evt.pageX;
          domStyle.top = evt.pageY;
      }
      else {
          domStyle.left = window.event.x;
          domStyle.top = window.event.y;
      }
  }
}

function dropIt() {
  if (domStyle) {
      domStyle.zIndex = 0;
      domStyle = null;
  }
}

function defaultEvents() {
  if (isLayers) {
  //Gives Navigator 4 global event
  → capturing
```

(code continues on next page)

4. `function dragIt(evt) {...}`

   Add the `dragIt()` function to the JavaScript. This function will be triggered every time the visitor moves the mouse. The function does not do anything unless the visitor clicks one of the chips, in which case the function moves the chip as the visitor moves the mouse.

5. `function dropIt() {...}`

   Add the `dropIt()` function to the JavaScript. This function is triggered when the visitor releases the mouse button. It resets the variable `domStyle` to `null` and replaces the element to the 0-level z-index.

6. `function defaultEvents() {...}`

   Add the `defaultEvents()` function to the JavaScript. This function is triggered by an `onLoad` event handler in the `<body>` tag of your document. When triggered, it sets which functions run when particular events (`onMouseDown`, `onMouseMove`, and `onMouseUp`) occur anywhere in the browser window (see "Creating a Global Event Handler" in Chapter 14).

7. `.chip {...}`

   Set up a class style to define the appearance of the magnetic poetry chips on the screen. Define the chips as being absolutely positioned with a z-index of 0.

8. `#chip1 {...}`

   Set up a different ID selector for each chip on the screen. Give each chip an initial top and left position.

continues on next page

9. onLoad="defaultEvents()"

In the <body> tag, add an onload event handler to trigger **defaultEvents()**.

10. <span id="chip1" class="chip">
→ One</span>

Set up layers for as many word chips as needed, each with its own unique ID.

✔ Tips

■ Note: Internet Explorer 4 has trouble redrawing elements as they move across the screen.

■ Due to a bug in Netscape 6, this function does not work in that browser version.

Code 25.9 *continued*

```
              code

        document.captureEvents
        → (Event.MOUSEDOWN | Event.MOUSEMOVE
        → | Event.MOUSEUP)
    }
    if (isDHTML){
    document.onmousedown = pickIt;
    document.onmousemove = dragIt;
    document.onmouseup = dropIt;
    }
}
        </script>
    <style type="text/css">
.chip {position: absolute;  z-index: 0;
→ color: black; font: bold 16pt
→ helvetica,sans-serif; background-color:
→ #999999;layer-background-color: #999999;
→ cursor: move;}
#chip1 {top: 123px; left: 225px;}
#chip2 {top: 5px; left: 25px;}
#chip3 {top: 200px; left: 45px;}
#chip4 {top: 55px; left: 55px;}
#chip5 {top: 150px; left: 60px;}
#chip6 {top: 75px; left: 125px;}
        </style>
</head>
<body onload="defaultEvents()">
        <span id="chip1"
class="chip">One</span>
    <span id="chip2" class="chip">Ring</span>
    <span id="chip3" class="chip">to</span>
    <span id="chip4" class="chip">Rule</span>
    <span id="chip5" class="chip">Them</span>
    <span id="chip6" class="chip">All</span>
</body>
</html>
```

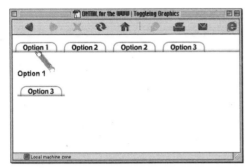

Figure 25.13 When the visitor places the mouse pointer on the Option 1 tab...

Figure 25.14 ...the tab switches its appearance.

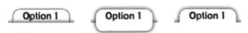

Figure 25.15 The three tab states: off, rdy (ready), and on.

Code 25.10 This code uses image swapping to change images, depending on the page displayed in the content frame.

```
<html>
<head>
   <script language="JavaScript">
var o1,o2,o3;
if (document.images){
imag = new Array();
   imag[0] = "media/o1_off.gif";
   imag[1] = "media/o1_rdy.gif";
   imag[2] = "media/o2_off.gif";
```
(code continues on next page)

Swapping Images

JavaScript rollovers are everywhere on the Web; they are the most popular way of giving visitors dynamic feedback about the link they are about to click. When the mouse pointer passes over a hypertext link (**Figure 25.13**), the graphic changes its appearance (**Figure 25.14**). Move the mouse pointer off the link, and the graphic changes back.

To set up image swapping:

1. o1_off.gif

   Create three version of each graphic button, one for each button state (**Figure 25.15**):

   ▲ off. Used when the button is not selected.

   ▲ rdy. Used when the mouse pointer is on the button and the button is ready to be selected.

   ▲ on. Used when the button is selected.

   Each version is used at different times, depending on what is happening on the screen (**Code 25.10**).

2. imag = new Array();

   The file names of the various graphics are stored in the imag array. Each graphic in the array has its own unique number—starting with 0, not 1. You can use this number to reference the graphic in the array.

   continues on next page

3. `im = new Array();`

To load each image into the browser, use the `im[]` array. The toggle function uses the `im[]` array to swap graphics back and forth. You can add as many different images as you want to the `imag[]` array for inclusion in the `ia[]` array, but each image needs a unique number. In this example, I am loading six graphics—an `off` and `rdy` (ready) version of each one.

4. `function toggleImage(imgName,num)`
`→ {...}`

Add `toggleImage()` to the JavaScript. This function is fairly straightforward. First, it makes sure the browser can swap images (`document.images`) and verifies that the image that is being referenced exists (`imgName`). Then it changes the source of the image called `imgName` to the source of the image in the array, referenced by the `num` variable.

Code 25.10 *continued*

```
imag[3] = "media/o2_rdy.gif";
imag[4] = "media/o3_off.gif";
imag[5] = "media/o3_rdy.gif";
im = new Array();
for (var i = 0; i < imag.length; i++)
{
im[i] = new Image();
im[i].src = imag[i];
}
}
function toggleImage(imgName,num){
    if (document.images && imgName){
        imgName.src = im[num].src;
        }
    return;
}

</script>
<style type="text/css">
body    {
    background: white url(media/bg.gif);
    margin-top: 10px
    }
</style>
<base target="content">
</head>
<body marginHeight="0" topmargin="0">
    <a href="option1.html"
    → onmouseover="toggleImage(o1,1)"
    → onmouseout="toggleImage(o1,0)">
        <img height="45" width="100"
        → src="media/o1_off.gif" border="0"
        → name="o1">
    </a>
    <a href="option2.html"
    → onmouseout="toggleImage(o2,2)"
    → onmouseover="toggleImage(o2,3)">
        <img height="45" width="100"
        → src="media/o2_off.gif"
        → border="0">
    </a>
    <img height="45" width="100"
    → src="media/o2_off.gif" border="0"
    → name="o2">
    <a href="option3.html"
    → onmouseout="toggleImage
    → (parent.content.document.o3,4)"
    → onmouseover="toggleImage
    → (parent.content.document.o3,5)">
        <img height="45" width="100"
        → src="media/o3_off.gif"
        → border="0">
    </a>
</body>
</html>
```

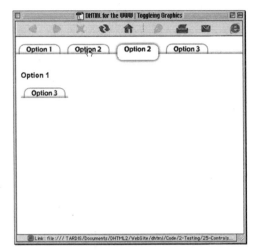

Figure 25.16 When the visitor mouses over the second option tab, the tab next to it changes.

To change an image:

1. `<img height="45" width="100"`
   `→ src="media/o1_off.gif" border="0"`
   `→ name="o1">`

   Set up an image, and give it a unique name.

2. `onmouseover="toggle(o1,1)"`

   Add an **onmouseover** event handler to a link around the graphic you created in step 1 to trigger the **toggleImage()** function. Include the name of the image you want to change and the number of the image (from the **imag[]** array) to which you want to change its source.

3. `onmouseout="toggle(o1,0)"`

   Add an **onmouseout** event handler to the link to trigger the **toggleImage()** function. Include the name of the image you want to change and the number of the image (from the **imag[]** array) to which you want to change its source.

   The image in this code has been given a name: **o1**. All images that will be changed need unique names. When the mouse pointer is placed over this graphic (**onmouseover**), the **toggleImage()** function is triggered, using **o1** for the **imgName** (the name of the image to be changed) and 1 for **num** (1 corresponds to the ready version of the graphic in the **imag[]** array). When the mouse pointer leaves the area of the graphic (**onmouseout**), the **toggleImage()** function is executed again to change the **o1** image again, replacing it with **imag[0]**, the off version of the graphic.

   No rule says you must change the image that the mouse pointer is on (**Figure 25.16**). You could have the **onmouseover** event handler change the source of another graphic on the screen. All that matters is what image name you include when you run the **toggleImage()** function.

SWAPPING IMAGES

To change a different image:

1. `<img height="45" width="100"`
   `→ src="media/o2_off.gif" border="0">`

   Set up an image, and include a link around it.

2. `onmouseover="toggleImage(o2,3)"`

   Add an `onmouseover` event handler to the link around the image you created in step 1 to trigger the `toggleImage()` function. Include the name of the image you want to change and the number of the image (from the `imag[]` array) to which you want to change its source.

3. `<img height="45" width="100"`
   `→ src="media/o2_off.gif" border="0"`
   `→ name="o2">`

   Set up the image to be changed from the link, and give it a unique name.

You can change images other than the one that the mouse is on, and you can even change images in other frames (**Figure 25.17**).

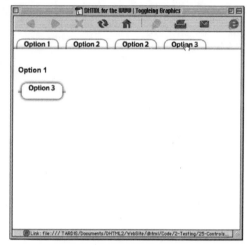

Figure 25.17 The tab for Option 3 changes the Option 3 tab in the bottom frame to the ready position.

Code 25.11 This code sets up a simple frameset with a menu at the top and the content frame below.

```
code
<html>
<frameset rows="55,*" border="0"
→ framespacing="0" frameborder="NO">

   <frame src="menu.html" name="menu"
   → scrolling="NO" noresize
   → marginHeight="0px" marginWidth="0px">

   <frame src="option1.html" name="content"
   → noresize>

</frameset>
</html>
```

Code 25.12 This sample content page includes a graphic that can be controlled from the menu.

```
code
<html>
<head>
   <style type="text/css">
body { background: white; }
   </style>
</head>
<body>
   <h2>Option 1</h2>

   <img height="45" width="100"
   → src="media/o3_off.gif" border="0"
   → name="o3">

</body>
</html>
```

To change an image in another frame:

1. `<frameset>`

   Set up your frame document, and give each frame a unique name (**Code 25.11**).

2. `<img height="45" width="100"`
   `→ src="media/o3_off.gif" border="0">`

   In the file menu.html, set up an image, and include a link around it (**Code 25.12**).

3. `onmouseout="toggle`
   `→ (parent.content.document.o3,4)"`

   Add an **onmouseover** event handler to the link around the image you created in step 1 to trigger the **toggleImage()** function. Include the name of the image you want to change and the number of the image (from the **imag[]** array) to which you want to change its source.

   The image name should also include a path to a graphic called **o3** in the frame called **content**. If that image does not exist, the toggle function ignores this rollover.

4. `<img height="45" width="100"`
   `→ src="media/o3_off.gif" border="0"`
   `→ name="o3">`

   In the file option1.html, set up the image that will be changed from the link, and give it a unique name.

✔ Tips

- What happens after you click the link? In the following section, I'll show you how to highlight the button for the content that is currently loaded and make sure the correct button is always highlighted for the correct content.

- You can also use image toggling to change multiple objects simultaneously. Just repeat the function in the same event handler, separating instances with a semicolon (;).

SWAPPING IMAGES

Creating a Smart Menu

In the preceding section, I showed you how to toggle between two graphics, depending on where the mouse pointer is. But you need to teach your Web site when to show a particular graphic, depending on which Web page is displayed. In other words, when a page loads into a frame, it tells the menu what section it is in, and the menu updates itself to indicate the correct section (**Figure 25.18**).

This technique is intended for use on Web sites that use frames to create the interface.

To create a smart menu:

1. o1_off.gif

Create three version of each graphic button, one for each button state (**Code 25.13**):

▲ off. Used when the button is not selected.

▲ rdy. Used when the mouse pointer is on the button and the button is ready to be selected.

▲ on. Used when the button is selected.

Each version is used at different times, depending on what is happening on the screen.

2. index.html

Set up a new frameset document (**Code 25.14**), with one frame (named menu) to hold the menu and another frame (named content) to hold the content.

3. menu.html

Set up a new HTML file, and save it as menu.html. Steps 4 through 10 apply to this file.

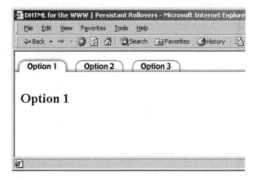

Figure 25.18 As soon as option1.html loads, it tells the menu which tab should be selected (in this case, Option 1).

Code 25.13 The menu contains the main site navigation, as well as the JavaScript that produces the rollover effect and sets the correct tab for the page displayed in the content frame.

```
<html>
<head>
    <script language="JavaScript">
var o1,o2,o3;
var optionCurrent;
var option;
var nowLoaded = 0;

if (document.images){
imag = new Array();
    imag[0] = "media/o1_off.gif";
    imag[1] = "media/o1_rdy.gif";
    imag[2] = "media/o1_on.gif";
    imag[3] = "media/o2_off.gif";
    imag[4] = "media/o2_rdy.gif";
    imag[5] = "media/o2_on.gif";
    imag[6] = "media/o3_off.gif";
    imag[7] = "media/o3_rdy.gif";
    imag[8] = "media/o3_on.gif";

    im = new Array();
    for (var i = 0; i < imag.length; i++)
    {
    im[i] = new Image();
```

(code continues on next page)

Code 25.13 *continued*

```
                         code
    im[i].src = imag[i];
    }
}

function toggleImage(imgName,num){
    if (document.images){
        if (optionCurrent == imgName.name) {
        → return;}
        imgName.src = im[num].src;
        }
    return;
}

function setButtons() {
  if (document.images) {
    option = parent.content.option;
        optionCurrent = 'o' + option;
        if (option == 1) { document.o1.src =
        → im[2].src } else { document.o1.src =
        → im[0].src  }
        if (option == 2) { document.o2.src =
        → im[5].src } else { document.o2.src =
        → im[3].src  }
        if (option == 3) { document.o3.src =
        → im[8].src } else { document.o3.src =
        → im[6].src  }
    }
}
    </script>
    <style type="text/css">
body { background: white url(media/bg.gif);
→ margin-top: 10px; }
    </style>
    <base target="content">
</head>
<body onload="setButtons(); nowLoaded = 1;"
→ marginHeight="0" topmargin="0">
        <a href="option1.html"
        → onmouseover="toggleImage(o1,1)"
        → onmouseout="toggleImage(o1,0)"
        → onclick="toggleImage(o1,0)">
            <img height="45" width="100"
            → src="media/o1_off.gif"
            → border="0" name="o1">
        </a>
```

(code continues in next column)

4. `var nowLoaded = 0;`

Declare your global variables, and initialize the variable **nowLoaded** to 0 (false). Content pages check this variable to make sure the menu has been loaded.

5. `imag = new Array();`

In menu.html, start a new array called **imag[]** to store the location of the graphics to be used. Each graphic location in the **imag[]** array has a unique number—starting with 0, not 1. You can use this number to reference the graphic in the array.

6. `im = new Array();`

To load each image into the browser, use the **im[]** array. The **toggleImage()** function uses the **im[]** array to swap graphics back and forth. You can add as many images as you want to the **imag[]** array for inclusion in the **ia[]** array, but each image needs a unique number.

continues on next page

Code 25.13 *continued*

```
                         code
        <a href="option2.html"
        → onclick="toggleImage(o2,3)"
        → onmouseout="toggleImage(o2,3)"
        → onmouseover="toggleImage(o2,4)">
            <img height="45" width="100"
            → src="media/o2_off.gif"
            → border="0" name="o2">
        </a>
        <a href="option3.html"
        → onclick="toggleImage(o3,6)"
        → onmouseout="toggleImage(o3,6)"
        → onmouseover="toggleImage(o3,7)">
            <img height="45" width="100"
            → src="media/o3_off.gif"
            → border="0" name="o3">
        </a>
</body>
</html>
```

7. `function toggleImage(imgName,num)` → `{...}`

Add `toggleImage()` to the JavaScript. This function is very much like the function in "Swapping Images" earlier in this chapter, except it checks whether the image to be changed is currently active. If so, the function does not toggle that graphic.

8. `function setButtons() {...}`

Add `setButtons()` to the JavaScript. This function turns on the menu button to reflect the page loaded in the content frame. It checks a variable called `option`, which it finds in the document loaded in the content frame. Depending on that value, the function turns on the appropriate menu tab and turns off the other tabs.

9. `onmouseover="toggle(o1,1)"` → `onmouseout="toggle(o1,0)"` → `onclick="toggle(o1,0)"`

Set up the menu links and graphics, adding `onmouseover`, `onmouseout`, and `onclick` event handlers to each link.

Remember that each graphic you use needs a unique name.

10. `onload="setButtons(); nowLoaded=1;"`

In the `<body>` tag, add an `onload` event handler that triggers the `setButtons()` function, and set the variable `nowLoaded` to 1 (true).

11. `option1.html`

Set up as many content pages as you need for the site (**Code 25.15**). All content pages in the Web site should include the code described in steps 12 through 15.

Code 25.14 This frameset sets up two frame rows: a narrow row on top for the menu and a row for the content, which fills the remaining space.

```
<html>
<frameset rows="55,*" border="0"
→ framespacing="0" frameborder="NO">
    <frame src="menu.html" name="menu"
    → scrolling="NO" noresize
    marginheight="0">
    <frame src="option1.html" name="content"
    → noresize>
</frameset>
</html>
```

Code 25.15 Every page on the site needs to contain the JavaScript on this page. Set the `option` variable to reflect the tab that should be selected in the navigation.

```
<html>
<head>
    <script language="JavaScript">
function doNothing() {};
var option = 1;
if (top.menu.nowLoaded) {
→ top.menu.setButtons(); }
    </script>
    <style type="text/css">
body { background: white; }
    </style>
</head>
<body onunload="doNothing();">
    <h2>Option 1</h2>
</body>
</html>
```

12. `function doNothing() {};`

Add **doNothing()** to all your content pages. This function itself does nothing. When it runs as the page unloads, however, it overcomes a bug in some versions of Internet Explorer that prevents the browser from re-executing JavaScript when the page is reloaded from the cache.

13. `var option = 3;`

Add the **option** variable to each content page. Its value should correspond to the menu option with which this page is associated.

14. `if (top.menu.nowLoaded)`
  → `{ top.menu.setButtons(); }`

Add code to your JavaScript that checks whether the menu is loaded and then runs the **setButtons()** function in the **menu** frame.

15. `onunload="doNothing();"`

In the **<body>** tag, add an **onunload** event handler to run the **doNothing()** function. This allows certain versions of Internet Explorer to re-execute JavaScript functions if the page is loaded from the cache.

✔ Tip

■ If you are familiar with JavaScript, you may wonder why this technique does not simply change the menu-option graphic to the on state through an **onclick** event handler. But what if visitors get to this page without clicking the menu option? They might arrive through a site map, from a link in the content frame rather than in the menu, or (more likely) by using the browser's Back button. The **onclick** event would never be triggered, and the menu-option graphic would not change. This system ensures that the correct menu option is always selected for the correct content.

SPECIAL EFFECTS

You don't need to have boring Web pages that sit there on the screen, waiting for the visitor to do something. In this chapter, I'll show you some of the fun effects you can achieve with CSS and DHTML.

Several of these effects may come under the label "stupid Web tricks," but they are all cool, and some may even be useful. A word of caution though: Use special effects judiciously, lest you annoy your visitors.

Creating Drop Caps

Drop-cap-style letters are a time-honored way of starting a new section or chapter of lengthy text. Medieval monks used drop caps with illuminated manuscripts—and now you can use them on the Web (**Figure 26.1**).

You create a drop cap by making the first letter of a paragraph larger than subsequent letters and moving the first several lines of text over to accommodate the larger letter.

To set a drop cap with the <span> tag:

1. p { font: normal 12px/14px helvetica,
   → arial,sans-serif; }

   Define the paragraph tag to display text in the style you want to use (**Code 26.1**). This example uses 10-point Helvetica with 12-point line spacing. (For help with font sizing, see "Setting the Font" in Chapter 3.)

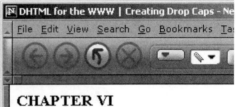

CHAPTER VI
Pig and Pepper

For a minute or two she stood looking at the h do next, when suddenly a footman in livery ca (she considered him to be a footman becaus judging by his face only, she would have called h at the door with his knuckles. It was opened by ar round face, and large eyes like a frog; and both fc powdered hair that curled all over their heads. Sh what it was all about, and crept a little way out of 1 Fish-Footman began by producing from under hi

Figure 26.1 A drop cap.

Code 26.1 The dropcap class can help draw attention to the first paragraph on the page.

```
<html>
<head>
    <style type="text/css">
p {font: 12px/14px helvetica,arial,sans-serif;}
.dropcap {
    font: bold 300% times,serif;
    color: red;
    float: left; }
    </style>
</head>
<body>
    <h3>CHAPTER VI<br>
    Pig and Pepper</h3>
    <p><span class="dropcap">F</span>or a minute or two she stood looking at the house, and
    → wondering what to do next, when suddenly a footman in livery came runningout of the wood-
    → (she considered him to be a footman because he was in livery: otherwise, judging by his face
    → only, she would have called him a fish)--and rapped loudly at the door with his knuckles. </p>
</body>
</html>
```

2. `.dropcap {font: bold 300% times, serif;`
`→ color: red; float: left;}`

Set up a class that defines its text as bold and three times larger than the text around it. Other text will flow around this emphasized text element to the right, because this drop-cap text will float to the left (see "Wrapping Text Around an Element" in Chapter 7).

3. `<p> <span class="dropcap">F</span>`
`→ or a minute or two...</p>`

To use the **dropcap** class to create drop-cap text, employ the **<span>** container in your HTML. In this setup, the letter appears as 30-point, dropped down so its top aligns with the tops of the rest of the characters.

✔ Tip

■ Internet Explorer renders floating letters with their baselines flush with the rest of the text (that is, the bottoms of letters on the same line). Therefore, the letter styled with **dropcap** does not actually drop down.

Not Really an Element

An easier way to create drop caps is to use the first-letter pseudo-element. A *pseudo-element* is a specific, unique part of an element—such as the first letter or first line of a paragraph—the appearance of which can be controlled independent of the rest of the element. You can use the first-letter pseudo-element to set the style of the first letter in a paragraph as follows:

`P:first-letter { font: bold 300% times, serif; 'float: left; }`

Another pseudo-element is **first-line**, which allows you to set the appearance of the first line of text.

Unfortunately, neither Netscape 4 nor Internet Explorer 4 supports pseudo-elements. Use them at your own risk.

Creating a Simple Drop Shadow

Another popular special effect on the Web is the drop shadow. Drop shadows make text (especially large headlines and titles) stand out from the rest of the page, adding emphasis and impact. Before CSS, however, the only way to create drop shadows for the Web was to create a graphic of the text and its shadow. Now, a little CSS trickery lets you do the same thing without resorting to graphics (**Figure 26.2**).

Figure 26.2 A drop-shadow effect.

To create a CSS drop shadow:

1. #title {...}

In your CSS rules list (**Code 26.2**), create three ID selectors called title, text, and shadow. title and text should be positioned relatively; shadow should be positioned absolutely and slightly offset from its top-left corner (see "Nesting an Absolute Element in a Relative Element" in Chapter 8).

Code 26.2 The text and shadow layers are nested in the title layer.

```
code
<html>
<head>
    <style media="screen" type="text/css">
#title  { font: bold 75px "Hoefler Text", serif, "Times New Roman", Georgia, Times; position:
→ relative; top: 5px; left: 5px; }
#text { position: relative; top: 0px; left: 0px; color: #000000; z-index:2; }
#shadow { position: absolute; top: 4px; left: 4px; color: #999999; z-index:1; }
    </style>
</head>
<body>
    <div id="title">
        <span ID="text">Alice in Wonderland</span>
        <span ID="shadow">Alice in Wonderland</span>
    </div>
    <p>Down, down, down. Would the fall <i>never</i> come to an end! 'I wonder how many miles I've
    → fallen by this time?'</p>
</body>
</html>
```

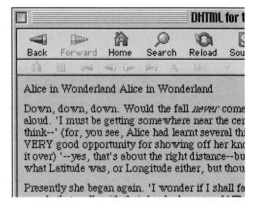

Figure 26.3 What a non-CSS-capable browser sees.

2. `<div id="title">...</div>`

Create a title layer. This layer will contain the foreground (`text`) and background (`shadow`) layers, and allow you to position these elements on the page as one unit.

3. `<span id="text">...</span>`

In the `title` layer, add the `text` layer for the foreground text.

4. `<span id="shadow">...</span>`

Immediately after the `text` layer, add the `shadow` layer, containing the same text as the `text` layer. This layer will be the text's shadow.

✔ Tips

■ Note: A non-CSS-capable browser reading a page that uses this drop-shadow technique will display the text one line after the next, which may not look very appealing (**Figure 26.3**).

■ You can play with different colors for the drop shadow or even use different fonts for the foreground text and the drop shadow if you are feeling like a complete nut.

■ You can create drop shadows with a fade if you use this technique with a bit of JavaScript (see the following section, "Creating an Advanced Drop Shadow").

Creating an Advanced Drop Shadow

Although the basic drop shadow is highly effective, this version goes one better. Instead of placing a single shadow below the text, the advanced drop shadow creates the illusion of a shadow fading into the page's background (**Figure 26.4**).

To add an advanced drop shadow:

1. `var shadowLength = 10;`

   Initialize the following variables in the JavaScript (**Code 26.3**):

   - ▲ `shadowLength`. Sets the number of iterations of the text. You can change this value. The higher the number, the farther the shadow will spread from the text.

   - ▲ `offsetLeft`. Sets how many spaces each iteration of the text should move to the left. You can change this value, but 1 is preferred for a smooth shadow.

   - ▲ `offsetTop`. Sets how many spaces each iteration of the text should move down. You can change this value, but 1 is preferred for a smooth shadow.

   - ▲ `oL`. Records the position of the left edge of the text. This variable sets the left position of each iteration of the text and should be set to 0 initially.

   - ▲ `oT`. Records the position of the top edge of the text. This variable sets the top position of each iteration of the text and should be set to 0 initially.

   - ▲ `bgR, bgG, bgB`. Sets the red, green, and blue background-color values. You can change these values. Values must be between 0 and 255 (see "Values and Units Used in This Book" in the introduction).

Figure 26.4 The advanced drop shadow. It is not quite as attractive as one created in Photoshop, but it appears much more quickly.

Code 26.3 The drop shadow is built from several layers of the same text, each layer's color slightly closer to the background color and its position offset slightly from the preceding layer.

```
<html>
<head>
   <script language="JavaScript">
var shadowLength = 10;
var offsetLeft = 1;
var offsetTop = 1;
oL = 0;
oT = 0;
var bgR = 255;
var bgG = 255;
var bgB = 255;
var shR = 0;
var shG = 0;
var shB = 0;
var fgR = 255;
var fgG = 0;
var fgB = 0;
var cR = shR;
var cG = shG;
var cB = shB;
zC = shadowLength;
var iR = Math.round((Math.abs(bgR - shR))/
→ shadowLength);
var iG = Math.round((Math.abs(bgG - shG))/
→ shadowLength);
var iB = Math.round((Math.abs(bgB - shB))/
→ shadowLength);

function colourShift () {
```

(code continues on next page)

Code 26.3 *continued*

```
                     code
   if ( cR >= bgR ) { cR  -= iR; }
   else { cR += iR; }
   if ( cG >= bgG
) { cG  -= iG; }
   else { cG += iG; }
   if ( cB >= bgB ) { cB  -= iB; }
   else { cB += iB; }
}

function writeLayer(layerPrefix,message) {
   document.writeln ('<div id="title">')
   document.writeln ('<span id="text">')
   document.writeln (message)
   document.writeln ('</span>')
   for (var i = 1; i <= shadowLength; i++) {
   document.writeln ('<span id="'+
→ layerPrefix + i + '">')
   document.writeln (message)
   document.writeln ('</span>')
}
document.writeln ('</div>')
}

function writeCSS(layerPrefix) {
   document.writeln ('#text{')
   document.writeln ('color: rgb(' + fgR + ',
→ ' + fgG  + ',' + fgB + ');')
   document.writeln ('position: relative;')
   document.writeln ('z-index: ' + zC + ';')
   document.writeln ('left: ' + oL + ';
→ top: ' + oT + ';')
   document.writeln ('}')
   for (var i = 1; i <= shadowLength; i++) {
      oL = oL + offsetLeft; oT = oT +
→ offsetTop; zC = zC - 1;
      document.writeln ('#'+ layerPrefix +
→ i + '{')
      document.writeln ('color: rgb(' + cR
→ + ',' + cG  + ',' + cB + ');')
      document.writeln ('position:
→ absolute;')
      document.writeln ('z-index: ' +
→ zC + ';')
      document.writeln ('left: ' + oL + ';
→ top: ' + oT + ';')
```

(code continues on next page)

▲ shR, shG, shB. Sets the red, green, and blue shadow-color values. You can change these values. Values must be between 0 and 255.

▲ fgR, fgG, fgB. Sets the red, green, and blue foreground-color values—the color of the text that the shadow will be below. You can change these values. Values must be between 0 and 255.

▲ cR, cG, cB. Records the red, green, and blue color values for the current shadow-layer iteration. Initially, these values are the same as the shadow colors but change with each iteration to fade into the background color.

▲ zC. Records the z-index value of each layer. Initially, this value should be the same as the shadowLength.

▲ iR, iG, iB. Records the amount by which the current red, green, and blue color of each layer should change from the preceding layer's color.

2. function colorShift() {...}

   Add colorShift() to the JavaScript. This function changes the red, green, and blue values of the current layer from the preceding layer.

3. function writeLayer(layerPrefix,
   → message) {...}

   Add writeLayer() to the JavaScript. Given the general name of each layer (layerPrefix) and the message to be written, this function writes each layer iteration for the shadow into the HTML code.

4. function writeCSS(layerPrefix) {...}

   Add writeCSS() to the JavaScript. Given the general name of each layer (layerPrefix), this function writes the CSS needed for each layer iteration, using the colorShift() function to change the color after each layer iteration is created.

continues on next page

5. `document.writeln('<style type=`
`→ "text/css">')`

Add JavaScript that writes CSS for the `<body>` tag, using the background-color variables from step 1 to define the background color of the page.

6. `writeCSS('shadow')`

Add a call to the `writeCSS()` function, passing it the general name of the shadow layers.

7. `#title {...}`

Add the ID title to your CSS. This step sets up a relatively positioned element for the drop shadow to be nested within so it can be positioned in the document.

8. `writeLayer('shadow','Alice In`
`→ Wonderland');`

In the body of your document, call the `writeLayer()` function, and pass it the general name of the shadow layers and the message to be created.

✔ Tips

- This trick works only if the background is a solid color; otherwise, the fade will look chunky.

- By changing the offset variables, you can create some interesting effects with a '70s flavor (**Figure 26.5**).

Code 26.3 *continued*

```
            document.writeln ('}')
            colourShift();
                }
        }
        }
    </script>
    <script language="JavaScript">
document.writeln ('<style type="text/css">')
document.writeln ('body {')
document.writeln ('background-color: rgb(' +
→ bgR + ',' + bgG  + ',' + bgB + ');')
document.writeln (' }')
writeCSS('shadow')
document.writeln ('</style>')
    </script>
    <style type="text/css">
#title  { font: bold 75px "Hoefler Text",
→ serif, "Times New Roman", Georgia, Times;
→ position: relative; top: 5px; left: 5px }
    </style>
</head>
<body>
    <script language="JavaScript">
writeLayer('shadow','Alice in Wonder Land');
    </script>
    <p>Down, down, down. Would the fall
    → <i>never</i> come to an end! 'I wonder
    → how many miles I've fallen by this
    → time?'</p>
</body>
</html>
```

Figure 26.5 The advanced drop shadow with the `offsetLeft` set to 5. Funky!

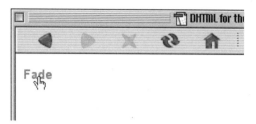

Figure 26.6 The text is nowhere to be seen as the visitor rolls over the link.

Figure 26.7 The text is in mid-fade.

Figure 26.8 The text is at full strength.

Code 26.4 Like the advanced drop shadow, fading text is built from several layers of text. The layers are shown one at a time, so the text appears to either fade up when the link is rolled over, or fade down when the mouse rolls out.

```
code
<html>
<head>
    <script src="findDOM.js"></script>
    <script language="JavaScript">
var domTop;
var domNew;
var layerAlpha = 1;
var layerOmega = 60;
var layerCurrent =null;
var layerNumberUp = null;
```

(code continues on next page)

Fading HTML Text

Building on the advanced drop shadow, you can make HTML text appear to fade up or down without using an animated GIF (**Figures 26.6**, **26.7**, and **26.8**). One warning, this is buggy in Netscape 4 for Windows.

To add fading text:

1. `<script src="findDOM.js"></script>`

   In any JavaScript function that addresses an object on the screen directly, you need to include the findDOM code (see "Using the Cross-Browser DOM" in Chapter 11). To do so, include it in an external text file and then import that file into the page in which it will be used (**Code 26.4**).

2. `var domTop;`

   In your JavaScript, initialize the following variables:

   ▲ `domTop`. Records the Document Object Model (DOM) of the top layer showing.

   ▲ `domNew`. Records the DOM of the new layer to be shown.

   ▲ `layerAlpha`. Records the number of the current layer.

   ▲ `layerOmega`. Records the maximum number of layers. This variable controls how many layer iterations will be shown during the fade, so the larger the number, the smoother (and slower) the fade.

   ▲ `layerCurrent`. Records the name (ID) of the current layer showing.

   ▲ `layerNumberUp`. Records the number of the current layer showing, if the function `fadeText()` is fading the text up to the foreground color.

continues on next page

▲ `layerNumberDown`. Records the number of the current layer showing, if the `fadeText()` function is fading the text down to the background color.

▲ `delay`. Sets the amount of delay between running a function recursively (see "Making a Function Run Again" in Chapter 14). You can change this value. A larger number means a slower fade.

▲ `bgR`, `bgG`, `bgB`. Sets the red, green, and blue background-color values. You can change these values. Values must be between 0 and 255.

▲ `fgR`, `fgG`, `fgB`. Sets the red, green, and blue foreground-color values—the color from which the text will fade up or down. You can change these values. Values must be between 0 and 255.

▲ `cR`, `cG`, `cB`. Records the red, green, and blue color values for the current shadow-layer iteration. Initially, these values are the same as the shadow colors but change with each iteration to fade into the background color.

▲ `iR`, `iG`, `iB`. Records the amount by which the current red, green, and blue color of each layer should change from the preceding layer's color.

3. `function fadeText(layerPrefix, → direction) {...}`

   Add `fadeText()` to the JavaScript. Given a direction to fade—`0` to go up from background to foreground or `1` to go down from foreground to background—this function prepares the variables and then runs `fadeUp()` or `fadeDown()`, depending on which direction is indicated.

Code 26.4 *continued*

```
                    code
var layerNumberDown = null;
var delay = 75;
var bgR = 255;
var bgG = 255;
var bgB = 255;
var fgR = 0;
var fgG = 0;
var fgB = 0;
var cR = bgR;
var cG = bgG;
var cB = bgB;
var iR = Math.round((Math.abs(bgR - fgR))/
→ layerOmega);
var iG = Math.round((Math.abs(bgG - fgG))/
→ layerOmega);
var iB = Math.round((Math.abs(bgB - fgB))/
→ layerOmega);

function fadeText(layerPrefix,direction) {
    if (layerCurrent == null) {
    if (direction == 0 ) {
        layerCurrent = layerPrefix +
        → layerAlpha;
        layerNumberUp = layerAlpha;
        fadeUp(layerPrefix);
    }
    else {
        layerCurrent = layerPrefix +
        → layerOmega;
        layerNumberDown = layerOmega;
        fadeDown(layerPrefix);
    }
}
else {
    if (direction == 0 ) {
        layerNumberUp = layerNumberDown + 1;
        layerNumberDown = layerAlpha;
        fadeUp(layerPrefix);
        }
    else {
        layerNumberDown = layerNumberUp - 1;
        layerNumberUp = layerOmega;
        fadeDown(layerPrefix);
    }
    }
}

function fadeUp(layerPrefix) {
```

(code continues on next page)

Code 26.4 *continued*

```
                    code
    layerPrevious = layerCurrent;
    layerCurrent = layerPrefix +
  → layerNumberUp;
    domTop = findDOM(layerPrevious,1);
    domNew = findDOM(layerCurrent,1);
      domTop.visibility = 'hidden';
    domNew.visibility = 'visible';
    domTop.zIndex = '0';
    domNew.zIndex = '100';
    layerNumberUp++;
    if (layerNumberUp <= layerOmega) {
        code2run = 'fadeUp("' + layerPrefix
      → + '")';
        setTimeout(code2run,delay);
    }
}

function fadeDown(layerPrefix) {
  → layerPrevious = layerCurrent;
    layerCurrent = layerPrefix +
  → layerNumberDown;
    domTop = findDOM(layerPrevious,1);
    domNew = findDOM(layerCurrent,1);
    domTop.visibility = 'hidden';
    domNew.visibility = 'visible';
    domTop.zIndex = '0';
    domNew.zIndex = '100';
    layerNumberDown--;
    if (layerNumberDown >= layerAlpha) {
        code2run = 'fadeDown("' +
      → layerPrefix + '")';
        setTimeout(code2run,delay);
    }
}

function colourShift () {
    if ( cR >= fgR ) { cR  -= iR; }
    else { cR += iR; }
    if ( cG >= fgG ) { cG  -= iG; }
    else { cG += iG; }
    if ( cB >= fgB ) { cB  -= iB; }
    else { cB += iB; }
}
function writeLayer(layerPrefix,message) {
    for (var i = 1; i <= layerOmega; i++) {
        document.writeln ('<span id="'+
      → layerPrefix + i + '"
      → class="fadeText">')
        document.writeln (message)
```

(code continues on next page)

4. `function fadeUp(layerPrefix) {...}`

   Add `fadeUp()` to the JavaScript. This function flips up the series of layers, showing and hiding each one, creating the illusion that the text is fading from the background color to the foreground color.

5. `function fadeDown(layerPrefix) {...}`

   Add `fadeDown()` to the JavaScript. This function flips down the series of layers, showing and hiding each one, creating the illusion that the text is fading from the foreground color to the background color.

6. `function colorShift () {...}`

   Add `colorShift()` to the JavaScript. This changes the red, green, and blue values of the current layer from the preceding layer for use in the CSS.

7. `function writeLayer(layerPrefix, message) {...}`

   Add `writeLayer()` to the JavaScript. Given the general name of each layer (`layerPrefix`) and the message to be written, this function writes each layer iteration for the fade into the HTML code.

8. `function writeCSS(layerPrefix) {...}`

   Add `writeCSS()` to the JavaScript. Given the general name of each layer (`layerPrefix`), this function writes the CSS needed for each layer iteration, using the `colorShift()` function to change the color after each layer iteration is created.

9. `document.writeln ('<style type= "text/css">')`

   Add JavaScript that writes CSS for the `<body>` tag, using the background color variables from step 1 to define the background color for the page.

continues on next page

10. `writeCSS('f')`

Add a call to the `writeCSS()` function, passing it the general name you used to create the IDs.

11. `#title {...}`

Add the ID title to your CSS. This step sets up a relatively positioned element for the drop shadow to be nested within so it can be positioned in the document.

12. `onmouseover="fadeText('f',0)"`

Trigger the `fadeText()` function , passing it the general name (ID) of the fading object and the direction in which you want it to fade. 0 fades from background to foreground; 1 fades from foreground to background.

13. `<div id="title">...</div>`

Set up a CSS layer called `title`, and place the JavaScript from step 10 in this layer.

14. `writeLayer('f','DHTML Rules.');`

In the body of your document, call the `writeLayer()` function, and pass it the general name you used to create the IDs and the message to be created. This step creates the layers that create the fade illusion.

✔ Tip

- Because the text is not truly transparent, this technique will not work unless the background is a solid color.

Code 26.4 *continued*

```
                          code
        document.writeln ('</span>')
    }
}

function writeCSS(layerPrefix) {
    for (var i = 1; i <= layerOmega; i++) {
        document.writeln ('#'+ layerPrefix +
         → i + '{')
        document.writeln ('color: rgb(' +
         → cR + ',' +  cG  + ',' + cB + ');')
        document.writeln ('}')
        colourShift();
    }
}
    </script>
    <script language="JavaScript">
document.writeln ('<style type="text/css">')
document.writeln ('body {')
document.writeln ('background-color: rgb(' +
 → bgR + ',' +  bgG  + ',' + bgB + ');')
document.writeln ('color: white;')
document.writeln (' }')
document.writeln ('.fadeText {')
document.writeln ('font-size: xx-large;')
document.writeln ('font-family:  "arial
 → Black",Arial, Helvetica, Geneva, sans-serif;')
document.writeln ('position: absolute;')
document.writeln ('visibility: hidden;')
document.writeln ('top: -12px;')
document.writeln ('left: -3px;')
document.writeln ('}')
writeCSS('f')
document.writeln ('</style>')
    </script>
    <style type="text/css">
#title { font: bold 75px "Hoefler Text",
 → serif, "Times New Roman", Georgia, Times;
 → position: relative; top: 5px; left: 5px }
    </style>
</head>
<body>
    <h2><a href="#" onmouseover="fadeText
    ('f',0)" onmouseout="fadeText('f',1)">
     → Fade</a></h2>
    <div id="title">
        <script language="JavaScript">
writeLayer('f','DHTML Rules.');
        </script>
    </div>
</body>
</html>
```

Figure 26.9 This technique creates a flashlight effect. The text is black on a black background. The white graphic moves below the text but above the background, causing the text to show up only when the mouse is over it.

Follow the Mouse Pointer

Like scroll bars (see "Creating Your Own Scroll Bars" in Chapter 25), the mouse pointer is part of the user interface that gives designers limited control. Although some browsers also let you control the pointer's appearance to a limited degree (see "Changing the Mouse Pointer's Appearance" in Chapter 5), you are stuck with the pointers provided by the browser.

By using a bit of DHTML, however, you can create a layer that follows the mouse on the screen. In browsers that allow you to set the pointer's appearance to none, you can replace the pointer with a graphic of your own devising (**Figure 26.9**).

To create an object that follows the mouse pointer:

1. `<script src="findDOM.js"></script>`

   In any JavaScript function that addresses an object on the screen directly, you need to include the findDOM code. To do so, include it in an external text file and then import that file into the page in which it will be used (**Code 26.5**).

2. `var evt = null;`

   In the JavaScript, initialize the following variables:

   ▲ `evt`. Sets the event variable to `null`.

   ▲ `isNS`. Sets a variable to record whether the browser being used is Netscape (1) or not (0).

3. `if (navigator.appName.indexOf`
   `→ ('Netscape') != -1) {isNS = 1;}`

   Test to see whether the browser being used is a Netscape browser (any version; see "Detecting the Browser's Name and Version" in Chapter 12). Reset the variable `isNS` to 1 if the browser is Netscape-compatible.

4. `function defaultEvents(evt) {...}`

   Add `defaultEvents()` to the JavaScript. This function sets up a global event handler (see "Creating a Global Event Handler" in Chapter 14); whenever the mouse moves, the `followMe()` function executes.

5. `function followMe(evt) {...}`

   Add `followMe()` to the JavaScript. This function moves a specific object (in this case, called `spotLight`) to wherever the mouse pointer is, minus 150 pixels. Because the object in question is a 300-px-by-300-px graphic, the mouse pointer appears in the middle of the object.

Code 26.5 A global event handler allows you to track the path of the mouse and move an object along with it.

```
<html>
<head>
    <script language="javascript"
    → src="findDOM.js"></script>
    <script language="javascript">
var evt = null;
var isNS = 0;

if (navigator.appName.indexOf('Netscape')
→ != -1) {isNS = 1;}

function defaultEvents(evt) {
    if (isNS) {
        document.captureEvents
        → (Event.MOUSEMOVE)
    }
    if (isDHTML){
        document.onmousemove = followMe;
    }
}

function followMe(evt) {
    if (isNS) event = evt;
        domStyle = findDOM('spotLight',1);
    if (event.pageX != null) {
        domStyle.left = event.pageX - 150;
        domStyle.top = event.pageY - 150;
        return;
    }
    else {
        domStyle.left = event.x - 150;
        domStyle.top = event.y - 150;
        return;
    }
}
    </script>
    <style media="screen" type="text/css">
```

(code continues on next page)

Code 26.5 *continued*

```
#spotLight {
    position: absolute;
    top: 20px;
    left: 20px;
    z-index: 0;
#content {
}
    font: bold 50px fantasy;
    position: absolute;
    top: 100px;
    left: 100px;
    z-index: 100;
    }
body {
    background-color: black;
    color : black;
    cursor: none;
    }
    </style>
</head>
<body onload="defaultEvents(event)">
    <span id="spotLight">
        <img src="spotLight.gif" width="300"
        → height="300">
    </span>
    <div id="content">Are you afraid of the
    → dark?</div>
</body>
</html>
```

6. #spotLight {...}

Set up the ID for the object you will be controlling with the mouse's movement, making it absolutely positioned. The initial top and left positions do not matter, because they will change as soon as the visitor moves the mouse pointer.

7. onload="defaultEvents(event)"

When the page loads, the default events need to be initialized, so place an onload event handler in the <body> tag to run the defaultEvents() function.

8. <span id="spotLight">...</span>

Set up the layer that will be moved by the mouse movement. Although this example places a graphic in this layer, you can use HTML text, GIF animations, or anything else that can go in a CSS layer.

✔ Tips

■ Although you can place anything you want in the layer to be moved, larger objects take longer for the computer to draw and redraw, so their movement will appear slower and choppier than that of smaller items.

continues on next page

■ You can combine this technique with a variety of other techniques for some stunning effects. You might use layers in different z-indexes (see "Stacking Objects [3-D Positioning]" in Chapter 8) to create a puzzle Web page (**Figure 26.10**). Or you can use a PNG graphic (see "Creating Transparent Graphics in PNG Format" later in this chapter) to create a crosshair target (**Figure 26.11**).

Figure 26.10 The screen is a mess of overlapping text, with a hole that moves around below the mouse pointer until the visitor finds the magic link.

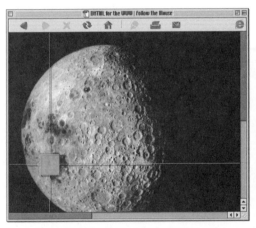 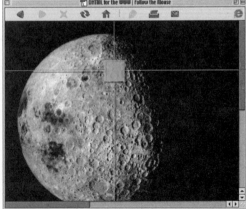

Figure 26.11 The crosshair moves over the intended target. I used a PNG graphic in this example to get the transparent middle and drop shadow, so this graphic will not work in every browser (see "Creating Transparent Graphics in PNG Format" later in this chapter).

Floating Objects

This technique is a real eye-catcher. The objects spin around on the screen, speeding up and slowing down. The effect doesn't accomplish much, but it looks cool (**Figure 26.12**).

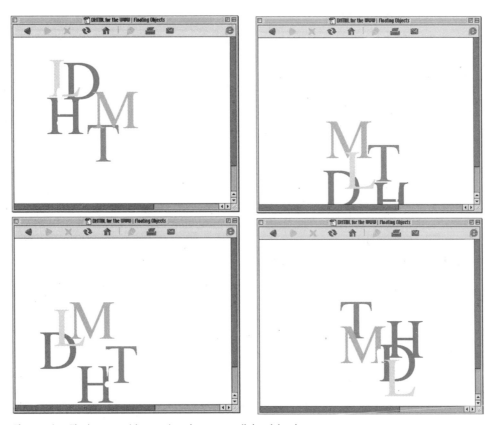

Figure 26.12 The letters swirl around on the page until the visitor leaves.

To set up floating objects:

1. `<script src="findDOM.js"></script>`

In any JavaScript function that addresses an object on the screen directly, you need to include the findDOM code. To do so, include it in an external text file and then import that file into the page in which it will be used (**Code 26.6**).

2. `var tall = 200;`

In the JavaScript, initialize the following variables:

▲ `tall`. Sets the height of the area in which the objects will float. The objects can float this many pixels to the left or right of the Xpos. You can change this value. The larger the number, the farther objects move above or below the center.

▲ `wide`. Sets the width of the area in which the objects will float. The objects can float this many pixels above or below the Ypos. You can change this value. The larger the number, the farther objects move to the left or right of the center.

▲ `step`. Sets the increment for the nextStep variable. You can change this value. The smaller the number, the slower the objects will float.

▲ `delay`. Controls the delay when the function loops (see "Making a Function Run Again" in Chapter 14). You can change this value. The larger the number, the slower the objects will float.

▲ `nextStep`. Controls the current speed of the objects.

▲ `numObjects`. Sets the number of objects being floated. Set this variable to the number of objects you will be controlling.

▲ `Xpos`. Sets the position from the left of the page around which the objects will center. You can change this value.

Code 26.6 The floating objects follow an elliptical orbit around a center point.

```
<html>
<head>
    <script src="findDOM.js"></script>
    <script language=JavaScript>
var tall = 200;
var wide = 200;
var step = .25;
var delay = 50;
var nextStep = 0;
var numObjects = 6;
var Xpos = 200;
var Ypos = 200

function objectsFloat() {
for (var xx = 1 ; xx < (numObjects + 1) ;
→ xx++ ) {
var objectID = 'object' + xx;
domStyle = findDOM(objectID,1)
domStyle.top = Ypos +Math.cos((20*Math.sin
→ (nextStep/(30+xx)))+xx*70)*tall*(Math.sin
→ (10+nextStep/10)+0.2)*Math.cos((nextStep+
→ xx*55)/10);
domStyle.left = Xpos +Math.sin((20*Math.sin
→ (nextStep/30))+xx*70)*wide*(Math.sin
→ (10+nextStep/(10+xx))+0.2)*Math.cos
→ ((nextStep+ xx*55)/10);
}
nextStep += step;
setTimeout('objectsFloat()', delay) ;
}
```

(code continues on next page)

Code 26.6 *continued*

```
[========= code =========]
    </script>
</head>
<body onload="objectsFloat()">
    <div id="object1" style="position:
    → absolute; left: 300; top: 140;
    → visibility:
visible;font: 136px times;
→ color:#000000;">D</div>
    <div id="object2" style="position:
    → absolute; left: 690; top: 240;
    → visibility:
visible;font: 136px times;
→ color:#333333;">H</div>
    <div id="object3" style="position:
    → absolute; left: 400; top: 340;
    → visibility:
visible;font: 136px times;
→ color:#666666;">T</div>
    <div id="object4" style="position:
    → absolute; left: 400; top: 340;
    → visibility:
visible;font: 136px times;
→ color:#999999;">M</div>
    <div id="object5" style="position:
    → absolute; left: 400; top: 340;
    → visibility:
visible;font: 136px times;
→ color:#CCCCCC;">L</div>
    <div id="object6" style="position:
    → absolute; left: 400; top: 340;
    → visibility:
visible;font: 136px times;
→ color:#FFFFFF;">!</div>
</body>
</html>
```

▲ `Ypos`. Sets the position from the top of the page around which the objects will center. You can change this value.

3. `function objectsFloat() {...}`

Add `objectsFloat()` to the JavaScript. This function repositions each object, using a formula that causes them to appear to spin in an elliptical orbit around `Xpos/Ypos`. The function loops recursively until the page is unloaded.

4. `onload="objectsFloat()"`

In the `<body>` tag of the Web page, add an `onload` event handler to trigger the `objectsFloat()` function.

5. `<div id="object1" style="position:`
`→ absolute; left: 300; top: 140;`
`→ visibility: visible;font: 136px`
`→ times; color:#000000;">...</div>`

Set up the CSS layers for the objects that you will be floating, using a `<div>` tag defined with an ID and style attributes (see "Adding CSS to an HTML Tag" in Chapter 2). The style defines the object as being positioned absolutely, includes an initial top and left position, and includes any other definitions desired.

✔ Tips

■ Although this example triggered the floating objects with the `onload` event handler, you can trigger the floating from any event handler you choose.

■ You can place any content in the CSS layer, but the larger the object, the choppier the animation will appear.

■ I placed the style definitions within the `<div>` tag for each of the six layers. But I could have just as easily have set up six different IDs in a `<style>` tag or used an external CSS file (see "Adding CSS to a Web Page" and "Adding CSS to a Web Site" in Chapter 2).

Creating Transparent Graphics in PNG Format

The most promising alternative to GIF is PNG (Portable Network Graphics), a standardized, patent-free graphic format supported by the World Wide Web Consortium (W3C). This format has several features that make it a superior choice over GIF.

Most important, this format allows you to create transparent graphics. Rather than being solid, the graphics' colors are translucent, allowing content below them to show through—something that GIF cannot do (**Figure 26.13**). The following tasks describe how to create PNG graphics using either Adobe Photoshop or Macromedia Fireworks.

To create a PNG graphic in Photoshop:

1. Open a new graphic document in RGB mode at 72 dpi, and set the background to transparent (**Figure 26.14**).

    Allow extra working space in defining the initial size of the graphic.

GIF ⌐   PNG ⌐

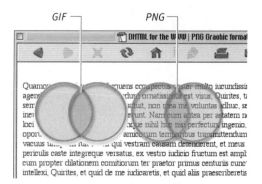

Figure 26.13 Both images are the same, but the first graphic was saved as a GIF and the second as a PNG. Notice that the GIF image covers the text even in transparent areas, while the text shows through the PNG.

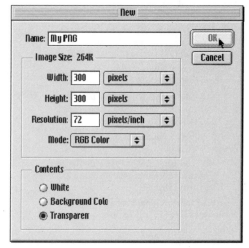

Figure 26.14 Photoshop's New dialog box. The new image should be 72 dpi, RGB, with a transparent background.

CREATING TRANSPARENT GRAPHICS IN PNG FORMAT

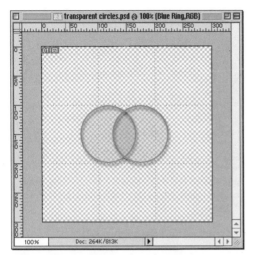

Figure 26.15 The image in Photoshop: two intersecting rings with their interior opacity set to 25%. The rings also have a slight drop shadow.

2. Create a graphic.

The graphic can use drop shadows and other transparency effects, and different layers can have different opacities (**Figure 26.15**). When the image is complete, crop the image or use the slice tool to get the desired size.

3. Choose File > Save for Web.

The Save for Web dialog box opens.

4. From the Settings drop-down menu, choose PNG-24, check the Transparency checkbox, and click OK (**Figure 26.16**).

The Save Optimized As dialog box opens.

5. Type the name of the image, preserving the .png extension.

6. Navigate to the folder in which you want to save the image, and click Save (**Figure 26.17**).

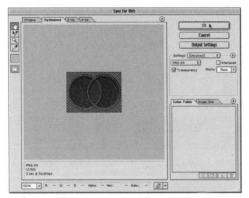

Figure 26.16 Photoshop's Save for Web dialog box. The image format needs to be set to PNG-24.

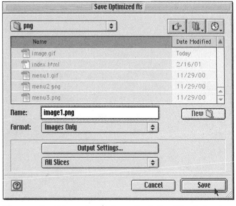

Figure 26.17 Photoshop's Save Optimized As dialog box.

To create a PNG graphic in Fireworks:

1. Open a new graphic document at 72 dpi, and set the background to transparent (**Figure 26.18**).

   Allow extra working space in defining the initial size of the graphic.

2. Create a graphic.

   The graphic can use drop shadows and other transparency effects, and different layers can have different opacities (**Figure 26.19**). When the image is complete, crop the image or use the slice tool to get the desired size.

3. In the Optimize (Document) control panel, set the format to PNG 24 (**Figure 26.20**). If you don't see the Optimize control panel, select Window>Optimize and it should appear.

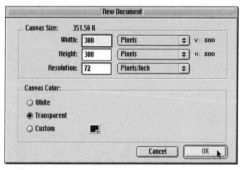

Figure 26.18 Fireworks' New Document dialog box. The new image should be 72 dpi with a transparent background.

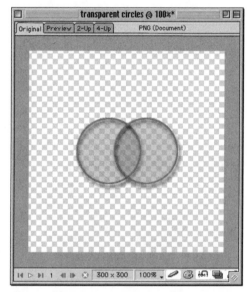

Figure 26.19 The image in Fireworks: two intersecting rings with their interior opacity set to 25%. The rings also have a slight drop shadow.

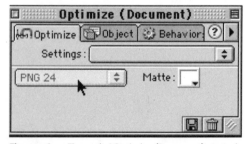

Figure 26.20 Fireworks' Optimize (Document) control panel. The image format should be set to PNG 24.

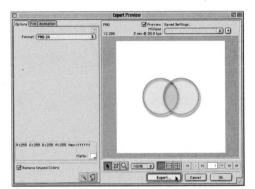

Figure 26.21 Fireworks' Export Preview dialog box. If you forgot to set the image format to PNG 24 in step 3, you can do it here as well.

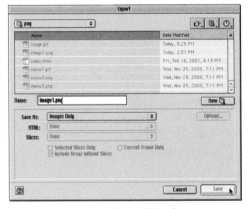

Figure 26.22 Fireworks' Export dialog box.

4. Choose File > Export Preview.

   The Export Preview dialog box opens (**Figure 26.21**).

5. Make sure the Format drop-down menu is set to PNG 24; then click Export.

   The Export dialog box opens.

6. Type the name of the image, preserving the .png extension.

7. Navigate to the folder in which you want to save the image, and click Save (**Figure 26.22**).

CREATING TRANSPARENT GRAPHICS IN PNG FORMAT

To use a PNG graphic on a Web page:

◆ `<img src="image1.png" width="164"`
   `→ height="116" border="0"`
   `→ alt="Two Circles">`

Type the `<img>` tag, and use the URL of the PNG image you created in the preceding exercise as the source (**Code 26.7**). Because PNG is just another image format, you can use the `<img>` tag to include PNG graphics. Because some browsers do not support this format fully—or even at all— you may want to include `alt` text.

✔ Tips

■ Unfortunately, the PNG format has two major drawbacks that have prevented it from wide adoption: (1) It cannot create animations, and (2) it is not supported in browsers before Version 4. In fact, many of PNG's best features (including transparency) are not supported by many of the browsers that can display this format, so use it with caution.

■ With PNG, you no longer have to worry about the background color you set when you created the image. The antialiased pixels adapt to any background.

Code 26.7 The code shows a PNG graphic being placed in a CSS layer, which is in turn positioned over the text.

```
<html>
<head>
    <style type="text/css">
body  { color: black; font-size: 14px;
→ line-height: 16px; font-family: Times,
→ "Times New Roman", Georgia, serif;
→ background-color: white; }
#overlay  { position: absolute; top: 25px;
→ left: 25px; visibility: visible; }
    </style>
</head>
<body>
    <div id="overlay">
        <img src="image1.gif" width="164"
        → height="116" border="0" alt="Two
        → Circles">
    <img src="image1.png" width="164"
    → height="116" border="0" alt="Two
    → Circles">
    </div>
    <p>Quamquam mihi semper frequens
    → conspectus vester multo iucundissimus,
    → hic autem locus ad agendum
    → amplissimus...</p>
</body>
</html>
```

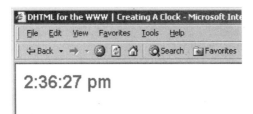

Figure 26.23 The clock, displaying the visitor's local time.

Code 26.8 The code writes itself into a layer recursively, updating the time every second.

```
                        code
<html>
<head>
    <script>
function countThis(){
    if (!document.layers&&!document.all)
    → return
    var Digital=new Date();
    var hours=Digital.getHours();
    var minutes=Digital.getMinutes();
    var seconds=Digital.getSeconds();
    var dn="am"
    if (hours>12){
        dn="pm"
        hours=hours-12
    }
    if (hours==0) hours=12;
    if (minutes<=9) minutes="0"+minutes;
    if (seconds<=9) seconds="0"+seconds;
    countDown='<span class="clockStyle">'
    → +hours+':'+minutes+':'+seconds+'
    → '+dn+'</span>';
    if (document.layers){
        document.layers.clock.document.
        → write(countDown)
document.layers.clock.document.close()
}
    else if (document.all)
    → clock.innerHTML=countDown
    setTimeout("countThis()",1000)
}
```

(code continues on next page)

Creating a Clock

As Groucho Marx said, "Time flies like an arrow, and fruit flies like a banana." If you are designing a site where users may enter time-sensitive information, or if you just want to remind visitors of how much time they are spending on the Web, you may want to include a clock on your Web page.

This clock displays the local time reported by the visitor's computer (**Figure 26.23**). This function does not work in Netscape 6.

To add a clock to your Web page:

1. `function countThis(){...}`
   Add `countThis()` to the JavaScript. This function checks the hours, minutes, and seconds reported by the computer's clock, translates this data from military format to a.m./p.m. format, and writes that information in the **counter** CSS layer. The function runs recursively until the page is unloaded (**Code 26.8**).

2. `#clock {...}`
   Create an ID called **clock**, which defines the clock's layer. Give this layer a position, width, and height, depending on the font size you define in **clockStyle** (step 3).

3. `.clockStyle {...}`
   Create a class called **clockStyle**, which defines the appearance of the clock. The clock can be small or large, depending on the font size.

4. `onLoad="countThis()"`
   Add the **onload** event handler to the `<body>` tag, and have it trigger the **countThis()** function. This step starts the clock.

   continues on next page

CREATING A CLOCK

5. `<div id="clock"></div>`

Create the clock layer: a `<div>` tag with `id` set to `clock` and `class` set to `clockStyle`.

✔ Tip

■ This time is very different from the server and GMT time code I showed you in "Using Server-Side Includes" in Chapter 23. This clock shows (and updates every second) the local time as set on the visitor's computer. Thus, if a visitor has their time set incorrectly, this clock will display the wrong time.

Code 26.8 *continued*

```
          </script>
          <style type="text/css">
#clock {position: absolute; top: 10px;
→ left: 10px; height: 20px; width: 200px;
→ z-index: 201; }
.clockStyle { font: bold 25px
→ helvetica,arial; }
          </style>
</head>
      <body onLoad="countThis()">
      <div id="clock"></div>
      </body>
</html>
```

MULTIMEDIA

Ever since the Web has become a predominant medium, the big promise has been "in a few months, we'll have multimedia just like CD-ROMs." And after a few months, the promise was still "in a few months, we'll have multimedia just like CD-ROMs." And after a few more months...

Today, we still don't have anything approaching the performance of multimedia delivered on CD-ROM. Although Macromedia Flash can do some impressive things, video and sound still lag far behind.

Sound and moving images, collectively referred to as multimedia, come at a high price for the amount of information conveyed. Due to their raw size, multimedia files can take a large chunk of time to move across the Web, even over the fastest Internet connections. In addition, they usually deliver subpar results compared with other media, such as TV, CD, and DVD. Still, multimedia promises new levels of dynamic interactivity on the Web—after the bandwidth dilemma is sorted out.

In this chapter, I'll introduce some of the top contenders for adding multimedia to your Web site. This chapter does not examine each topic thoroughly; instead, it tells you about some of the possibilities.

Adding Sound

Both Netscape and Internet Explorer come with built-in sound capabilities, making it easy to embed in a Web page sound files that can play in the background (**Figure 27.1**), or that users can control.

This section shows you how to place the sound file in a Web page by using two tags — <object> and <embed>—simultaneously. Although the <embed> tag is more universally recognized by browsers, the <object> tag is the standardized tag and will be used increasingly in the future. Adding both versions now should not interfere with the playback and should ensure the greatest compatibility (**Code 27.1**).

Figure 27.1 Although no visual cues let you know that a sound is playing on this page, the sound of distant alien winds is playing in the background.

Code 27.1 The sound file is included on the page, but the controls are hidden. Only one set of tags is needed, but including both the <object> and <embed> tags ensures future compatibility.

```
<html>
<head>
    <style type="text/css">
body { background-image:
→ url(mars1_pathfinder.jpg); }
    </style>
</head>
<body>
    <h1>Welcome to my world...</h1>
    <object width="100" height="100">
        <param name="hidden" value="true">
        <param name="loop" value="true">
        <param name="autostart" value="true">
        <param name="src" value="ambiant.wav">
        <embed src="ambiant.wav" width="100"
        → height="100" autostart="true"
        → loop="true" hidden="true">
    </object>
</body>
</html>
```

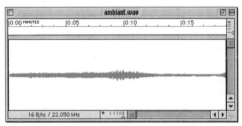

Figure 27.2 A visual representation of a sound file. This is what you would see if you opened the file in a sound editing program.

Table 27.1

Important Sound Attributes		
PARAMETER NAME	**VALUES**	**WHAT IT DOES**
src	\<url\>	The location of the sound file
hidden	true false	Whether the controls show up on the screen
loop	true false	Whether the sound repeats
autostart	true false	Whether the sound plays immediately after the page loads
pluginpage	\<url\>	Location of page to find sound plug-in

To add ambient sound to a Web page:

1. `ambiant.wav`

   First, you need a sound file to be played (**Figure 27.2**). The file can be in a variety of formats, including WAV (.wav), MIDI (.mid), AU (.au), and QuickTime (.mov).

2. `<object>`

   In the `<body>` of your HTML document, add the `<object>` tag to open an object container.

3. `<param name="hidden" value="true">`

   Within the object container, add the parameters for the object, using the `<param>` tag. **Table 27.1** lists common parameters and values to define for sound.

4. `<embed src="ambiant.wav"`
   `→ autostart="true" loop="true"`
   `→ hidden="true">`

   Within the object container, add the `<embed>` tag, defining its attributes the same way you defined the parameters in step 3.

5. `</object>`

   Close the object container.

✔ Tips

■ The download times for sound files are high even for a short audio clip. (The 10-second loop I used in this example is larger than 800 KB.) You can further compress the sound in other ways, such as by using MP3 files, but not all browsers support newer, better sound formats.

■ Not only would you potentially annoy your visitors with long download times, but to many people, sound files are the aural equivalent to the `<blink>` tag. If you use sound, make sure it is for a good reason.

ADDING SOUND

487

Adding a GIF Animation

Remember when you got your first paperback dictionary as a kid? The first thing I did with mine (it was 1977) was create flip movies of X-wing and TIE fighters battling in the margins. I would draw one small picture in the right margin of the first page; draw another picture just like it but moved up or down slightly on the next page; and so on for several dozen pages. When I flipped through the pages of the dictionary, I had my movie of the X-wing swooping in and destroying the TIE fighter.

The Graphic Interchange Format—GIF, to its friends—allows you to set up your own flip-book animation. Although the tools, the medium, and the method of distribution have radically changed since my dictionary flip book, the technique for creating animation is pretty much the same: You draw a picture on one layer, draw the same picture on the next layer but move it just slightly, and so on. When you play back these images, the object appears to be moving.

A variety of tools allow you to create GIF images and animations, but Macromedia Fireworks and Adobe ImageReady both include drawing and animation functions in the same package.

To create a GIF animation in Fireworks:

1. In Fireworks, open a new document at 72 dpi, and set the canvas to the desired size (**Figure 27.3**).

   As with all graphics, larger canvas sizes mean larger files and longer download times.

2. In the Optimize palette, choose animated GIF from the top drop-down menu (**Figure 27.4**).

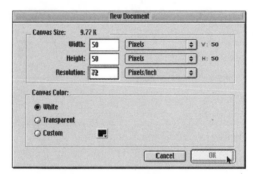

Figure 27.3 The New Document dialog box in Fireworks. Make sure the new document's resolution is set to 72 dpi.

Figure 27.4 The image type needs to be set to Animated GIF.

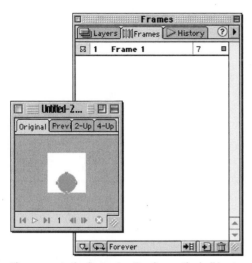

Figure 27.5 In the first animation frame, the ball is at the bottom of the image.

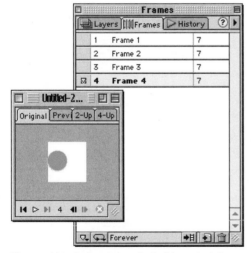

Figure 27.6 In the last frame, the ball is on the left side of the screen, after having traveled to the right and top in previous frames.

3. Add an image to the first frame of the animation (**Figure 27.5**).

4. Add more frames, with images in each frame.

The easiest way to do this is to simply duplicate the first frame and then move the object from one frame to the next (**Figure 27.6**). You can also use the Frame palette to set the animation to play once or loop.

5. When you finish creating your animation, choose File > Export.

The Export dialog box opens.

6. Type the name of the image (making sure to preserve the .gif extension), navigate to the folder in which you want to save the image, and click Save.

To create a GIF animation in ImageReady:

1. In ImageReady, open a new document and set the canvas to the desired size (**Figure 27.7**).

    As with all graphics, larger canvas sizes mean larger files and longer download times.

2. Add an image to the first frame of the animation (**Figure 27.8**).

3. Add more frames, with images in each frame.

    The easiest way to do this is to simply duplicate the first frame and then move the object from one frame to the next (**Figure 27.9**). You can also use the Frame palette to set the animation to play once or loop.

4. When you have finish creating your animation, choose File > Save Optimized.

    The Save Optimized dialog box opens.

5. Type the name of the image (making sure to preserve the .gif extension), navigate to the folder in which you want to save the image, and click Save.

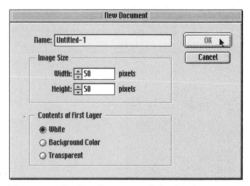

Figure 27.7 The New Document dialog box in ImageReady. The program assumes 72 dpi for all images.

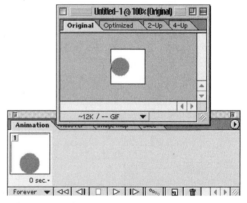

Figure 27.8 In the first animation frame, the ball is at the bottom of the image.

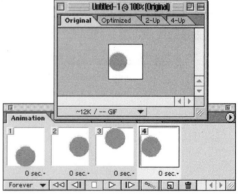

Figure 27.9 In the last frame, the ball is on the left side of the screen, after having traveled to the right and top in previous frame.

Code 27.2 In the code, an <img> link to an animated GIF is identical to an <img> link to any GIF.

```
                        code
<html>
<body>
    <img src="redBall.gif" width="50"
    → height="50" border="0">
</body>
</html>
```

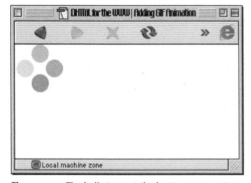

Figure 27.10 The ball starts at the bottom; moves to the right, to the top, and to the left; and then starts all over again.

To add a GIF animation to your Web page:

◆ <img src="redBall.gif" width="50"
  → height="50" border="0">

Adding a GIF animation to a Web page works just like adding any other GIF image (**Code 27.2** and **Figure 27.10**).

✔ Tips

■ If you do not already own ImageReady or Fireworks, an assortment of free or inexpensive GIF animation tools are available on the Web. For the Mac, I recommend GIFBuilder, and for Windows, I recommend GIF Construction Set (see Appendix E). You can download both of these programs from www.download.com.

■ Remember that although an animated GIF may occupy the same physical space as a similar static GIF, each frame of the GIF is an entire image, adding that much more to the file size and download time.

ADDING A GIF ANIMATION

What is GIF animation good for?

GIF animations have been with us for a while—you have no doubt seen them gaping or blinking at you on pages around the Web. Yes, they add noise to more Web pages than I care to think about, but that does not mean they cannot be used to make Web pages more informative, attractive, and dynamic. You just need to know how to use them effectively.

I have placed examples of each of the following ideas online—check out `www.webbedenvironments.com/dhtml/gifanimate` to see them in action.

JavaScript rollovers. Most Web sites use JavaScript rollovers to change a button's graphic when the visitor places the mouse over it (**Figure 27.11**). This technique gives visitors visual feedback about the button they are about to click (see "Swapping Images" in Chapter 25). Because these graphics are GIFs, you can use an animated GIF for the rollover. I created two graphics, one for the button's off state and one for the ready state (when the mouse rolls over it). The off state is a static arrow; the ready state flashes the arrow on and off.

Note: Netscape 4 seems to have problems if you use too many animated GIFs in rollovers on the same page. I recommend using one rollover graphic (such as the arrow) and reusing it on the page.

ADDING A GIF ANIMATION

Figure 27.11 This example acts like a normal JavaScript rollover, but the new image is an animated GIF that flashes on and off.

Backgrounds. For a long time, animated GIFs did not work as background graphics; at least, they would not animate. You would see either the first or last frame of the animation (depending on the browser) as the tiling background graphic, but nothing else happened. Both browsers, however, now support animated background GIFs (**Figure 27.12**). Animation in a background can be highly distracting, though, so use this feature sparingly.

Illustrations. One of the most obvious, yet overlooked, uses for animated GIFs is to improve illustrations (**Figure 27.13**). For example, illustrating a step-by-step process (such as how to install RAM in your computer) is difficult with static images. You can demonstrate the process far more clearly by using GIF animation, showing the actual movement required to insert a RAM module and then snap it into place.

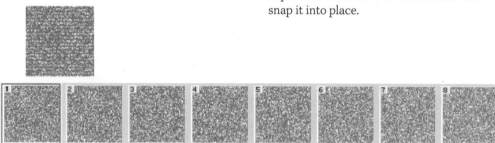

Figure 27.12 Each frame contains visual noise—which, when tiled in a background, looks like television static.

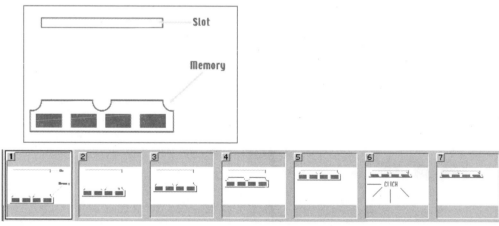

Figure 27.13 The illustration shows the movement needed to snap the memory chip into the slot.

Slide shows. If you want to display several images in a limited amount of space, you can use GIF animation to set up a slide show (**Figure 27.14**). Rather than show fluid motion, as in the preceding examples, you simply place each image in its own frame and then set how much time you want to pause before the next image appears. If you loop this setup, the slide show will continue infinitely. Depending on the images you are using, though, looping can lead to large files that take forever to download. Remember that each frame of a GIF animation is a GIF, and the file size adds up as you include more frames.

Figure 27.14 These are some snapshots I took in England.

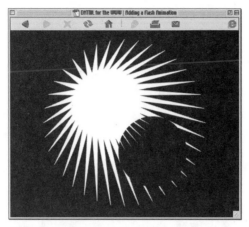

Figure 27.15 The Flash animation in mid-play. The moon has started gliding across the surface of the sun.

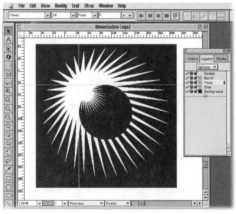

Figure 27.16 Although Flash has some fairly sophisticated drawing tools and can even render some complex gradients, I created the logo in another vector drawing program. This file included each of the elements to be animated in separate layers: star, moon, and burst.

Adding a Flash Animation

Flash originally was intended to offer an alternative animation format to GIF animation for the Web. Although it can offer much more than that now, Flash is still an excellent choice for adding simple animations with a small file size, and you can still use it for that purpose in conjunction with DHTML.

For the Flash animation shown in **Figure 27.15**, I wanted to add movement to a logo. The logo is a moon covering a sun, with a starburst glow coming off the edge of the moon. I wanted to animate the moon slowly moving across and then eclipsing the sun.

To create a Flash animation:

1. Create the Flash images from scratch, or import vector graphics from other programs by choosing File > Import in Flash (**Figure 27.16**).

continues on next page

2. In the Import dialog box, make sure you preserve the layers from your imported file, then click OK (**Figure 27.17**).

All of the layers you created in the original document should be represented in Flash's timeline window (**Figure 27.18**).

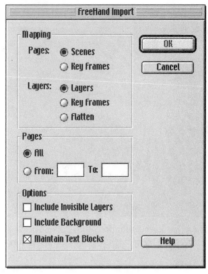

Figure 27.17 The Import dialog box allows you to preserve layers created in other programs (in this case, FreeHand) for use in Flash.

Keyframe

Timelines

Layers

Stage

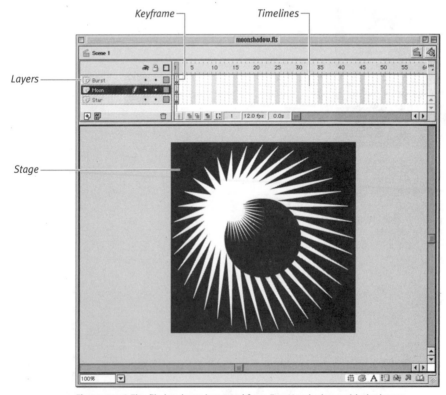

Figure 27.18 The file has been imported from FreeHand, along with the layers.

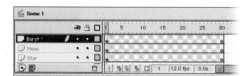

Figure 27.19 Like a filmstrip, a Flash animation is made up of still frames. As each frame plays back in sequence, the result is the illusion of action. In Flash, you set up keyframes to define the starting and stopping points of the action. For this movie, the animation lasted about 2.5 seconds, so I set keyframes by selecting the first frame of all three layers and inserted a keyframe into the 30th frame (2.4 seconds later).

3. To specify the length of the animation, select the frames for each layer below the time you want to use for the duration, then choose Insert > Keyframe (**Figure 27.19**).

This step establishes a stopping point for the animation.

4. To animate an object, select a starting-point frame in the layer that contains the object you want to animate, and move the object on the stage to its starting position (**Figure 27.20**).

If the frame is not currently a keyframe, choose Insert > Keyframe.

continues on next page

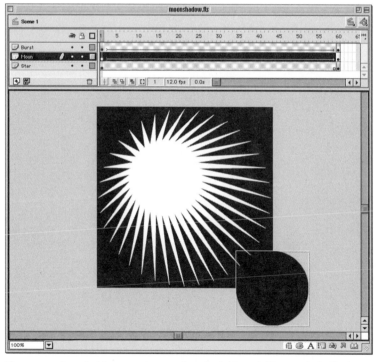

Figure 27.20 I wanted the moon to move from the bottom-right corner to its final position below the starburst. To do this, I set its starting position by selecting frame 1 in the moon layer, clicking the moon, and moving it down to the position where I wanted it to start.

ADDING A FLASH ANIMATION

5. Select the frames between the starting and stopping points of the animation, then open the Frame palette and choose Motion from the Tweening drop-down menu (**Figure 27.21**).

   Flash calculates a straight path between the starting and stopping positions and fills in the intervening frames.

6. To preview the animation, choose Control > Play.

   You can save the Flash file in its native format to edit it later. To use it as an animation on the Web, however, you have to export the Flash movie in Shockwave format (.swf).

7. Choose File > Export Movie to display the Export dialog box, type a file name (making sure to preserve the .swf extension), and click Save.

   The program displays a new dialog box, asking you about the export options.

8. Click OK to accept the default options.

Now you need to place the animation that you just created in a Web page.

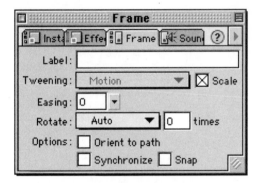

Figure 27.21 In the Frame palette, you can set tweening. This specifies how the frames in between the two keyframes should act, changing an object's position (motion) or shape.

Table 27.2

Important SWF Attributes		
PARAMETER NAME	VALUE(S)	WHAT IT DOES
movie	\<url>	The location of the .swf file
quality	best high auto high auto low low	The quality at which the animation is rendered
loop	true false	Whether the animation repeats
play	true false	Whether the animation plays immediately after the page loads
pluginpage	\<url>	Location of page to find Flash plug-in

To embed the Flash animation in a Web page:

1. **\<object>**

   In the **\<body>** of your HTML document, add the **\<object>** tag to open an object container (**Code 27.3**).

2. **\<param name="movie" value="logo.swf">**

   Within the object container, add the parameters for the object, using the **\<param>** tag. **Table 27.2** lists parameters and values to define for sound.

   continues on next page

Code 27.3 The Shockwave file (.swf) created in Flash is being included in the Web page and will resize itself to fill the available window space.

```
<html>
<head>
   <style type="text/css">
body { background-color: black }
   </style>
</head>
<body>
   <div align="center">
      <object codebase="http://download.macromedia.com/pub/shockwave/cabs/flash/
      → swflash.cab#version=4,0,2,0" width="400" height="400" align="middle"
      → name="MoonshadowNM">
         <param name="loop" value="false">
         <param name="movie" value="logo.swf">
         <param name="quality" value="best">
         <param name="play" value="true">
         <embed src="logo.swf" type="application/x-shockwave-flash" width="400" height="400"
         → pluginspage="http://www.macromedia.com/shockwave/download/index.cgi?P1_Prod_Version=
         → ShockwaveFlash" quality="best" play="true" align="middle" name="MoonshadowNM"
         → loop="false">
      </object>
   </div>
</body>
</html>
```

ADDING A FLASH ANIMATION

3. <embed>

Within the object container, add the <embed> tag, defining its attributes the same way you defined the parameters in step 2.

4. </object>

Close the object container.

✔ Tips

■ Although the tag pairs are redundant, including both the <object> and <embed> tags ensures forward compatibility. Most browsers today use the <embed> tag, but the <object> tag is the officially sanctioned standard and will be used in future browsers.

■ Look at the final result, and notice that no matter how the browser window is sized, the Flash animation resizes to fit in the window. I set the width and height attributes to 95%, which fills most of the window regardless of the window's size. Why not use 100%? This setting sometimes causes the movie to be clipped by the browser window's edges. At 95%, close is close enough.

■ Not only does a GIF animation not resize to fill the available space, but the same animation as a GIF is 51 KB vs. 5 KB for the .swf file.

■ You can use a Flash animation for most of the same things as a GIF animation (refer to the sidebar "What Is GIF Animation Good For?" earlier in this chapter).

Figure 27.22 The video plays back in the window. In this example, the controls have been removed. This setup looks cleaner, but it prevents the visitor from changing the sound or backing the movie up to watch it again.

Adding Video

Video has been available over the Web since the mid-1990s. Although the size, quality, and speed of Web video have improved, it still lags far behind video over satellite or cable TV. But the Web does offer certain advantages for delivery that are not available in other media. Most obvious: You do not have to own a TV station to broadcast (**Figure 27.22**).

You can broadcast movies over the Web in several formats, including RealMedia, Windows Media, and MPEG. In this example (**Code 27.4**), I'll show you how to use QuickTime.

Code 27.4 The QuickTime video is being included in the page. The text will float around it to the right.

```
<html>
<head>
    <style type="text/css">
body { color: #9c6; font-size: 24px; font-family: "Times New Roman", Georgia, Times, serif;
→ background-color: #600; text-align: center }
    </style>
</head>
<body>
    <object style="float: left" width="240" height="180">
        <param name="loop" value="true">
        <param name="playeveryframe" value="true">
        <param name="cache" value="true">
```

(code continues on next page)

To add a QuickTime movie:

1. `JocelynWeb.mov`

   First, you need a QuickTime movie to play. Many software programs can create these movies, but my favorite is iMovie from Apple (**Figure 27.23**).

2. `<object>`

   In the `<body>` of your HTML document, add the `<object>` tag to open an object container.

3. `<param name="src"`
   `→ value="JocelynWeb.mov">`

   Within the object container, add the parameters for the object, using the `<param>` tag. **Table 27.3** lists common parameters and values to define for QuickTime video.

4. `<embed>`

   Within the object container, add the `<embed>` tag, defining its attributes the same way you defined the parameters in step 3.

5. `</object>`

   Close the object container.

Figure 27.23 iMovie is a fun and simple way to create QuickTime movies on the Mac.

Code 27.4 *continued*

```
                                     code
        <param name="controller" value="false">
        <param name="autoplay" value="true">
        <param name="src" value="JocelynWeb.mov">
        <embed style="float: left" src="JocelynWeb.mov" width="240" height="180" autoplay="true"
        → controller="false" cache="true" type="video/quicktime" playeveryframe="true"
        → loop="true">
    </object>
    <p>A Day in the Life...<br>
    Jocelyn Cranford Teague</p>
</body>
</html>
```

Table 27.3

Important QuickTime Attributes		
PARAMETER NAME	VALUES	WHAT IT DOES
src	<url>	The location of the QuickTime file to be played
cache	true false	Whether the movie should be saved to the visitor's cache for faster playback
loop	true false	Whether the sound repeats
autoplay	true false	Whether the sound plays immediately after the page loads
playeveryframe	true false	Prevents skipping but may slow playback
volume	0 to 100	Controls volume
pluginpage	<url>	Location of page to find QuickTime plug-in

✔ Tips

■ Although the tag pairs are redundant, including both the <object> and <embed> tags ensures forward compatibility. Most browsers today use the <embed> tag, but the <object> tag is the officially sanctioned standard and will be used in future browsers.

■ You can wrap text around the video (or any <object> tag, for that matter) by including the float property in the <object> and <embed> tags (see "Wrapping Text Around an Element" in Chapter 7).

■ You can have sound in the same file as the video, but it will increase the file size.

■ To learn more about making iMovies, check out Scott Smith's *Making iMovies*, also from Peachpit Press.

ADDING VIDEO

Adding a Java Applet

Java is a programming language that allows you to incorporate small programs (called *applets*) into your Web pages. Although I don't have the space in this book to show you how to create Java applets, you can find plenty of free applets on the Web, and they are easy to place in your Web pages. Java is great for adding everything from chat rooms to search engines to clocks to your Web site (**Figure 27.24**).

To add a Java applet to your Web page:

1. `BillsClock.class`

   First, create or download a Java applet.

2. `<applet>`

   Type the `<applet>` tag in the `<body>` of your HTML document (**Code 27.5**), and include a `code` attribute that includes the URL of the Java applet, the `width` and `height`, and the `codebase` (if applicable).

Figure 27.24 The Java clock is ticking away. I got this free Clock applet by William Giel from Freeware Java.

What Is the Difference Between Java and JavaScript?

Java is a *programming* language developed by Sun Microsystems that you can use to write standalone software applications that do not require a Web browser. In addition, you can use Java to write applets (small applications) that run on a Web page.

JavaScript is a *scripting* language developed by Netscape Communications Corp. that controls the HTML on a Web page. It is primarily intended to be used in a Web browser.

Scripting languages and programming languages may be able to do similar things. Scripting languages generally are easier to learn and use but more limited in what they can accomplish.

Code 27.5 The `<applet>` tag is only the tip of the Java iceberg. The real Java code is in the `class` file that's being imported.

```
                      code
<html>
<head>
   <style type="text/css">
body { color: #9f3; font-weight: bold;
→ font-size: 24px; font-family: Arial,
→ Helvetica, Geneva, sans-serif; background-
→ color: #000; text-align: center }
   </style>
</head>
<body>
   <applet code="BillsClock.class"
   → width="300" height="300"
   → codebase="bills_clock"
   → alt="Clock"></applet>
   <p>Greenwich Mean Time</p>
</body>
</html>
```

✔ Tips

- You can find free Java applets in a variety of places on the Web. Freeware Java (www.freewarejava.com) is where I got Bill's clock, shown in Figure 27.24. It was created by William Giel.

- Whether a visitor's browser can run the Java applet depends on several factors, including the level of Java support in her operating system.

ADDING A JAVA APPLET

DEBUGGING YOUR CODE

28

If you are using CSS or DHTML to create your Web pages, eventually you will have bugs. Like death and taxes, problems with your code are inescapable.

I have tested and retested the code in this book on the most popular browsers and operating systems available and hope that it is as bug-free as humanly possible. You will inevitably have to adapt the code for your own use, however. You will have to change variables, values, URLs, and styles. You may have to combine code from different examples. You may even have to write your own functions from scratch.

This means bugs.

In this chapter, I'll guide you through some of the most common problems, help you identify and fix them, and (I hope) keep you from smashing your monitor with a heavy mallet when things go wrong.

Troubleshooting CSS

All too often, you carefully set up your style-sheet rules, go to your browser, and see... nothing. Don't worry, this happens to everyone.

Check the following

There are many things you might have done that are preventing your style-sheet rules from working properly; most of them are easily spotted. **Figure 28.1** points out some common problems you may encounter.

♦ **Are the properties you are using available for your platform and browser?** Many properties are not supported by Internet Explorer and/or Netscape, depending on the operating system being used. Check Appendix B to see whether the property works with the intended browser and OS.

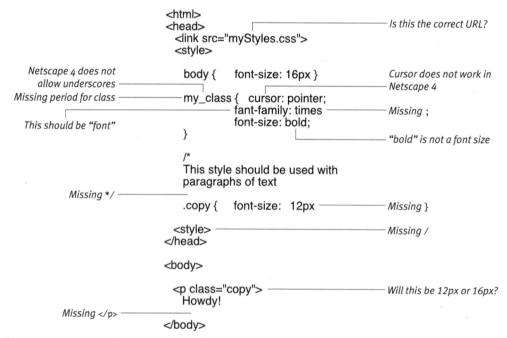

Figure 28.1 Errors are inevitable, but don't let them ruin your day. This figure shows examples of some of the most common CSS problems you may encounter.

◆ **Does your selector contain typos?**
If you forget the opening period or number sign (#) for classes and IDs, they won't work. Also, Netscape 4 does not allow underscores in IDs or classes.

◆ **Do the properties contain typos?**
Typos in one property can cause the entire rule to fail.

◆ **Are the values that you are using permitted for that property?**
Using improper values may cause a definition to fail or behave unpredictably.

◆ **Are you missing any semicolons?**
A missing semicolon at the end of a definition will cause the entire rule to fail.

◆ **Did you open and close the definition list with curly brackets?** If not, there is no telling what will happen.

◆ **Did you remember to close all your multi-line comment tags?** If not, the rest of the CSS is treated as a comment (see "Adding Comments to CSS" in Chapter 2).

◆ **Are the HTML tags set correctly in the document?** Remember that you have to use an end </p> to make the paragraph tag work properly with CSS (see "Kinds of HTML Tags" in Chapter 1).

◆ **If your rules are in the head, did you use the <style> tag correctly?**
Typos in the <style> style tag mean that none of the definitions is used (see "Adding CSS to a Web Page" in Chapter 2).

continues on next page

TROUBLESHOOTING CSS

◆ **If you are linking or importing style sheets, are you retrieving the correct file?** Check the exact path for the file. Also, remember that you should not include the `<style>` tag in an external CSS file (see "Adding CSS to a Web Site" in Chapter 2).

◆ **Do you have multiple, perhaps conflicting, rules for the same tag?** Check your cascade order (see "Determining the Cascade Order" in Chapter 2).

If all else fails, try these ideas

If you've looked for the above errors and still can't get your code to work, try these ideas.

◆ **Delete the rules and retype them.** When you can't see what's wrong, retyping code from scratch sometimes fixes it.

◆ **Test the same code on another browser and/or OS.** It's possible that a property is buggy and doesn't work correctly in your browser. It's even possible that the browser does not allow that property to work with that tag.

◆ **Give up and walk away from the project.** Just joking, though you might want to think about taking a 15-minute break before looking at the problem again.

◆ **If nothing else works, try a different solution to the design problem.**

Figure 28.2 The W3C's CSS Validator.

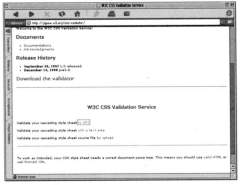

Figure 28.3 I want the validator to check out a CSS file online.

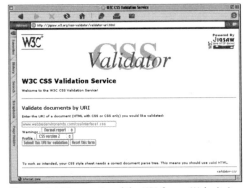

Figure 28.4 I have entered the URL for my Web site's external CSS file.

Validating Your CSS

Although both Dreamweaver and GoLive will make sure your CSS code is accurate, the World Wide Web Consortium (W3C) provides a Web site called the CSS Validator that lets you check your CSS to confirm that it meets the requirements set in the W3C standards (**Figure 28.2**).

To use the W3C's CSS Validator:

1. Point your Web browser to jigsaw.w3.org/css-validator/.

2. Specify the method by which you want to validate your CSS (**Figure 28.3**).

    You can enter a URL (*by URI*), enter the CSS code directly in a form (*with a text area*), or upload your file(s) (*by upload*). In this example, you will submit a URL.

3. Enter the URL of the Web site or style sheet (**Figure 28.4**).

    I recommend entering the *exact* URL of the style sheet.

continues on next page

4. Specify how you want warnings to be presented and the type of validation you want to use (usually, CSS2), then click Submit This URI for Validation.

The validation takes only a few seconds. You are given a report of errors and other possible problems in your CSS (**Figure 28.5**).

✔ Tips

■ Anyone who creates a Web page can display the Made with CSS icon (**Figure 28.6**); however, only pages that pass muster with the CSS Validator should display the Valid CSS icon (**Figure 28.7**).

■ Although you do not have to have valid CSS for the browser to display your code, the validation process often helps locate code errors.

Figure 28.6 Say it loud, say it proud: made with CSS.

Figure 28.7 If your CSS passes muster, you too can display the Valid CSS icon.

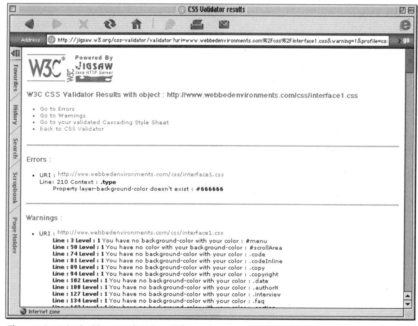

Figure 28.5 It looks like I need to do a little work to get my CSS up to snuff.

Figure 28.8 Type javascript: in the location bar.

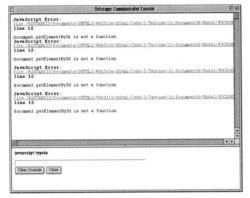

Figure 28.9 The error screen in Netscape 4.

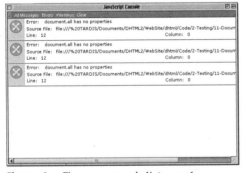

Figure 28.10 The error screen in Netscape 6.

Troubleshooting JavaScript

Although JavaScript is not a true programming language like Java (see the sidebar "What Is the Difference Between Java and JavaScript?" in Chapter 27), you still must use logic to construct the actions that should take place. Things inevitably go wrong.

Unlike CSS, though, JavaScript does not require you to eyeball the code to figure out what's wrong. Most browsers display an error message that details what went wrong and where.

To view JavaScript errors:

◆ In Netscape 4, type javascript: in the browser's location bar (**Figure 28.8**). A window like the one shown in **Figure 28.9** appears. It displays any JavaScript errors that occur in open windows.

◆ In Netscape 6, choose Tasks > Tools > JavaScript Console. A window like the one shown in **Figure 28.10** appears. It displays any JavaScript errors that occur in open windows.

continues on next page

◆ In Internet Explorer, JavaScript errors appear as soon as they occur unless you set your preferences not to show errors (**Figure 28.11**).

After the error has been detected and located, you can check the code and even use JavaScript to track down the problem (**Figure 28.12**).

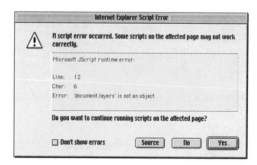

Figure 28.11 An error message in Internet Explorer.

```
<html>
<head>
  <script language="javascript" text="text/javascript">

  function myFunction(var1,var2,var3) {
    var myName = 'jason;
    if var1 == 5 {
    alert ('Got Here!')
    var1++;
    document.nextFrame.value1 = var1;
    else {
    if (myname == 'jocelyn') comment = 'tara';
    alert ('myName = ' + myName);
    }
  }
  </script>
</head>
<body>
  <a href="javascript:myFunction(1,2)">Click Me</a>
</body>
```

Missing ()
If alert appears then var1 = 5
Missing }
myname *is not the same as* myName

Missing '
Value1 *may or may not exist*

Alert displays the variables current value

Missing third value

Figure 28.12 These errors commonly crop up in JavaScript. Don't let this happen to you.

If you have an error, check the following

Look for these common problems:

- **Do you have matching curly brackets ({}) for every instance?** If either end is left out, the script will fail.

- **Do you have matching quotes (' ') for every instance?** If you do not close a quote string, the script will fail.

- **Have all referenced objects and variables loaded before being referenced?** This situation is called a timing problem. If a page in one frame attempts to reference a nonexistent object or an object that simply hasn't finished loading yet, the script will fail. One way around this problem is to test for the existence of the object or variable before trying to perform an action on it, as follows:

```
if (document.nextFrame.value1)
→ {document.nextFrame.value1 = x}
```

- **Have you used a reserved word for a variable?** Certain words, such as new, have a special meaning for JavaScript and cannot be used for variables. You can use derivations of these words, such as newObject; you just can't use the exact word. See Appendix C for a list of reserved words.

- **Do your variable names match?** A typo in a variable name may cause a function to fail or act unpredictably, but JavaScript is also case-sensitive, so even a difference in a letter's case will cause the function to think that it is dealing with different variables. The variable noWhere, for example, is completely different from nowhere.

continues on next page

◆ **Have you placed all the necessary values in the function call, and are they in the right order?** If not, your JavaScript may fail or act unpredictably. You wouldn't believe how many hours I've wasted debugging code only to realize that I simply placed my variables in the wrong order when I referenced the function.

◆ **Do your `if` statements have parentheses around their arguments?** I forget the parentheses all the time. Your `if` statements need to have the following structure:

```
if (argument) doThis;
```

◆ **Is your JavaScript running the correct code?** Sometimes, code that you expect to run does not run for some reason. The best way to test this situation is to put an alert in strategic places in the code to show what is running (and what is not). Place the following line in your code where you think the code might not be running:

```
alert('Got Here!');
```

If the code is running, the alert should appear.

◆ **Are your variables getting the right values?** Your variables may not get the values you expect them to get. Place an alert immediately after a variable to test its value, as follows:

```
alert('myVariable = ' + myVariable);
```

◆ **Is your logic sound?** Simply stated, you need to make sure that what you have programmed makes sense. If actions occur out of order for the desired effect, things will go wrong. Trace through your code as though you were the computer running it, keeping track of what variables have what values at a given time and whether the correct actions are executed at the correct time.

✔ Tips

■ Although you can use double quotes (`""`) or single quotes (`''`) in your JavaScript and HTML, I recommend sticking with single quotes for JavaScript and double quotes for HTML. This practice will help prevent a lot of confusion. I make fewer programming errors if I stick to this simple rule.

■ Although you do not have to use it, JavaScript has an accepted way of creating variable names, often referred to as JavaScript notation. Simply put, if you have multiple words in a variable, the first word is lowercase, and the first letter of each subsequent word is uppercase, with other letters in lowercase. So my last name—Cranford Teague—would be `cranfordTeague` in JavaScript notation.

Figure 28.13 In Internet Explorer 5 for Windows, the header looks fine with the line-height set to normal. However, in the Mac version, the lines of text knock together.

Cross-Browser Conundrums

HTML, CSS, JavaScript, and the Document Object Model are all referred to as *interpreted code*. That is, every browser that can understand these technologies follows a set of rules to help it translate and display the code you set up. Unfortunately, these rules can vary slightly or enormously from browser to browser.

A friend of mine was experimenting with CSS in his Web site, and the line-height was set to normal in every rule (see "Adjusting Leading" in Chapter 4). Although this setup looked perfectly fine in Internet Explorer 5 for Windows, in Internet Explorer 5 for the Mac, the headlines (which were multiple lines of large text) overlapped. Why? Apparently, when Microsoft programmers created Internet Explorer for Windows, they interpreted normal to mean that the browser should apply the current font size being used at that point in the page. Conversely, the Mac development team interpreted normal as meaning the default font size for the page. Thus, in Windows, the line-height would have been the same as the font size of the text being presented. But in the Mac version, the line-height would more than likely be around 12 points, causing the 36-point text lines to overlap (**Figure 28.13**).

I run across these problems all the time. Many of them are not really bugs—they're just slightly different ways that one browser interprets HTML, CSS, or JavaScript compared with other browsers, in much the same way that words (even in the same language) may mean different things in different countries (see the sidebar "Pants or Trousers?"). Although this situation usually is not life-threatening, it can be confusing, not to mention annoying. You can't do much to fix these problems—unless you reprogram the browsers and then install them on the computers of all the people who will be viewing your site. But you *can* work around the problems.

Cross-browser workarounds:

- **Adjust your code.** In my friend's case, he didn't need the `line-height: normal` definition, so he took it out. The layout looked fine in both browsers.

- **Tailor your code to the OS, the browser, or both.** I showed you how to do this in "Setting the CSS for the OS" in Chapter 22.

- **Rethink the method you are using to create the page.** Because Netscape 6 has difficulty displaying backgrounds and borders for nested CSS layers, if you require nested layers, you may have to forego border colors.

- **Live with it.** Some problems are just not worth the effort of fixing them. If a problem is small—for instance, one browser puts a few extra line breaks after an `<h1>` header, while another browser does not—you can be doing far better things with your time than trying to offset the problem in both browsers.

Pants or Trousers?

While I was a student living in London, I frequented a local pub (one of about six within a five-minute walk of my flat) on the banks of the Thames river. On one occasion, I was talking to some friends, and a drunken rugby player who was standing next to us sloshed lager on me. After the third time this happened, I stood up and started yelling at him, "Hey, do you want to clean my pants?" Unfortunately, I forgot that to a Brit, the word *pants* means *underwear*, whereas to an American, it means *trousers*. He and his six mates, who were not familiar with this little linguistic twist, tried to throw me into the Thames. Make no mistake about it—language can kill.

THE FUTURE 29
OF THE DYNAMIC WEB

Suppose you are doing a bit of work about the house, building that back deck you always wanted. A friend who has graciously agreed to help you measures the first board and tells you to cut another one to 350.3 centimeters. You look at your tape measure and realize that it uses inches, not centimeters. What do you do? Easy: Convert 350.3 centimeters to inches by dividing by 2.54. The result is about 138 inches. Cut the board, and you are in business.

What was wrong with good old inches, feet, and yards? These units were the standards for centuries. The problem was that the imperial measurement system had some rather vague and arbitrary conversions between smaller and larger units (I can never remember how many yards are in a mile, for example), whereas the metric system allows you to convert from smaller to larger units by moving the decimal (see the sidebar "All for a Lack of Standards").

Standards are great, but if we didn't try to improve our standards, we'd still be swinging from tree to tree, trying to figure out which one had the best bananas.

In the world of the Web, yesterday's bleeding-edge technology is today's standard. The stuff that crashes your browser now may well be the accepted norm with the next browser release. That said, these things can become standards only if we—the people creating for the Web—actually use them.

Why Standards Matter

The prime meridian and Greenwich Mean Time are standards that allow us to determine our position on Earth with pinpoint accuracy (**Figure 29.1**). These standards can be applied anywhere at any time by anybody; they are universally accessible and understood because everybody has agreed to do it that way. They allow ships to ply the seven seas without bumping into land (usually) and airplanes to fly in friendly skies without bumping into each other. And they have opened the world to travel not necessarily because they are a superior way of doing things, but simply because everyone has agreed to do things the same way. Sounds like a pretty good idea, doesn't it?

The idea of a standard was the principle behind the creation of the World Wide Web: Information should be able to be transmitted to any computer anywhere in the world and displayed pretty much the way the author intended it to look. In the beginning, only one form of HTML existed, and everyone on the Web used it. This situation didn't present any real problem, because almost everyone used Mosaic, the first graphics-based browser, and Mosaic stuck to this standard like glue. That, as they say, was then.

Along came Netscape, and the first HTML extensions were born. These extensions worked only in Netscape, however, and anyone who didn't use that browser was out of luck. Although the Netscape extensions defied the standards of the World Wide Web Consortium (W3C), most of them—or at least some version of them—eventually became part of that very standard. According to some people, the Web has gone downhill ever since.

The Web is a very public form of discourse, one the likes of which has not existed since people lived in villages and sat around the campfire telling stories every night. The problem is that without standards, not everyone in the

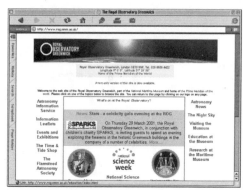

Figure 29.1 The Royal Observatory Greenwich Web site (www.rog.nmm.ac.uk).

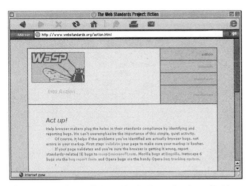

Figure 29.2 The Web Standards Organization: Making the Web safer for your code.

All for a Lack of Standards

A recent example of the problems that arise when standards are not embraced was the loss of a Martian space probe. The company that manufactured the probe was using imperial measurement, while NASA was using the metric system (the scientific standard). Because of this, the distance at which the probe was supposed to approach Mars was wildly inaccurate, and it smashed into the face of the red planet.

A slightly older case in point: On October 22, 1707, four Royal Navy ships miscalculated their position and crashed off the shores of Sicily, all for lack of a standard way to determine the meridian. Two thousand lives were lost. Makes your browser's crashing when it hits nonstandard JavaScript sound insignificant, doesn't it?

global village can make it to the Web campfire. You can use as many bleeding-edge techniques as you like. You can include Flash, JavaScript, VBScript, QuickTime video, layers, or data binding, but if only a fraction of browsers can see your work, you are keeping a lot of fellow villagers out in the cold.

In coding for this book, I spent a good 75% to 80% of the time trying to get the code to run as smoothly as possible in both Internet Explorer and Netscape. This situation holds true for most of my Web projects; most of the coding time is spent on cross-browser inconsistencies. If the browsers stuck to the standards, this time would be reduced to almost none.

Your safest bet as a designer, then, is to know the standards of the Web, try to use them as much as possible, and demand that the browser manufacturers use them as well. The Web Standards Project (`www.webstandards.org`) is a watchdog group working to make sure that browser manufacturers stick to the standards they helped create (**Figure 29.2**). Get involved.

WHY STANDARDS MATTER

Extensible Markup Language (XML)

The Standard Generalized Markup Language (SGML) is the grandfather of most markup languages used for both print and the Internet. SGML is the international standard used to define the structure and appearance of documents. Different SGMLs have been created for a variety of document types and for different specialties, such as physics, accounting, and chemistry. HTML is the Web's version of SGML. Compared with full-blown SGML, however, HTML is lacking in several key areas.

Most notably, HTML does not allow you to tell the browser anything about the information in the document except, to a very limited extent, in <meta> tags (see "Educating the Browser" in Chapter 24).

The Extensible Markup Language—XML, for short (www.w3.org/XML)—is another offshoot of SGML (**Figure 29.3**). Unlike HTML, XML gives Web designers the ability to not only define the structure of the page, but also to define what types of information is being presented. XML produces a Web page that works like a database and is convenient to search and manipulate. This is why XML is being touted as the greatest thing to happen to the Internet since HTML.

Extensible Style Language, or XSL (www.w3.org/Style/XSL; **Figure 29.4**), converts XML documents into other kinds of documents (such as HTML for display on the Web) or defines a page's output. XSL is not a replacement for CSS, however.

Figure 29.3 The W3C's XML Web site (www.w3.org/XML): a great place to begin your exploration of all things extensible.

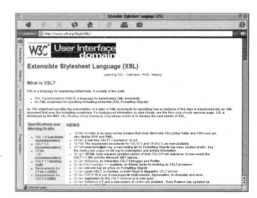

Figure 29.4 The XSL home page (www.w3.org/Style/XSL).

Code 29.1 The DTD tells you that identity is composed of name and organization; name is composed of real and alias; and real, alias, and organization are all PCDATA (alphanumeric characters).

```
code
<!ELEMENT identity (name,organization) >
<!ELEMENT name (real,alias) >
<!ELEMENT real (#PCDATA) >
<!ELEMENT alias(#PCDATA) >
```

Code 29.2 This code tags a person's identity with real name, an alias, and organization. It also includes a reference to a DTD called identity.dtd, which will be used to define the tags.

```
code
<?xml version="1.0" ?>
<!DOCTYPE identity SYSTEM "identity.dtd">
<identity>
<name>
<real>Doctor</real>
<alias>John Smith</alias>
</name>
<organization>UNIT</organization>
```

How does XML work?

XML works a lot like HTML and CSS. It is made up of tags that describe how a browser should render the document. The document's author creates his own tags to identify explicitly the content of the document and its various pieces. Then the author creates a Document Type Definition (DTD) file to define what those tags mean. The DTD sets out what names are being used as tags, what type of information the tag contains, and in what context the tag can be used.

Suppose you have a list: Doctor, John Smith, UNIT. At first glance, some of the items in the list have an obvious meaning: Doctor is a person's title, and John Smith is a name. But what is UNIT? Also, the first two items may be used in a way that is not obvious. To a computer, these items are just alphanumeric characters with no inherent meaning.

But you can use XML to define each of these items and to tell the document where to get the DTD document for this code (**Code 29.1**). Next, you set up the actual DTD document (**Code 29.2**).

Now the browser can tell the difference between the real name, the alias, and the person's organization. You could also tell the browser how each of these tags should be displayed.

continues on next page

EXTENSIBLE MARKUP LANGUAGE (XML)

✔ Tips

- From a graphic-design standpoint, XML may seem to be of little use. Sure, you can make your own tags and define what they look like, but you can do that with CSS, which is easier to use. But XML is being adopted as the foundation for several interesting new multimedia and graphic standards that are in the proposal stage. One of those standards, SVG, is discussed later in this chapter (see "Scalable Vector Graphics").

- Currently, XML requires a separate *parser* (a small application that tells the browser how to deal with XML) to run in most older browsers. Microsoft includes such a parser with Internet Explorer 4/5, but Netscape 4 does not.

XML, CSS, and the DOM

In Chapter 11, I showed you how to access the Document Object Model (DOM). Later chapters showed how to apply the DOM to change HTML objects on the Web page. The DOM is not only applicable to HTML, but also can be used with pages created with XML.

Likewise, CSS will work with an XML document. In fact, they are integral to XML's usefulness.

For more information on XML, check out Elizabeth Castro's book *XML for the World Wide Web*, also published by Peachpit Press.

Figure 29.5 The XHTML recommendation (www.w3.org/TR/xhtml1/).

Extensible Hypertext Markup Language (XHTML)

XML and XSL hold many promises for Web designers, not the least of which is the ability to separate the display of content from its actual layout (www.w3.org/TR/xhtml1/). Freeing the content from its layout means that rather than having to sweat the details on each page, you can control the layout for a site from a single location.

But how do you get Web designers to switch from HTML, with which they are comfortable, to the more complex XML?

The answer: XHTML.

XHTML (**Figure 29.5**) is a hybrid of the recently updated HTML 4.01 standard (www.w3.org/TR/html40/) and XML. Many people hope that XHTML will begin a relatively painless transition from HTML to XML.

XHTML uses the XML Document Type Definitions (DTD)—collections of declarations that tell the browser how to treat the structure, elements, and attributes of the tags that it finds in a document. XHTML uses all the same tags as the HTML DTD. The upshot is that although XHTML Web pages can use the strength of XML, the code will still work even if the browser does not understand XML.

Why make the change?

If the standards are so similar, why change? The W3C offers two good reasons:

- The *X* in *XHTML* stands for *extensible*, which means it is much easier to add new capabilities to XHTML than to HTML. The behavior of tags is defined in a DTD rather than by the individual browser, so XHTML will be more modular. Therefore, the capabilities of XHTML can be enhanced for future browsers or other Web-enabled devices without sacrificing backward compatibility.

- The W3C claims that by 2002, 75% of Web traffic will be on alternative platforms, such as TV sets, Palm Pilots, and tele-phones. If you think it is hard to code HTML for a few browsers, imagine coding for dozens of devices. A standard language is needed. In addition, because these devices will have a smaller bandwidth, the code will need to be as compact as possible—something for which XHTML is perfect.

The W3C hopes that if Web designers begin using XHTML now, they can began to reap the benefits of XML without having to give up the HTML skills they worked so long to develop. In fact, if you know HTML, you already know all the XHTML tags. The main thing you will have to learn is how these tags can (and cannot) be used. XHTML is a good deal stricter than HTML in terms of what it allows you to do, but these restrictions lead to cleaner, faster, easier-to-understand HTML code.

Converting HTML to XHTML

So what is the difference between HTML and XHTML? XHTML is far more restrictive than HTML. It will not allow you to bend the rules and get away with it. However, because XHTML shares the same tags as HTML, it's fairly easy to convert if you keep these points in mind:

- **No overlapping tags.** Most browsers do not care whether HTML tags are properly nested, so the following code works just fine:

  ```
  <p>Bad <b>Nesting</p></b>
  ```

  That is not the case in XHTML. The correct syntax would have to be this:

  ```
  <p>Good <b>Nesting</b></p>
  ```

- **Tags and attributes have to be lowercase.** XML is case-sensitive, so `<li>` and `<LI>` are different tags. Keep all your tags and attributes in lowercase, and you will be fine.

- **Always use an end tag.** Often, Web designers simply slam in a `<p>` tag to separate paragraphs. With XHTML, however, you would have to use this format:

  ```
  <p>Your text</p>
  ```

- **Use a space and slash in empty tags.** The preceding rule doesn't make much sense for `<br>` or `<li>` tags, which have no closing tag. Instead, include a space and then a slash in the tag to make it self-closing, as follows:

  ```
  <br />
  ```

- **Don't nest links.** The following doesn't work:

  ```
  <a src="this.html">This<a src=
  → "that.html">That</a></a>
  ```

  But why would you want to do that in the first place?

continues on next page

EXTENSIBLE HYPERTEXT MARKUP LANGUAGE (XHTML)

◆ **Use** id **and** name **together.** If you are identifying an element on the screen, such as a layer, use both the id and name attributes except in radio buttons, as follows:

```
<div id="object1" name="object"1">
→ </div>
```

◆ **Place attribute values in quotes.** If a tag has attributes in it, the values have to be in quotes. The following example is wrong:

```
<img src=myImage.gif />
```

Use this syntax instead:

```
<img src="myImage.gif" />
```

◆ **Encode the ampersand in URLs or other attribute values.** The ampersand (&) has to be coded as &. The following example is wrong:

```
<img src="bill&ted.gif" />
```

Use this syntax instead:

```
<img src="bill&amp;ted." />
```

◆ **Don't use HTML comments in script or style containers.** One trick I show you in this book is to place HTML comment tags immediately after <style> or <script> tags to hide the code from older browsers. For XHTML, do not do this. The following example is wrong:

```
<style> <!--
    p { font: times; }
//-->
</style>
```

Use this syntax instead:

```
<style>
    p { font: times; }
</style>
```

✔ Tip

■ It looks as though XHTML and CSS may be the future of Web design. Although browser manufacturers have been slow to adapt these standards, the W3C has made sure that XHTML will always be backward-compatible.

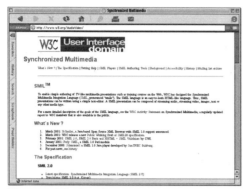

Figure 29.6 The SMIL home page
(www.w3.org/AudioVideo).

Synchronized Multimedia Integration Language (SMIL)

Synchronized Multimedia Integration Language, (or SMIL, which has the cute pronunciation "smile"), may end up being the HTML for creating multimedia events on the Web (www.w3.org/AudioVideo; **Figure 29.6**). As HTML does with text and graphics, SMIL uses tags to help define how your media files—audio, video, text, and static graphics (sorry, no smell yet)—should be laid out on the screen. More important from the standpoint of multimedia, SMIL also allows Web page designers to describe the temporal behavior of the presentation of those elements using timelines similar to those we saw in Dreamweaver and GoLive (Chapters 18 and 19) for creating DHTML animation.

SMIL is based on XML (see "Extensible Markup Language (XML) and Extensible Stylesheet Language (XSL)" earlier in this chapter), the same markup language from which HTML evolved. But do not be fooled: SMIL is not HTML—or even an extension of HTML. SMIL and HTML are two different file types and use different tags. At best, you could think of HTML and SMIL as being cousins.

Although HTML is great for laying out text and static graphics, it is not very good at presenting multimedia, even if you use JavaScript and DHTML. That's where SMIL enters the picture. To create robust, complex multimedia, you need a new system of markup tags designed specifically to deal with the problems of multimedia, including layout, chronology, bandwidth, and file format.

continues on next page

SMIL

SMIL provides Web designers exacting control of the layout of a multimedia document through CSS. As it does with HTML, CSS defines individual elements on the page that can be positioned, repositioned, shown, moved, removed, or replaced as needed. This arrangement is similar to the way that DHTML works with JavaScript.

The main difference is the way that SMIL code is created. Rather than being placed inside a `<style>` tag like CSS, SMIL code is placed inside of a `<layout>` tag to define different regions of the screen. You then use the SMIL tags to manipulate these regions as desired.

Besides the ability to move the elements around, you also need the ability to synchronize the various elements in a timeline. If you have ever worked with multimedia programs such as Macromedia Director and Macromedia Flash, or if you come from a movie or television background, you probably are familiar with the concept of the timeline. Timelines coordinate how the various pieces of a multimedia production work together chronologically.

SMIL includes several tags that allow Web designers to dictate when, where, and how the multimedia content is presented. You can specify when media clips start and stop, how long they run, and whether they loop. You can synchronize media clips to run simultaneously by using simple attributes in HTML-like tags. You don't need to resort to complex coding languages (such as JavaScript) or expensive software (such as Flash).

Another important impediment to high-quality multimedia on the Web is the disparity in bandwidth. Whereas a visitor on a T1 line might have no problem downloading a QuickTime video, a visitor with a 14.4 Kbps modem will. SMIL includes tags that provide different download options, depending on the bandwidth available to the visitor.

✔ Tip

- Will you be smiling or frowning on SMIL in the future? Sorry, I couldn't resist that one. The W3C now recommends it as a standard, and it is likely to be adapted by all major players in the World Wide Web game.

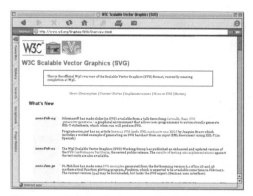

Figure 29.7 Find out what's new with SVG (www.w3.org/Graphics/SVG).

Figure 29.8 Sample SVG code generated in Adobe GoLive.

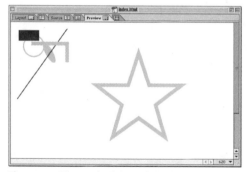

Figure 29.9 The result of the code in Figure 29.8 previewed in GoLive.

Scalable Vector Graphics (SVG)

The Scalable Vector Graphics format—SVG, for short—is a method of creating vector graphics on the Web (www.w3.org/Graphics/ SVG; **Figure 29.7**). Like Flash, rather than plotting each point in the graphic, SVG describes two points and then plots the path between them as a straight line or curve.

Unlike Flash, which uses an editor to create its files and hides much of the code used to create the graphics, SVG uses a variation of XML (**Figure 29.8**) to create its vector graphics (**Figure 29.9**). More important from a DHTML standpoint, SVG graphics can be scripted with the DOM and can include all the DHTML capabilities described in this book.

SVG is still only a W3C candidate recommendation, and although Adobe is offering an SVG browser plug-in, no browser has built-in SVG capabilities. Together with SMIL, however, SVG is poised to give Flash some competition.

What's Next: CSS Level 3

Never content to rest on its laurels, the W3C is already hard at work on another rendition of cascading style sheets: CSS Level 3 (**Figure 29.10**). Many of the problems that CSS2 does not adequately address will be solved in this upcoming version. (www.w3.org/TR/css3-roadmap).

Although the standard is still in the proposal stage, many of the additions to CSS3 sound very exciting.

Highlights of CSS3:

◆ **Columns.** The most exciting new feature proposed for CSS3 is the capability to create flexible columns for layout. As mentioned in the sidebar "Layout with CSS vs. Tables" in Chapter 21, CSS still cannot replace tables for multiple-column layout. Ideally, CSS3 will take care of this problem.

◆ **Web fonts.** Although CSS2 provides downloadable font capability (see "Downloading Fonts" in Chapter 3), it's still too hard to use. The W3C wants to make fonts more Web-friendly in CSS3.

◆ **Color profiles.** One common problem with graphics is that they may be darker or lighter, depending on the computer being used. CSS3 will allow authors to include color descriptions to offset this problem.

◆ **User interface.** CSS3 will add more pointers, form states, and ways to use visitor-dictated color schemes (see the sidebar "Using the Visitor's Styles" in Chapter 3).

◆ **Behaviors.** The most intriguing new capability that CSS3 might include uses CSS to dictate not only visual styles, but also the behavior of objects. This capability would provide further dynamic controls via CSS.

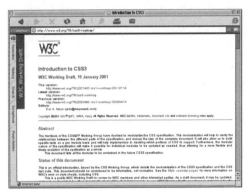

Figure 29.10 See the future of Web design: CSS Level 3 (www.w3.org/TR/css3-roadmap).

✔ Tip

■ The standards don't matter if the browsers do not support them. Remember that you have a voice. Visit The Web Standards Project (www.webstandards.org/) for more information on how to get involved with making the browser manufacturers live up to the promise of an open Web community.

The DHTML and CSS Browsers

For a browser to be considered DHTML- and CSS-capable, it must support the following technologies to some degree:

- **HTML.** HTML is the foundation of all DHTML. Support of the recent HTML 4 (currently at Version 4.01) standard is preferred.

- **JavaScript.** If HTML is the foundation, JavaScript is the cornerstone of DHTML.

- **CSS Level 1.** CSS provides much-needed style controls for Web layout, as well as the capability to define elements as objects on the screen.

- **CSS Positioning** or **CSS Level 2.** To move and change objects, the browser must support the positioning controls in either the early CSS-P standard—which was later integrated into CSS2—or CSS2.

- **DOM.** The browser must use some form of the Document Object Model. The standard version of the World Wide Web Consortium (W3C) is preferred (see "The W3C ID DOM" in Chapter 11).

The browsers discussed in this appendix meet (or will meet) these criteria.

Non-DHTML Browsers

Some browsers in use today do not run DHTML code, especially with the increase of Web access by hand-held devices. If you do not want to turn off a significant portion of your potential audience, your Web pages should work both with and without DHTML. It's a good idea to test your Web pages in as many Web browsers as possible before going live on the Web.

Internet Explorer

Microsoft's Internet Explorer has become the dominant browser on the Web, garnering the lion's share of Web traffic around the world. Although I recommend creating Web sites that are compatible across browsers and are as standards-compliant as possible, most of the people viewing your Web site are likely to be using some version of Internet Explorer.

Internet Explorer 4

Use of Internet Explorer 4 has diminished rapidly over the past two years, as most private and business users have upgraded to the more standards-compliant Internet Explorer 5. Version 4 was Microsoft's first serious contender as a Web browser, and despite the legal debates about its integration in the Windows operating system, Internet Explorer is the browser that began to turn the tide on the once-dominant Netscape browser.

Internet Explorer 4 adopted many of the W3C's standards. Although it was not perfect, it was the first browser to build its DHTML capabilities around those standards.

Internet Explorer 4 supports HTML, CSS1 (partial), CSS-P (partial), JavaScript, and the Internet Explorer Document Object Model (DOM).

Internet Explorer 5 (Windows)

Internet Explorer 5 was strategically integrated into the Windows operating system and now dominates the Web browser market.

There is little doubt that this browser is a huge step forward for standards compliance compared with Version 4. But Internet Explorer 5's implementations of CSS and the DOM are far from complete.

By integrating the browser further into the operating system, Microsoft managed to increase the divide between users of the Windows version of Internet Explorer and users of all other browsers, even Internet Explorer 5 for the Mac (discussed later in this appendix). In fact, Microsoft has only backhandedly implemented some of the most important standards, such as the W3C DOM and HTML 4, and has already drawn the ire of many developers such as the Web Standards Project (`www.webstandards.org/wfw/ieah.html`).

Although Internet Explorer 5.5 improves on the standards compliance of Version 5, it relies on proprietary technologies such as VBScript and Active X. Internet Explorer still has a long way to go.

Internet Explorer 5 (Windows) supports HTML 4 (partial), CSS1 (partial), CSS2 (partial), XML (partial), JavaScript, PNG (partial), and the W3C DOM (partial).

Internet Explorer 5 (Mac)

Besides the fact that they were both made by Microsoft, the Mac and Windows versions of Internet Explorer 5 have only two things in common: They are both Web browsers, and they are both called Microsoft Internet Explorer 5. Beyond that, Internet Explorer 5 for the Mac is as different from the Windows version as Mac OS is from Windows.

The first thing you notice about Internet Explorer 5 when you launch it is the iMac-inspired interface. It is an early indication not only of an entirely new GUI, but also of a new user experience that builds on the strengths of the Mac. Unlike past browsers, which were merely ports of the Windows version, Internet Explorer 5 is Mac from the ground up.

From a developer's standpoint, Internet Explorer 5 for the Mac is an important leap forward, not because it introduces any amazing new technologies (as Netscape did with frames and JavaScript), but because it follows the rules.

Internet Explorer 5 for the Mac supports HTML 4, CSS1, CSS2 (partial), XML, JavaScript, PNG, and the W3C DOM.

Netscape Navigator

Although the company that made this ground-breaking product has been acquired by America Online, Netscape will always be remembered as the browser that popularized the Web. The Web browser itself was renamed Navigator with Version 3. Because most people still refer to the browser by its company's name, however, I refer to the browser as *Netscape* throughout this book.

Netscape 4

Netscape 4 lasted for more than four years as Netscape's flagship Web product and became the workhorse browser for many Web designers, despite its shaky and incomplete support of Web standards. To be fair, however, many of the standards used today either did not exist or were in nascent form when Netscape 4 appeared on the scene.

Netscape 4 introduced its own flavor of DHTML that relied on the `<layer>` tag (see Chapter 16). This technique never caught on, though, and Netscape has since abandoned it in favor of the standards set forth by the W3C.

Netscape 4 supports HTML, CSS1 (partial), CSS-P (partial), JavaScript, and the Netscape Layers DOM.

Netscape 6

Netscape 6 (yes, 6, not 5) was built around the Gecko rendering engine, which was created to comply with the latest Web standards. This news is welcome to the Web-development community, which has been suffering for years trying to make incompatible browsers play nicely on Web sites.

Gecko is an amazing piece of work, and the many people who devoted their time and effort to its creation should be proud of their craftsmanship. It's small, extremely fast, and one of the most standards-compliant rendering engines available.

But the interface is crowded with menus, buttons, and assorted options that have no clear hierarchy. Most of the menus at the bottom of the interface are nothing but glorified bookmark links to Netscape's Web pages, and I have found no way to customize these links to suit the user's needs. Although the My Sidebar feature is a step in the right direction, it seems to exist primarily to funnel Web surfers to Netscape and its affiliates, rather than to provide useful and truly customized tools that make surfing easier.

Netscape 6 supports HTML 4, CSS1, CSS2 (partial), XML, JavaScript, PNG (partial), and the W3C DOM.

Other Browsers

Believe it or not, there are more than two browsers available to the Web public. While Netscape and Internet Explorer are primary browsers you need to think about when constructing your DHTML Web site, two other contenders are making their mark: Opera (Mac/Windows) and iCab (Mac).

Opera (Mac/Windows)

Opera Software (www.opera.com) set out with a mission to create a completely standards-compliant browser. With Version 5 of the Opera browser, the company is closer than ever to hitting the moving target that is Web standards. Although the browser is not perfect, Opera considers W3C standards as being not just a good idea, but the law.

In addition, Opera is small (around 2 MB to download without Java), renders pages extremely fast, and includes strong security.

Although it started as a Windows-only browser, Opera has added several other platforms (including EPOC, Linux, and Mac) and is working on a version for BeOS. Currently, the Mac version is still in beta, and some of the standards seem to be missing or incomplete.

Opera 5 supports HTML 4, CSS1, CSS2 (partial), JavaScript, XML, and the W3C DOM (partial).

iCab (Mac)

iCab (www.icab.de) is what a Web browser should be. It is small—a mere 900 KB download. It is fast, with pages seeming to appear as soon as you click a link. It is smart, with more options than any other browsers I have seen. It adheres to the standards, following the W3C's recommendations to the letter. It does everything that a Web surfer needs it to do—or at least it will when it gets out of beta. Currently, the browser is still in development and lacks certain key features, such as CSS and full JavaScript support.

Which mega-corporation is creating this insanely great new browser? Actually, iCab is the work of one guy in Germany, Alexander Clauss, and a few of his friends.

Although developers will enjoy its strong adherence to the W3C standards, the current beta version of iCab—without full JavaScript, CSS, or DHTML—probably will not be your everyday browser. Future plans include all this and more.

iCab supports HTML 4 and JavaScript (partial), and plans to add CSS1 and CSS2 in upcoming releases.

CSS
Quick Reference

B

Chapters 3 through 9 present the properties that can be used with CSS. In this appendix, those properties are represented in a slightly more concise format, which also includes information about a property's inheritance and the HTML tags to which the property can be applied.

- **Table B.1** describes font controls (Chapter 3).

- **Table B.2** describes text controls (Chapter 4).

- **Table B.3** describes list and mouse controls (Chapter 5).

- **Table B.4** describes color and background controls (Chapter 6).

- **Table B.5** describes margin and border controls (Chapter 7).

- **Table B.6** describes positioning controls (Chapter 8).

- **Table B.7** describes visibility controls (Chapter 9).

- **Table B.8** describes pseudo-elements and pseudo-classes (see the sidebars "Not Really a Class" in Chapter 24 and "Not Really an Element" in Chapter 26).

Quick Reference

You'll find information about the applicability of each property in the various types of HTML tags. Each property is described in terms of what it can be used with, whether the property is inherited by its child elements, and whether the property is supported by various browsers and operating systems.

Properties marked with a **P** in the browser columns are partially implemented or buggy in one or both operating systems. I generally recommend not using these properties.

Keep in mind that each browser has several versions, even within a single version number. There is not a Netscape 4, for example, but several versions (4.06, 4.5, and 4.7), with slight differences among them. The information presented in this appendix generally should be correct, but if you want to test the CSS capabilities of your own browser, check out the World Wide Web Consortium's (W3C) test suite:

`http://www.w3.org/Style/CSS/Test/`

This utility will help you confirm which properties work in your browser.

Legend

■	Mac and Windows
○	Neither
W	Windows only
M	Mac only
P	Problems
All	Property can be applied to any HTML tag
Block	Property can be applied only to block-level tags
Inline	Property can be applied only to inline tags

Boldface indicates the default value of that property.

Table B.1

Font Controls

Name	Value	Applies To	Inherited	N4	N6	IE4	IE5
font-family	<family-name>	All	Yes	■	■	■	■
	serif			■	■	■	■
	sans-serif			■	■	■	■
	cursive			M	■	■	■
	fantasy			M	■	■	■
	monospace			■	■	■	■
font-style	**normal**	All	Yes	■	■	■	■
	italic			■	■	■	■
	oblique			○	■	■	■
font-variant	**normal**	All	Yes	○	■	■	■
	small-caps			○	■	P	■
font-weight	**normal**	All	Yes	■	■	■	■
	bold			■	■	■	■
	bolder			W	■	■	■
	lighter			○	■	■	■
	100-900*			■	■	■	■
font-size	<length>	All	Yes	■	■	■	■
	<percentage>			■	■	■	■
	smaller			■	■	■	P
	larger			■	■	■	P
	xx-small			■	■	P	■
	x-small			■	■	P	■
	small			■	■	P	■
	medium			■	■	P	■
	large			■	■	P	■
	x-large			■	■	P	■
	xx-large			■	■	P	■
font	<font-style>	All	Yes	■	■	■	■
	<font-variant>			○	■	P	■
	<font-weight>			■	■	■	■
	<font-size>/<lineheight>			■	■	P	■
	<font-family>			■	■	■	■

Requires the visitor's computer to have display-weighted fonts available

Table B.2

Text Controls

Name	Value	Applies To	Inherited	N4	N6	IE4	IE5
word-spacing	**normal**	All	Yes	○	■	M	M
	<length>			○	■	M	M
letter-spacing	**normal**	All	Yes	○	■	■	■
	<length>			○	■	■	■
vertical-align	**baseline**	Inline	No	○	■	■	■
	<percentage>			○	■	○	M*
	sub			○	■	■	■
	super			○	■	■	■
	top			○	■	○	M**
	text-top			○	■	○	M**
	middle			○	■	○	M**
	bottom			○	■	○	M**
	text-bottom			○	■	○	M**
line-height	**normal**	All	Yes	■	■	■	■
	<number>			■	■	■	■
	<length>			P	■	■	■
	<percentage>			P	■	■	■
text-decoration	**none**	All	No	■	■	■	■
	underline			■	■	■	■
	overline			○	■	■	■
	line-through			■	■	■	■
	blink			■	■	○	○
text-transform	**none**	All	Yes	■	■	■	■
	capitalize			■	■	■	■
	uppercase			■	■	■	■
	lowercase			■	■	■	■
text-align	left	Block	Yes	■	■	■	■
	right			■	■	■	■
	center			■	■	■	■
	justify			P	■	W	■
text-indent	<length>	Block	Yes	■	■	■	■
	<percentage>			■	■	■	■
white-space	**normal**	Block	Yes	■	■	○	■**
	pre			■	■	○	■*
	nowrap			○	■	○	■**

Mac only; not available in Windows
**IE5.5 for Windows*

CSS QUICK REFERENCE

Table B.3

List and Mouse Controls

Name	Value	Applies To	Inherited	N4	N6	IE4	IE5
list-style-type	**disc**	All*	Yes	■	■	■	■
	circle			■	■	■	■
	square			■	■	■	■
	decimal			■	■	■	■
	lower-roman			■	■	■	■
	upper-roman			■	■	■	■
	lower-alpha			■	■	■	■
	upper-alpha			■	■	■	■
	none			■	■	■	■
list-style-image	**none**	All*	Yes	○	■	■	■
	url(<url>)			○	■	■	■
list-style-position	**outside**	All*	Yes	○	■	■	■
	inside			○	■	■	■
list-style	<list-style-type>	All*	Yes	■	■	■	■
	<list-style-position>			○	■	■	■
	<list-style-image>			○	■	■	■
cursor	**auto**	All	Yes	○	■	■	■
	crosshair			○	■	■	■
	hand**			○	○	■	■
	pointer			○	■	■	■
	move			○	■	■	■
	n-resize			○	■	■	■
	ne-resize			○	■	■	■
	e-resize			○	■	■	■
	se-resize			○	■	■	■
	s-resize			○	■	■	■
	sw-resize			○	■	■	■
	w-resize			○	■	■	■
	nw-resize			○	■	■	■
	text			○	■	■	■
	wait			○	■	■	■
	help			○	■	■	■

*In Netscape and IE, applies only to the <list> tag. In standard CSS, these properties can be applied only to tags that include display:_list-item; in the definition.

**IE only. Same as pointer.

Table B.4

Color and Background Controls

NAME	VALUE	APPLIES TO	INHERITED	N4	N6	IE4	IE5
color	<color>	All	Yes	■	■	■	■
background-color	**transparent**	All	No	■	■	■	■
	<color>			■	■	■	■
background-image	**none**	All	No	■	■	■	■
	url(<url>)			■	■	■	■
background-repeat	**repeat**	All	No	■	■	■	■
	repeat-x			P	■	■	■
	repeat-y			P	■	■	■
	no-repeat			■	■	■	■
background-attachment	**scroll**	All	No	○	■	■	■
	fixed			○	■	■	■
background-position	<percentage>	Block	No	○	○	○	■
	<length>			○	■	■	■
	top			○	■	■	■
	center			○	■	■	■
	bottom			○	■	■	■
	left			○	■	■	■
	center			○	■	■	■
	right			○	■	■	■
background	<background-color>	All	No	■	■	■	■
	<background-image>			■	■	■	■
	<background-repeat>			■	■	■	■
	<background-attachment>			○	■	■	■
	<background-position>			○	■	■	■

Table B.5

Margin and Border Controls

Name	Value	Applies To	Inherited	N4	N6	IE4	IE5
margin-top, -right, -bottom, -left	<length>	All	No	P	■	P	■
	<percentage>			P	■	P	■
	auto			P	■	P	■*
margin	<length>	All	No	■	■	○	■
	<percentage>			■	■	○	■
	auto			○	■	○	■*
padding-top, -right, -bottom, -left	<length>	All	No	P	■	P	■
	<percentage>			P	■	P	■
padding	<length>	All	No	P	■	P	■
	<percentage>			P	■	P	■
border-color	<color>	All	No	P	■	■	■
border-style	none	All	No	■	■	■	■
	dotted			○	■	M	■*
	dashed			○	■	M	■*
	solid			■	■	■	■
	double			■	■	■	■
	groove			■	■	■	■
	ridge			■	■	■	■
	inset			■	■	■	■
	outset			■	■	■	■
border-top, -right, -bottom, left-width	medium	All	No	■	■	P	■
	<length>			■	■	P	■
	thin			■	■	P	■
	thick			■	■	P	■
border-width	medium	All	No	■	■	P	■
	<length>			■	■	P	■
	thin			■	■	P	■
	thick			■	■	P	■
border-top, -right, -bottom, -left	<border-width>	All	No	○	■	P	■
	<border-style>			○	■	P	■
	<color>			○	■	P	■
border	<border-width>	All	No	P	■	P	■
	<border-style>			P	■	P	■
	<color>			■	■	P	■

IE5.5 for Windows

(table continues on next page)

Table B.5

Margin and Border Controls	*continued*						
NAME	**VALUE**	**APPLIES TO**	**INHERITED**	**N4**	**N6**	**IE4**	**IE5**
width	**auto**	Block	No	P	■	P	■
	<length>			P	■	P	■
	<percentage>			P	■	P	■
height	**auto**	Block	No	○	■	P	■
	<length>			○	■	P	■
float	**none**	All	No	■	■	■	■
	left			P	■	P	■
	right			P	■	P	■
clear	**none**	All	No	■	■	■	■
	left			P	■	M	■
	right			P	■	M	■
	both			■	■	■	■
display	**block**	All	No	P	■	■	■
	inline			○	■	W	■
	list-item			P	■	M	M
	none			■	■	■	■

*IE5.5 for Windows

Table B.6

Positioning Controls							
NAME	**VALUE**	**APPLIES TO**	**INHERITED**	**N4**	**N6**	**IE4**	**IE5**
position	**static**	All	No	■	■	■	■
	absolute			■	■	■	■
	relative			■	■	■	■
	fixed			○	○	○	■*
left	**auto**	All**	No	■	■	■	■
	<length>			■	■	■	■
	<percentage>			■	■	■	■
top	**auto**	All**	No	■	■	■	■
	<length>			■	■	■	■
	<percentage>			■	■	■	■
bottom	**auto**	All**	No	○	■	○	■
	<length>			○	■	○	■
	<percentage>			○	■	○	■
right	**auto**	All**	No	○	■	○	■
	<length>			○	■	○	■
	<percentage>			○	■	○	■
z-index	**auto**	All	No	■	■	■	■
	number			■	■	■	■

* Mac only; not available in Windows
** The position *property for the element must also be set to* absolute *or* relative.

Table B.7

Visibility Controls

NAME	VALUE	APPLIES TO	INHERITED	N4	N6	IE4	IE5
clip	auto	All*	No	■	■	○	■
	<shape>			■	■	○	■
overflow	visible	All*	No	■	■	○	■
	hidden			■	■	○	■
	scroll			■	■	○	■
	auto			■	■	○	■
visibility	inherit	All	Yes**	■	■	■	■
	visible			■	■	■	■
	hidden			■	■	■	■
	hide			■	○	○	○
	show			■	○	○	○

*The position property for the element must also be set to absolute or relative.
**If visibility is set to inherit.

Table B.8

Pseudo-Classes and Pseudo-Elements

NAME	VALUE	APPLIES TO	INHERITED	N4	N6	IE4	IE5
:link	—	Anchor	Yes	■	■	■	■
:active	—	Anchor	Yes	○	■	■	■
:visited	—	Anchor	Yes	○	■	■	■
:hover	—	All	Yes	○	■	■	■
:first-line	—	Block	No	○	■	○	■*
:first-letter	—	Block	No	○	■	○	■*

*IE5.5 for Windows

DHTML
QUICK REFERENCE

Chapter 11 presents the most common event handlers that you will use regularly to construct your DHTML (see "Understanding Event Handlers"), and Chapter 12 details all the information about your Webbed environment that you can learn and change. The tables in this appendix present that information in a form that you can read quickly.

Table C.1

Common Event Handlers

NAME	WHEN IT HAPPENS	APPLIES TO
onLoad	After an object is loaded	Documents and images
onUnload	After the object is no longer loaded	Documents and images
onFocus	When an element is selected	Documents and forms
onBlur	When an element is deselected	Documents and forms
onMouseOver	When the mouse pointer passes over an area	All*
onMouseOut	When the mouse pointer passes out of an area	All*
onClick	When the mouse button is clicked over an area	All*
onMouseDown	While the mouse button is pressed	All*
onMouseUp	When the mouse button is released	All*
onMouseMove	As the mouse is moved	Document
onKeyDown	While a keyboard key is pressed	Forms and Document
onKeyUp	When a keyboard key is released	Forms and Document
onKeyPress	When a keyboard key is pressed and immediately released	Forms and Document
onResize**	When the browser window or a frame is resized	Document
onMove***	When the browser window is moved	Document

Available only for anchor links and images in Netscape 4
**Not supported by Internet Explorer 4*
***Not supported by Internet Explorer 4/5 or by Netscape 6*

Table C.2

System Properties

TO FIND	NAME	VALUE	COMPATIBILITY
Operating System	navigator.appVersion	<string>	IE3, N2
Screen Width (total)	screen.width	<pixels>	IE4, N4
Screen Height (total)	screen.height	< pixels>	IE4, N4
Screen Width (live)	screen.availWidth	< pixels>	IE4, N4
Screen Height (live)	screen.availHeight	< pixels>	IE4, N4
Number of Colors	screen.colorDepth	<number>	IE4, N4

Table C.3

Browser Properties

TO FIND	NAME	VALUE	COMPATIBILITY
Browser Name	navigator.appName	<string>	IE3, N2
Browser Version	parseInt(navigator.appVersion)	<number>	IE3, N2
Browser Window Width	window.outerWidth	<pixels>	N4
Browser Window Height	window.outerHeight	<pixels>	N4

Table C.4

Page Properties

To Find	Name	Value	Compatibility
URL	self.location	<string>	IE3, N2
Title	document.title	<string>	IE3, N2*
Visible Width	window.innerWidth	<pixels>	N4
	document.body.clientWidth	<pixels>	IE4
Visible Height	window.innerHeight	<pixels>	N4
	document.body.clientHeight	<pixels>	IE4
Scroll Position Left	window.pageXOffset	<pixels>	N4
	document.body.scrollLeft	<pixels>	IE4
Scroll Position Top	window.pageYOffset	<pixels>	N4
	document.body.scrollTop	<pixels>	IE4

Buggy in Mac version of Netscape 4; returns file name instead of title.

Table C.5

Object Properties

To Find	Name	Value	Compatibility
Width	offsetWidth	<length>	IE4, N6
	width	<length>	N4
Height	offsetHeight	<length>	IE4, N6
	height	<length>	N4
Left Position	offsetLeft	<length>	N6
	pixelLeft	<length>	IE4
	left	<length>	N4
Top Position	offsetTop	<length>	N6
	pixelTop	<length>	IE4
	top	<length>	N4
Z-Index	zIndex	<number>	IE4, N4
Visibility	visible		IE4, N4
	hidden		IE4, N4
	show		N4 (only)
	hide		N4 (only)
Clip	clip[]	<array>	IE
Clip Top	clip.top	<pixel>	N4*
Clip Left	clip.left	<pixel>	N4*
Clip Bottom	clip.bottom	<pixel>	N4*
Clip Right	clip.right	<pixel>	N4*
Clip Width	clip.width	<pixel>	N4*
Clip Height	clip.height	<pixel>	N4*

• *Although clip values can be determined in Internet Explorer, it requires processing the clip array. See "Finding an Object's Visible Area" in Chapter 12.*

Reserved Words

When you are creating CSS class, CSS ID, or JavaScript variable names, keep in mind that the browser has dibs on certain words. I recommend not using these.

That said, it is OK to combine different words to form compound words, even if both words are on the reserved list. Although new and label would not make good variable names, for example, newLabel would be fine.

JavaScript and Java reserved words

The following words are part of the JavaScript or Java language and should be avoided at all costs.

abstract	finally	short
boolean	float	static
break	for	super
byte	function	switch
case	goto	synchronized
catch	if	this
char	implements	throw
class	import	throws
comment	in	transient
const	instanceOf	true
continue	int	try
debugger	interface	typeof
default	label	var
delete	long	void
do	native	while
double	new	with
else	null	
enum	package	
export	private	
extends	protected	
false	public	
final	return	

Other words to avoid

Although not officially on the reserved list, these words are used by JavaScript and will cause problems if you use them.

Remember that Netscape is case-sensitive, so capital letters make a difference. `history`, for example, is not the same as `History`.

alert	event	length	outerHeight	Select
Anchor	evt	Link	outerWidth	self
Area	FileUpload	location	Packages	setInterval
arguments	find	Location	pageXoffset	setTimeout
Array	focus	locationbar	pageYoffset	status
assign	Form	Math	parent	statusbar
blur	Frame	menubar	parseFloat	stop
Boolean	frames	MimeType	parseInt	String
Button	Function	moveBy	Password	Submit
callee	getClass	moveTo	personalbar	sun
caller	Hidden	name	Plugin	taint
captureEvents	hide	NaN	print	Text
Checkbox	history	navigate	prompt	Textarea
clearInterval	History	navigator	prototype	toolbar
clearTimeout	home	Navigator	Radio	top
close	Image	netscape	ref	toString
closed	Infinity	Number	RegExp	unescape
confirm	innerHeight	Object	releaseEvents	untaint
constructor	innerWidth	onBlur	Reset	unwatch
Date	isFinite	onError	resizeBy	valueOf
defaultStatus	isNaN	onFocus	resizeTo	watch
document	java	onLoad	routeEvent	window
Document	JavaArray	onUnload	scroll	Window
Element	JavaClass	open	scrollBars	
escape	JavaObject	opener	scrollBy	
eval	JavaPackage	Option	scrollTo	

BROWSER-SAFE FONTS

I showed you the browser-safe fonts in Chapter 3 ("Using Browser-Safe Fonts"). This appendix shows the fonts with samples of what each font looks like, weights and styles that the font includes, and the generic font family name.

✔ Tip

- You can use CSS to make any font bold or italic. Fonts that include bold, italic, or bold italic versions, however, generally look better on the screen.

Table D.1

Microsoft Internet Explorer (Mac and Windows)			
NAME	WEIGHTS & STYLES	GENERIC FAMILY	EXAMPLE
Andale Mono		Monospace	ABCDEFGHIJKLMNOPQRSTUVWXYZ abcdefghijklmnopqrstuvwxyz 1234567890
Arial Black		Sans-serif	**ABCDEFGHIJKLMNOPQRSTUVWXYZ abcdefghijklmnopqrstuvwxyz 1234567890**
Comic Sans MS	bold	Cursive	ABCDEFGHIJKLMNOPQRSTUVWXYZ abcdefghijklmnopqrstuvwxyz 1234567890
Georgia*	bold, italic, bold italic	Serif	ABCDEFGHIJKLMNOPQRSTUVWXYZ abcdefghijklmnopqrstuvwxyz 1234567890
Impact		Sans-serif	ABCDEFGHIJKLMNOPQRSTUVWXYZ abcdefghijklmnopqrstuvwxyz 1234567890
Minion Web*	bold, italic	Serif	ABCDEFGHIJKLMNOPQRSTUVWXYZ abcdefghijklmnopqrstuvwxyz 1234567890
Trebuchet MS*	bold, italic, bold italic	Sans-serif	ABCDEFGHIJKLMNOPQRSTUVWXYZ abcdefghijklmnopqrstuvwxyz 1234567890
Verdana	bold, italic, bold italic	Sans-serif	ABCDEFGHIJKLMNOPQRSTUVWXYZ abcdefghijklmnopqrstuvwxyz 1234567890
Webdings		Fantasy	

As of IE5

Table D.2

Mac OS			
NAME	WEIGHTS & STYLES	GENERIC FAMILY	EXAMPLE
Apple Chancery*		Cursive	ABCDEFGHIJKLMNOPQRSTUVWXYZ abcdefghijklmnopqrstuvwxyz 1234567890
Capitals*		Serif	ABCDEFGHIJKLMNOPQRSTUVWXYZ ABCDEFGHIJKLMNOPQRSTUVWXYZ 1234567890
Charcoal		Sans-serif	ABCDEFGHIJKLMNOPQRSTUVWXYZ abcdefghijklmnopqrstuvwxyz 1234567890
Chicago		Sans-serif	ABCDEFGHIJKLMNOPQRSTUVWXYZ abcdefghijklmnopqrstuvwxyz 1234567890

As of Mac OS 8.5

Table D.2

Mac OS *continued*			
NAME	WEIGHTS & STYLES	GENERIC FAMILY	EXAMPLE
Courier	bold, italic, bold italic	Monospace	ABCDEFGHIJKLMNOPQRSTUVWXYZ abcdefghijklmnopqrstuvwxyz 1234567890
Gadget*		Sans-serif	ABCDEFGHIJKLMNOPQRSTUVWXYZ abcdefghijklmnopqrstuvwxyz 1234567890
Geneva		Sans-serif	ABCDEFGHIJKLMNOPQRSTUVWXYZ abcdefghijklmnopqrstuvwxyz 1234567890
Helvetica	bold, italic, bold italic	Sans-serif	ABCDEFGHIJKLMNOPQRSTUVWXYZ abcdefghijklmnopqrstuvwxyz 1234567890
Hoefler Text*	bold, italic, bold italic	Serif	ABCDEFGHIJKLMNOPQRSTUVWXYZ abcdefghijklmnopqrstuvwxyz 1234567890
Monaco		Monospace	ABCDEFGHIJKLMNOPQRSTUVWXYZ abcdefghijklmnopqrstuvwxyz 1234567890
New York		Serif	ABCDEFGHIJKLMNOPQRSTUVWXYZ abcdefghijklmnopqrstuvwxyz 1234567890
Palatino	bold, italic, bold italic	Serif	ABCDEFGHIJKLMNOPQRSTUVWXYZ abcdefghijklmnopqrstuvwxyz 1234567890
Sand*		Cursive	ABCDEFGHIJKLMNOPQRSTUVWXYZ abcdefghijklmnopqrstuvwxyz 1234567890
Skia*		Sans-serif	ABCDEFGHIJKLMNOPQRSTUVWXYZ abcdefghijklmnopqrstuvwxyz 1234567890
Symbol		Fantasy	ABXΔEΦΓHIϑKΛMNOΠΘPΣTYςΩΞΨZ αβχδεφγηιφκλμνοπθρστυϖωξψζ 1234567890
Techno		Serif	ABCDEFGHIJKLMNOPQRSTUVWXYZ abcdefghijklmnopqrstuvwxyz 1234567890
Textile*		Cursive	ABCDEFGHIJKLMNOPQRSTUVWXYZ abcdefghijklmnopqrstuvwxyz 1234567890
Times	bold, italic, bold italic	Serif	ABCDEFGHIJKLMNOPQRSTUVWXYZ abcdefghijklmnopqrstuvwxyz 1234567890

As of Mac OS 8.5

Table D.3

Windows OS			
NAME	WEIGHTS & STYLES	GENERIC FAMILY	EXAMPLE
Abadi MT Condensed Light*		Sans-serif	ABCDEFGHIJKLMNOPQRSTUVWXYZ abcdefghijklmnopqrstuvwxyz 1234567890
Arial	bold, italic, bold italic	Sans-serif	ABCDEFGHIJKLMNOPQRSTUVWXYZ abcdefghijklmnopqrstuvwxyz 1234567890
Arial Black*		Sans-serif	ABCDEFGHIJKLMNOPQRSTUVWXYZ abcdefghijklmnopqrstuvwxyz 1234567890
Book Antiqua*	bold, italic, bold italic	Serif	ABCDEFGHIJKLMNOPQRSTUVWXYZ abcdefghijklmnopqrstuvwxyz 1234567890
Calisto MT*	bold, italic	Serif	ABCDEFGHIJKLMNOPQRSTUVWXYZ abcdefghijklmnopqrstuvwxyz 1234567890
Century Gothic*	bold, italic, bold italic	Sans-serif	ABCDEFGHIJKLMNOPQRSTUVWXYZ abcdefghijklmnopqrstuvwxyz 1234567890
Comic Sans MS*	bold	Cursive	ABCDEFGHIJKLMNOPQRSTUVWXYZ abcdefghijklmnopqrstuvwxyz 1234567890
Copperplate Gothic Bold		Serif	ABCDEFGHIJKLMNOPQRSTUVWXYZ ABCDEFGHIJKLMNOPQRSTUVWXYZ 1234567890
Copperplate Gothic Light		Serif	ABCDEFGHIJKLMNOPQRSTUVWXYZ ABCDEFGHIJKLMNOPQRSTUVWXYZ 1234567890
Courier New	bold, italic, bold italic	Monospace	ABCDEFGHIJKLMNOPQRSTUVWXYZ abcdefghijklmnopqrstuvwxyz 1234567890
Lucida Console*		Monospace	ABCDEFGHIJKLMNOPQRSTUVWXYZ abcdefghijklmnopqrstuvwxyz 1234567890
Lucida Handwriting Italic*		Cursive	ABCDEFGHIJKLMNOPQRSTUVWXYZ abcdefghijklmnopqrstuvwxyz 1234567890
Lucida Sans Unicode*	italic	Sans-serif	ABCDEFGHIJKLMNOPQRSTUVWXYZ abcdefghijklmnopqrstuvwxyz 1234567890
News Gothic MT*	bold, italic	Sans-serif	ABCDEFGHIJKLMNOPQRSTUVWXYZ abcdefghijklmnopqrstuvwxyz 1234567890
OCR A Extended*		Monospace	ABCDEFGHIJKLMNOPQRSTUVWXYZ abcdefghijklmnopqrstuvwxyz 1234567890

* As of Windows 98

Table D.3

Windows OS *continued*			
NAME	WEIGHTS & STYLES	GENERIC FAMILY	EXAMPLE
Symbol		Fantasy	ΑΒΧΔΕΦΓΗΙϑΚΛΜΝΟΠΘΡΣΤΥςΩΞΨΖ αβχδεφγηιϕκλμνοπθρστυϖωξψζ 1234567890
Tahoma*	bold	Sans-serif	ABCDEFGHIJKLMNOPQRSTUVWXYZ abcdefghijklmnopqrstuvwxyz 1234567890
Times New Roman	bold, italic, bold italic	Serif	ABCDEFGHIJKLMNOPQRSTUVWXYZ abcdefghijklmnopqrstuvwxyz 1234567890
Verdana*	bold, italic, bold italic	Sans-serif	ABCDEFGHIJKLMNOPQRSTUVWXYZ abcdefghijklmnopqrstuvwxyz 1234567890
Webdings*		Fantasy	
Wingdings		Fantasy	

* As of Windows 98

TOOLS OF THE TRADE

I use lots of tools for Web design—not only the high-end stuff like FreeHand, Photoshop, Dreamweaver, and GoLive, but also smaller programs that make my life much easier. Some are freeware or shareware programs; others are Web sites. Here are a few of my favorites.

Software

One of the greatest features that the Web offers is the capability to download software quickly and easily. This feature has led to an explosion of programs that would have had too small an audience to make it onto the shelves of your local store, but are nonetheless indispensable for Web designers.

Screen Ruler (Mac/Win)

www.kagi.com/microfox

Some ideas are so obvious, so simple, and yet so brain-bitingly useful that you kick yourself every time you use them for not having thought them up yourself. Screen Ruler (**Figure E.1**) is just such an invention. It places a ruler (in the form of a long yellow graphic) on your screen, which you can use anywhere and at any time, independent of other programs being run. Screen Ruler is indispensable for figuring out positioning in your browser window, from how far over you need to nudge a graphic to make it fit to how wide a table needs to be to accommodate your text.

Pixel Spy (Mac) and Color Picker (Win)

shakti.cc.trincoll.edu/~bhorling/pixelspy/
chunting.uhome.net/colorpk.zip

Like ScreenRuler, Pixel Spy (**Figure E.2**) and Color Picker (**Figure E.3**) are examples of obvious but amazing little devices. When you select any pixel on the screen, these tools will give you that pixel's color in hex, RGB, CMYK, and a few other formats. They also find the closest match to that color in the list of browser-safe colors. Get these programs if you always have to match colors in browser windows or between programs.

Figure E.1 Screen Ruler.

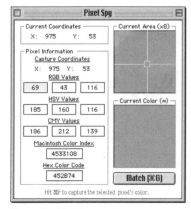

Figure E.2 Pixel Spy.

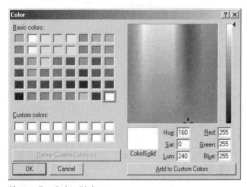

Figure E.3 Color Picker.

SOFTWARE

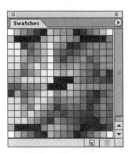

Figure E.4 Visibone's CLUT in Photoshop.

frames					
8 frames	Length : 1.60 s		Size : 35x35		Loop : forever
Name	Size	Position	Disp.	Delay	Transp.
Frame 1	35x35	(0 ; 0)	N	10	W
Frame 2	34x34	(1 ; 1)	N	10	1
Frame 3	19x22	(11 ; 7)	N	10	W
Frame 4	34x34	(1 ; 1)	N	50	1
Frame 5	34x34	(1 ; 1)	N	10	1
Frame 6	19x22	(11 ; 7)	N	10	W
Frame 7	34x34	(1 ; 1)	N	10	1
Frame 8	19x22	(11 ; 7)	N	50	W

b_rdy.gif	1 / 8

Figure E.5 GIFBuilder.

Browser-safe color palettes (Mac/Win)
www.lynda.com/files/CLUTS
www.visibone.com/swatches

Lynda Wynman, who is credited with popularizing the concept of browser-safe colors, has placed copies of the color palette for use in several programs—Photoshop, FreeHand, Paint Shop Pro, and Illustrator—in one place for you to download. I recommend using the Visibone swatch collection, which presents the colors in a user-friendlier format (**Figure E.4**).

You can use these color-lookup tables (CLUT, for short) with your graphics software to ensure that you always have quick and easy access to the safe colors.

GIFBuilder (Mac) and GIF Construction Set (Win)
homepage.mac.com/piguet/gif.html
www.mindworkshop.com/alchemy/gifcon.html

Despite the fact that far more complex and sophisticated programs for creating animated GIFs are on the market, you can't beat GIFBuilder (**Figure E.5**) and GIF Construction Set (**Figure E.6**) for putting together a nice quick animation straight out of Photoshop. One of GIFBuilder's lesser-known but choicest features is the capability to take a layered Photoshop file and make each layer an animation frame. On top of all that, these programs are free.

Figure E.6 GIF Construction Set.

SOFTWARE

GraphicConverter (Mac) and LView Pro (Win)

www.lemkesoft.de/us_gcabout.html

www.lview.com

Although the program is not nearly as sophisticated as Photoshop in terms of graphics editing, I have used GraphicConverter (**Figure E.7**) to open files in formats and strangely encoded file types that sent its more sophisticated rival fleeing in panic. In addition, GraphicConverter can batch-convert any number of graphic files from one file format to another with great control.

Figure E.7 GraphicConverter.

Figure E.8 Webmaster's Color Lab.

Figure E.9 Color Mix.

Online

In addition to offering software that you can download, plenty of Web sites provide functions and services that you can use to improve your own Web site.

Webmaster's Color Lab

www.visibone.com/colorlab/

How do you define the color palette for your Web site? It helps to place colors next to each other and see how they work together. Visibone has created a very useful tool called Webmaster's Color Lab to help you do just that (**Figure E.8**). In one frame, you have a well-organized color wheel that contains all the browser-safe colors. Clicking one of these colors causes a swatch of that color to appear in an adjacent frame. As you click more colors, they appear next to the previous swatch. Even better, though, an example of all of the previous colors appears in the swatch for comparison.

ColorMix

www.colormix.com/

Tired of the same old 216 browser-safe colors? ColorMix (**Figure E.9**) allows you to combine two or three browser-safe colors to form thousands of new colors. ColorMix takes a small dot of each color and places the dots side by side. Your eye then blends the colors. This effect does not look as smooth as a solid color, and some combinations look very strange. Still, this tool is a neat way to add a bit of variety to your Web site.

CSS1 Test Suite

www.w3.org/Style/CSS/Test

How do you know what CSS capabilities your favorite browser supports? Run it through the W3C's CSS1 Test Suite (**Figure E.10**). Every CSS attribute is represented. This tool is especially useful if you are creating a site with CSS or DHTML and need to make sure the CSS you want to use will actually work before you go to all the trouble of creating the Web site.

Web Site Garage

websitegarage.netscape.com

Tune up your up Web site in the Web Site Garage (**Figure E.11**). Give this tool your site's URL, and it will deliver a free report on the site, rating browser compatibility, load time, dead links, spelling, and HTML on a scale from excellent to poor. If you pay $10 a month, you also get access to several online applications that allow you to optimize your Web site to its fullest potential. I ran my site through Web Site Garage and got an overall rating of good. I'm hoping for excellent by next month .

Radio Free Underground

www.stitch.com/studio/

All right, this site is not really a design tool, but I always find it easier to work with some good tunes playing. Radio Free is the place to get them (**Figure E.12**). You select a music style (Goth, Techno, '80s, Ambient, and so on), and the site puts together a mix of 40 to 50 songs that reflects your musical preferences. Then it plays the songs through your RealAudio Player in stereo. Every time you run it, the mix is different. As the Moz said, "Hang the DJ."

Figure E.10 W3C's CSS1 Test Suite.

Figure E.11 Web Site Garage.

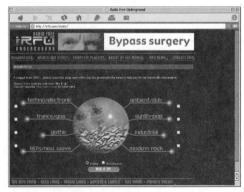

Figure E.12 Radio Free Underground.

FURTHER RESOURCES

I hope this book has opened your eyes to the possibilities of DHTML and CSS, and given you the foundation you need to build your own Web site with these tools. But this book should only be the beginning. The Web is full of resources to help you become a better Web designer.

This appendix is a small sample of the Web sites, books, and other publications that I find indispensable.

Web Sites: Technology and Standards

As complete as I tried to make this book, there is always more to know. These sites should help guide you to everything you could want to know about DHTML and CSS.

World Wide Web Consortium

www.w3.org

If you are looking for the source of all standards, this site is the place to go. Whether you need information on the most recent work being done to update the Document Object Model or the final recommendations for CSS Level 1, this site is the alpha and omega (**Figure F.1**).

BuildingTheWeb.com

www.buildingtheWeb.com

This site is the most useful resource for finding resources on the Web. More than just a site of links, BuildingTheWeb.com includes well-structured lists based on important topics. Each link to an external site includes a well-researched abstract to help you find the best resources for your needs (**Figure F.2**).

HTML Help by the Web Design Group

www.htmlhelp.com

This site is where I first learned CSS myself. After I slogged my way through the W3C's turgid specification, HTML Help made some sense of it all. This site may not be the most attractive one on the Web, but don't be fooled—it is stocked with some of the clearest explanations of Web standards available (**Figure F.3**).

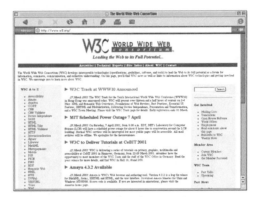

Figure F.1 The World Wide Web Consortium.

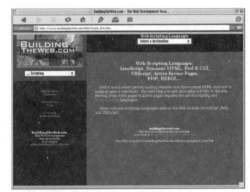

Figure F.2 Building The Web.com.

Figure F.3 HTML Help.

Figure F.4 The Web Standards Project.

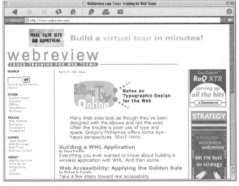

Figure F.5 WebReview.com.

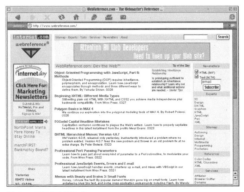

Figure F.6 WebReference.com.

The Web Standards Project

www.webstandards.org

This watchdog group does not set the standards; it watches the browser manufacturers and agitates when they go astray. The Web Standards Project does more than just complain, however. The group has started a browser-upgrade campaign to help designers stick to the standards (**Figure F.4**).

WebReview

www.webreview.com

WebReview provides Web-design professionals articles on a variety of topics, including coding, design tips, and editorials. This site is a great place to visit if you want to stay abreast of changes in the industry (**Figure F.5**).

WebReference

www.webreference.com

WebReference concentrates on the nuts and bolts of front-end Web design, providing in-depth articles on the practical use of DHTML, CSS, and other technologies (**Figure F.6**).

Apple Developer Connection — Internet Developer

developer.apple.com/internet

Although slanted toward Web designers who use the Mac, the ADC site includes information that any Web designer can apply, written by some of the best minds in the industry (**Figure F.7**).

Dynamic Drive

www.dynamicdrive.com

This site offers just DHTML stuff. If you are looking for innovative uses for your new DHTML skills, this is the best place to start (**Figure F.8**).

DHTML Frequently Asked Questions

www.faqts.com/knowledge_base/index.phtml/fid/128

This site is one of my favorites. If you have a question about DHTML (or CSS or JavaScript, for that matter), it probably will be listed here, along with the answer (**Figure F.9**).

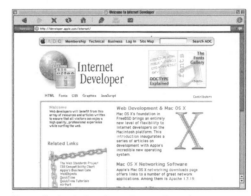

Figure F.7 Apple Developer Connection – Internet Developer.

Figure F.8 Dynamic Drive.

Figure F.9 DHTML FAQ.

Figure F.10 DHTML for the World Wide Web (2nd Edition).

DHTML for the World Wide Web

www.webbedenvironments.com/dhtml

The support site for this book includes all the code presented in the book; you can view the code online and download it. In addition, I will place updates and corrections on this site (**Figure F.10**).

Web Sites: Design and Theory

Creating an effective Web site takes more than just knowing how the code works. You also have to understand how to put the pieces together in a user-friendly design.

GlassDog

www.glassdog.com/design-o-rama

This site is a smart yet entertaining place to learn about Web-site design. GlassDog talks to you as though you are an intelligent human being, rather than a mindless drone, and still manages to slip in all the raw information you need. (**Figure F.11**).

Scott McCloud

www.scottmccloud.com

Scott is an accidental Web guru. Although he is a renowned comic-book artist (*ZOT!* is a must-read), his book *Understanding Comics* became an instant classic in the burgeoning Web-design industry in the mid-1990s. Although his Web site concentrates primarily on Web-based comic books, its message is relevant to anyone who wants to learn more about design for the Web (**Figure F.12**).

The Argus Center for Information Architecture

argus-acia.com

The Web is increasingly becoming a place where people go to get things done with online applications. The design of such applications requires that you understand more than just visual design, but you should also understand user-centered design, usability, and information architecture. The ACIA site provides outstanding articles that will help you understand the role of an information architect in building Web sites (**Figure F.13**).

Figure F.11 Glass Dog.

Figure F.12 Scott McCloud's Online Comics.

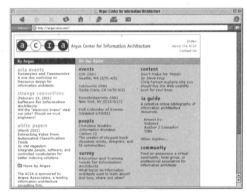

Figure F.13 Argus Center for Information Architecture.

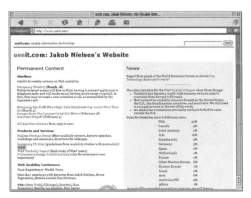

Figure F.14 Jakob Nielsen's Useit.com.

Figure F.15 Web Page Design for Designers.

Useit.com
www.useit.com

Like the ACIA, Jakob Nielsen's Useit.com site provides articles that help readers make better Web sites through usability theory. Although I do not always agree with the conclusions Nielsen draws from his own theories, his ideas usually are intriguing (**Figure F.14**).

Web Page Design for Designers
www.wpdfd.com

Joe Gillespie is a designer's designer, and his site is chock-full of articles to help designers make the transition from print to the Web. Even seasoned veterans of the Web wars will find much to read here (**Figure F.15**).

Web Sites: Examples

The number of sites using DHTML to create their interfaces is growing every day. Here are a few that I recommend reviewing.

Splatterpunk

www.splatterpunk.com

This site is a project by Adobe to show off the capabilities of its software, including GoLive. It includes some pretty neat DHTML tricks (**Figure F.16**).

Sandman Film

www.sandmanfilm.org

I created this site for an independent film by my brother David, using DHTML scrolling techniques. The site has a "zoetropic" effect in which two frames slide horizontally back and forth, depending on which section you want to view (**Figure F.17**).

Coma2

www.coma2.com

Coma2 bills itself as a "collection of media artists." This portfolio site uses DHTML in clever and innovative ways. In addition, several of the sites to which the portfolio links use DHTML (**Figure F.18**).

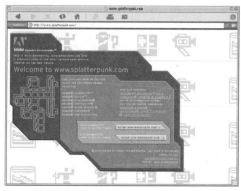

Figure F.16 Splatterpunk.

Figure F.17 The Sandman.

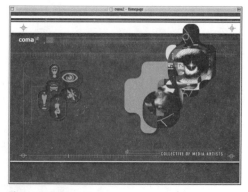

Figure F.18 Coma2.

Figure F.19 Kaliber 1000.

Kaliber 10000

www.k1ok.com

Kaliber 10000, also known as K10K, is a popular destination for Web designers looking for cutting-edge Web design ideas that work. This site is a great place to pick up ideas for integrating DHTML into your site's interface (**Figure F.19**).

Books, Magazines, and Other Publications

Although the Web happens on the screen, many great print publications can help you as well.

Visual Explanations

Although words seem to dominate our lives, it is surprising how much more information we derive from visual cues than from letters. Edward Tufte's book *Visual Explanations: Images and Quantities, Evidence and Narrative* (Graphics Press) deals with the complexities of conveying information through a visual medium and the important role that visual communication plays in our lives.

Understanding Comics

I mentioned Scott McCloud's excellent Web site earlier in this appendix; his book *Understanding Comics* (Kitchen Sink Press) is also worthy of mention. Although ostensibly about comic books, the book is really about visual communication. If you are looking for a captivating introduction to the wonders of sharing information through images rather than letters, I highly recommend this book.

Invisible Computer

Donald A. Norman's basic message in his book *Invisible Computer: Why Good Products Can Fail, the Personal Computer Is So Complex and Information Appliances Are the Solution* (MIT Press) is that people don't want to use computers; they want to get things done. We tend to forget that when we think of all the things a computer can do. *Invisible Computer* is a great book about the philosophy of creating products to be distributed through the computer medium.

Figure F.20 Cre@te Online's Web site.

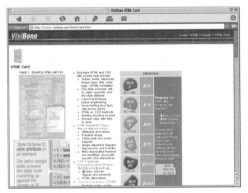

Figure F.21 Visibone's HTML and CSS Reference Card Web site.

Create Online

www.createonline.co.uk

Each month, this magazine is full to the spine with tips and step-by-step instructions, as well as articles examining a range of issues that are important to Web designers. Although *Create Online* is published in the United Kingdom, I have found it in many bookstores in the United States (**Figure F.20**).

Visibone HTML and CSS Card

www.visibone.com/html

Visibone HTML and CSS Card is the perfect cheat sheet for anyone who creates code for the Web. These four pages contain virtually everything you need to know about HTML tags and CSS properties, including attributes, values, browser compatibility, bugs, and special characters. This card is a must-have for all Web designers (**Figure F.21**).

INDEX

: (colon), 19
, (commas), 40
; (semicolon), 13, 18, 44, 183, 184, 509
// characters, 54
/* characters, 54
< > (chevrons), xvi, 184
{ } (curly brackets), 21, 509, 515
( ) parenthesis, 160, 516
" " (quotation marks), xix, 19, 183, 516
& (ampersand), 528
= (equal sign), 19, 183
(number sign), xvii, 34, 509
' (single quotes), 19, 389, 515, 516
_ (underscore), 509
3-D positioning
    finding object position, 224–225
    setting for objects, 240–242
    stacking objects, 151–152

A

<a> tag, 41, 395
absolute length values, xvi
absolute positioning, 139, 141, 143
ActiveX controls, 297
ActiveX technology, 170
addARule() function, 278–279
Adobe Acrobat, 384
Adobe GoLive, 305–318
    creating animation with, 316–318
    CSS and, 310–315
    interface overview, 306–309
    tools, 309
Adobe LiveMotion, 173
Adobe Photoshop, 356, 478–479
alignment, text, 83–86. See also positioning
    controls
ampersand (&), 528

anchor tag, 395
animateObject() function, 254, 255–256
animation
    creating with Dreamweaver, 330–332
    creating with Fireworks, 488–489
    creating with Flash, 495–500
    creating with GoLive, 316–318
    creating with ImageReady, 490
    DHTML animation, 316–318
    GIF animation, 488–494
    objects, 254–256
<applet> tag, 504, 505
applets, 504–505
attributes. See properties
AU format, 487

B

Back button, 346, 433
background-attachment property, 112
background-color property, 110
background-image property, 112
background-position property, 113
background property, 106–108
background-repeat property, 112, 113
backgrounds, 106–113
    animated GIFs in, 493
    background controls, 542
    color in, 107, 109–111, 384, 483
    cross-browser issues, 107
    defining, 106–108
    images in, 107, 108, 111–113, 384
    Netscape and, 110
    PNG format and, 482
    properties, 109–113
    repeating, 113
    sidebars, 368–369
bandwidth, 530

blandTrans() filter, 298
<blink> tag, 487
blinking text, 90
block-level tags, 14, 37–38
<blockquote> tag, 31
blurOn() function, 302
blurring items, 301
<body> tag, 19, 30, 45, 145
<bold> tag, 4, 29
bold text, 29, 71–72
bookmarks, 380–382
border-color property, 114, 127
border property, 124–128
border-style property, 127
border-width property, 128
borders
    border controls, 543–544
    color of, 114, 124, 127
    decorating, 126–128
    described, 117
    finding in objects, 228–231
    Netscape 4 and, 125, 128
    remote controls and, 409
    setting, 124–125
    tables, 131–132

 tag, 156
breadcrumb menus, 415–420
browsers. *See* Web browsers
bugs, 172, 193, 507–518
bulleted lists, 97, 98–101
bullets, 97, 98, 100–101

C

Caption key word, 75
cascade order, 49–50
Cascading Style Sheets. *See* CSS
CD-ROMs, 485
changeStyle() function, 274–275
changeWindowSize() function, 272
changeWindowsSize() function, 270, 271
child tags, 41
chrome, 409
clamshell menus, 345, 411–414
class rules, 31
class selectors, 31–32
classes
    applying to HTML tags, 31, 32
    changing for objects, 276–277
    copy class, 31, 67, 74, 363
    defining, 31–32
    dependent classes, 31
    described, 11
    hypertext class, 438

menu class, 417
    naming, 32
    pseudo-classes, 395, 545
    relElement class, 154
    vs. IDs, 34
Clear button, 445
clear property, 135
client-side code, 168
clip area, 160–161
clipLayer() function, 295
clocks, Web page, 483–484
clockStyle() function, 483, 484
closeWindow() function, 266, 267, 268, 408–409
CLUT (color lookup tables), 561
code. *See* HTML code
code attribute, 504
colon (:), 19
color
    background color, 107, 109–111, 384, 482
    borders, 114, 124, 127
    browser-safe colors, xvii, 561, 563
    color controls, 542
    CSS3 and, 532
    detecting monitor colors, 210–211
    drop shadows, 463, 464, 466
    foreground color, 114
    HTML code, xix
    links, 396, 397, 398
    nested elements and, 114
    pixels, 560
    transparent, 384
    values, xvi
color lookup tables (CLUT), 561
Color Picker program, 560
color property, 114
ColorMix Web site, 563
colorShift() function, 465, 469
columns, 532
commas (,), 40
comment tags, 509
comments, 54, 509, 528
containers, 117, 502
content
    dynamic, 261–263
    dynamic Web sites and, 348, 357
    importing external content, 288–289,
        385–391
    nonlayer content, 296
    pop-up windows, 268–269
    preparing, 357
controls, 425–457. *See also* positioning controls;
        visibility controls
    ActiveX controls, 297
    Back button, 433

background controls, 542
border controls, 543–544
color controls, 542
drag-and-drop feature, 446–448
font controls, 57–75, 539
forms, 441–445
image swapping, 449–453
margin controls, 543–544
mouse controls, 102–103, 541
Next button, 433
pop-up hypertext, 438–440
remote controls, 407–410
removing, 434
scroll bars, 426–432
site controls, 323
slide shows, 434–437
smart menus, 454–457
text controls, 77–94, 540
conventions, xvi–xix
copy class, 31, 67, 74, 363
counterSPACE Web site, 57
countThis() function, 483
cross-browser DHTML, 170
cross-platform issues. See also Mac OS platform;
    Windows platform
  browser problems, 172, 363, 517–518
  DHTML problems, 172
  dynamic capabilities, 167
  setting CSS for operating system, 362–363
  support for properties, 508
crosshair target, 474
CSS (Cascading Style Sheets). See also style
    sheets; styles
  adding comments to, 54
  adding to HTML tags, 18–19
  adding to Web pages, 20–22, 234, 310
  adding to Web sites, 23–28
  basics, 17–56
  browser support for, 9, 10, 13, 15, 17, 533
  cascade order, 49–50
  changing CSS definitions, 274–275
  described, 6–8, 170
  DOM and, 524
  Dreamweaver and, 324–329
  dynamic techniques, 273–281
  external style sheets, 24–28
  formatting CSS definitions, 21–22
  general syntax, 18
  GoLive and, 310–315
  hiding from incompatible browsers, 22, 421
  HTML 4.01 and, 10
  Inspector palette and, 312–313
  line breaks and, 22
  Netscape bug fix, 360–361
  overview, 3–15

ownership of, 7–8
printing, 51–53
properties, 7
quick reference, 537–545
rules, 11–13
setting for operating system, 362–363
strategies for, 55–56
troubleshooting, 508–510
validating, 511–512
versions of, 9–10
  vs. font tags, 62
  vs. HTML tags, 17
  vs. tables, 358
  XML and, 524
CSS Editor, Dreamweaver, 326–327
.css extension, 28
CSS files
  external, 362
  global CSS files, 55
  linking to, 311, 325
  order of, 53
  setting up, 311, 325
CSS layers. See also layers; Netscape layers
  adding to Web pages, 314–315, 328–329
  properties, 315, 329
  vs. Netscape layers, 179, 283, 284
CSS Level 1 (CSS1), 9
CSS Level 2 (CSS2), 9
CSS Level 3 (CSS3), 10, 532
CSS-P (CSS-Positioning), 9
CSS-Positioning (CSS-P), 9
CSS rules, 11–13
  adding, 278–279
  basic syntax, 12
  cascade order, 49–50
  conflicting, 510
  defining bold text, 72
  defining fonts, 61–62
  defining kerning, 78
  defining leading, 80–81
  defining minicaps, 73
  defining multiple font attributes, 74–75
  defining page breaks, 94
  defining tags, 39–40
  defining text alignment, 83–84
  defining text case, 82
  defining text decoration, 89–90
  defining text indentation, 87–88
  defining vertical alignment, 83–84
  defining word spacing, 79
  in document heads, 13
  eliminating, 280–281
  embedded rules, 13
  external files and, 13, 17
  external rules, 13

in HTML tags, 13
multiple, 510
CSS value tables, xviii
CSS1 (CSS Level 1), 9
CSS1 Test Suite, 564
CSS2 (CSS Level 2), 9
CSS3 (CSS Level 3), 10, 532
curly brackets { }, 21, 509, 515
cursive fonts, 58
cursor attribute, 103
CyberStudio. *See* Adobe GoLive

D

debugging code, 507–518
decorative fonts, 58
defaultEvents() function, 252–253, 447, 448, 472
definitions
    changing for objects, 274–275
    described, 12
    forcing use of, 44
    grouping, 40
    !important value, 43–44
    semicolons in, 13
delayHide() function, 399, 401
<description> tag, 424
DHTML (dynamic HTML), 165–302
    advanced techniques, 247–272
    advantages, 171–172
    basics, 233–246
    browser support, 171, 186, 205
    cross-browser DHTML, 170
    described, 168
    disadvantages, 172
    flavors of, 169–170
    goals of, 168
    Microsoft-specific, 169, 170
    Netscape-specific, 169
    overview, 167–176
    quick reference, 547–551
    resources, xxi–xxii, 568, 569
    vs. Flash, 173–176
disabled property, 281
display property, 137–138, 159, 414
<div> tag, 32, 35, 37, 38, 42, 145
Document Object Model (DOM), 177–202. *See also* objects
    capabilities, 179
    creating objects, 180
    cross-browser DOM, 194–198, 217
    described, 170, 177
    detecting DOM type, 192–193
    event handlers, 181–184
    feature sensing, 191–193
    Internet Explorer DOM, 189
    Netscape Layer DOM, 187–188
    overview, 178–179
    process, 185–190
    setting up, 186
    W3C ID DOM, 190
    XML and, 524
Document Type Definition (DTD), 523, 525
DOM. *See* Document Object Model
doNothing() function, 457
downloading files, 174, 487
downloading fonts, 63–64
drag-and-drop objects, 446–448
dragIt() function, 447
Dreamweaver, 319–332
    creating animation with, 330–332
    CSS and, 324–329
    CSS Editor, 326–327
    interface, 320–323
    keyframes, 330, 332
    site controls, 323
    styles and, 325
    Timelines window, 330, 332
    tools, 323
drop caps, 460–461
drop shadows, 462–466
dropIt() function, 447
DTD (Document Type Definition), 523, 525
dynamic content, 261–263. *See also* content
dynamic CSS, 273–281
dynamic functions, 248–250
dynamic headers/footers, 370–371
dynamic HTML. *See* DHTML
dynamic Web sites, 335–358
    content on, 348, 357
    creating, 347–358
    design, 351, 352–356
    future of, 519–532
    guidelines, 339
    templates for, 357

E

#echo tag, 388
elements. *See also* objects
    background color, 110
    blurring, 301
    borders, 124–125
    box concept, 116–117
    controlling in other frames, 261–263
    defining as objects, 178, 180
    defining clip area of, 160–161

INDEX

defining overflow control, 162–163
defining padding, 129–130
defining z-index, 151–152
described, 116
display mode, 137–138
drag-and-drop feature, 446–448
events and, 260
fading, 298
height of, 118–120
identifying, 178
margins, 121–123
nesting, 153–156
positioning, 139–156
pseudo-elements, 545
setting visibility of, 158–160
wave filter for, 302
width of, 118–120
wrapping text around, 133–134
<embed> tag, 486, 487, 500, 503
embedded rules, 13
.eot format, 64
equal sign (=), 19, 183
errorOn() function, 253
errors, 508–509, 513–516. *See also* bugs
event handlers
    DOM, 181–184
    global, 252–253
    onClick, 457
    onLoad, 268, 269, 477, 483
    onMouseover, 451–453
    onUnload, 267
events
    detecting, 183–184
    elements and, 260
    Internet Explorer and, 182
    JavaScript and, 182, 183
    mouseover events, 181, 284
    Netscape and, 182
    onClick event, 258, 402
    onResize event, 361
    passing to functions, 251
Extensible Hypertext Markup Language
        (XHTML), 14, 525–528
Extensible Markup Language (XML), 522–524
Extensible Stylesheet Language (XSL), 7, 522
extensions
    .css extension, 28
    .swf extension, 173
external documents, 13
external rules, 13
external style sheets, 24–28

F

fadeDown() function, 468, 469
fadeElement() function, 298
fadeText() function, 467, 468, 470
fadeUp() function, 468
fading items, 298
fading text, 463, 467–470
fantasy fonts, 58
files
    CSS files. *See* CSS files
    downloading, 174, 487
    external files, 13, 17
    HTML files, 21–22, 389
    JavaScript files, 361, 389
    links to, 26–27, 311
    Shockwave files, 499
    sound files, 486, 487
fillScreen() function, 272
fillScreenWindowsSize() function, 270
filters
    blandTrans() filter, 298
    RevealTrans() filters, 299–300
    visual filters, 170, 297–302
    wave filter, 302
findBottom() function, 222, 223
findBrowserHeight() function, 212
findBrowserWidth() function, 212
findClip functions, 228–231
findColors() function, 211
findDOM() function, 194–202, 261
findDOMFrame() function, 263
findHeight() function, 218, 219
findLayer() function, 224, 240, 241
findLeft() function, 220, 255
findLivePageHeight() function, 213
findLivePageWidth() function, 213–214, 438
findObject() function, 259–260
findRight() function, 222, 223
findScrollLeft() function, 216
findScrollTop() function, 216–217
findTop() function, 220, 221, 255
findVisibility() function, 226, 227
findWidth() function, 218, 219
findXCoord() function, 257
findYCoord() function, 257
Fireworks, 480–481, 488–489
fixed positioning, 144–145, 366
Flash
    advantages, 173–174
    animation, 495–500
    described, 173
    disadvantages, 173–174, 176
    vs. DHTML, 173–176

Flash plug-in, 60
flashlight effect, 471–474
float property, 133–136, 503
floating box, 308, 314–315
floating objects, 475–477
floating position, 134
floating text, 134, 135–136
followMe() function, 472
font attribute, 75
font families, 58
font-family values, 62
font property, 61
font-size property, 68
font-size values, 68, 74
font-style element, 69
font-style values, 70, 73, 74
font tag, 62
font values, 75
font-variant property, 73
font-variant values, 74
font-weight property, 72
font-weight values, 72, 74
@fontface statement, 63
fonts, 57–75. *See also* text
    blinking text, 90
    bold text, 29, 71–72
    browser-safe fonts, 65–66, 553–557
    cross-platform issues, 64, 66
    CSS3 and, 532
    cursive fonts, 58
    decorative fonts, 58
    defining in rules, 61–62
    downloading, 63–64
    drop caps, 460–461
    fading, 463, 467–470
    fantasy fonts, 58
    font controls, 57–75, 539
    font families, 58
    font-weight value, 72
    graphic text, 59–60
    HTML text, 59
    Internet Explorer, 64, 66
    italic font, 69–70
    minicaps, 73
    monospace fonts, 58
    multiple values, 74–75
    Netscape, 64
    oblique fonts, 69
    overline text, 90
    sans-serif fonts, 58
    serif fonts, 58
    size, 67–68
    strikethrough font, 89, 90
    underline text, 70, 89, 90, 398
    using on Web, 59–60
    using visitor's styles, 75
    vector text, 60
    Web browsers and, 62, 64
footers, dynamic, 370–371
foreground color, 114
formats
    AU format, 487
    .eot format, 64
    MPEG format, 501
    PNG format, 482
    QuickTime format, 487
    TrueType format, 64
    WAV format, 487
forms, 441–445
frame borders, 371–373
frames
    bookmarking, 380–382
    closing, 374–379
    collapsible, 375–379
    controlling elements in, 261–263
    dynamic content between, 261–263
    navigation and, 384
    opening, 374–379
    referencing framed pages, 380–382
framesets
    nested framesets, 374–379
    placing pages in, 381–382
functions. *See also specific functions*
    dynamic functions, 248–250
    findClip functions, 228–231
    JavaScript functions, 251
    making recursive, 248–250
    passing events to, 251

G

GIF animation, 488–494
GIF Construction Set program, 491, 561
GIF images, 478
GIFBuilder program, 491, 561
global CSS files, 55
global style sheets, 55
GoLive. *See* Adobe GoLive
graphic text, 59–60
GraphicConverter program, 562
graphics. *See also* images
    backgrounds, 107, 108, 111–113, 384
    creating headlines, 364–365
    in frame borders, 372–373
    PNG graphics, 478–482
    resizing, 120
    SVG (Scalable Vector Graphics), 10, 60, 531

text in, 384
transparent, 384, 478–482
vector graphics, 10, 60, 531
XML and, 524

H

hanging indents, 99
<head> tag, 21
headers
    dynamic, 370–371
    fixed, 366–367
headlines, 364–365
height property, 118–120
history element, 433
history.go() method, 433
HTML
    converting to XHTML, 527–528
    described, 3
    resources, 566
    vs. SGML, 522
    vs. XML, 522
HTML 4.01, 10
HTML code
    client-side code, 168
    color of, xix
    conventions, xix
    debugging, 507–518
    dynamic Web sites, 357
    sample code to download, xxii
    viewing hidden code, 390–391
HTML documents, 389
HTML selectors, 11, 30, 31, 40, 42
HTML tags. *See also* HTML code; *specific tag*
    names
    adding CSS to, 18–19
    applying classes to, 31, 32
    applying IDs to, 34
    block-level tags, 14, 37–38
    child tags, 41
    defining in context, 41–42
    defining/redefining, 29–30
    defining with same rules, 39–40
    font tags, 62
    inheriting properties, 45–46
    inline tags, 15, 35–36
    managing property values, 47–48
    nested tags, 41, 45–46, 116
    overriding, 47–48
    parent tags, 41, 42, 45–46, 48
    redefining, 29–30
    replaced tags, 15
    rules in, 13, 510

setting font style, 70
setting individual style properties, 18–19
setting styles in HTML documents, 21–22
styles applied to, 6
syntax, 509
types of, 14–15
uppercase *vs.* lowercase, xix, 14–15
vs. containers, 117
vs. CSS, 17
vs. selectors, 12–13
vs. style sheets, 10
HTML text, 59
hypertext. *See also* links
    described, 336, 339
    pop-up hypertext, 438–440
    vs. navigation links, 338
hypertext class, 438

I

iCab browser, 422, 536
Icon key word, 75
id attribute, 38, 528
ID rules, 11, 34
ID selectors, 33–34
if statements, 516
<iframe> tag, 386–387
<ilayer> tag, 284, 285, 287, 386–387
image swapping, 449–453
ImageReady, 490
images. *See also* graphics
    animated GIFs in, 493
    background images, 107, 108, 111–113, 384
    GIF images, 478
    identifying, 178
    PNG images, 478–482
    pre-loading, 138
    resizing, 120
    slide shows, 434–437, 494
    SVG (Scalable Vector Graphics), 10, 60, 531
    swapping, 186
<img> tag, 482
iMovies, 502, 503
@import statement, 23, 27
!important value, 43–44, 49
importing
    external content, 288–289, 385–391
    external CSS files, 28
    external JavaScript files, 389
    external style sheets, 27
    style sheets, 510
indenting text, 87–88, 99
inline tags, 15, 35–36

Inspector palette, 312–313
interactive Web sites, 337, 350
Internet. *See* Web sites
Internet Explorer. *See also* Web browsers
    adding rules, 278–279
    backgrounds and, 107
    browser-safe fonts, 554
    clipping values, 228
    CSS-P support, 9
    CSS support, 13
    CSS1 support, 9
    CSS2 support, 9
    CSS3 support, 10
    detecting, 204–205
    DHTML, 170
    disabling style sheets, 280–281
    DOM and, 177, 179
    drop caps and, 461
    eliminating rules, 280–281
    events and, 182
    fixed position and, 144, 145
    font issues, 64, 66
    overview, 534
    versions of, 534
    z-index and, 224
Internet Explorer 4
    drag-and-drop feature and, 448
    lists and, 95
Internet Explorer DOM, 189
Internet Explorer for Windows, 297–302
interpreted code, 517
italic text, 69–70

J

Java, 504, 550
Java applets, 504–505
JavaScript
    accessing layers with, 290–293
    class names and, 32
    described, 170
    errors, 513–516
    events and, 182, 183
    feature sensing, 191
    ID selectors and, 33, 34
    importing into HTML documents, 389
    modifying layers with, 294–295
    naming conventions, 275
    reserved words, 550
    rollovers, 186, 449–453, 492
    troubleshooting, 513–516
    vs. Java, 504
    words to avoid, 551

JavaScript files, 361
JavaScript functions, 251
JavaScript notation, 516
JavaScript objects, 186
JavaScript style sheets (JSS), 10, 169
JSS (JavaScript style sheets), 10, 169
justifying text, 83, 84

K

kerning, 78
keyframes, 330, 332, 497
<keywords> tag, 424

L

layer-background-color attribute, 110
<layer> tag, 188, 284, 285, 290
layers
    accessing through JavaScript, 290–293
    changing source file of, 293
    CSS layers. *See* CSS layers
    floating box, 314–315
    modifying with JavaScript, 294–295
    nested, 199–202
    Netscape. *See* Netscape layers
layout, 340–342, 358
layout grid, 354, 356
<layout> tag, 530
leading, 80
letter-spacing property, 78
letterforms. *See* fonts
letters, 78, 460–461
<li> tag, 95, 96, 98
line-height property, 80–81
lines
    breaking, 22
    height, 80–81
    spacing, 80–81
<link> tag
    adding CSS to Web sites, 23
    contextual selectors, 42
    importing CSS files, 28
    linking to CSS files, 27
    printing and, 53
    setting up, 422–423
    support for, 424
links. *See also* hypertext; navigation
    <a> tag and, 41
    color of, 396, 397, 398
    to CSS files, 26–27, 311
    to external style sheets, 25, 26–27

in fixed headers, 367
guidelines, 343–346
nested, 527
to pop-up text, 439
pseudo-classes, 395
relationships between, 422
return-to-top links, 345
states for, 394, 397
to style sheets, 25
styles for, 394–398
underlined text and, 90, 398
vs. hypertext, 338
Linux platform, 207
list-style-image property, 100–101
list-style-image value, 97
list-style-position property, 99
list-style-position value, 96
list-style property, 96–101
list-style-type value, 96
lists, 96–101, 541
LiveMotion, 173
LiveScreenHeight variable, 209
LiveScreenWidth variable, 209
LView Pro program, 562

M

Mac OS platform. *See also* cross-platform issues
Apple Developer Connection Web site, 568
browser-safe fonts, 554–555
font issues, 64, 66, 554–555
iCab browser, 422, 536
Internet Explorer, 534
Netscape Navigator, 535
Opera Web browser, 204–205, 536
screen dimensions, 208
magnifyWindowsSize() function, 270, 271
margin property, 121–123
margins. *See also* padding
defining left and top margins, 146–148
defining right and bottom margins, 149–150
described, 117
elements, 121–123
margin controls, 543–544
negative margins, 122
paragraph indents and, 88
setting on one side, 123
tables, 131–132
vs. padding, 129, 130
menu class, 417
Menu key word, 75

menus
breadcrumb menus, 415–420
clamshell menus, 345, 411–414
drop-down menus, 399–403
sliding menus, 404–406
smart menus, 454–457
menuToggle() function, 377, 378
Message-box key word, 75
meta data, 422–424
<meta> tag, 300, 422, 423, 424
methods, 294. *See also specific methods*
Microsoft, 7–8, 169, 170
minicaps, 73
monitors. *See also* screen
browser-safe colors, xvii
detecting number of colors, 210–211
screen dimensions, 208–209, 214
monospace fonts, 58
Mosaic Web browser, 520
mouse controls, 102–103, 541
mouse events, 181, 284. *See also* events
mouse pointer
changing appearance of, 102–103
finding on-screen position, 257–258
objects that follow pointer, 471–474
mouseover events, 181
moveBy() function, 238, 239
moveBy method, 264, 265
moveObject() function, 263
moveObjectBy() function, 238–239
moveObjectTo() function, 236–237, 441, 442
moveTo method, 264, 265
movies, 501–503
MPEG format, 501
multimedia
animation, 488–500
on CD-ROM, 485
Flash *vs.* DHTML, 176
Java applets, 504–505
movies, 501–503
slide shows, 434–437, 494
SMIL, 529–530
sound, 486–487
video, 501–503
music, 564

N

name attribute, 528
navigation, 393–424
Back button, 346, 433
breadcrumb menus, 415–420
clamshell menus, 345, 411–414

navigation *continued*
   Clear button, 445
   described, 393
   drop-down menus, 399–403
   dynamic headers/footers, 371
   frames and, 384
   guidelines, 343–346
   links. *See* links
   meta data and, 422–424
   noise, 401
   for nondynamic browsers, 421
   remote controls, 407–410
   sidebars, 368–369
   site maps, 353
   sliding menus, 404–406
   smart menus, 454–457
   Submit button, 445
nested framesets, 374–379
nested items
   color and, 114
   elements, 114, 153–156
   layers, 199–202
   links, 527
   tags, 41, 45–46, 116
Netscape. *See also* Web browsers
   background color in, 110
   backgrounds and, 107
   clipping area and, 161
   clipping values, 228
   CSS bug fix, 360–361
   CSS-P support, 9
   CSS support, 13, 15
   CSS1 support, 9
   CSS2 support, 9
   CSS3 support, 10
   detecting, 204–205
   DHTML, 169
   DOM and, 177, 179
   events and, 182
   existing property values and, 48
   finding window dimensions, 212
   fixed position and, 144, 145
   font issues, 64
   layers and, 169
   overview, 535
   page titles and, 215
   scrolling and, 217, 244
   standards and, 520
   styles and, 19
   versions of, 535
   z-index and, 224
Netscape 4
   borders and, 125, 128
   DHTML and, 233

   fonts and, 64
   ID selectors and, 36
   @import statement and, 27, 28
   !important value and, 44
   layers and, 199–202, 283
   linked style sheets and, 28
   list-style-image property and, 101
   lists and, 95, 98, 101
   margins and, 122
   media-based CSS and, 53
   recursive calls and, 250
   setting widths, 120
   styles and, 19
   tables and, 132
Netscape 6
   drag-and-drop feature and, 448
   layers and, 169
Netscape Layer DOM, 187–188
Netscape layers, 283–296. *See also* CSS layers;
     layers
   accessing with JavaScript, 290–293
   attributes, 286, 288–289
   creating, 285–287
   described, 283, 284
   expanding, 295
   importing external content, 288–289
   modifying with JavaScript, 294–295
   nested layers, 199–202
   Netscape 4 and, 199–202
   object methods, 294
   object properties, 291
   setting up, 287
   support for, 169
   vs. CSS layers, 179, 283, 284
newspaper style text, 83
Next button, 433
Nielsen, Jakob, 176
<noframes> tag, 296
<nolayer> tag, 284, 285, 296, 386
<noscript> tag, 421
nowrap value, 92
number sign (#), xvii, 34, 509

O

object containers, 117, 502
<object> tag, 486, 487, 500, 503
objects. *See also* Document Object Model;
     elements
   animating, 254–256
   behavior of, 532
   changing class, 276–277
   changing definition, 274–275

changing position, 236–239
changing visibility area, 245–246
changing visibility state, 234–235
creating, 180
defining elements as, 178, 180
defining IDs for, 33–34
described, 180
drag-and-drop feature, 446–448
fading between, 298
finding 3-D position, 224–225
finding borders of, 228–231
finding bottom and right positions, 222–223
finding dimensions of, 218–219
finding top and left positions, 220–221
finding visibility of, 226–227
finding visible area of, 228–231
finding z-index of, 224–225
floating objects, 475–477
following mouse pointer, 471–474
identifying on screen, 259–260
JavaScript objects, 186
properties, 549
referenced, 515
setting 3-D position, 240–242
stacking, 151–152
wave filter for, 302
objectsFloat() function, 477
oblique fonts, 69
onClick event, 258, 402
onClick event handler, 457
onLoad event handler, 268, 269, 477, 483
onMouseover event handler, 451–453
onResize event, 361
onUnload event handler, 267
openRemote() function, 407–409
openWindow() function, 266, 267, 269
Opera Web browser, 204–205, 536
operating system
    detection of, 206–207
    Java support, 505
    setting CSS for, 362–363
overflow control, 162–163
overflow property, 162–163
overline text, 90

P

<p> tag, 6, 11, 30, 38, 43
padding, 117, 129–130. *See also* margins
padding property, 130
page-break property, 93–94
page breaks, 93–94, 384
pageTitle variable, 215

pageURI variable, 215
paragraphs
    indenting text, 87–88
    margins, 88
    white space in, 91–92
parent tags, 8, 41, 42, 45–46
parenthesis ( ), 160, 516
parser, 524
passItOn() function, 251
Photoshop. *See* Adobe Photoshop
pickIt() function, 446
pixel-depth values, 211
Pixel Spy program, 560
pixels, 68, 211, 560
plug-ins, 171, 174
PNG graphics, 478–482
points, 68
popMenu() function, 399–403
popUp() function, 438, 439
position property, 144, 160
positioning controls, 139–156. *See also*
        alignment; controls
    3-D positioning, 151–152
    absolute positioning, 143
    browser window, 140–141
    defining left and top margins, 146–148
    defining right and bottom margins, 149–150
    fixed positioning, 144–145, 366
    keywords and, 113
    listed, 544
    relative positioning, 143
    setting positioning type, 142–145
    static positioning, 143
<pre> tag, 91, 92
printing
    CSS, 51–53
    improving appearance of printed pages,
        383–384
    setting page breaks for, 93–94, 384
    Web pages, 383–384
problems. *See* troubleshooting
properties. *See also specific properties*
    adding to layers, 288–289
    backgrounds, 109–113
    conventions, xviii
    CSS layers, 315, 329
    CSS properties, 7
    described, 12
    improper values, 509
    inheriting from parent, 45–46
    managing, 47–48
    objects, 549
    percentages, xvii
    quick reference, 537–545

properties *continued*
    support for, 508
    system properties, 548
    units, xvi–xvii
    values, xvi–xvii
    Web browsers, 548
    Web pages, 549
properties toolbar, Dreamweaver, 322
pseudo-classes, 395, 545
pseudo-elements, 461, 545

Q

QuickTime attributes, 503
QuickTime format, 487
QuickTime movies, 501–503
quotation marks (" "), xix, 19, 183, 516
quotes ('), 19, 389, 515, 516

R

Radio Free Underground, 564
RealMedia, 501
relative length values, xvi
relative positioning, 139, 141, 143
relElement class, 154
reloadPage() function, 361
remote controls, 407–410
replaced tags, 15
reserved words, 515
resizeBy() method, 271
resizeTo() method, 271, 295
resources, 565–575
    books, 574
    magazines, 575
    Web site for this book, xxi–xxii
    Web sites (examples), 572–573
    Web sites (references), 566–571
RevealTrans() filters, 299–300
rollovers, 186, 449–453, 492
rules, CSS. *See* CSS rules

S

sans-serif fonts, 58
Scalable Vector Graphics (SVG), 10, 60, 531
screen. *See also* monitors
    dimensions, 208–209, 214
    finding mouse pointer position, 257–258
    identifying objects on, 259–260
    setting window position, 265
Screen Ruler program, 560

ScreenHeight variable, 209
ScreenWidth variable, 209
<script> tag, 360, 389, 390
scroll bars, 426–432
scroll() function, 427, 429
scroll position, 216–217
scrolling Web pages, 243–244
scrollPageTo() function, 243–244
scrollTo() function, 243
selectors
    block-level tags, 14, 37–38
    decorating text, 89–90
    defining floating position, 134
    defining multiple list attributes, 96–97
    defining white space for, 92
    described, 12
    display mode, 137–138
    inline tags, 15
    replaced tags, 15
    typos in, 509
    vs. HTML tags, 12
    vs. tags, 12–13
semicolon (;), 13, 18, 44, 183, 184, 509
serif fonts, 58
server-side includes (SSIs), 388
servers, Web, 388
setButtons() function, 456–457
setClass() function, 276–277
setClip() function, 228, 230, 245–246
setLayer() function, 224, 225, 240, 242
setMenu() function, 404–406
setTimeout() function, 250
setVisibility() function, 226, 227, 234, 235
SGML (Standard Generalized Markup
    Language), 522
shadows, drop, 462–466
Shockwave file (SWF), 499
showDim() function, 219
showMenu() function, 416–420
showPos() function, 221, 223
showVisibility() function, 227
sidebars, 368–369
single quotes ('), 19, 389
site maps, 353
slide shows, 434–437, 494
slideMenu() function, 405
Small-Caption key word, 75
SMIL (Synchronized Multimedia Integration
    Language), 529–530
sound, 176, 486–487, 503, 564
sound attributes, 487
sound files, 486, 487
spacing, 78–81
<span> tag

creating drop caps, 460–461
inline tags, 35, 36
sliding menus and, 406
special effects, 459–484
   clocks, 483–484
   crosshair target, 474
   drop caps, 460–461
   drop shadows, 462–466
   fading text, 467–470
   flashlight effect, 471–474
   floating objects, 475–477
   Internet Explorer for Windows, 297–302
   objects that follow mouse pointer, 471–474
   rollovers, 186, 449–453, 492
   slide shows, 434–437, 494
   transition effects, 299–300
   transparent graphics, 478–482
SSIs (server-side includes), 388
stacking objects, 151–152
Standard Generalized Markup Language
   (SGML), 522
standards, 8, 519–521, 534, 567
startAnimate() function, 254, 255, 256
startScroll() function, 428, 430, 431
static positioning, 143
Status-bar key word, 75
stopScroll() function, 429, 431
storyboard, 355
strikethough text, 89, 90
style property, 19, 94, 302
style sheets. *See also* CSS
   author-defined *vs.* user-defined, 44, 49
   comments in, 54
   disabling, 280–281
   global style sheets, 55
   importing, 510
   JavaScript, 10
   linking to, 25, 510
   specifying for medium, 52–53
   troubleshooting, 508–510
   user-defined *vs.* author-defined, 44, 49
   vs. HTML tags, 10
<style> tag
   CSS rules and, 35, 509
   external CSS files and, 24
   placement of, 56
   setting styles with, 21, 27
   typos in, 509
styles. *See also* CSS (Cascading Style Sheets)
   described, 5
   Dreamweaver and, 325
   general syntax, 18, 19
   links, 394–398
Submit button, 445

subscript text, 86
superscript text, 86
SVG (Scalable Vector Graphics), 10, 60, 531
swapForm() function, 444
swapLayer() function, 241, 242
SWF attributes, 499
.swf extension, 173
SWF (Shockwave file), 499
Synchronized Multimedia Integration Language
   (SMIL), 529–530
system properties, 548

T

tables, 131–132, 358
templates, Web page, 357
text, 77–94. *See also* fonts
   alignment, 83–86
   blinking text, 90
   bold text, 29, 71–72
   condensing, 81
   decorating, 89–90
   double-spaced, 81
   drop caps, 460–461
   drop shadows, 462–466
   fading text, 463, 467–470
   floating text, 134, 135–136
   graphic text, 59–60
   in graphics, 384
   HTML text, 59
   indenting, 87–88, 99
   italic font, 69–70
   justifying, 83, 84
   kerning, 78
   leading, 80
   overlapping, 122
   overline text, 90
   page breaks, 93–94
   preventing from wrapping, 135–136
   setting text case, 82
   spacing, 80–81
   strikethrough, 89, 90
   subscript text, 86
   superscript text, 86
   text controls, 77–94, 540
   underline text, 70, 89, 90, 398
   vector text, 60
   white space and, 91–92
   word spacing, 79
   wrapping, 99, 133–134
text-align property, 83–84
text-decoration property, 89–90
text-indent property, 87–88

INDEX

text-transform property, 82
timelines, 332, 530
Timelines window, Dreamweaver, 330, 332
timing problems, 515
<title> tag, 215
toggleImage() function, 450, 451, 453, 456
toggleLayerViz() function, 292, 293
toggleVisibility() function, 234–235
toggleWindow() function, 266, 267
tools
    Dreamweaver, 323
    GoLive, 309
    for Web design, 559–564
ToolTips, 439
transition effects, 299–300
transparent colors, 384
transparent graphics, 478–482
troubleshooting
    bugs, 172, 193, 507–518
    cross-browser problems, 172, 363, 517–518
    CSS, 508–510
    JavaScript, 513–516
    timing problems, 515
TrueType format, 64
type styles, 58
typoGRAPHIC Web site, 57
typography, 57, 77. *See also* fonts; text

U

underlined text, 70, 89, 90, 398
underscore (_), 509
Universal Resource Identifiers (URIs), 215
Universal Resource Locators. *See* URLs
URB() function, 427, 429, 432
URIs (Universal Resource Identifiers), 215
URLs (Universal Resource Locators)
    described, xvii, 215
    global, xvii
    local, xvii
    viewing external content, 390–391
    vs. URIs, 215
URT() function, 427, 430, 431

V

values, 12
variables, 515–516
vector graphics, 10, 60, 531
vector text, 60
vertical-align property, 85–86
video, 501–503

visibility controls, 157–163. *See also* controls
    changing object visibility area, 245–246
    changing object visibility state, 234–235
    clip area, 160–161
    finding object visibility, 226–227
    Internet Explorer for Windows, 297–302
    listed, 545
    overflow controls, 162–163
    setting element visibility, 158–160
visibility property, 138, 158–159, 234
Visibone Web site, 561, 563, 575
visual filters, 170, 297–302
void() function, xvii

W

W3C CSS Validator, 511–512, 538
W3C CSS1 Test Suite, 538, 564
W3C ID DOM, 190
W3C (World Wide Web Consortium), 4, 7–10, 566
WAV format, 487
wave filter, 302
Web browsers, 533–536. *See also* Internet Explorer; Netscape
    browser-safe colors, xvii, 561, 563
    browser-safe fonts, 65–66, 553–557
    browser sensing, 205
    bugs in, 172, 193
    changing window size, 270–272
    closing window, 266–267
    controls. *See* controls
    conventions, xviii
    cross-browser DOM, 194–198, 217
    cross-browser problems, 172, 363, 517–518
    cross-platform problems, 172
    CSS styles and, 9
    CSS support, 9, 10, 13, 15, 17, 533
    detecting monitor colors, 210–211
    detecting operating system, 206–207
    detecting type and version, 204–205
    detecting visible page dimensions, 213–214
    DHTML flavors, 169–170
    DHTML support, 171, 186, 205
    feature sensing, 191–193, 205
    finding mouse pointer position, 257–258
    fonts and, 62, 64
    hiding CSS from, 22, 421
    iCab browser (Mac), 422, 536
    meta data and, 422–424
    Mosaic Web browser, 520
    moving browser window, 264–265
    non-DHTML browsers, 533

nondynamic browsers, 421
nonlayer browsers, 296
opening new window, 266–269
Opera browser, 204–205, 536
pop-up window content, 268–269
properties, 548
reserved words and, 550–551
screen dimensions and, 208–209, 214
viewing source code, 390–391
windows in. *See* windows, browser
Web design tools, 559–564
Web designers, xv
Web pages
    adding clock to, 483–484
    adding CSS layers to, 314–315, 328–329
    adding CSS to, 20–22, 310, 324
    adding global event handlers, 252–253
    adding new rules to, 278–279
    animation in. *See* animation
    assembling, 358
    detecting visible page dimensions, 213–214
    finding location and title, 215
    improving appearance of printed pages,
        383–384
    Java applets in, 504–505
    layout of, 359–384
    linking to external CSS file, 311
    properties, 549
    referencing framed pages, 380–382
    scroll position, 216–217
    scrolling in, 243–244
    sound in, 176, 486–487, 564
    templates, 357
    transitions between, 299–300
    using cross-browser DOM in, 197–198
    using PNG graphics on, 482
    video in, 501–503
    viewing hidden code, 390–391
Web servers, 388
Web Site Garage, 564
Web sites
    adding CSS to, 23–28
    Apple Developer Connection Web site, 568
    Argus Center for Information Architecture,
        570
    audience, 349, 351
    building, 357–358
    BuildingTheWeb.com, 566
    Cascading Style Sheets home page, 9
    ColorMix Web site, 563
    Coma2 Web site, 572
    content for. *See* content
    control pads, 410
    controls, Dreamweaver, 323

counterSPACE Web site, 57
CSS1 Test Suite, 564
design, 351, 352–356
DHTML FAQs, 568
DHTML for the World Wide Web, 569
downloading fonts from, 63–64
dynamic. *See* dynamic Web sites
Dynamic Drive Web site, 568
Dynamic HTML Guru Web site, 569
features of, 350
Freeware Java, 505
GlassDog Web site, 570
HTML Help Web site, 566
interactive Web sites, 337, 350
Internet Developer Web site, 568
Kaliber 10000 Web site, 573
layout, 340–342, 358
layout grid, 354, 356
navigation, 393–424
navigation guidelines, 343–346
outline for, 352
page breaks in, 93–94, 384
planning, 347–356
purpose of, 349, 350
Radio Free Underground, 564
resources, 566–573
Sandman Film Web site, 572
Scott McCloud Web site, 570
screen dimensions and, 208–209, 214
site maps, 353
SMIL home page, 529
Splatterpunk Web site, 572
spotlights, 410
storyboard, 355
testing, 358
for this book, xxi–xxii
tours, 410
typoGRAPHIC Web site, 57
typography on, 58–60
Useit.com, 571
users *vs.* visitors, 351
Visibone Web site, 561, 563, 575
Web Page Design for Designers, 571
Web Site Garage, 564
Web Standards Project, 8, 521, 532, 567
Webmaster's Color Lab, 563
WebReference Web site, 567
WebReview Web site, 567
World Wide Web Consortium, 4, 9, 566
XML Web site, 522
XSL home page, 522
Web standards, 8, 519–521, 534, 567
Web Standards Project, 8, 521, 532, 534, 567
Webmaster's Color Lab, 563

WEFT program, 64
whichLayer() function, 225
white space, 91–92
white-space attribute, 91–92
width property, 118–120
windows, browser
    changing size, 270–272
    closing, 266–267, 408
    Flash animation and, 500
    opening, 266–267
    overview, 140–141
    pop-up, 268–269
    toggling, 266, 267, 268
    x and y coordinates in, 257–258
Windows Media, 501
Windows platform. *See also* cross-platform
        issues
    browser-safe fonts, 556–557
    font issues, 64, 66
    Internet Explorer, 534
    Netscape Navigator, 535
    Opera Web browser, 204–205, 536
    screen dimensions, 208
    special effects for, 297–302
word spacing, 79
word-spacing property, 79
World Wide Web Consortium. *See* W3C
wrapping text, 99, 133–136
writeCSS() function, 465, 466, 469
writeLayer() function, 465, 466, 469, 470

X

x coordinates, 257
XHTML (Extensible Hypertext Markup
        Language), 14, 525–528
XML (Extensible Markup Language), 522–524
XSL (Extensible Stylesheet Language), 7, 522

Y

y coordinates, 257

Z

z-index
    3D objects and, 240–242
    defining, 151–152
    finding in objects, 224–225
z-index property, 240, 242